Description and Explanation in Korean Linguistics

Description and Explanation in KOREAN Linguistics

edited by
Ross King

East Asia Program
Cornell University
Ithaca, New York 14853

The Cornell East Asia Series is published by the Cornell University East Asia Program and has no formal affiliation with Cornell University Press. We are a small, non-profit press, publishing reasonably-priced books on a wide variety of scholarly topics relating to East Asia as a service to the academic community and the general public. We accept standing orders which provide for automatic billing and shipping of each title in the series upon publication.

If after review by internal and external readers a manuscript is accepted for publication, it is published on the basis of camera-ready copy provided by the volume author. Each author is thus responsible for any necessary copy-editing and for manuscript formatting. Submission inquiries should be addressed to Editorial Board, East Asia Program, Cornell University, Ithaca, New York 14853-7601.

Cover design: Karen K. Smith.

Number 98 in the Cornell East Asia Series.
© 1998 Ross King. All rights reserved
ISSN 1050-2955
ISBN 1-885445-56-3 hc
ISBN 1-885445-98-9 pb

13 12 11 10 09 08 07 06 05 04 03 02 01   10 9 8 7 6 5 4 3 2 1

CAUTION: Except for brief quotations in a review, no part of this book may be reproduced or utilized in any form, without permission in writing from the author. Please address inquiries to Ross King in care of East Asia Program, Cornell University, 140 Uris Hall, Ithaca, NY 14853-7601.

Dedication

This volume is dedicated to the memory of:

Seok Choong Song (Oct. 2, 1927 - Aug. 27, 1996)
First ICKL President, 1975-1977

Han-kon Kim (Nov. 18, 1931 - Nov. 18, 1996)
Fifth ICKL President, 1984-1986

John H. Koo (Feb. 1, 1932 - May 26, 1997)
Tenth ICKL President, 1994-1996

Contents

Contributors x

Introduction 1

PHONETICS and PHONOLOGY 9

1
The Effects of Prosodic Structure and Consonant Phonation on Vowel FØ in Korean: An Examination of Bilabial Stops
  David James Silva 11

2
Phonological Incorporation of the Korean Glottal Approximant
  Gregory K. Iverson and Young-Key Kim-Renaud 35

3
Umlaut Uniformity in Korean and Old High German
  Gregory K. Iverson and Shinsook Lee 51

4
Phonological Aspects in Causative Suffixation
  Sang-Cheol Ahn 67

SYNTAX 85

5
Negative Polarity Items in Korean and English
  Susumu Kuno 87

6
Case Assignment in the *siphta* Construction and its Implications for Case on Adverbials
  Soowon Kim and Joan Maling 133

7
Anaphoric Dependencies and Predication
  Hyunoo Lee 169

8
A Minimalist Approach to Case Alternation in the Context of Korean Exceptional Case Marking
  Kwangho Lee 185

9
Prominence of an Antecedent and its Effect on Anaphor Binding in Korean
  Chan Chung 219

10
Affectedness and the Degree of Transitivity in Korean: A Functional-Typological Approach
  Jae-Hoon Yeon 241

11
Coordinated Clauses and their Tense: The Korean Data and the Labelled Deductive Model
  Mark Vincent 259

**SEMANTICS, PRAGMATICS
and GRAMMATICALIZATION** 283

12
A Pragmatic Analysis of the Postpositional Marker *Nun*
  Seungja Choi 285

13
Conditional Forms and Meanings in Korean
    Chang-Bong Lee 311

14
Towards a Unified Analysis of *khenyeng*
    Yoon-Suk Chung 329

15
From Quotation to Sentence-Final Particle: The Analysis of *-ko* in Modern Korean
    Sung-Ock S. Sohn 351

Index 369

Contributors

Ahn, Sang-Cheol
(SCAHN@NMS.KYUNGHEE.AC.KR)
Dept. of English, Kyung Hee University
1 Hoegi-dong, Tongdaemun-gu
Seoul 130-701, Korea
(O)(82-2)-961-0446; (F)(82-2)-965-8004

Choi, Seungja
Yale University
East Asian Languages and Literatures
P. O. Box 1504A Yale Station
New Haven, CT 06520-7425
(O)(203)-432-2860; (F)(203)-432-64729

Chung, Chan
(CCHUNG@KOWON.DONGSEO.AC.KR)
Dept. of English, Dongseo University
2 Churye-dong, Sasang-gu
Pusan 617-716, Korea
(O)(82-51)-327-3750; (F)(82-51)-312-2389

Chung, Yoon-suk
(yschung@garnet.berkeley.edu)

Iverson, Gregory K.
(iverson@uwm.edu)
Dep't. of Foreign Languages & Linguistics
University of Wisconsin-Milwaukee
Milwaukee, WI 53201-0413, USA

Kim, Soowon
(soowon@u.washington.edu)
Dept. of Linguistics, GN-40
A210 Padelford Hall
University of Washington, Seattle
Seattle, Washington
(O)(206)-685-7978; (F)(206)-685-7978

King, Ross
(jrpking@unixg.ubc.ca)
Department of Asian Studies
University of British Columbia
Asian Centre, 1871 West Mall
Vancouver, British Columbia V6T 1Z2
CANADA(O)(604)-822-54281 (F)(604)-822-8937

Kim-Renaud, Young-Key
(KIMRENAU@GWIS.CIRC.GWU.EDU)
Dept. of East Asian Languages and Literatures
George Washington University
Washington, DC 20052, USA
(O)(202)-994-7107; (F)(202)-994-1512

Kuno, Susumu
(kuno@fas.harvard.edu)
Dept. of Linguistics
Harvard University
Cambridge, MA 02138

Lee, Chang-Bong
3801 Conshohockan Ave. No. 306
Philadelphia, PA 19131
tel./fax215-878-1424

Lee, Hyunoo
(HYLEE@DRAGON.INHA.AC.KR)
Dept. of English Education, Inha University
Inchon 420-751, Korea
(O)(82-32)-860-7857; (F)(82-32)865-3857

Lee, Kwangho
Honam University
English Department
Kwangsan-gu, Seobong-dong 59-1
Kwangju City 506-090, Korea

Maling, Joan
(maling@volen.brandeis.edu)
Program in Linguistics, Volen Center, MS-013
Brandeis University
Waltham, MA 02454-9110
(O)(781)-736-3261; (F)(781)-736-2398

Silva, David James
(david@ling.uta.edu)
Program in Linguistics
University of Texas at Arlington
Box 19559 - Hammond Hall 408
Arlington, TX 76019-0559
(O)(817)-272-5334; (F)(817)-272-2731

Sohn, Sung-Ock
(Sohn@humnet.ucla.edu)
Dept. of East Asian Languages and Cultures
290 Royce, Box 951540
Los Angeles, CA 90095-1540

Vincent, Mark
(M.A.Vincent@durham.ac.uk)
Dept of Theology, University of Durham
Abbey House, Palace Green
Durham, DH1
England, UK
(O)(+44)-191-514-4620; (F)(+44)-1723-585691

Yeon, Jae-hoon
(jy1@soas.ac.uk)
Dept of East Asia/Centre for Korean Studies
SOAS, University of London
Thornhaugh Street, Russell Square
London WC1H OXG, UK
(O)(+44)-171-323-6177; (F) (+44)-171-323-6179

Introduction

Ross King

This volume contains fifteen papers originally presented at the Ninth International Conference on Korean Linguistics, held at the School of Oriental and African Studies (SOAS), University of London, from 20-22 July, 1994. The papers range in coverage from phonetics and phonology, to syntax, semantics, pragmatics and grammaticalization, and were selected from the more than sixty papers presented at the conference. Each paper has been subjected to anonymous peer review by an international panel of readers. The 1994 conference also included a number of interesting and important papers in the fields of Korean dialectology and Korean historical and comparative linguistics, but resource constraints have militated against producing a second volume devoted to these subjects.

The biennial ICKL conferences are the official assemblies of the International Circle of Korean Linguistics (ICKL). As Young-key Kim-Renaud (1994) has already noted, the quality and quantity of ICKL papers in recent years have risen dramatically. This volume, like hers, bears witness to the same "dynamic and lively state" of Korean linguistics in the international linguistics arena today. Thus, while the volume contains new research by established scholars like Gregory Iverson, Young-key Kim-Renaud, Susumu Kuno, and Joan Maling, it is perhaps more significant that the bulk of the papers are by young scholars who have recently finished or are just now finishing their doctorates. Relative newcomers to the field include Hyunoo Lee, Kwangho Lee, Chan Chung, Jae-Hoon Yeon, Mark Vincent, Chang-Bong Lee and Yoon-suk Chung. It is a testament to the growing quality of the field that so many young scholars survived the review process to appear in the volume.

Besides new faces, this volume also includes some new approaches. For example, Vincent's paper on "Coordinated Clauses and their Tense. . ." is the first paper ever to appear in the Labelled Deductive Model framework using Korean data. Sung-ock Sohn's paper on "The Evolution of the Quotative Constructions in Korean" is one of very few papers that have appeared to date on grammaticalization in Korean.

Another important feature of many of the papers in this volume is the extent to which the authors have included or appealed to cross-linguistic and typological data. Thus, Iverson and Lee's paper uses data from both Korean and Old High German to study umlaut phenomena, Susumu Kuno's paper contrasts Korean and English data on negative polarity items, Hyunoo Lee's paper interweaves data from English and Toba Batak in its discussion of anaphora, and Jae-Hoon Yeon's data brings in data from a wide variety of languages in an explicitly functional-typological approach.

Other papers in the volume work within longer established and/or more mainstream frameworks and attempt either to use Korean data to develop a particular theoretical model, or to use a particular theoretical model to solve a problem in Korean. In the phonetics and phonology section, David Silva's paper makes two contributions: it shows how a sensitivity to Korean prosodic structure is vital to understanding certain phonetic processes in Korean, and it also demonstrates how exploitation of better quantitative tools can bolster qualitative descriptions. The three papers in phonology proper all use feature geometry and underspecification theory. Iverson and Kim-Renaud combine certain Korean-specific properties like non-release of syllable-final consonants with more general considerations of syllable contact and marked vs. unmarked structure to present an analysis of Korean aspiration. Iverson and Lee's contribution uses a similar framework to tackle the problem of umlaut blocking in both Old High German and modern Korean. They show how universal constraints on autosegmental association explain why palatals in Korean and /h/ in Old High German block umlaut. Sang-cheol Ahn offers a synchronic, dissimilation-based analysis of a thorny problem usually seen as having only a diachronic solution: the allomorphy in the Korean causative suffix.

The first five papers in the syntax section of the volume either work within, or seek to challenge, Chomsky's Government and Binding framework, or refinements to it like the Minimalist program. Susumu Kuno's paper, one of the keynote addresses at the 1994 conference, is a thorough investigation of negative polarity items (NPIs) in Korean. Kuno uses new data from Korean and English to challenge the checking theory proposed by Chomsky and Lasnik (1993). Thus, he casts doubt in the latters' assumption that the NPI licensing condition in English can be stated at S-structure alone, at LF alone, or at S-structure and LF alone. Kuno proposes a number of new generalizations for NPIs in Korean, and proposes a new two-step approach to NPI licensing: NPI Licensing at D-structure, and an Anti-Superiority Condition on Licensees at S-structure.

Soowon Kim and Joan Maling use evidence from the nominative-accusative case-marking alternation in the Korean *siphta* construction and from the case behavior of durational adverbials to argue that the *siphta* construction involves Aspect Phrase-complementation, which yields two different structures depending on whether the complement Aspect Phrase is fully specified as [-complete]. These two different structures explain the case marking alternation. In addition, the authors suggest that durational adverbials get ACC from Aspect—like verbal objects, they delimit the event of the clause they occur in. They provide evidence that Aspect in Korean is a functional category heading its own projection above VP, and claim that the Korean data provide strong evidence for the view that adverbials are assigned case syntactically, just like verbal arguments.

Hyunoo Lee's paper uses evidence from Korean anaphora to support the claim that there is no universal structural relation that relates referentially dependent items (RDIs) to their antecedent. He proposes a Principle of Referential Autonomy (PRA), from which he then derives the Anaphora Asymmetry Universal, the strongest generalization that constrains the anaphor-antecedent relations in natural languages. Lee's new axiom of semantic interpretation accounts for the fact that RDIs and their antecedents are "asymmetrically" distributed in the sentence.

Kwangho Lee's paper analyzes Korean exceptional case-marking structures in sentences like the following:

(1) a. Mary-ka [$_{CP}$[$_{C'}$ [$_{AGRsP}$ John-ul   cengcikha-ess]-tako]]   mit-ess-ta.
         -Nom   -Acc honest-Past-Comp   believe-Past-Dec
    'Mary believed that John was honest.'

Kwangho Lee tries to account for Korean ECM in terms of the SPEC-head relation by raising the Accusative Case-marked embedded subject to SPEC of the matrix AGRoP, as suggested in Chomsky's latest minimalist framework (Chomsky 1993). According to Lee, in Korean ECM constructions CP-deletion has to occur after COMP-lowering due to the lack of the semantic content of the complementizer node selected by Korean bridge verbs. Lee's new analysis of the case-marking in the Korean ECM constructions allows for Watanabe's (1993) Three-Layered Case Theory to apply in compliance with Chomsky's minimalist framework. Lee also extends his approach to an account of Case alternation in Korean Periphrastic Causative constructions.

Chan Chung's paper discusses the dichotomy of syntactic vs. discourse anaphors with respect to Korean data. He uses principles of obliqueness, presupposition of contrastive focus and linear precedence to define notions of syntactic and discourse 'prominence' for antecedents in Korean anaphora, thereby reformulating the conditions for anaphor binding in Korean.

Jae-Hoon Yeon's paper is written from a functional-typological perspective rather than a formal one, and presents useful new data from Korean and a number of other languages on the problem of semantic contrasts between total affectedness of object-space and partial affectedness of locative-space. Thus, Yeon's paper is a Korean-centered contribution to the study of the transitivity continuum, a research tradition that usually cites Hopper and Thompson (1988) as its starting point. Yeon's paper casts new light on the areas of affectedness, case-marking in causative constructions, and possessor ascension in Korean.

Mark Vincent's paper is a novel attempt to examine Korean data using the Labelled Deductive Systems (LDS) framework being developed by Gabbay and Kempson at the University of London. Vincent studies the presence and/or absence of tense in certain clause-coordinating structures in Korean, focussing in particular on on -*ko* linkage. Vincent takes issue with previous GB analyses of tense in Korean like Shin (1988), and throws new light on clause union in Korean. Specifically, he tries to show how an LDS account of clause union avoids the problems with an overly simplistic coordinate vs. subordinate dichotomy, and provides a better way of handling the low specificity and underdeterminacy of many connective patterns.

The third and final section of the volume contains papers on semantics, pragmatics and grammaticalization. Seungja Choi's paper on the "Pragmatic Analysis of the Postpositional Marker *nun*" takes issue with Whitman's (1989) syntactic hypothesis of a licensing relationship between modals and topic phrases whereby topic phrases occur in constructions with overt heads in COMP, and this overt head is a modal element in Japanese and Korean. Choi argues that it is actually the relative accessibility of the discourse entity referred to by the *nun*-marked element that makes the occurrence of *nun*-marked phrases, whether topic or contrastive, more felicitous. Choi criticizes previous studies for failing to capture the link between contrast and the familiarity of the discourse entity, and proposes that the shared core of these two seemingly distinctive functions is the accessibility of the discourse entity; thus, she presents 'topic' *nun* and 'contrastive' *nun* as one unified phenomenon.

Chang-Bong Lee's paper is a semantic approach to conditionals in Korean. He studies the form and meaning of the two most common Korean conditional markers, -*(u)myen* and -*tamyen*, and concludes that, contrary to prior claims, -*(u)myen* is not a ubiquitous conditional marker in Korean and the realis domain cannot be a conditional target in Korean. The author also finds that *-tamyen* is favored over *-(u)myen* when the speaker views the content of the protasis as (highly) hypothetical. Chang-Bong Lee presents his paper as an interesting addition to the cross-linguistic study of conditionals—Korean provides an example of a language where one and the same morpheme functions as a 'given that *p*' clause marker as well as a conditional marker, and Korean is described as a language that employs two different conditional constructions to express different degrees of hypotheticality.

Yoon-suk Chung's paper is a thorough new study of the hitherto poorly described Korean delimiter *khenyeng*. By arguing that *khenyeng* is a "proposition conjunction" and a negative polarity trigger (hence, negative conjunction), and by analyzing its meaning in terms of scalar semantics, Chung provides a unified account of what have traditionally been considered two different uses of *khenyeng*. Thus, Chung's paper is at once an important new study of a specific Korean delimiter and a contribution to the analysis of scalar operators in general.

Sung-Ock Sohn's paper uses authentic conversational data to examine the interplay between *ha-* 'say' verb deletion in Korean and the grammaticalization of sentence-final particle *-ko*. Sohn finds that, in line with recent research on grammaticalization showing unidirectionality in semantic changes, the grammatical extension of the Korean quotative marker *-ko* moves toward speaker-based meaning. Her analysis of the processes of reanalysis and analogy whereby particle *-ko*, originally linking a quoted message and the 'say' verb *ha-*, becomes a sentence-final particle enhancing the speaker's point of view is consistent with cross-linguistic studies on the development of reported speech.

Apart from generally accepted spellings of proper names and individual preferences for the spelling of certain scholars' names, and some instances of phonetic transcription, the Yale system of romanization has been employed throughout the volume.

As organizer of the ninth ICKL meeting, I received assistance, both moral and financial, from a great many sources. On behalf of ICKL, I gratefully acknowledge the generous financial support of the Korea Research Foundation, the British Academy, the SOAS Research Committee, the Korean Embassy (London), Korean Services Travel (New Malden, UK), and Routledge Publishers. I am grateful to my former SOAS colleagues Martina Deuchler, Young Sook Pak, Keith Howard, Jae-Hoon Yeon, Patrick Quow and Liz Parkin for their support during the conference, and would also like to thank SOAS students Andrew Pratt, David Swinburn, Andy Wong, and Ji Yong Shin for their efforts.

I feel particularly fortunate to have had the benefit of the wisdom and experience of my colleagues and friends S. Robert Ramsey and Young-Key Kim-Renaud, and of my teacher Samuel E. Martin, in planning the conference and this volume. Professors Sang-Oak Lee of Seoul National University and Sang-cheol Ahn of KyungHee University were particularly helpful in organizing the participants from Korea.

Much of the initial planning and editing of this volume was carried out at the University of California-Berkeley during the academic year 1994-1995. I am grateful to Professor Hong Yung Lee and the Centre for Korean Studies for hosting me that year as a Korea Foundation Postdoctoral Fellow, and also wish to thank Jonathan Petty and David Moon for their assistance on this and other projects that year. Most recently, UBC student Bob Armstrong has logged nearly a hundred hours preparing the final camera-ready copy for this volume, and I thank him for his patience and good humor. Thanks also to Karen Smith of the Cornell East Asia series for her good-natured and expert guidance.

Finally, the authors and the editor dedicate this volume to the memory of three colleagues lost in the space of just nine months during the academic year 1996-1997. Seok Choong Song, Professor Emeritus of Michigan State University, passed away in August of 1996 at the age of sixty-eight. Professor Han-Kon Kim of Brigham Young University passed away in November of 1996 at the age of sixty-five, and John H. Koo, Professor Emeritus of the University of Alaska-Fairbanks, passed away in May of 1997 at the age of sixty-five. All three scholars had made valuable contributions to our field, all three were still busy in their research, and all three were former presidents and active members of ICKL. All three will be missed.

References

Chomsky, N. A Minimalist Program for Linguistic Theory. In *The View from Building 20*, edited by K. Hale and S. J. Keyser, Cambridge, Mass.: MIT Press. 1-52, 1993.

Chomsky, N. and H. Lasnik, The Theory of Principles and Parameters. In *Syntax: An International Handbook of Contemporary Research Vol. 1*, edited by J. Jacobs, A. van Stechow, W. Sternefeld, and T. Vennemann, Walter de Gruyter, Berlin, 506-569, 1993.

Hopper, P. J. and Thompson, S. A. Transitivity in Grammar and Discourse. *Language* 56. 251-299, 1980.

Kempson, Ruth and Gabbay, Dov. *How we Understand Sentences. And Fragments too: Natural Language Interpretation as Labelled Natural Deduction.* SOAS draft ms, 1993.

Kim-Renaud, Young-key. (ed.) *Theoretical Issues in Korean Linguistics.* Palo Alto, CA: Center for the Study of Language and Information, 1994.

Shin Sung-ock. *Tense and Aspect in Korean.* Ph.D. dissertation, University of Hawaii, 1988.

Watanabe, A. *AGR-Based Case Theory and Its Interaction with the A-bar System.* Ph.D. dissertation. MIT, 1993.

Whitman, John. Topic, Modality, and IP Structure. *Harvard Studies in Korean Linguistics* III, pp. 341-356, 1989.

PHONETICS and PHONOLOGY

1
The Effects of Prosodic Structure and Consonant Phonation on Vowel FØ in Korean: An Examination of Bilabial Stops

David James Silva

Introduction[1]

The literature on Korean phonetics includes a number of claims regarding the effects that consonants have on adjacent vowels. For example, C-W Kim (1965) comments on the relationship between phonation and FØ, writing that the rate of vocal cord vibration of a vowel following a lax stop is slower than that of a vowel following either an aspirated or reinforced stop. Han and Weitzman (1967) report that for vowels following either an aspirated or a reinforced (tense) consonant, the onset value of the fundamental frequency (FØ) is relatively higher than for vowels following a lax stop. These authors conclude, however, that the considerable overlapping of the value ranges for FØ suggests that "the onset values of fundamental frequency

---

[1] This paper is based on data that were originally intended to appear in my 1992 Ph.D. dissertation (but did not); as such, all of the thanks that appear there apply here. In particular, I would like to acknowledge the financial support of the Korean-American Educational Foundation, the United States Fulbright Commission, the Cornell Graduate School, the Cornell Department of Modern Languages and Linguistics, and the Scientific Foundation of Sigma Xi. For their support of subsequent work on this project, I would like to thank the University of Texas at Arlington's College of Liberal Arts and the UTA Program in Linguistics. Finally, thanks go to an anonymous reviewer for comments both critical and constructive. Despite the support of such an illustrious cast, I am certain any number of infelicities of style and analysis appear herein, all of which I claim as my own.

cannot be too significant a cue in the distinction of stop consonants" (1967: 22). In each case, the point is clear: phonation type has an effect on the FØ contours of the following vowel.

While these previous studies have proven to be important foundational work in Korean phonetics, each is characterized by circumstances that limit interpretation. In C-W Kim's (1965) case, for example, the speech of only one subject was analyzed, thereby making cross-speaker generalizations difficult. In the case of Han and Weitzman's series of studies (1965, 1967, 1970), multiple speakers were involved; there is, however, the possibility of gender and dialect effects, as the speaker pool is not as homogeneous as might otherwise be expected. Additionally, the quantitative techniques employed in both sets of experiments were quite limited; while each study presents copious raw data, the bulk of the subsequent analysis is typically limited to qualitative generalizations. One reason for this limitation lies in the fact that different speakers employ different FØ ranges. Finally, neither study takes serious account of potential effects of prosodic structure, which have more recently been shown to be significant in Korean phonology and phonetics (Cho 1987, 1990; Jun 1993; Silva 1992); it seems important, then, for one to consider the role of prosody when examining consonant-vowel interactions such as those affecting FØ.

This paper address these latter two points: the development of more revealing statistical measures for the data and the role of prosody in the analysis. The major findings to be presented are summarized below:

(1) (a) Individual differences in FØ can be factored out of the analysis by converting the raw FØ data into standard score measurements; these measurements, though not direct representations of FØ, provide a reliable basis for comparing the behaviors of different speakers, thereby making comparisons possible.

(b) In most cases, phonation and prosody must be considered together in order to reasonably characterize FØ effects; the two factors interact.

Prior to addressing these two particular issues, let us now turn to a brief discussion of the methodology employed in the current study.

Methodology[2]

The data for this study come from five male speakers of standard Seoul Korean, ranging in age from 19 to 37 years. Each speaker was

---

[2] The data for the current study come from a more comprehensive investigation of prosodic and phonation effects in Korean; see Silva (1992) for further details.

recorded in a sound attenuated booth located in the Cornell University Phonetics Laboratory using a Marantz cassette recorder and a Sennheiser microphone at a standard tape speed (7.5 ips). Speakers were asked to read five sets of randomly ordered cards, each with a short sentence rendered in Korean script (*hankul*), at a self-selected speed.

Each of the test sentences contained a target segment—the low unrounded vowel /a/ [3]—preceded by one of the three underlying bilabial stops—lax /p/, aspirated /pʰ/ and reinforced /pp/. In addition, the target sequences (e.g., /...pa.../) were situated in three different prosodic positions: at the edge of a phonological phrase and the edge of a word (hereafter phrase-edge or PE); within a phonological phrase but at the edge of a word (word-edge or WE); and the position within a word (word-internal or WI) [4]. Finally, the target sequences appeared after both a vowel and a nasal. The combination of these three factors—phonation type, prosodic position, and preceding segment—yielded eighteen (18) test sentences (all rendered in Yale Romanization):

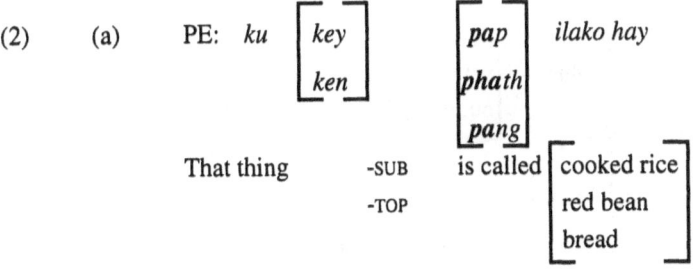

---

[3] In one case the target vowel is /e/ [ə] (/apeci/ = [abədʒi]); this was to ensure that all the words were meaningful.

[4] See Selkirk (1986) and Selkirk and Tateishi (1988a, 1988b) for discussion regarding the general nature of prosodic constituency as assumed herein; see Silva (1989) and Silva (1992) for a more detailed discussion of prosodic phrasing in Korean.

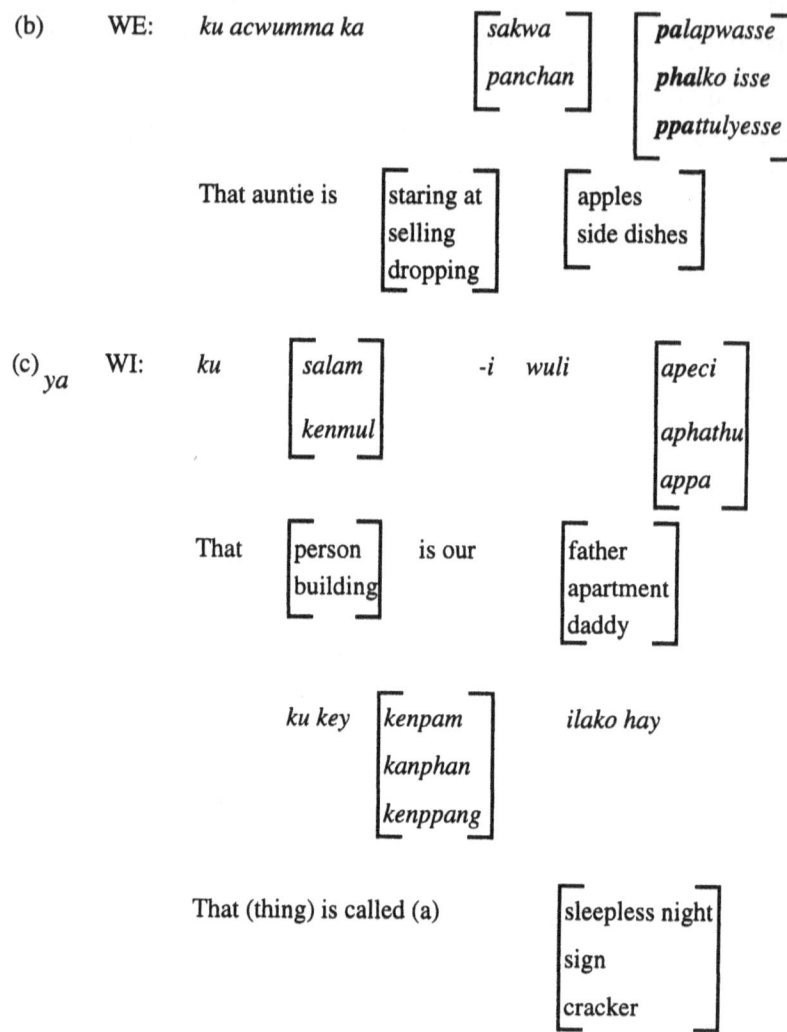

These sample sentences, when read five times each by the five speakers ultimately provided 442 usable tokens for the analysis.

The data were digitized on a Sun workstation at a sampling rate of 12,000 samples/second. For each token, waveforms, spectrograms, and pitch tracks were created using Entropics Waves+ software. FØ values were calculated by means of an automated pitch tracking algorithm, using a frame size of 1/1000 second [5]. FØ measurements were taken at three points during the vowel following the bilabial stop: at vowel onset, at the midway point of the vowel (50% of the vowel), and at a point 10% into the vowel duration. From these values were extracted the four sets of data on which the present study is based:

(3)   a.   (Relative) FØ at vowel onset
       b.   (Relative) FØ at the midway point of the vowel (i.e., the steady state)
       c.   Change in FØ during the first 10% of the vowel
       d.   Change in FØ during the first 50% of the vowel

Prior to considering the results, however, it will be necessary to explain further the statistical technique used to normalize the FØ data collected from the five subjects.

Normalizing FØ Values

Speakers of any language will differ from one another with regard to FØ, both in terms of an overall average FØ value (i.e., some speakers have "higher" or "lower" voices than others) and in terms of the range of FØ values (i.e., some speakers employ a narrow, "monotonic" range while others use a wider range). This individual variation can make cross-speaker comparisons difficult to generalize appropriately. Consider the data given in Table 1, FØ measurements (in Hertz) for the test sentence *ku key ... ilako hay* 'that thing is (a) ...'.

As can be discerned from Table 1, Speaker 3 has a relatively "higher pitched" voice than Speaker 5. Looking specifically at the mean FØ following lax /p/, we find that Speaker 3's value (152.2 Hz) is considerably higher than that of Speaker 5 (113.6 Hz). Similarly, we find that for the mean FØ following aspirated /ph/, Speaker 3's value (182.0 Hz) is higher than that of Speaker 5 (153.0). Note, moreover, the striking overlap in the two speakers' behavior—a value of 152-153 Hz corresponds to different linguistic categories in each case. Situations such as these indicate that a quantitative analysis of FØ for multiple speakers must reasonably account for inherent variation across subjects, lest the results obtained be deemed contradictory or misleading.

---

[5] The resulting FØ data were then checked for anomalous values; in those few cases in which the pitch tracker was clearly in error, measurements were recalculated manually.

TABLE 1

FØ (Hz) at Vowel Onset after Bilablial Stops at Phrase-Edge Position between Vowels

Test Sentence: *ku key pap/phath/ppang ilako hay*. Both speaker and phonation are signficant effects (p ≤ 0.0001) as is the interaction between the two (p ≤ 0.05).

(numbers in *italics* = standard deviations; total n = 442)

	lax /p/	aspirated /ph/	reinforced /pp/
Speaker 1	128.6	166.0	147.6
	16.6	*12.1*	*4.5*
Speaker 2	130.6	183.9	178.7
	6.6	*7.6*	*12.9*
Speaker 3	152.2	182.0	161.9
	10.8	*9.3*	*9.7*
Speaker 4	108.1	172.4	146.3
	9.0	*14.0*	*41.5*
Speaker 5	113.6	153.0	154.8
	6.4	*11.4*	*17.7*
Average (Pooled)	126.6	171.5	157.8
	18.5	*15.4*	*23.1*

To factor out individual speaker effects, I normalized the FØ data for each set of measurements (i.e., FØ at onset, FØ at steady state, etc.) for each speaker by converting each value to a Z-score. The Z-score represents a particular data point's distance from the mean value for all the data points collected from each individual speaker. As such, Z-scores are not given in terms of Hertz but rather in terms of standard deviations about the mean.

While statistical tests performed on Z-scores do not provide direct insight into the actual FØ values for particular tokens, they provide important data regarding relative FØ values. In other words, the use of Z-scores allows us to establish a baseline value for each speaker (for a particular point in time) and then to align these baseline values for the purposes of comparison.

The normalized values appear in Table 2. An examination of these data reveal that when the preceding segment is the lax bilabial /p/, the FØ value at vowel onset is below the average FØ value used by each individual speaker: each of the relative values are below the adjusted mean of zero (0.0). When the preceding segment is aspirated, however, the FØ at onset is relatively higher for all speakers: the average pooled Z-score equals 1.244. In the case of a preceding reinforced stop, the average relative score is somewhat higher than average (average pooled Z = 0.643).

These adjusted scores are noteworthy in that they provide some clear quantitative confirmation of observations made by both C-W Kim (1965) and Han and Weitzman (1967): that lax stops are associated with relatively lower FØ values and so-called "tense" stops (a term for grouping the aspirated and reinforced segments) are associated with relatively higher FØ values. By normalizing the raw data for FØ, one can indeed factor out individual differences and focus on relative, general trends in the data.

TABLE 2

Relative FØ (Z-Score) for Vowel Onset after Bilabial Stops at Phrase-Edge Position between Vowels

Test sentence: *ku key pap/phath/ppang ilako hay*. Only phonation is significant (p≤ 0.0001); neither speaker effects nor the interaction between the two are significant (p>0.17 in each case).

(numbers in italics = standard deviations; total n = 442)

	lax /p/	aspirated /ph/	reinforced /pp/
Speaker 1	-0.308	1.423	0.570
	0.769	*0.562*	*0.209*
Speaker 2	-0.941	1.025	0.832
	0.244	*0.281*	*0.474*

TABLE 2 (cont.)

	lax /p/	aspirated /ph/	reinforced /pp/
Speaker 3	-0.444	1.137	0.680
	0.571	*0.493*	*0.512*
Speaker 4	-0.656	1.732	0.762
	0.333	*0.520*	*1.541*
Speaker 5	-0.840	0.925	1.006
	0.287	*0.511*	*0.792*
Average (Pooled)	-0.648	1.244	0.643
	0.503	*0.511*	*0.835*

Results
FØ at Vowel Onset

The first set of data to consider are those for the relative values of FØ at vowel onset. A repeated measures ANOVA indicates that there are no significant between-speaker effects for the Z-score values of FØ at vowel onset ($p = 1.00$) but that within-speaker effects are significant ($p = 0.0001$). This finding is critical to the analysis, as it indicates that the five subjects behave consistently. It is thus possible to pool their data and focus specifically on the linguistic factors that give rise to the observed within-speaker effects.

A three-way factorial ANOVA of the pooled data indicates that phonation, prosody, and preceding segment are all significant ($p \leq 0.0035$). Moreover, one finds significant interactions between phonation and prosody ($p = 0.0001$) and prosody and preceding segment ($p = 0.0001$); all other interactions are not significant at the level $p \geq 0.05$. Further statistical analysis (post-hoc tests) reveals that the effects of preceding segment are significant only in WI (word-internal) position; as such, effects of preceding segment can be collapsed in PE and WE position. The relevant data appear in Table 3; all effects are significant at the level $p \leq 0.01$[6]. Mean values for each of the cells in Table 3 is graphically presented in Figure 1.

Looking first at the effects of consonant phonation on FØ, we find there is a general pattern whereby the lax stop /p/ is associated with lowest

---

[6] Note that in each of the Z-Score tables, the grand mean (lower right hand box) is always zero; this reflects the use of the zero-value as a consistent baseline in the analysis.

relative value (in every case, the FØ value at onset is below the zero baseline), the reinforced stop is associated with mid-range values, and the aspirated stop is associated with the highest relative values. One point at which pattern appears to break down is WI position when a nasal consonant precedes; here, the mean value for the reinforced stop is slightly higher than that of the aspirated.

TABLE 3

Mean Values of the Standard Score (Z-score) for the Value of FØ at Vowel Onset

Data for all speakers pooled. Numbers in italics = n/cell.

Prosodic Environment → Preceding Segment →		PE Both	WE Both	WI V	WI N	Mean fl
Phonation	p	-0.69	-0.89	-0.90	-0.20	-0.73
		50	*50*	*25*	*22*	*147*
	ph	1.30	0.48	-0.50	0.20	0.55
		50	*48*	*25*	*25*	*148*
	pp	0.54	0.25	-0.86	0.30	0.17
		50	*47*	*25*	*25*	*147*
	Mean	0.42	0.04	-0.75	0.11	0.000
		150	*145*	*75*	*72*	*442*

Source	df	Σsquares	F	p
phonation	2	132.2	150.7	0.0001
prosody	2	45.5	51.8	0.0001
preceding segment	1	6.3	14.3	0.0002
phonation X prosody	4	34.1	19.4	0.0001
phonation X preceding	2	0.1	0.1	0.9441
prosody X preceding	3	24.9	28.3	0.0001
pho X pros X prec	4	4.0	2.3	0.0623
error	424	186.1		

FIGURE 1

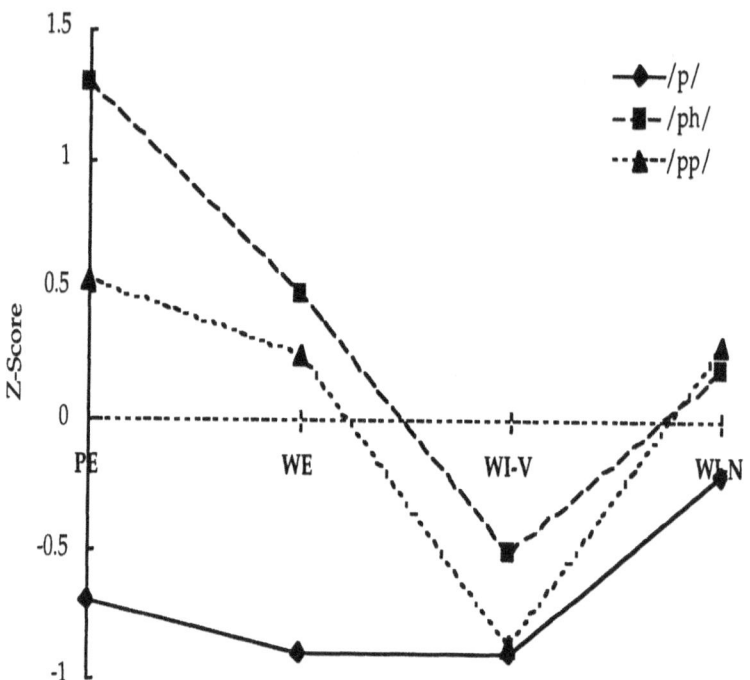

Figure 1: Average Z-Score Equivalents of FØ for Vowel Onset

Explanation for these patterns may lie in the different glottal configurations for each stop type at release. As suggested by C-W Kim (1965), the vocal cord vibration of the lax stop is slower than that of the aspirated and reinforced stop because of a relatively lower volume and speed of airflow over the glottis at the time of release. In terms of relative FØ values, this would result in lower values for lax stops as opposed to aspirated and reinforced stops, as is the case above. This line of reasoning finds additional support in a number of other sources, among them Dart 1987, Hirose et al. 1974, and Kagaya 1974.

In differentiating between aspirated and reinforced stops, one might propose the following. In the case of the aspirated stops, the wide-open glottal configuration evident at release (see C-W Kim 1970 for cineradiographic data) provides for a larger than normal degree of airflow through the glottis at the point of vowel onset, thereby enhancing the speed of vocal cord vibration. Vibration is further enhanced by the fact that the vocal folds are in the [+stiff] position (see Halle and Stevens 1971). In the case of the reinforced stops, there may be conflicting conditions in the glottis at the point of vowel onset. On the one hand, the glottal tension associated with the Korean reinforced stops ([+stiff]) would serve to enhance the rate of vocal fold vibration, thereby raising FØ. On the other hand, the rate of airflow across the glottis at vowel onset is curbed by the fact that the vocal folds are approximated at the point of consonant release (Halle and Stevens' [+constricted]); this dampening of airflow would serve to slow down vocal cord vibration thereby lowering FØ. As the data indicate, the end result is a relatively moderate rate of vocal cord vibration, as evidenced by the intermediate FØ values.

As for the effects of prosody, Figure 1 shows a general trend whereby distance from the left edge of a phonological phrase is inversely related to relative FØ values. This type of effect, whereby phonological and phonetic phenomena are enhanced at prosodic left edges in Korean has been predicted by Kim-Renaud (1974), who argues that certain prosodic positions (e.g., the edge of a phonological phrase) are to be considered as strengthening environments. The further one moves away from phrasal edges and towards the middle of prosodic constituents (from PE to WE to WI position), the more likely it is that strengthening processes give way to those involving weakening, or lenition (e.g., intervocalic stop voicing; see Silva 1992).

A striking anomaly in this otherwise reasonable pattern occurs when the target vowel is preceded by a nasal-stop sequence in the WI position (the column labeled WI-N): In these cases, the values are higher than would perhaps be expected. In accounting for this situation, let us briefly consider an alternative approach to the notion of prosody.

A second possible source of explanation for these data can be garnered by considering the overall semantic/intonational context in which each target segment was uttered. Consider, for example, the sentences in which the target appears in PE position: *ku key/ken X ilako hay* 'that thing is called X'. In each case, the target is the initial segment of the word with the greatest (and, in some cases, the only) semantic import; not surprisingly, each also appears at the intonational peak of the utterance. For sentences in which the target appears in WE position (e.g., *ku acwumma-ka sakwa X...sse* 'that auntie is X-ing the apples'), the target segment appears closer to the end of the sentence. Moreover, the target occurs after the intonational peak of the sentence, which, in this case, is aligned with the word *sakwa* 'apple'. Below are listed the frame sentences for the lax /p/, each marked with the point at which the intonational peak occurs (by means of an asterisk above); the target segments have been double-underlined:

(4) PE: V_ V   ku key <u>p</u>ap ilako hay *over p*

       N_ V   ku ken <u>p</u>ap ilako hay *over p*

   WE: V_V   ku acwumma ka sakwa <u>p</u>alapwasse *over p*

       N_V   ku acwumma ka panchan <u>p</u>alapwasse *over p*

   WI: V_V   ku salami uri <u>p</u>eciya *over p*

       N_V   ku key ken <u>p</u>am ilako hay *over p*

Analysis indicates that distance from the intonational peak of the utterance appears to have an effect on the FØ properties of the target segment. Not surprisingly, as the target vowel's distance from intonational peak increases, its relative FØ value tends to decrease (Table 4).

At this juncture, we are left with a question: what are the relative contributions of syntactically-determined prosodic structure (of the sort PE/WE/WI) and broader intonational patterns? Attempting to address this particular issue extends beyond the more narrowly defined scope of the current work. Of concern to us here, however, is the finding that the effects of phonation type on adjacent vowels can not reasonably be understood without taking into account the prosodic properties of the utterance as a whole. We leave the task of untangling the complex interactions among sentential intonation patterns, semantic/intonational prominence, speaker intent, and syntactically-determined prosodic categories to future work.

TABLE 4

Mean Values of the Standard Score (Z-score) for FØ at Vowel Onset, Revised

In this table, Prosodic Environment and Preceding Segment have been replaced by a measure of "Distance From Intonational Peak", measured in terms of the number of syllables separating the target vowel and the intonational peak of the utterance.

Data for all speakers pooled. Numbers in italics = n/cell.

Distance from Peak (in syllables) "→"		Zero	One	Two	Three+	Mean
Phonation	p	-0.70	-0.21	-0.90	-1.03	-0.74
		50	*22*	*50*	*25*	*147*
	ph	1.37	0.19	0.48	-0.51	0.56
		50	*25*	*48*	*25*	*148*
	pp	0.59	0.33	0.25	-0.87	0.18
		50	*24*	*47*	*26*	*147*
	Mean	0.42	0.12	-0.07	-0.80	0.000
		150	*71*	*145*	*76*	*442*

Source	df	Σsquares	F	p.
phonation	2	82.3	93.6	0.0001
distance from peak	3	76.7	58.1	0.0001
phonation X distance	6	35.7	13.5	0.0001
error	430	189.1		

In accounting for the data regarding the higher than unexpected values for relative FØ in the context of a nasal-plus-stop context, it perhaps worthwhile to pursue a more phonological orientation. One can begin by pointing to languages in which one finds consonantal "strengthening" in such an environment. (Numerous examples come from Bantu—e.g., in Lumasaaba, [+cont] —> [–cont] after a nasal (Carr 1993:296ff).[7]) If the phonological arguments for post-nasal fortition are adopted here, it would follow that any of the Korean bilabial stops should take on more "fortis" characteristics in the context / [+nasal] __ . The data presented herein support such an analysis; examining the standardized FØ at onset in WI position, we consistently find higher values for targets following nasal-stop clusters.

Further pursuit of this line of reasoning might lead one to consider the possibility that in these WI nasal-stop clusters, we might find evidence of a phonological rule of tensification (perhaps through the presence of some phonologically unrealized consonant morpheme or the infamous "sai-sios"). Under such a hypothesis, one would posit that the bilabial stop in *kenpam* 'sleepless night' would be phonologically changed to a reinforced segment. Unfortunately, the FØ data do not reasonably support such a hypothesis—while mean relative FØ value is, in fact, higher in this case (-0.20 as compared to a value of -0.90 for a word such as *apeci*), it does not approximate the value for /pp/ under the same conditions (as in *kenppang*, value = 0.30). Whatever phonologically-based fortition effects might contribute to the data in this situation are not necessarily of a categorical nature.

With an eye towards a more phonetically oriented account of these nasal-stop data, one might wish to pursue a far more speculative analysis, one which appeals to the role of airflow. When the target vowel is preceded by two oral segments (here, a vowel plus a bilabial stop), oral air pressure during stop closure increases, which in turn leads to a reduction in the airflow across the glottis, thus inhibiting vocal cord vibration. Upon stop release, the vocal folds start up from a static position, which means that the FØ at vowel onset will be damped. When the preceding sequence is comprised of a nasal-oral, however, the buildup in air pressure above the larynx will take significantly longer, given the airflow into the nasal cavity. This situation promotes airflow across the glottis, thereby enhancing vocal cord vibration at vowel onset, which in turn gives rise to higher than expected FØ values. It is critical to note that the proposed scenarios take place only in WI position, suggesting that coarticulation effects are strictly local: the presence of a word-level or higher prosodic boundary between the nasal and bilabial segments is sufficient to override any coarticulation effects. This point comes through in the statistical analysis in that preceding segment (be

---

[7] My thanks to the anonymous reviewer for suggesting this line of reasoning.

it vowel or nasal stop) has no effect on FØ in PE and WE positions. In the absence of appropriate airflow data from Korean, such a tentative and theoretical account awaits future empirically based evaluation.

FØ at Vowel Steady State

As was the case in the immediately preceding section, a repeated measures ANOVA of the Z-score of FØ halfway through the following vowel shows no significant between-speaker effects ($p = 1.00$) but significant within-speaker effects ($p = 0.0001$). Also, phonation and prosody are significant factors while previous segment yields significant effects only in WI position ($p \leq 0.01$). Finally, significant interaction occur between phonation and prosody ($p = 0.001$). Mean values for normalized FØ appear in Table 5.

The discussion of the FØ values during the steady state essentially parallels that for FØ at vowel onset. The phonation effects are as before: lax stops are associated with lower relative FØ values, aspirated stops with higher values, and reinforced stops with intermediate values. The prosodic effects are likewise similar: as one moves away from PE position and towards the center of each word, the relative FØ values fall [8]. Once again, the exception to this general pattern involves the WI-Nasal column, which shows the same raising effect as above. In sum, we see that phonation and prosodic effects carry into the steady state of the vowel.

---

[8] Statistical analysis based on distance from the intonational peak yields similar results: we find lower relative values for FØ as we move away from the most prominent element in the utterance. Patterns attributable to phonation differences remain similar as well, as we find the lax, reinforced and aspirated stops yielding lower, intermediate, and higher relative FØ values, respectively.

TABLE 5

Mean Values of the Z-score for the Value of FØ during the Steady State (50% mark)

Data for all speakers pooled. The n/cell are same as those given in Table 3.

Prosodic Environment →		PE	WE	WI	
Mean					
Preceding Segment →		Both	Both	V	N
Phonation	p	-0.809	-0.846	-0.909	-0.153
-0.741					
	ph	1.450	0.408	-0.552	0.317
0.582					
	pp	0.853	0.105	-1.153	0.156
0.154					
	Mean	0.498	-0.123	-0.871	0.118
0.000					

Source	df	Σsquares	F	p
phonation	2	130.8	183.2	0.0001
prosody	2	60.4	84.6	0.0001
preceding segment	1	7.4	20.8	0.0002
phonation X prosody	4	50.4	35.3	0.0001
phonation X preceding	2	0.2	0.2	0.7978
prosody X preceding	3	29.1	40.8	0.0001
pho X pros X prec	4	2.5	1.7	0.1429
error	424	151.4		

FIGURE 2

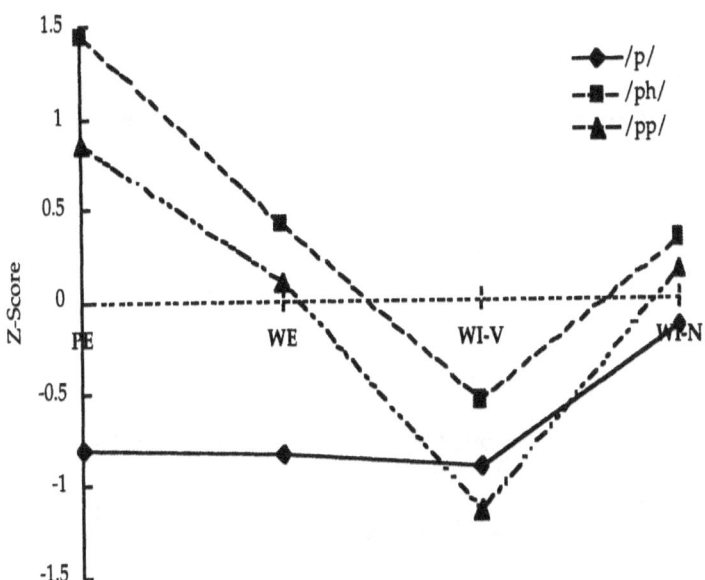

Figure 2: Average Z-Score Equivalents of FØ for Steady State (50%)

Change in FØ during first 10% of vowel

A repeated measures ANOVA indicates that change in FØ during the first 10% of the vowel following the target consonant exhibits between speaker effects (p = 0.0008)[9]. Separate ANOVAs for each subject reveal that the only contributing factor to the analysis is phonation type. As indicated in Table 6, moreover, phonation is a significant factor for only three of the subjects (1, 3, 5). Further exploration of the data reveal that the

---

[9] This statistic indicates that when pooling the data for all speakers, the resulting model may not be reliable. Bearing this limitation in mind, let us consider the results of a three-way ANOVA on the pooled data. According to the ANOVA, there are no significant differences due to prosody (p = 0.7736) or preceding segment (p = 0.4266). Only phonation plays a significant role (p = 0.0001). As indicated in Table 5, the largest change in FØ occurs in reinforced stops, which show a 10 Hz drop. Aspirated and lax stops likewise show initial drops in FØ -- aspirated: 5.5 Hz drop; lax: 3.8 Hz drop. These latter figures are not significantly different at p = 0.05.

FØ change during the first 10% of the vowel following lax and aspirated consonants is not significantly different; values for Scheffe F-tests indicate that at the 95% confidence level, the relevant distinction to be made is that be reinforced and non-reinforced segments. Looking at the numbers themselves, we find a greater drop in FØ for reinforced segments during the early stages of the vowel. Hence we conclude that a sharp drop in the fundamental frequency at the initial stages of vowel production can be correlated with the tenseness of the preceding consonant; it is not clear, however, that all speakers behave consistently with respect to this phenomenon.

TABLE 6

Mean Values of the FØ Excursion during the first 10% of the Following Vowel (Hz)

Individual ANOVAs for each speaker reveal that only phonation type is a significant factor (and only for speakers 1, 3, 5). Moreover, a Scheffe F-test indicates that values in boxes for speakers 1, 3, and 5 are not significantly different (at 95%), thus indicating that reinforced segments behave differently from lax/aspirated for these three subjects.

Numbers in italics are standard deviations.

Subject →	1	2	3	4	5	Pooled Means
Phonation p	-5.0	-6.7	-0.8	-0.9	-2.4	-3.8
	8.1	*8.1*	*3.9*	*5.8*	*4.0*	
ph	-9.0	-6.5	-0.4	-6.0	-6.4	-5.5
	10.2	*12.2*	*1.6*	*8.5*	*9.1*	
pp	-17.6	-10.1	-7.7	-3.9	-11.1	-10.1
	13.7	*11.7*	*17.8*	*15.1*	*16.2*	
p-value (for phonation)	0.0001	0.557	0.009	0.201	0.025	

Change in FØ during first 50% of vowel

A repeated measures ANOVA on the change in FØ over the first 50% of the following vowel exhibits between speaker effects (p = 0.0001) but no significant within speaker effects (p = 0.6918). ANOVAs run on data for each individual speaker, however, reveals there to be a limited number of cases in which phonation is a significant effect. (Prosody and preceding segment were not significant (p =0.05) for any subject.) For speakers 2 and 3, there are no effects of phonation: by the midway point of the vowel, any effect that phonation my have had on the change in FØ are no longer relevant. While such findings may not be surprising in the case of speaker 2 (who showed no prosody effects for the FØ change during the first 10% of the vowel), they are more striking for speaker 3. In his case, we can argue that the changes in FØ associated with particular phonation types are relevant only in the earlier stages of vowel production—i.e., the effects are primarily an issue of consonant-to-vowel transition.

For speakers 1, 4, and 5, we find that phonation is a significant effect (p ≤ 0.003). Scheffe F-tests further reveal the nature of these effects to be somewhat idiosyncratic. For speaker 1, we find that the effect of a lax stop (a drop of 8.3 Hz) is distinct from those of reinforced and aspirated stops (which manifest a drop of 19.4 Hz and 16.7 Hz, respectively)[10,1]. For speaker 4, effects of aspiration and reinforcement are distinct, while other comparisons are not; for speaker 5, only the effects of lax and reinforced consonants prove significantly different.

Given these idiosyncratic behaviors, it is no surprise to learn that an examination of the pooled data (which admittedly must be viewed with caution) indicate no factors too significant in the analysis. Perhaps more revealing, however, is a comparison of the FØ contours for the three phonation types. Assuming that the overall FØ drop into the steady state is a on average 10 Hz (as suggested by the pooled data), we see that for reinforced stops, the vast majority of the FØ drop occurs in the first 10% of the vowel. (Recall that at the 10% mark, vowels following a reinforced stop had experienced a 10 Hz drop.) The FØ contour for an aspirated segment is more gradual, with approximately 55% of the drop occurring during the first 10% of the vowel, leaving the remaining 45% to occur over next 40% of the vowel duration. Lastly, the FØ contour for a vowel following a lax stop is the least abrupt, with only 38% of the drop occurring in the first 10% of the vowel duration. These generalized values are schematized in Figure 3.

---

[10] As above, discussions of data based on the results of the Scheffe F-test are taken to be significant at the 95% level.

TABLE 7

Mean Values of the FØ Excursion during the first 10% of the Following Vowel (Hz)

Individual ANOVAs for each speaker reveal that only phonation type is a significant factor (and only for speakers 1, 4, 5).

Numbers in italics are standard deviations.

Subject →		1	2	3	4	5	Pooled Means
Phonation	p	-8.3 *8.7*	-10.8 *9.5*	-2.3 *4.2*	-6.7 *7.6*	-7.3 *5.5*	-7.1
	ph	-16.7 *9.9*	-14.8 *12.2*	-4.0 *3.6*	-11.2 *9.6*	-13.2 *11.6*	-11.9
	pp	-19.4 *15.1*	-11.8 *11.5*	-5.3 *20.6*	-0.2 *15.2*	-19.2 *17.5*	-11.2
p-value (for phonation)		0.001	0.347	0..647	0.001	0.003	

FIGURE 3

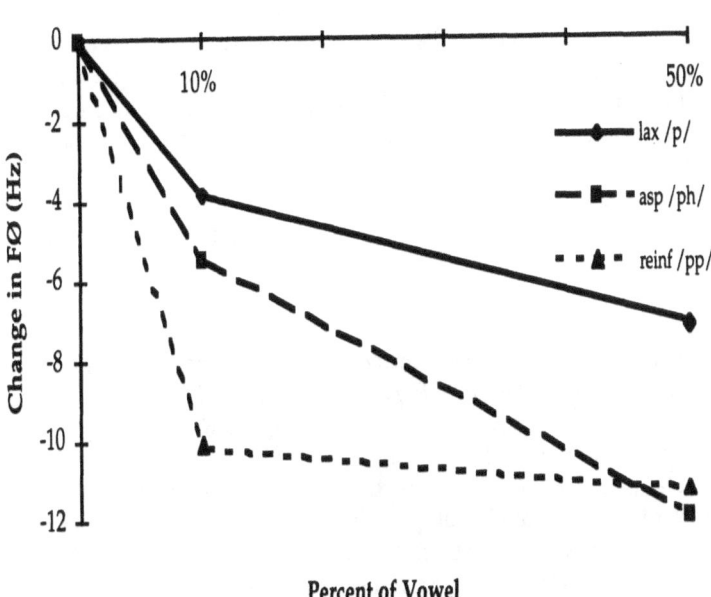

Figure 3: Schematized FØ Contours.

Note how the reinforced stop produces an immediate and sharp drop in FØ, while the lax stop produces a more gradual FØ change.

Conclusions

The work presented here confirms the previous qualitative observations made regarding the effects that phonation type has on the FØ of the following vowel, providing quantitative support. More specifically, we find that all three phonation types in Korean—lax, aspirated, and reinforced—exert statistically different effects on the following vowel. This finding does little to support claims in the literature (e.g., that of C-W Kim) that the reinforced and aspirated stops can be viewed as a natural class defined by the feature [±tense] or [±fortis]. In addition, this study bolsters previous claims regarding prosody made by Cho, Jun, and Silva by providing additional evidence in support of the notion that prosodic structure is a vital factor in understanding how phonological and/or phonetic processes operate in Korean. Moreover, the data support the general taxonomy of strong vs. weak positions in Korean originally made by Kim-Renaud. Finally, this work reinforces the notion that a more detailed understanding of speaker behavior can be obtained by exploiting more thoroughly the statistical tools available to the linguist. In this way, we can provide additional empirical evidence to support qualitative descriptions. This final point is of critical importance when considering the ways in which basic research can inform those who work on applications; given the emphasis on the role of the computer in tasks such as speech modeling and recognition, it is doubtless that sound quantitative models of human speech will continue to play a key role in future applied work.

References

Beckman, M. and J. Kingston. Introduction. In *Between the Grammar and the Physics of Speech—Papers in Laboratory Phonology* I, edited by J. Kingston and M. Beckman, Cambridge, UK: Cambridge University Press, 1-16, 1990.

Carr, Philip. *Phonology*. New York: St. Martin's Press, 1993.

Cho, Y-M. Y. Phrasal phonology of Korean. *Harvard Studies in Korean Linguistics* II, edited by S. Kuno, I-H Lee, J. Whitman, S-Y Bak, and Y-S Kang,Cambridge, MA: Department of Linguistics, Harvard University, 328-340, 1987.

Cho, Y-M. Y. Syntax and phrasing in Korean. *The Phonology-Syntax Connection*, edited by S. Inkelas and D. Zec,Chicago: University of Chicago Press, 47-62, 1990.

Chomsky, N. and M. Halle. *The Sound Pattern of English*. Cambridge, MA: MIT Press, 1968.

Dart, S. An aerodynamic study of Korean stop consonants: Measurements and modeling. *Journal of the Acoustical Society of America* 81.1, 138-147, 1987.

Halle, M. and K. Stevens. A note on laryngeal features. *MIT Research Laboratory of Electronics Quarterly Report* 101, 198-213, 1971.

Han, M. S. and R.S. Weitzman. Acoustic characteristics of Korean stop consonants. *Studies in the Phonology of Asian Languages* III. Los Angeles, CA: University of Southern California, Acoustic Phonetics Research Laboratory, 1965.

Han, M. S. and R.S. Weitzman. Acoustic features in the manner differentiation of Korean stop consonants. *Studies in the Phonology of Asian Languages* V. Los Angeles, CA: University of Southern California, Acoustic Phonetics Research Laboratory, 1967.

Han, M. S. and R.S. Weitzman. Acoustic features of Korean /P,T,K/, /p,t,k/ and /p^h,t^h,k^h/. *Phonetica* 22, 112-128, 1970.

Hirose, H., C. Y. Lee, T. Ushijima. Laryngeal control in Korean stop production. *Journal of Phonetics* 2, 145-152, 1974.

Huffman, M. Implementation of Nasal: Timing and Articulatory Landmarks. *UCLA Working Papers in Phonetics* 75. Los Angeles, CA: University of California Los Angeles, Phonetics Laboratory, 1990.

Jun, S-A. The prosodic structure of Korean–in terms of voicing. *ICKL 7: Papers for the Seventh International Conference on Korean Linguistics*, edited by E-J Baek,Toronto: International Circle of Korean Linguists and Osaka University of Economics and Law (University of Toronto Press), 87-104, 1990.

Jun, S-A. *The Phonetics and Phonology of Korean Prosody*. PhD dissertation, The Ohio State University, 1993.

Kagaya, R. A fiberscopic and acoustic study of the Korean stops, affricates, and fricatives. *Journal of Phonetics* 2, 161-180, 1974.

Kim, C-W. On the autonomy of the tensity feature in stop classification. *Word* 21, 339-359, (Reprinted in C-W Kim 1988, 12-33.), 1965.

Kim, C-W. A theory of aspiration. *Phonetica* 21, 107-116. (Reprinted in C-W Kim 1988, 73-82.), 1970.

Kim, C-W. *Sojourns in Language*. Seoul: Tower Press, 1988.

Kim-Renaud, Y-K. Korean Consonantal Phonology. PhD dissertation, University of Hawaii, 1974.

Kohler, K. J. Phonetic explanation in phonology: the feature fortis/ lenis. *Phonetica* 41, 150-174, 1984.

Nespor, M. and I. Vogel. *Prosodic Phonology*. Dordrecht: Foris Publications, 1986.

Selkirk, E. O. On derived domains in sentence phonology. *Phonology Yearbook* 3, 371-405, 1986.

Selkirk, E. O. On the nature of prosodic constituency: a comment on Beckman and Edwards's paper. In *Papers in Laboratory Phonetics*, edited by, M. Beckman and J. Kingston, Cambridge, UK: Cambridge University Press, 179-200, 1987.

Selkirk, E. O. and K. Tateishi. Syntax and phonological phrasing in Japanese. *Essays in Honor of S. Y. Kuroda*, edited by, C. Georgopoulos and R. Ishihara, Dordrecht: Reidel, 1988a.

Selkirk, E. O. and K. Tateishi. Constraints on minor phrase Formation in Japanese. *Proceedings of CLS* 24, 316-336, 1988b.

Silva, D. J. Determining the domain for intervocalic stop voicing in Korean. *Harvard Studies in Korean Linguistics III*, edited by S. Kuno et al, Cambridge, MA: Department of Linguistics, Harvard University, 177-188, 1989.

Silva, D. J. A comparison of Korean and Japanese pitch-accent from a prosodic perspective. *Japanese/Korean Linguistics*, edited by H. Hoji, Stanford, CA: SLI, 182-205, 1990.

Silva, D. J. A prosody-based investigation into the phonetics of Korean stop voicing. *Harvard Studies in Korean Linguistics IV*, edited by S. Kuno et al. Cambridge, MA: Department of Linguistics, Harvard University, 1991.

Silva, D. J. *The Phonetics and Phonology of Stop Lenition in Korean.* Ithaca, NY: DMLL Publications, 1992.

2
Phonological Incorporation of the Korean Glottal Approximant

Gregory K. Iverson and *Young-Key Kim-Renaud*

1. Phenomenon

Among the general phonological properties of /h/ in Korean is a symmetrical, bidirectional effect of aspiration on adjacent lax stops: Heteromorphemic sequences of /h/ plus /p, t, k/ emerge as aspirated /ph, th, kh/ ([p^h, t^h, k^h]), the same as sequences of /p, t, k/ plus /h/.[1] For example, the cluster consisting of a lax velar stop /k/ followed by the glottal approximant /h/ is merged into a single aspirated stop /kh/ [k^h] in the pronunciation of [sok^{h}i] 'fast' adv., which derives from underlying /sok+hi/; with identical results, the reverse sequence of /h/ plus /k/ also merges into /kh/ [k^h], as in the realization of underlying /coh + ko/ as [cok^{h}o] 'good-and'.[2] These and some similar examples are listed in (1).

---

[1] Many of the ideas behind the general focus of this paper were developed on the basis of initial conversations and electronic correspondence with Hyang-Sook Sohn. However, circumstances have forced the current authors (who bear all responsibility for any errors or infelicities that may follow) to complete the study without her. We also wish to thank Ross King and an anonymous reviewer for their thoughtful comments and suggestions.

Yale romanization is used throughout for transliteration of Korean words, except in those cases where another personally preferred or generally accepted romanization is known to us. In presenting linguistic data, however, we have used broad phonetic or phonemic representations in order to avoid possible confusion in understanding the facts. Most of the symbols employed in this paper are essentially like the ones used by Kim-Renaud (1974), and differ only slightly from the IPA symbols: we use [ë] for IPA [v], for example, [š] for IPA [ʃ], [Ñ] for [ŋ], [ʉ] for [ɯ], etc.

(1) Aspiration Merger

a.

/ip + hak/	-->	[ipʰak] 'admission [enter-school]'
/cap + hi/	-->	[capʰi] 'hold-PASSIVE'
/sip + ho/	-->	[šipʰo] 'ten-number'
/kkoc + hi/	-->	[k'ocʰi] 'insert-PASSIVE'
/sok + hi/	-->	[sokʰi] 'fast-ADVERBIAL'

b.

/coh + ko/	-->	[cokʰo] 'good-and'
/noh + ke/	-->	[nokʰe] 'lay-IMPERATIVE'
/nah + ta/	-->	[natʰa] 'give birth-DECLARATIVE'
/neh + ca/	-->	[nëcʰa] 'insert-SUGGESTIVE'
/suh + pëm/	-->	[supʰëm] 'male-tiger'

In some earlier accounts, e.g., Martin (1951), this phenomenon was taken to be the result of a metathesis placing /h/ after the stop, thus merging /h/-plus-stop with sequences of stop-plus-/h/. The metathesized clusters then equated with the class of phonemically aspirated stops, since aspiration was considered to be a separate, coarticulated glottal segment. Current interpetations of Korean phonology, however, including the more recent work of Martin (1986), hold that aspiration may be interpreted as a laryngeal gesture inherent in the articulation of the stop itself (as per C.-W. Kim 1970 and many subsequent studies). On this view, with aspiration represented by a feature rather than a segment, the observed effect of /h/ on adjacent lax stops would appear to be the result, not of metathesis, but of a mirror-image coalescence of /h/-plus-stop and stop-plus-/h/ into a single aspirated stop (Kim-Renaud 1974, K.-H. Kim 1987, Sohn 1987, Cho 1990).

---

[2] There are other, morphologically sensitive alternations associated with /h/ in Korean (viz., verb-stem final h-deletion and affix-final h-deletion as described in Kim-Renaud 1986, Ch. 5); our concern here, however, lies in the purely phonological or phonetic adjustments involving /h/, i.e., in "...prevalent, automatic processes" that apply irrespective of lexical category (Kim-Renaud 1986:78).

2. Proposal

The present paper develops and motivates an alternative to the coalescence as well as the metathesis analysis. In brief, it is hypothesized that a conventional assimilation takes place in either of the orders involving sequences of /h/ and a lax stop, according to which all the specified features and structures of the left segment spread into the underspecified portions of the right one. This monodirectional operation is motivated by language-specific properties of Korean, particulalry syllable-final unreleasing, as well as by more general considerations of syllable contact and the spread of marked into unmarked structure. The resulting bisegmental representations are then subject to further, independently motivated adjustments, including the obligatory neutralization of syllable-final /h/ to [t] in (extra-)careful speech (/coh + kho/ --> /cot + kho/), the optional regressive assimilation of place of articulation features in stop clusters (/cot + kho/ --> /cok+ kho/), and the stylistically governed simplification of long segments (/cok+kho/ --> [cok^{h}o]) observable in casual or sloppy speech. In addition, geminate or long aspirated stops are also possible realizations of the underlying order of stop-plus-/h/ (/ip + hak/ --> /ip + phak/, /sok + hi/ --> /sok + khi/), though in more rapid speech these too are pronounced with single, short aspirated stops ([ip^{h}ak], [sok^{h}i]). The frequently cited single segment reductions listed in (1) thus form only part of the story relating to the phonological incorporation of /h/ in stop clusters: underlying sequences of stop-plus-/h/ actually may surface with either long or short aspirated stops, as exemplified in (2a), and /h/-plus-stop sequences can emerge in any one of the three form types listed in (2b) (the ⁿ' symbol indicates unreleased articulation of the preceding stop).[3]

(2) Variation: EXTRA CAREFUL   CAREFUL   CASUAL
a.   /ip + hak/   -->   ....[ip⁀p^{h}ak].........[ip^{h}ak⁀]
     /cap + hi/   -->   ....[cap⁀p^{h}ⁱi].........[cap^{h}ⁱi]
     /sip + ho/   -->   ....[šip⁀p^{h}o].........[šip^{h}o]
     /kkoc + hi/   -->   ....[k'oc⁀c^{h}i].........[k'oc^{h}i]
     /sok + hi/   -->   ....[sok⁀k^{h}i].........[sok^{h}i]

---

[3] Facts such as these are reviewed, in part, under the rubrics "conflation" and "compression" in Martin (1986:120, 1992:51-52).

	Variation:		EXTRA CAREFUL	CAREFUL	CASUAL
b.	/coh + ko/	-->	[coťkʰo]............	[cokˀkʰo]......	[cokʰo]
	/noh + ke/	-->	[noťkʰe]............	[nokˀkʰe]......	[nokʰe]
	/nah + ta/	-->	............[naťtʰa]............		[natʰa]
	/neh + ca/	-->	............[nëïcʰa]............		[nëcʰa]
	/suh + pem/	-->	[suˀpʰëm]............	[supˀpʰëm]......	[supʰëm]

3. Analysis

The variants in (2b) all derive from familiar independent generalizations in Korean phonology if it is first assumed, as will be motivated below, that a stem-final /h/ induces aspiration in immediately following lax stops, e.g. /h+k/ --> /h+kh/. An intermediate representation like /coh + kho/ < /coh + ko/ will then be subject to syllable-final neutralization in the same way as are the word-final illustrations in (3).

(3) Coda Neutralization

/p	pp	ph/	-->[pˀ]	/iph/	-->	[ipˀ]	'leaf'
/t	tt	th/	-->[tˀ]	/nath/	-->	[natˀ]	'each'
/c	cc	ch/	-->[tˀ]	/nach/	-->	[natˀ]	'face'
/s	ss/		-->[tˀ]	/nas/	-->	[natˀ]	'sickle'
/h/	-->		[tˀ]	/nah/	-->	[natˀ]	'give birth'
/k	kk	kh/	-->[kˀ]	/pok/	-->	[pokˀ]	'happiness, good luck'

The neutralizations in (3) are motivated by the phonetic implementation constraint presented in (4).

(4) Syllable-final Nonrelease
Oral contact in syllable-final consonants may not be immediately released.[4]

Following a line of reasoning in Korean phonology beginning with Kim-Renaud (1974), we interpret nonrelease in terms of the maintenance (preceded by imposition of closure, in the case of continuants) of oral contact throughout the segment's articulation.[5] The phonological consequence of such unreleasing, in terms of a feature-geometric model of the kind employed

---

[4] Iverson & Sohn (1994) point out that the nonrelease restriction also extends to nasals and the liquid, thus accounting for the occurrence of (centrally) unreleased allophones of syllable-final sonorant consonants, too; in the case of the liquid phoneme, syllable-final nonrelease results in a lateral ([l]) rather than in the continuously released allophone ([r]).

by Iverson & Kim (1987), for example, is that 'all terminal features are delinked in syllable-final position'. Thus syllable-final labials and velars lose their distinctive laryngeal properties–[spread glottis] or [constricted glottis]–to emerge as neither aspirated nor glottally tense, as do the coronals, whose [continuant] quality in fricatives or affricates also disappears in favor of the phonologically featureless, unmarked obstruent in Korean. This obstruent, by general default interpretation, is the lax coronal stop [t] (cf. Kim-Renaud 1974, Martin 1982, and Iverson 1989 regarding Korean, or Paradis & Prunet 1991 for elaboration of the crosslinguistically unmarked status of coronals). With respect to /h/, neutralization by delinking results in the default consonant [t], too, since /h/, a glottal approximant marked only for the terminal features [continuant] and [spread glottis], has no inherent place of articulation features. Hence /coh + kho/ --> [cot̚kʰo], the "...slow, bookish, emphatic pronunciation..." of /coh + ko/ (Kim-Renaud 1974:124), and so on.

Another variant of the /h/-plus-stop type of cluster consists in the sequence of an unreleased stop and a following homorganic aspirated stop, as in [cok̚kʰo]; in forms like these, we assume the coda-neutralized /h/ --> /t/ has further undergone regressive assimilation in place of articulation. Place assimilation, by which labials assimilate to velars and coronals assimilate to both labials and velars, is a very general and independent process in Korean (Kim-Renaud 1974, Cho 1988, Avery & Rice 1989); some illustrations are given in (5).[6]

(5)   Place of Articulation Assimilation
/pan + myen/   -->   [pammyën]   'on the other hand'
                                  (< 'opposite' + 'side')
/han + kang/   -->   [haŋgaŋ]   'Han River'
/pat + ko/   -->   [pak̚k'o]   'receive-and'
/os + pota/   -->   [op̚p'oda]   'clothes-than'
/ep + ko/   -->   [ëk̚k'o]   'carry-and'
/kam + ki/   -->   [kaÑgi]   'cold' (< 'feeling' + 'air, breath, wind')

---

[5] The absence of immediate release thus reduces perceptual cues, which is the reason for restructuring in many free-standing forms like nouns. A partial phonetic definition of syllable-final unreleasing may lie in a recent study by Silverman & Jun (1994) demonstrating that some word-internal consonantal sequences involve a high degree of gestural overlap as well as gestural reduction. However, this observation needs to be further researched in relation to unreleasing of word-final consonants, which show the same phonological behavior as the word-internal syllable-final consonants.

By virtue of the same assimilation, then, formal speech variants like [cok̚kʰo] 'good-and' (or, vacuously, [nat̚t̚ʰa] 'give birth-DECLARATIVE) derive from intermediate structures in which the coda /h/ has been neutralized to /t/: /coh + kho/ --> /cot + kho/ --> [cok̚kʰo] (/nah + tha/ --> /nat + tha/ --> [nat̚t̚ʰa]).

The final variant of the forms in (2b) is also due to operation of an independent principle, in this case to the reduction of geminate obstruents that takes place in casual, rapidly spoken speech (Kim-Renaud 1974:241-243, 1987:351). In fast speech, accidental geminates arising from the juxtaposition of morphemes as well as geminates derived either through assimilation (as in (5)) or through the process which accounts for the fact that long forms in (2a) (see below) may be pronounced as short. Some examples of the ensuing variation are given in (6).

(6)   Geminate Reduction
a. /ip + pota/   -->   [ip̚p'oda] ~ [ip'oda]   'mouth-rather than'
    /path + to/   -->   [pat̚t'o] ~ [pat'o]   'field-also'
    /mek + ko/   -->   [mëk̚k'o] ~ [mëk'o]   'eat-and'
b. /pat + ko/   -->   [pak̚k'o] ~ [pak'o]   'receive-and'
    /kot + palo/   -->   [kop̚p'aro] ~ [kop'aro]   'straight'
    /ep + ko/   -->   [ëk̚k'o] ~ [ëk'o]   'carry-and'

4. Generalization

In conjunction with three separate generalizations of Korean phonology, then--Coda Neutralization, Place Assimilation, Geminate Reduction--the pronunciation variants involving underlying obstruent clusters

---

[6] Place assimilation is variable, and is considerably more likely to affect the lesser marked coronals than the more marked labials. Nonetheless, (extra-)careful pronunciation of final /h/ as [t] is possible even in preconsonantal position, as Kim-Renaud (1974:185, fn. 18) verified in a series of tests with native speakers of the Standard Seoul dialect and recently confirmed using a slightly different methodology. Throughout, unassimilated [t] deriving from /h/ was judged no less natural than syllable-final [t] originating from other sources, e.g., in [ut̚k'ine] (rather than [uk̚k'ine]) < /wus-ki-ney/ 'Don't you make me laugh!' and [kut̚k'e] (rather than [kuk̚k'e]) < /kwut-key/ 'firmly', considered to be equally as natural (or unnatural) as [cot̚kʰo] (rather than [cok̚kʰo]) < /coh-ko/, etc. In word-final position, however, the conversion of /h/ to [t] often results in restructuring due to the absence of supporting alternations, e.g., [hiɯt̚] is the invariant pronunciation today of historical /hiuh/ 'name of the letter *h*', as cited, for example, in the 1962 edition of North Korea's *Korean Language Dictionary (Cosenmal sacen)*, p. 4038 (though Martin et. al. 1967:1779 still list the word as pronounced with final [h], as [hiɯh]).

with /h/ can all be explained. The necessary initial supposition is that /h/, on the one hand, induces aspiration in an immediately following stop (cf. (2b)), and, on the other hand, serves as a docking site for the assimilatory extension of the oral features of an immediately preceding stop (cf. (2a)). In terms of present programs for the geometric representation of phonological features (Clements 1993, Clements & Hume 1994), the trigger for the variation noted in (2) lies in the rightward spreading of specified into unspecified structure: Either the glottal approximant's [spread glottis] gesture spreads into the unmarked Laryngeal constituent of the following stop, or the stop's Oral Cavity configuration spreads into the underspecified root node of the following glottal approximant. For example, the specified laryngeal quality of /h/ extends into the unmarked Laryngeal node of a following /k/, as shown in (7a), and the specified oral qualities of /k/ extend into a following /h/, which is not marked for Oral Cavity features, as illustrated in (7b).

(7)   a. /h + k/ --> /h + kh/   b. /k + h/ --> /k + kh/

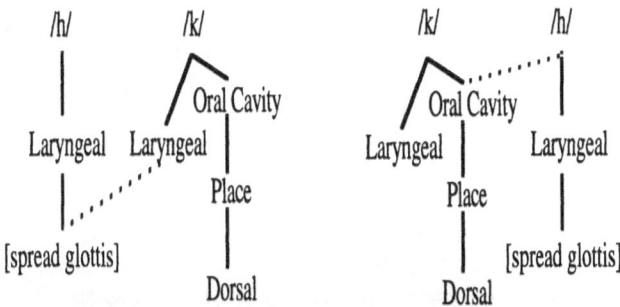

Just as /k/ acquires the aspiration or [spread glottis] property of /h/ in an /h + k/ sequence, then, /h/ acquires the oral properties of /k/ in a /k + h/ sequence.[7] The effect of these adjustments is to 'improve the sonority

---

[7] We consider that the [continuant] quality of /h/ is redundant in geometric representation since this segment is otherwise represented only for the Laryngeal node; in stops, the phonological absence of [continuant] specification (versus its presence in fricatives and affricates) is the unmarked case. Hence the spread of the Oral Cavity node of /k/ rightward into /h/ results in the phonemic representation of an aspirated stop, not an aspirated fricative, which would be ruled out in Korean by Structure Preservation in any event (see also footnotes 7 and 8 below).

relations' between the termination of one syllable and the beginning of the next.[8] In particular, parallel to several other Korean assimilations as analyzed by Iverson & Sohn (1994), the strengthening to /kh/ of both onset /k/ in /h + k/ and onset /h/ in /k + h/ reflects the frequently cited preference expressed in the Syllable Contact Law formulated by Murray & Vennemann (1983:520) (cf. also Vennemann 1988):

(8) Syllable Contact Law
The preference for a syllable structure A.B, where A and B are marginal segments and *a* and *b* are the Consonantal Strength values of A and B, respectively, increases with the value of *b* minus *a*.

As Murray & Vennemann clarify (cf. also Clements 1993, and numerous earlier sources), Consonantal Strength is merely the inverse of sonority, i.e., the greater the value of one the less is the value of the other:

(9)   SONORITY SCALE   STRENGTH HIERARCHY
      0. Obstruents   0. Glides
         0.0 Tense/Aspirated   1. Liquids
         0.5 Lax   2. Nasals
      1. Nasals   3. Obstruents
      2. Liquids   3.0 Lax
      3. Glides   3.5 Tense/Aspirated

---

[8] As Hyang-Sook Sohn has pointed out to us, it might be expected that underlying aspirated stops should also trigger the rightward extension of [spread glottis] into a following lax stop, but this does not happen: /kiph + ta/ --> [kipt'a] (cf. (11)), not *[kipt^{h}a]. Phonetically, this would appear to be due to the interruption of airflow in the aspirated stop, making spread of the open glottis gesture less dynamically motivated than in the case of the orally uninterrupted /h/. Phonologically, we note that the structure of /h/ as given in (7) refers to only a single line of autosegmental association between the Laryngeal node and the root element to which it is attached, whereas an aspirated stop (as in the output of (7a)) includes association lines between the root element and the Oral Cavity node as well as the Laryngeal node; by terms of the Autosegmental Linking Constraint (Hayes 1986), or Uniformity Condition (Kenstowicz 1994), the rule of Aspiration Adjustment described in (12) will affect only clusters that include /h/ as the segment containing [spread glottis], not phonemically aspirated stops as well, because the only association the rule need refer to relative to this feature is the single line between the root element and the Laryngeal node in /h/, not the multiple lines of association involved in the representation of an aspirated stop.

At the point of contact between syllables, then, segments in codas are preferred which have a lower numeric rating in the strength hierarchy (higher value on the sonority scale), and segments in onsets are preferred which have a higher index in the strength hierarchy (lower value on the sonority scale). For example, coda obstruents in Korean assimilate to nasals, as exemplified in (10a), and to the liquid, as exemplified in (10b). This assimilation improves the sonority profile of the syllables in contact because it weakens the coda consonant to a sonorant. Putting it generally, the consonantal strength difference between an onset sonorant and a coda sonorant is more nearly optimal than that between an onset sonorant and a coda obstruent:[9]

(10) Sonority Assimilation
    a. /han-kuk + mal/ -->[haŋguŋmal] 'Korean language'
       /aph + nal/ -->[amnal] 'future' (< 'front-day')
       /path+ nongsa/ -->[pannoŋsa] '(dry) field farming'
    b. /tikut + liul/ -->[tigɨlliɨl] 't...l' (sequence in alphabet)
       /pep-lyul/ -->[pěmnyul] 'law'
       /pak-lam/ -->[paŋnam] 'exhibition'

The same principle provides motivation for other, apparently nonassimilatory processes in the language. Thus it is widely maintained that the tense and aspirated obstruents of Korean are phonologically 'stronger' than the unmarked lax ones to which the marked obstruents neutralize in syllable codas (cf. (3)). An otherwise rather mysterious phenomenon in the language, the post-obstruent tensing of syllable-initial lax obstruents exemplified in (11) (cf. also relevant obstruent clusters in (5) and (6)), accordingly takes its motivation too from the Syllable Contact Law. Specifically, tense obstruents are rated higher on the strength hierarchy (3.5) than are lax obstruents (3.0), hence the syllable contact situation between coda and onset is improved if the onset member in the sequence is strengthened, in this case by becoming glottally tense, the strongest category in the hierarchy.[10]

---

[9] In the heterorganic clusters of stop plus liquid illustrated in (10b), the result of 'assimilation' is a default sequence of otherwise occurring nasals rather than a sequence of liquids whose first member is noncoronal (which is not a possible segment in Korean). Nasal plus liquid clusters assimilate in the same way, defaulting to nasality throughout when the cluster is not strictly coronal (/sam-Lyu/ --> [samnyu] 'third-rate') but retaining approximant qualities in homorganic, coronal clusters (/chen-Li/ --> [cʰělli] 'natural law'); in liquid plus nasal clusters, however, assimilation is progressive: /sel + naL/ --> [sěllal] 'New Year's Day' (cf. Iverson & Sohn 1994).

(11) Post-obstruent Tensing
/cap + ko/   --> [cap̚k'o]   'catches-and'
/kiph + ta/ --> [kip̚t'a]   'deep-DECLARATIVE'
/kkoch + to/ --> [k'ot̚t'o]   'flowers-also'
/kkak + ca/ --> [k'ak̚c'a]   'shear-IMPERATIVE'

On the common assumption expressed in (9) that aspirated stops also rank higher in consonantal strength than lax stops, a motivation emerges as well for the aspiration related changes illustrated in (7).[11] Thus, a syllable contact of the form /h + k/ is improved by strengthening the lax syllable-initial stop in the sequence to an aspirate (cf. (7a)), which, moreover, facilitates recovery of the underlying /h/ since that segment itself actually surfaces as an unreleased stop; similarly, the contact in a /k + h/ sequence is improved by strengthening the inherently weak glottal approximant in the syllable onset to a true stop (cf. (7b)). Because there is no other assimilatory, higher sonority source for syllable contact improvement of the kind exemplified in (9), yet the requirement for nonrelease in coda consonants remains in force, the most direct, simplest way available to improve the /h + k/ or /k + h/ contact is to extend marked coda features into unmarked onset positions. Thus while lax obstruents are made glottally tense when following unreleased stops (cf. (11)), syllable-final /h/, which itself neutralizes to a stop (cf. (4)), induces aspiration rather than tensification in the following obstruent.[12] Tensing is defined on a much broader class of segments than are the adjustments reflected in (7), however, hence--in the spirit of the familiar 'Elsewhere Condition' (Kiparsky 1973)–the aspiration phenomenon predictably takes precedence. The rule which triggers the assimilations illustrated in (7) can then be summed up as in (12).

[10] Kim-Renaud (1974:129-132) hypothesizes that this tensing results from heightened oral air pressure caused by unreleasing of the preceding consonants.

[11] If the post-obstruent stop is aspirated to begin with, of course, tensification does not take place, because aspirated stops already occupy the strongest, lowest-sonority category along with tense consonants.

[12] If the following obstruent type does not participate in the aspiration contrast, however, as with the two fricatives /s/ and /ss/ [s'] (there is no /sʰ/ phoneme in Korean, cf. Iverson 1983), then tensification holds sway—the principle of Structure Preservation (Kiparsky 1985) precludes the production of an aspirated fricative; in these cases, coda-neutralized /h/ merges functionally with underlying /t/, which also attracts into itself the continuant property of the following fricative: /kwut+so/ --> [kuss'o] 'It's hardening!', /coh + so/ --> /cot + so/ --> [coss'o] 'OK!'.

(12) Aspiration Adjustment
In a heterosyllablic cluster containing /h/ and a lax consonant, spread marked features from the coda to the onset.

This monodirectional operation copies the Laryngeal feature [spread glottis] from /h/ into a following lax stop, thus aspirating it, but it also copies the Oral Cavity properties of a syllable-final stop into a following /h/, strengthening the /h/ to an aspirated stop. Both aspects of the structural change are motivated by the Syllable Contact Law since they result in enhanced consonantal strength in onsets, and both conform to Cho's (1988, 1990) insightful observation that Korean assimilations always involve the spread of marked into unmarked structure. Independent generalizations of Korean phonology then come into play to account for the coda neutralization of /h/ to /t/, for the assimilation of this /t/ to marked place of articulation in a following consonant, and for the simplification of homorganic obstruents via degemination in fast speech.

5. Alternatives to assimilation

Under the now conventional coalescence analysis, however, which merges the two input segments into a single aspirated stop directly, forms with geminate or long stops like [cok̚kʰo] < /coh + ko/ and [cap̚pʰi] < /cap + hi/ would have to be accounted for by inserting a segment (or a mora) before the derived aspirated stop. It turns out that a form of stop gemination is a necessary process in the language in any event because medial, syllable-initial tense or aspirated (i.e. marked) obstruents may be lengthened for emphasis even when no /h/ precedes: [ap̚p'a] < /appa/ 'daddy', [ak̚k'a] < /akka/ 'before'. Expressive gemination could not explain forms like [cot̚kʰo], however, since the [t̚] in the [t̚kʰ] cluster does not share its place of articulation with the following stop. Nor could variants of the [cot̚kʰo] type be explained by claiming that the segment inserted is the unmarked obstruent /t/, because [t] never shows up as an alternative to underlying /p/ or /k/, i.e. *[cat̚pʰi] is not a possible realization of /cap + hi/ (cf. (13a)), nor *[at̚p'a] of /appa/ (cf. (13b)), etc. Alternatively, if the [t] in words like [cot̚kʰo] is due to syllable-final neutralization of /h/, as in the assimilation analysis developed in the present paper, then the coalescence approach would not be able to derive aspiration in the following stop because neutralization converts the underlying /h/ in /coh + ko/ to an unaspirated [t] (cf. (13c)); if the /h/ instead first coalesces with the /k/ to produce [kʰ], conversely, then /h/ would no longer be available to be neutralized into [t] (cf. (13d)). These dilemmas do not arise under the assimilation analysis just presented (cf. (13e)), which retains the bisegmental skeletal structure of the input representations while spreading material specified in the left segment into positions underspecified in the right segment.

(13)   Coalescence vs. Assimilation
a. /h/-Cluster variation via optional assimilation and degemination:
/coh + ko/-->   /cot + kho/-->   [cok̚k^{h}o] ~ [cok^{h}o], also [cot̚k^{h}o]
/cap + hi/-->   /cap + phi/-->   [cap̚p^{h}i] ~ [cap^{h}i] (not *[cat̚p^{h}i])

b. Emphatic lengthening:
/appa/ 'daddy'   -->[ap'a] (BASE) ~ [ap̚'p'a] (EXPRESSIVE) (not *[at̚'p'a])
/akka/ 'before'   -->[ak'a] (BASE) ~ [ak̚'k'a] (EXPRESSIVE) (not*[at̚'k'a])

c.   If Coalescence: /coh + ko/ --> [cok^{h}o], but then no [cot̚k^{h}o].
d.   If Coda Neutralization: /coh + ko/ --> *[cotko], then no [cok^{h}o].
e.   If Aspiration Assimilation and Coda Neutralization: cf. (13a).

The aspiration adjustments as described for obstruents are also relevant to clusters involving /h/ and sonorant consonants, though in these cases there is no neutralization since Korean does not contrast voiced with voiceless or aspirated sonorants, perhaps explaining why there has been little descriptive awareness of this phenomenon in the literature on Korean phonology. For example, an underlying sequence of liquid plus /h/, as in /mal + ha + ta/ 'speak' (< 'language+do+DECLARATIVE'), is realized in careful speech unremarkably as [malhada], but in faster speech styles it emerges with the liquid properties having extended into the /h/, as in [mall̥ada] = [mal̥l̥ada]; simplifying further, the geminate liquid may reduce to a single consonant parsing as onset to the following syllable: [mar̥ada] (Iverson & Sohn 1994). Similarly, a casual speech rendition of /sil-hyen/ 'realization, actualization' would be [šir̥yën], with aspiration merged into the liquid now occupying syllable-initial position, though more careful pronunciations like [šil̥yën] and [šilhyën] are also possible.[13] We represent voiceless sonorants, like aspiration, in terms of the feature [spread glottis] (cf. Clements 1985, Cho 1991, Iverson & Salmons 1994), thus the [spread glottis] articulation which identifies /h/ extends into the liquid, causing it too to become voiceless, or 'aspirated'. As illustrated in the summary in (14), other sonorant plus /h/ sequences undergo the same process, e.g., /an + ha + ko/ 'NEGATIVE-do-and'

---

[13] There is regional/dialectal variation in these forms. Within a word, a liquid preceding underlying /h/ may be parsed as a syllable onset in Standard Korean, but in such dialects as Kyengsang it is more often parsed as a coda. Thus it is quite common to find the voiceless liquid in Kyengsang, but not in the standard Seoul dialect.

has variants of the form [anhago], [anɦago], [aŋago]. In /h/ plus sonorant sequences, on the other hand, the (morphophonemic) coda neutralization of /h/ to /t/ takes precedence and feeds into other assimilations of the language, thus bleeding any possibility of the rightward spread of /h/ into a sonorant, e.g., /swuh + nom/ 'male creature' appears with voiced nasals throughout, [sunnom].

(14) Sonorant clusters with /h/
/mal + ha + ta/   -->   [malhada] ~ [mallʰada] = [malḷada] ~ [maɾada]
/sil-hyen/   -->   [šilhyən] ~ [šillʰyən] = [s*ilḷyən] ~ [s*iɾyən]
/an + ha + ko/   -->   [anhago] ~ [annʰago] = [annago] ~ [aŋago]
/swuh + nom/   -->   /swut+nom/   -->   [sunnom]

6. Conclusion

To summarize and conclude, this paper has argued for an alternative to the traditional coalescence (or metathesis) analysis of /h/-incorporation in Korean consonant clusters. Specifically, it has been proposed here that a conventional assimilation takes place in either of the orders involving sequences of /h/ and a lax stop, according to which all the specified features and structures of the left segment spread into the underspecified portions of the right one, underscoring Cho's (1988, 1990) suggestion that Korean assimilations always involve the spread of marked into unmarked structure. This monodirectional operation copies the Laryngeal feature [spread glottis] from /h/ into a following lax stop, thus aspirating it, but it also extends the Oral Cavity properties of a syllable-final stop into a following /h/, strengthening the /h/ to an aspirated stop; additionally, in the case of a liquid or a nasal preceding the glottal approximant, the spread of Oral Cavity features into /h/ produces segment types which are novel in Korean, viz., voiceless sonorant consonants (illustrated in (14)). Each aspect of the structural change of the /h/-incorporation process is motivated by considerations of syllable contact, moreover, since the rule regularly results in enhanced consonantal strength (= lowered sonority) in syllable onsets. The resulting bisegmental representations are subject to other, independently motivated adjustments, including the obligatory neutralization of syllable-final /h/ to [t] in careful speech, the optional regressive assimilation to marked place of articulation features in stop clusters, and the stylistically governed simplification of long segments. But /h/-incorporation itself may be construed as a simple, unified process of marked-into-unmarked progressive assimilation, affecting sequences of /h/ plus stop as well as stop plus /h/.

References

Avery, P. and K. Rice. Segment Structure and Coronal Underspecification. *Phonology* 6, pp.179-200, 1989.

Cho, Y.-M. Y. Korean Assimilation. *Papers from the West Coast Conference on Formal Linguistics* 7.41-52, 1988.

Cho, Y.-M. Y. *Parameters of Consonantal Assimilation.* Ph.D. Dissertation, Stanford University, 1990.

Cho, Y.-M. Y. 'Voiceless' Sonorants are Aspirates, paper presented at the 65th Annual Meeting of the Linguistic Society of America, Chicago, 1991.

Clements, G. N. The Geometry of Phonological Features. *Phonology Yearbook* 2. 225-252, 1985.

Clements, G. N. Lieu d'articulation des consonnes et des voyelles: une théorie unifiée. In *Architecture des représentations phonologiques*, edited by B. Laks and A. Rialland, Collection Sciences du Langage. Paris: CNRS Editions, pp. 101-145, 1993.

Clements, G. N. and E. V. Hume. The Internal Organization of Speech Sounds. To appear in *A Handbook of Phonological Theory*, edited by J. Goldsmith, London: Blackwell, 1994.

Hayes, B. Inalterability in CV Phonology. *Language* 62.321-352, 1986.

Iverson, G. K. Korean *s*. *Journal of Phonetics* 11.191-200, 1983.

Iverson, G. K. On the Category Supralaryngeal. *Phonology* 6.285-304, 1989.

Iverson, G. K. and K.-H. Kim. Underspecification and Hierarchical Feature Representation in Korean Consonantal Phonology. *CLS* 23:2.(*Chicago Linguistic Society: Papers from the Parasession on Autosegmental and Metrical Phonology*, edited by A. Bosch, et al. Chicago: University of Chicago.), 182-198, 1987.

Iverson, G. K. and J. C. Salmons. Aspiration and Laryngeal Representation in Germanic. *Phonology* 12. 369-396, 1995.

Iverson, G. K. and H.-S. Sohn. Liquid Representation in Korean. In *Theoretical Issues in Korean Linguistics*, edited by Y.-K. Kim-Renaud, Stanford University: Center for the Study of Language and Information, pp. 79-100, 1994.

Kenstowicz, M. *Phonology in Generative Grammar.* Cambridge, MA: Blackwell Publishers, 1994.

Kim, C.-W. A Theory of Aspiration. *Phonetica* 21.107-116. Reprinted in *Sojourns in Language I (Collected Papers by Chin-W. Kim)*. Seoul: Tower Press, pp. 73-82, 1988, 1970.

Kim, K.-H. *The Phonological Representation of Distinctive Features: Korean Consonantal Phonology*. Ph.D. Dissertation, University of Iowa, 1987.

Kim-Renaud, Y.-K. *Korean Consonantal Phonology*. Ph.D. Dissertation, University of Hawaii, 1974.

Kim-Renaud, Y.-K. *Studies in Korean Linguistics*. Seoul: Hanshin, 1986.

Kim-Renaud, Y.-K. Fast Speech, Casual Speech, and Restructuring. *Harvard Studies in Korean Linguistics* 2.341-359, 1987.

Kiparsky, P. 'Elsewhere' in Phonology. In *A Festschrift for Morris Halle*, edited by S. R. Anderson and P. Kiparsky, New York: Holt, Rinehart and Winston, pp.93-106, 1973.

Kiparsky, P. Some Consequences of Lexical Phonology. *Phonology Yearbook* 2.85-138, 1985.

Martin, S. E. Korean Phonemics. *Language* 27.519-533, 1951.

Martin, S. E. Features, Markedness, and Order in Korean Phonology. In *Linguistics in the Morning Calm*, edited by I.-S. Yang, Seoul: Hanshin Publishing Company, pp. 601-618, 1982.

Martin, S. E. Phonetic Compression and Conflation in English and in Korean. In *Studies in Korean Language and Linguistics*, edited by N.-K. Kim, Los Angeles: University of Southern California East Asian Studies Center, pp.118-124, 1986.

Martin, S. E. *A Reference Grammar of Korean*. Tokyo: Charles E. Tuttle Publishing Co., Inc, 1992.

Murray, R. W. and T. Vennemann. Sound Change and Syllable Structure in Germanic Phonology. *Language* 59.514-528, 1983.

Paradis, C. and J.-F. Prunet. *The Special Status of Coronals: Internal and External Evidence*. New York: Academic Press, 1991.

Silverman, D. and J. Jun. Aerodynamic Evidence for Articulatory Overlap in Korean. *Phonetica* 51.210-220, 1994.

Sohn, H.-S. *Underspecification in Korean Phonology*. Ph.D. Dissertation, University of Illinois, 1987.

Vennemann, T. *Preference Laws for Syllable Structure and the Explanation of Sound Change—with Special Reference to German, Germanic, Italian, and Latin*. Berlin: Mouton, 1988.

Dictionaries Cited

DPRK [Democratic People's Republic of Korea] Academy of Science, Language and Literature Research Institute (compiled). *Cosenmal Sacen [Korean Language Dictionary]*. Phyengyang: Academy of Science Publishing Co, 1962.

Martin, S. E., Y.-H. Lee and S.-U. Chang. *A Korean-English Dictionary.* New Haven & London: Yale University Press, 1967.

3
Umlaut Uniformity in Korean and Old High German

Gregory K. Iverson and *Shinsook Lee*

Introduction.*

In Old High German, the central and southern variety of German recorded in manuscripts dating from the 8th–12th Centuries, certain consonant clusters exerted an umlaut-hindering effect in the assimilation of /a/ to [e]. In particular, umlaut failed to occur when a cluster containing /h/ intervened between the triggering segment, an /i/ or /j/ in the next syllable, and the target back vowel.[1] In some present-day varieties of Korean, similarly, there exists a synchronic umlaut phenomenon whereby back vowels are fronted before /i/ in the next syllable, and this process too is inhibited by certain intervening consonants—specifically, by palatals (Hume 1990, Lee 1994). The present paper develops an account of umlaut blocking in Korean which draws parallels to the feature-geometric analysis of umlaut in Old High German recently worked out by Iverson, Salmons & Davis (1994). In both languages, it will be argued, umlaut is free to take place across consonants just in case those consonants are phonologically independent of the vowels involved in the assimilation. In Old High German, tautosyllabic /h/ likely

---

* We wish to thank members of the audience at the presentation of this paper in London for their helpful and insightful comments, especially Sang-Cheol Ahn, Young-mee Yu Cho, Chin-Wu Kim, David Silva, and Young-Key Kim-Renaud.

[1] The blocking of umlaut in Old High German is treated in detail by Iverson, Salmons & Davis (1994). In southern varieties of the language, where the blocking effect was most pervasive, clusters of liquid plus consonant also inhibited umlaut, which Iverson, Salmons & Davis attribute to the vocalization of syllable-final liquids in Upper German in conjunction with operation of the autosegmental line crossing prohibition.

shared oral properties with the vowel that was nominally subject to umlaut, and in Korean, the vowel which would otherwise trigger umlaut shares place of articulation features with a preceding palatal consonant. In both cases, suspension of the application of umlaut may be attributed to operation of the Autosegmental Linking Constraint (Hayes 1986), also known as the Uniformity Condition (Kenstowicz 1994). This principle holds that, in the structural descriptions of phonological rules, lines of autosegmental association must be interpreted as exhaustive. The applicational consequence is that geometrically shared configurations will satisfy a rule's structural requirements only if they are specifically referred to by the rule. Under the Uniformity Condition, umlaut does not apply over syllable-final /h/ in Old High German, or over palatal consonants preceding /i/ in Korean, because the rule does not explicitly make reference to their shared or multiply associated properties.

The paper first lays out the umlaut situation as it is generally thought to have developed in the history of German, then turns to parallels in modern Korean. Throughout, a geometric scheme of representation is assumed in which vowels and consonants are characterized in terms of the same features, following Clements (1993) and Clements & Hume (1995).

1. Medieval German.

In the philological tradition of studies on Old High German, 'primary' umlaut is the term reserved for the process first indicated in the 8th Century which converts /a/ to [e] before /i/ or /j/ in the next syllable. In contrast to 'secondary' umlaut as recorded later in Middle High German (see below), this assimilation failed to occur when a cluster of the shape /hC/ intervened between the triggering segment and the target back vowel; hence fronting was not marked in forms like *naht/nahti* 'night' sg./pl., but it was marked in forms like *gast/gesti* 'guest' sg./pl. (Braune 1987), as seen in comparison of the forms in (1) versus those in (2).

(1) OHG primary umlaut
   gast/gesti   'guest' sg./pl.
   anst/ensti   'mercy' sg./pl.
   lamb/lembir   'lamb' sg./pl.
   leggen (< lagjan) 'lay' inf.
   faru/feris/ferit   'drive' 1/2/3 sg.

(2) Umlaut failure in OHG
   maht/mahti   'power' sg./pl.
   mahtig   'power' adj.
   naht/nahti   'night' sg./pl.
   gislahti   'race, tribe'
   wahsan/wahsit 'grow'inf./3sg.

The grapheme *h* in *ht* and *hs* clusters likely no longer represented a Germanic velar fricative [x], but had already been weakened to the glottal approximant [h] in Old High German (Braune 1987). Following Clements (1985), Keating (1988), Iverson (1989), and many earlier general phonetics descriptions, the oral properties of [h] may be understood as derivative of those of the neighboring tautosyllabic vowel. Thus the [h] in English *heat* is palatal, like the /i/ following, whereas the [h] in *hot* is retracted or dorsal, the same as the following /a/. Indeed, as has often been pointed out, a word like *heat* could as well be transcribed as [i̯it] (= [çit]), or *hot* as [a̯at] (= [hat]), in order to show explicitly that the segmental qualities of [h], apart from voicelessness, are the same as those of the tautosyllabic vowel. Assuming that Old High German was no different in this respect, syllable-final [h] in words like *mahtig* would also have had the same oral features as the neighboring vowel, i.e., [mah.tig] = [maa̯.tig].²

Under the model of segment representation put forward by Clements (1993), the same place of articulation features are used in the description of both consonants and vowels. The features vary in their geometric organization, however: vowel place features are subsumed under the category of V-Place, whereas consonant features fall under C-Place, the general place constituent to which V-Place is also subordinated (cf. also Archangeli & Pulleyblank 1987). Thus labial consonants and rounded vowels are both [labial], but in consonants this feature falls under the C-Place node, in vowels and glides under the V-Place node; similarly, central consonants and front vowels are both [coronal] (under C-Place for consonants, V-Place for vowels), back consonants and back vowels are both [dorsal], and consonants and vowels with retracted tongue root (e.g., pharyngeals) are both [radical]. V-Place also identifies vocalic articulations in consonants: Plain consonants have only a C-Place specification, but secondarily articulated (palatalized, velarized, etc.) consonants, as well as vowels and glides, carry V-Place as a daughter of C-Place. These relationships are illustrated in the geometric comparison in (3), adapted from Clements (1993).

---

² In syllable-initial position, [h] would have taken on the qualities of the vowel following, e.g., in *slahit* 'hit' 3.sg., [sla.hit] = [sla.jit]. Intervocalic *h* thus also exerted an umlaut-blocking effect, but only in Upper German (Bavarian and Alemannic *slahan/slahit*), not in Central German (Franconian *slahan/slehit*); we assume that *h* < /x/ had already weakened to phonetic [h] in syllable onsets in Upper German, but remained a velar fricative in that position in Franconian.

(3)   Plain Consonant vs. Vowel vs. Secondary Consonant Articulation

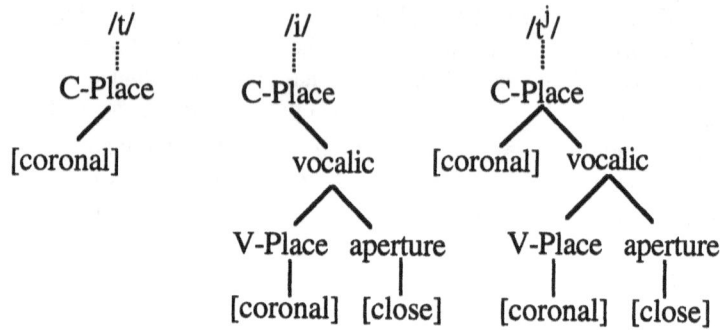

The rule of primary umlaut in Old High German under the geometry in (3) would have had the effect of spreading the [coronal] property of the vowel /i/ (or the glide /j/) backward into a preceding short /a/, an open aperture (low) dorsal (back) vowel. Considerations of structure-preservation cause the output vowel also to rise to mid front [e] (cf. Iverson & Salmons 1994), but the basic fronting action of the rule is as laid out in (4).

(4)   Old High German Primary Umlaut (of short /a/)

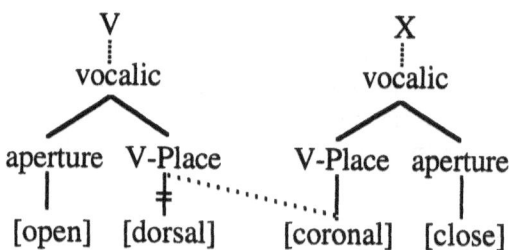

Consonants were free to intervene between the target and the trigger, both singly and in clusters (cf. (1)), but not if the cluster contained /h/ (cf. (2)). Irrespective of whether alveolars are underspecified for place of articulation features, as assumed here and elsewhere, or are provided at the outset with the articulator feature [coronal], as in (3), the basis for the blocking of umlaut appears to lie in the fact that [h] universally takes its oral properties from the vowel of the syllable in which it occurs. That is, the vocalic node of /a/ in an Old High German word such as *mahti* presumably extended into the (interpolated) C-Place position of the syllable-final /h/, as illustrated in (5).

(5)   Umlaut Blocking over /h/

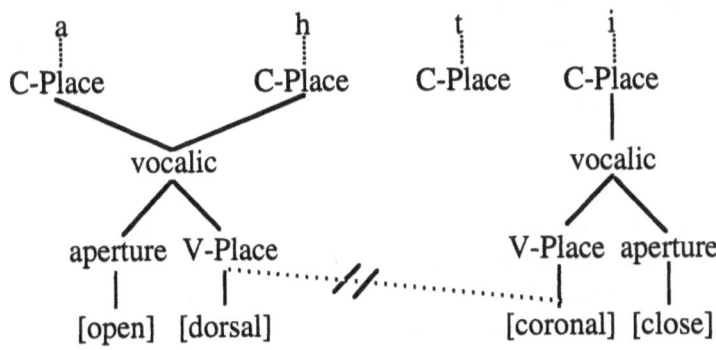

No line-crossing violation would occur if [coronal] were to spread leftward into the V-Place constituent of a shared configuration such as in (5), yet spreading is blocked nonetheless. The reason for umlaut blocking over /h/ is not due to the presence of INTERVENING vocalic structure, however, which would invoke the familiar autosegmental line crossing prohibition, but rather to the existence of SHARED vocalic structure. This circumstance brings to the fore another aspect of the general theory of phonological representation, specifically, the Autosegmental Linking Condition. As articulated by Hayes (1986) (cf. the similar constraint put forward by Steriade & Schein 1986), this condition on rule application holds that "lines of autosegmental association are interpreted as exhaustive", thus requiring a one-for-one match in association lines between structural descriptions and representations. We cite the constraint here from Kenstowicz (1994:413) under the rubric of the Uniformity Condition, generalizing it in the manner of the original Autosegmental Linking Condition so as to be relevant to the trigger as well as the target of phonological rules (we substitute the word "affect" for Kenstowicz's "change"):

(6) Uniformity Condition:
   In order to affect the feature content of a segment [A], every skeletal slot linked to [A] must satisfy the rule.

This principle was introduced into the theory in order to explain the 'geminate inalterability' phenomenon: rules which modify (and hence are defined on) single segments linked by only one association line to the skeletal tier do not affect otherwise identical geminate segments, which are linked to the skeletal tier by two lines of association (cf. Hayes 1986, Kenstowicz 1994 for numerous illustrations). In Old High German, the Uniformity Condition has the consequence that primary umlaut is inapplicable over /h/, because the vocalic structure in the neighboring vowel is shared with the /h/ by universal pattern of phonetic implementation. The rule of primary umlaut in (4) necessarily shows association of the vocalic node with only a single V element because long vowels were not subject to primary umlaut, which means that the rule refers just to vocalic structures that are not shared with any other skeletal slot. But the vocalic node of /a/ in (5) IS shared, namely, with the following /h/. By terms of the Uniformity Condition, then, an /h/ sharing oral properties with a tautosyllabic vowel will automatically block primary umlaut into that vowel, because no shared configuration relating to vocalic structure is referred to in the umlaut rule.[3]

By the time of the Middle High German period (beginning in the 12th Century), umlaut had become a much more general process, affecting all of the back vowels, both long and short: /o/ --> [ö], /o:/ --> [ö:] (ô --> œ), /u/ --> [ü], /u:/ --> [ü:] (û --> iu), /a:/ -->[ä:] (â --> æ). Short /a/ before clusters which had blocked umlaut in Old High German was affected at this stage of the language, too, but in this case the product, known as 'secondary umlaut', was the low vowel ä (= [æ]) rather than the mid vowel e (Paul 1975). Some examples for comparison between Old and Middle High

---

[3] Steriade (1987) observes that harmony processes that totally assimilate one vowel to another freely take place over just laryngeal consonants (/h, ʔ/), a phenomenon which she terms 'translaryngeal harmony', but that partial vocalic assimilations, such as is the case here with umlaut, generally apply over the whole range of consonant types. Translaryngeal harmony falls out from the phonological representation of laryngeals as not having any inherent place structure, i.e., these segments are transparent at underlying level to the spread of the vocalic node from one vowel to another because they have no vocalic or other place node of their own. At the level of phonetic representation, however, where the implementation of /h/ involves sharing of vocalic properties with a neighboring vowel, /h/ blocks the spread of vowel features via segmental rules which are defined on the skeletal tier, like Old High German primary umlaut (which was itself introduced at the phonetic level, cf. Iverson & Salmons 1994).

German relative to primary umlaut are given in (7a), to secondary umlaut in (7b), and to other instances of nonprimary umlaut in (7c).

(7) Old High German   Middle High German
a. gast/gesti   gast/geste   'guest' sg./pl.
   kraft/krefti   kraft/krefte   'force' sg./pl.
   grabu/grebis/grebit   grabe/grebest/grebit   'bury' 1/2/3 sg.

b. maht/mahti   maht/mähte   'power' sg./pl.
   mahtig   mähtec   'power' adj.
   gislahti   geslähte   'race, tribe'
   naht/nahti   naht/nähte   'night' sg./pl.

c. sun/suni   sun/süne   'son' sg./pl.
   mohta/mohtî   mohte/möhte   'might' indic./subj.
   hôrjen/hôrta   hœren/hôrta   'hear' inf./pret.
   tât/tâti   tât/tæte   'deed' sg./pl

These developments have been reviewed repeatedly in the literature on Germanic linguistics. The most interesting and important consequence from the present point of view is that a simplification of the primary umlaut rule given in (4) for Old High German, which affected only short /a/, results directly in the more general Middle High German secondary and nonprimary umlaut phenomenon, which held for all back vowels–including those instances of /a/ which had been exempted by blocking in Old High German. This result comes about without stipulation: because the Middle High German version of umlaut had to affect both long and short vowels, there could have been no motivation for including lines of autosegmental association between the skeletal tier and the segmental level of feature representation. Umlaut was thus free to apply across an intervening [h] in Middle High German, despite continued validity of the Uniformity Condition, because the V-Place docking site in the formulation of secondary and nonprimary umlaut was not restricted to any single segmental representation. That is, even a shared vocalic node was a proper recipient of the spread of [coronal] under conditions of umlaut in Middle High German, because that version of the rule, given in (8), affected all back vowels, long as well as short, and hence was not autosegmentally linked with the CV skeleton.

(8)   Umlaut (Secondary and Nonprimary)

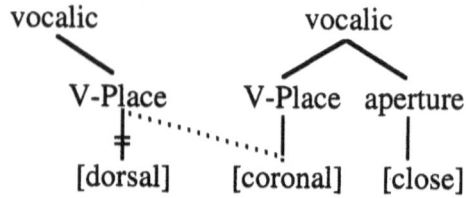

      [dorsal]   [coronal] [close]

The addition of rule (8) to the phonology of medieval German thus had the natural consequence that environments in Old High German which blocked primary umlaut by virtue of the Uniformity Condition became transparent to the more general secondary and nonprimary implementation of the process in Middle High German. Umlaut in the modern language is no longer phonologically motivated, of course, but rather now is triggered by morphological properties (cf. *Vater/Väter* 'father' sg./pl., etc.); nonetheless, its lengthy and well documented history offers striking confirmation of certain principles that govern phonological representation, in particular, the Uniformity Condition.

2. Korean.

Umlaut in the Kyengsang and Cella dialects of Korean (Hume 1990, Kang 1991, Lee 1993, 1994), though sociolinguistically variable and subject to considerable lexical exceptionality, is structurally remarkably parallel to the situation in medieval German. Indeed, forms appear to derive from the same general rule as in (8), some examples of which are given in (9).

(9)   a.   Umlaut across noncoronal consonants:

/api/	-->	[æbi]	'father'
/koki/	-->	[kegi]	'meat'
/emi/ [əmi]	-->	[emi]	'mother'
/cwuk + i + ta/	-->	[cigida]	'kill-DECLARATIVE'

     b.   Umlaut across anterior coronal consonants:

/mati/	-->	[mædi]	'knot'
/melmi/	-->	[melmi]	'vertigo'
/canti/	-->	[cændi]	'lawn'

c. Umlaut is blocked across an underlying palatal consonant:

/kachi/ --> [kacʰi] (*[kæcʰi]) 'value'
/taci + ta/ --> [tajida] (*[tæjida]) 'mince-DECL'
/keci/ --> [kəji] (*[keji]) 'beggar'

d. Lexical exceptions to umlaut:[4]

/salphi + ta/ --> [salpʰida] (*[sælpʰida]) 'search-DECL'
/napi/ --> [nabi] (*[næbi]) 'butterfly'
/moki/ --> [mogi] (*[megi]) 'mosquito'

Back vowels are fronted (and unrounded, for most umlauting speakers) before an /i/ in the next syllable. Underlying palatals, however, as exemplified in (9c), regularly interrupt the spread of vocalic coronality, just as intervening clusters with /h/ blocked umlaut in Old High German.[5] The reason why particularly palatals block umlaut in Korean does not appear to be a function of the prohibition on autosegmental line crossing, as suggested by Hume (1990) and Kenstowicz (1994), because that explanation requires that otherwise unmotivated V-Place structure be associated with the intervening palatals, which are primary palatal (nonanterior coronal), not secondary palatalized, articulations. That is, the structure of Korean palatal consonants is as presented in (10a), not as in (10b), because these sounds are nonanterior coronals rather than secondarily articulated alveolars.

(10) a. Palatal consonant   b. Palatalized consonant

---

[4] Some speakers may accept umlaut in these forms (cf. Kenstowicz 1994:470); the point is just that there is no phonological basis for the exclusion of umlaut among speakers who do not.

[5] Modern Korean umlaut, like nonprimary umlaut in Middle High German, requires no link to the skeletal tier, hence there is no reason that an intervening /h/ should interfere with the process in this language, either (but cf. King 1991, 1994 for the inhibitory role played by instances of "ghost" or historically deleted /h/ in the Hamkyeng dialect). In medial position /h/ undergoes a variety of incorporation and neutralization processes when next to a consonant (e.g., /coh + ko/ 'good-and' —> [cot̚kʰo], [cok̚kʰo], [cokʰo]; cf. Iverson & Kim-Renaud 1994), and when between vowels it typically deletes (e.g., /coh + una/ 'good-but' —> [couna]), though it may be retained in especially careful speech ([cohuna]). In either case, umlaut appears to be possible for Kyengsang speakers ([ceuna], [cehuna]).

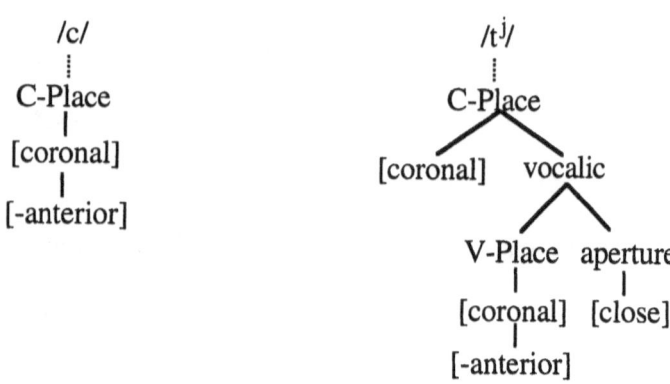

There are perhaps other ways to distinguish plain palatals from palatalized alveolars, but the important point is that no phonetic reason exists for ascribing vocalic structure to the Korean palatal series /c ch cc/ ([c c^h c']). Additionally, though the specification of [-anterior] under the [coronal] articulator is certainly redundant in vowels, the nonanterior phonetic quality of coronal (front) vowels constitutes an important, albeit predictable property relative to consonant assimilation, as shown by Lee (1994) and recapitulated below–hence its inclusion in the vocalic representation of (10b). If vocalic structure is not present in Korean palatals, however, the fact that these segments block umlaut cannot be attributed to the familiar autosegmental line crossing prohibition, because without V-Place structure standing in the way of the spread of other V-Place features, the coronal articulator identified in rule (8) would propagate through any intervening consonants, palatal or otherwise. On the common assumption that anterior coronals are underspecified in Korean, i.e., that alveolars are not marked for place of articulation features, umlaut is correctly predicted to take place in words like /mati/ 'knot'; but it would also appear to be incorrectly predicted to occur in words like /kachi/ 'value', because palatals in Korean are not secondary articulations. These effects are illustrated in (11) and (12).

(11)   Umlaut over place-underspecified alveolars (correct)

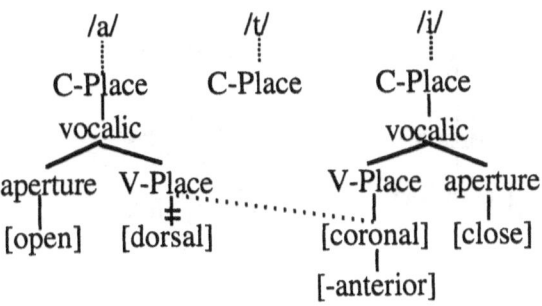

(12)   Umlaut over place-specified palatals (incorrect)

              /a/   /cʰ/   /i/

      C-Place   C-Place   C-Place

       vocalic   [coronal]   vocalic

aperture V-Place [-anterior] V-Place aperture

  [open] [dorsal]   [coronal] [close]

                                      [-anterior]

In fact, however, the ungrammatical consequence in (12) will be avoided if the Obligatory Contour Principle is taken into account, the universal constraint which prohibits the representation of adjacent identical specifications within morphemes (cf. McCarthy 1986, others). The V-Place specifications for front vowels accordingly must be shared with the C-Place constituent in a preceding palatal consonant since these feature properties of the two adjacent segments, though of differing geometric affiliation, are identical. The unifying effect of the Obligatory Contour Principle operating on morpheme-internal sequences of palatal consonant plus front vowel is illustrated in (13).

(13)   Obligatory Contour Principle effect on tautomorphemic /...ci.../

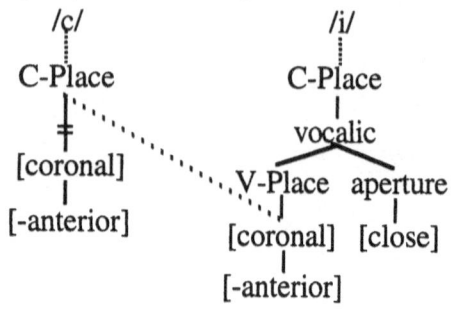

The reason palatal consonants block umlaut in Korean is now clear, and identical to why intervening clusters with /h/ blocked primary umlaut in Old High German–namely, the Uniformity Condition inhibits application to structures whose lines of autosegmental association are not explicitly mentioned in the rule. Thus, by virtue of the Obligatory Contour Principle, the feature configuration targeted for spread in the rule of umlaut ([coronal]) is shared in Korean representations containing a preceding underlying palatal consonant. The rule of umlaut as given in (8) refers to only one line of association relating to [coronal], however, hence its application is suspended in representations in which this feature is associated with two skeletal elements.

In contrast to possible alternative interpretations in terms of the autosegmental line crossing prohibition (which in any case would misrepresent palatals as secondary rather than primary articulations), the Uniformity Condition also entails that DERIVED palatals block the application of umlaut. Thus, as has often been described, alveolars become true palatals in position before /i/ in the next morpheme, and even within the same morpheme if no neutralization results (Iverson 1993). The rule of alveolar palatalization is given in (14), with both neutralizing and allophonic examples of the phenomenon listed in (15). As with the underlying palatals, these derived instances of nonanterior coronals inhibit umlaut.

(14)   Palatalization of alveolars

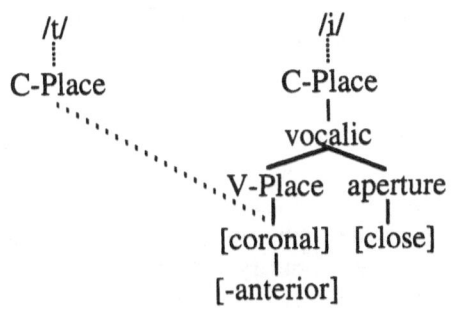

(15) a. Neutralizing palatalization:
    /pat^h+ i/   -->[pac^{h}i] (*[pæc^{h}i])   'field-SUBJECTIVE'
    /mat + i/   -->[maji]   (*[mæji])   'eldest-NOMINAL'
    /tot + i/   -->[toji]   (*[teji])   'rise-NOMINAL'
    /kath + i/   -->[kac^{h}i] (*[kæc^{h}i])   'same-ADVERBIAL'
                                                   (='together')
    /puth + i/   -->[puc^{h}i] (*[pic^{h}i])   'adhere-CAUSATIVE'

    b. Allophonic palatalization:
    /si/   -->[ši]   (*[si])   'poem'
    /os + i/   -->[oši]   (*[eši])   'clothes-SUBJECTIVE'
    /epsi/   -->[əpši]   (*[epši])   'without'
    /mun + i/   -->[muñi]   (*[miñi])   'door-SUBJECTIVE'
    /holli/   -->[hoλλi]   (*[heλλi])   'seduce'

In merging nonanterior coronals with underspecified alveolars through spread of the [coronal] node (with its redundant subordinate) from a following high vowel, the independent palatalization process given in (14) produces a shared feature configuration of the same kind as results from operation of the Obligatory Contour Principle in sequences of palatal plus front vowel, shown in (13). Thus both derived and basic palatals share coronal properties with a following high front vowel, and both, under the Uniformity Condition, are opaque to umlaut in virtue of their [coronal] node's multiple autosegmental association.

3. Conclusion.

Umlaut blocking in both Old High German and modern Korean derives from the Uniformity Condition, a universal constraint on phonological structure that requires a one-for-one match in autosegmental association between rule and representation. Because alveolars assimilate to a following /i/ in Korean, the [coronal] property of derived palatals is shared with that vowel, just as is a [coronal] specification among morpheme-internal sequences of underlying palatal and front vowel--due then, however, to operation of the Obligatory Contour Principle. In both cases, the reason that the general rule of umlaut in (8) does not apply over palatals in Korean is that these consonants are not autosegmentally independent of the vowel whose features they share, and on which the application of umlaut is defined.[6] For the same reason, the special rule of primary umlaut in (4) in Old High German does not apply over /h/. This segment takes on the oral properties of its tautosyllabic vowel and so shares vocalic structure with it, but the rule of primary umlaut is applicable only if relevant vocalic structure is not shared. The similarities in rule applicational restriction are not due to any genetic affinity between these two languages, of course, or to any likely contact between them; rather, they reflect the operation of principles of phonological organization and representation which appear to be valid for all languages.

---

[6] This effectively removes the reservations registered in Iverson (1993) over context-sensitive radical underspecification of the Korean palatals. The proposal advanced by Kiparsky (1993) was to specify underlying palatals everywhere except in the environment of a following /i/, where their palatal qualities could be provided by the palatalization rule; alveolars, on the other hand, were to be underspecified everywhere except again in the environment of a following /i/, where they would be marked for nonanterior coronality in order to escape the effects of palatalization (under terms of the derived environment constraint). As developed in the present paper, however, alveolars remain phonologically underspecified in all environments, while the OCP effect on underlying palatal plus front vowel sequences results in the seeming 'underspecification' of palatals before /i/--in actuality, palatals are specified for place of articulation features even here, but these features are shared with the following vowel.

References

Archangeli, Diana, & Douglas Pulleyblank. Maximal and Minimal Rules: Effects of Tier Scansion, *NELS* 17.16-35, 1987.

Braune, Wilhelm. *Althochdeutsche Grammatik.* (14th edition edited by Hans Eggers,[1st edition by Braune 1886]). Tübingen: Niemeyer, 1987.

Clements, George N. The Geometry of Phonological Features. *Phonology Yearbook* 2.225-252, 1985.

Clements, George N. Lieu d'articulation des consonnes et des voyelles: une théorie unifiée. In *Architecture des représentations phonologiques*, edited by B. Laks and A. Rialland, Collection Sciences du Langage. Paris: CNRS Editions, pp. 101-145, 1993.

Clements, George N. & Elizabeth Hume. The Internal Organization of Speech Sounds. In *The Handbook of Phonological Theory*, edited by John Goldsmith, Cambridge, Mass: Blackwell, pp. 245-306, 1995.

Hayes, Bruce. Inalterability in CV Phonology. *Language* 62.321-351, 1986.

Hume, Elizabeth. Front Vowels, Palatal Consonants, and the Rule of Umlaut in Korean, *NELS* 20.230-243, 1990.

Iverson, Gregory K. On the Category Supralaryngeal. *Phonology* 6.285-303, 1989.

Iverson, Gregory K. (Post)Lexical Rule Application, in *Studies in Lexical Phonology (Phonetics and Phonology*, vol. 4), edited by S. Hargus and E. Kaisse, San Diego: Academic Press, pp. 255-275, 1993.

Iverson, Gregory K. & Young-Key Kim-Renaud. Phonological Incorporation of the Korean Glottal Approximant, this volume, 39-50, 1997.

Iverson, Gregory K. & Joseph C. Salmons. The Primacy of Primary Umlaut. *Beiträge zur Geschichte der deutschen Sprache und Literatur* 118. 69-86, 1996.

Iverson, Gregory K., Joseph C. Salmons & Garry W. Davis. Blocking Environments in Old High German Umlaut. *Folia Linguistica Historica* 15.131-148, 1994.

Kang, Y. S. *Phonology of Consonant-Vowel Interaction: With Special Reference to Korean and Dependency Phonology*. Ph.D. dissertation, University of Illinois–Urbana-Champaign, 1991.

Keating, Patricia A. Underspecification in Phonetics. *Phonology* 5.275-292, 1988.

Kenstowicz, Michael. *Phonology in Generative Grammar*. Cambridge, Mass: Blackwell, 1994.

Kim, Kee-Ho. *The Phonological Representation of Distinctive Features: Korean Consonantal Phonology.* Ph.D. dissertation, University of Iowa, 1987.

Kim-Renaud, Young-Key. *Korean Consonantal Phonology.* Ph.D. dissertation, University of Hawaii, 1974.

King, Ross. *Russian Sources on Korean Dialects.* Ph.D. dissertation, Harvard University, 1991.

King, Ross. Dialect Elements in Soviet Korean Publications from the 1920's. *NSL7: Linguistic Studies in the non-Slavic Languages of the Commonwealth of Independent States and the Baltic Republics,* edited by H. Aronson, Chicago: Chicago Linguistic Society, pp. 151-183, 1994.

Kiparsky, Paul. Blocking in Nonderived Environments. In *Studies in Lexical Phonology (Phonetics and Phonology,* vol. 4), edited by S. Hargus and E. Kaisse, San Diego: Academic Press, pp. 277-313, 1993.

Lee, Shinsook. On the Representation of Front Vowels in Korean, paper presented at ESCOL 1993. Columbus: The Ohio State University, 1993.

Lee, Shinsook. *Theoretical Issues in Korean and English Phonology.* Ph.D. dissertation, University of Wisconsin–Madison, 1994.

McCarthy, John. OCP Effects: Gemination and Antigemination. *Linguistic Inquiry* 17.207-263, 1986.

Paul, Hermann. *Mittelhochdeutsche Grammatik.* (21st ed.) Tübingen: Niemeyer, 1975.

Schein, Barry & Donca Steriade. On Geminates. *Linguistic Inquiry* 17.691-744, 1986.

Steriade, Donca. Locality Conditions and Feature Geometry. *NELS* 17.595-617, 1987.

Vennemann, Theo. *Preference Laws for Syllable Structure—With Special Reference to German, Germanic, Italian, and Latin.* Berlin: Mouton de Gruyter, 1988.

4
Phonological Aspects in Causative Suffixation

Sang-Cheol Ahn

1. Introduction

Traditional Korean grammar (cf. Choy 1971) recognizes seven lexical causative suffixes (*-i, -hi, -li,-ki, -wu, -kwu, -chwu (or -hwu)*) and four passive suffixes (*-i, -hi, -li, -ki*). There has been, however, no explanation why such variants occur in different environments. The purpose of this paper, therefore, is to describe how the various allomorphic forms of the causative suffix surface phonologically. As the variation is much simpler in passives than in causatives, I will mainly deal with causatives. In order to explain this allomorphic variation phonologically, I will employ the general concepts of Feature Geometry and Underspecification, but with slight modifications. Here I will claim that the underlying representation of the causative suffix has an initial consonant whose feature specification is filled in by dissimilatory phonological processes.

2. Earlier Studies
2.1. Underlying Representation

There has been much controversy over the issue of whether all the causative suffixes can be derived from a single underlying representation. The earliest approach to this issue was made by K-M. Lee (1972:94-95), claiming that the underlying form of the suffix can be historically reconstructed as */ɣi/, which underwent the diachronic change * $\gamma i > gi > ɦi > i$.

From a synchronic point of view, however, C-W. Kim (1973:140-141) stated that the various causative forms in Korean can be derived from the single underlying form /hi/. In order to claim this, he considered the following variants as causative suffixes in Korean.

(1)
-*hi* after stem-final lax stops and affricates (e.g. tat-hi-ta 'close')
-*ki* after stem-final nasals   (e.g. kam-ki-ta 'wash hair')
-*i* after stem-final vowels   (e.g. po-i-ta 'see')

(1) illustrates that the affix -*hi* is attached to a stem-final consonant if it can be aspirated, but -*ki* is attached if the stem-final consonant cannot be aspirated. He thus claims that, as *k* is the phoneme closest to *h*, there should be a way to adjust *h* to *k* in the context in which it cannot contribute to aspiration of the preceding consonant and thereby describe causative formation in Korean as a single process. He also claims that deriving -*i*- from -*hi*- is no problem as intervocalic /h/ is deleted elsewhere in Korean.

(2)
coh-uni [cohini] --> [coini] 'be good', noh-ala --> [noara] 'put (it) down'

This proposal, however, may have several problems. First, it is not desirable to invoke an adjustment rule like the *h* -> *k* change without some other motivation. Second, it requires a readjustment rule which is an instance of absolute neutralization (cf. Kiparsky 1973). Third, since only causative /h/ undergoes readjustment, but not other cases of underlying /h/, the to-be adjusted /h/s must be marked diacritically. The phonology would become too unconstrained if we were to allow this sort of adjustment. Furthermore, the data Kim uses are not sufficient to propose a phonological generalization, for there are other causative forms: -*li*, -*wu*, -*kwu*, -*chwu*.

Bak (1982) also tried to show that the causative affixation is phonologically conditioned by positing /hi/ as the underlying representation. Thus he proposes the following rule to account for the *hi* -> *i* change.

(3)   *h*-deletion: h --> ø / [+voice] (+)___[-cons]
        (e.g. po- -hi- -ta/ -> [po- -i- -da] 'show')

Like C-W. Kim, Bak claims that this *h*-deletion rule is productive in Korean phonology. Moreover, he posits another *h*-deletion rule which is marked for verbal roots which end with -*ki*.

(4)   *h*-deletion (minor): h -> ø / k + ___]caus
        (e.g. cwuk-hi-ta -> [cug-i-da] 'kill')

As mentioned above, being attached to the plain plosive /k/, the suffix-initial /h/ might otherwise cause aspiration without this rule. Thus, an additional function of this rule seems to be the blocking of possible aspiration in this environment.

Furthermore, Bak proposes an additional rule to change -*hi* to -*ki*.

(5)   Velarization rule: h ---> k / $\begin{bmatrix} \text{nasal} \\ \text{s} \end{bmatrix}$ (+) ___

Finally, he also suggested the following rule for -*li* suffixation, assuming that -*li* is derived from -*i*.

(6)   *l*-gemination: l ---> ll / [+syll] (+) ___[+syll]

Therefore, it would appear that Bak's proposal is just a formalized version of C-W. Kim's adjustment approach.

2.2. Allomorphy Rules

Considering the problems of the earlier studies, Ahn (1989, 1992) presumed there was no possible way to derive the various causative forms from one source, and proposed instead the following allomorphy rules to predict the various causative forms, in which the -*i* allomorph is regarded as the default case.[1]

First, it was proposed that the minor cases of apparent -*kwu* and -*chwu* suffixation be listed in the lexicon, since there are only four examples found for each case.

(7)   sot-kwu-ta 'raise',   tot-kwu-ta 'encourage'[2]
        il-kwu-ta 'plow',   tal-kwu-ta 'heat'

(8)   nac-chwu-ta 'lower',   kac-chwu-ta 'install'
        nuc-chwu-ta 'postpone',   mac-chwu-ta 'assemble'

In the case of (8), it was also mentioned that these are cases where -*hi* suffixation is expected.[3] If -*hi* is used, however, the /c + hi/ sequence would create two palatal consonants in a row, [c + c^h], which is prohibited by the Obligatory Contour Principle. (McCarthy 1986)[4]

---

[1] The data were mainly drawn from Han (1984).

[2] This is not a genuine counterexample since *tot-wu-ta* is often used alternatively.

[3] From a synchronic point of view, these forms can be regarded as semantically noncompositional. In other words, they can be viewed as simple verbs not implying any process of causative suffixation.

For the minor cases of -*wu* [-u] suffixation, the following rule was proposed:

(9)   [CAUS] --> u / $\begin{bmatrix} + \text{syll} \\ - \text{back} \end{bmatrix}$ + _____

(10)   kki-wu-ta,   kali-wu-ta,   chi-wu-ta,   nayli-wu-ta [nɛriuda]
         chi-wu-ta,   pi-wu-ta,   phi-wu-ta,   i-wu-ta
         mey-wu-ta [meuda],   kkay-wu-ta [k'ɛuda],
         sey-wu-ta [seuda]

Note that these are cases where -*i* suffixation is predicted, since -*i* is suffixed after a vowel-final root. Therefore, these were interpreted as a case of the OCP prohibiting a [-back][-back] sequence.

As for the major cases, we have -*i*, -*hi*, -*li*, -*ki* suffixations, for which the following allomorphy rules were proposed.

(11)   [CAUS] --> hi / $\begin{bmatrix} -\text{cont} \\ - \text{tense} \\ -\text{back} \end{bmatrix}$ + _____

     (e.g. ppop-hi-ta, kwup-hi-ta, cap-hi-ta, ep-hi-ta [əphida],
         kwut-hi-ta, tat-hi-ta, mac-hi-ta, anc-hi-ta, etc.)

(12)   [CAUS] -> ki / {[+nasal], [+cons, +cont]} + _____

     (e.g. wus-ki-ta, ssis-ki-ta, as-ki-ta, kam-ki-ta, sin-ki-ta, an-ki-ta,
         etc.) (exceptions: tut-ki-ta [tɨtkida], math-ki-ta)

(13)   [CAUS] -> i, elsewhere

What we see here is that -*ki* and -*hi* suffixations, along with the -*kwu*, -*wu*, and -*chwu* suffixations, are considered to be the special cases. Thus the special allomorphy rules (11) and (12) apply first. Otherwise, we get -*i*

---

[4] Obligatory Contour Principle (McCarthy 1986):
     At the melodic level, adjacent identical elements are prohibited.

suffixation by the Elsewhere Condition (Kiparsky 1982). Therefore, after a tensed plosive or a vowel, we suffix -*i* as the default value.

Here it should be noted that there are many counterexamples, as shown in (14a), which take -*i*, rather than the predicted -*hi*, unlike the other examples shown in (14b). There was no explanation for this problem in earlier studies.

(14) a. mek-i-ta [məgidə], cwuk-i-ta, sak-i-ta, ssek-i-ta [s'əgidə], nok-i-ta
      b. palk-hi-ta, ik-hi-ta, ilk-hi-ta, kulk-hi-ta [kɨlkʰidə]

Notice, however, that all the verbs in (14a) end with the velar consonant /k/. In the next section, I will show that these cases show a transitional stage of allomorphy in which the suffix-initial consonant -*h* is disappearing due to dissimilation, since the back consonant -*h* is immediately following a back vowel and another back consonant /k/.[5]

Finally, as for the -*li* suffixation, it was assumed that -*li* is derived from -*i* by *l*-gemination, following Bak's earlier proposal.

(15) l --> ll / ___ + i]caus

      (e.g. nol-li-ta, wul-li-ta, nul-li-ta [nɨllidə], mal-li-ta, tol-li-ta, kolh-li-ta, kkwulh-li-ta, etc.)[6]

As for rule ordering, this rule follows *u* [ɨ-]-deletion and *h*-deletion.

---

[5] In passives, where only four suffixal variants exist, this dissimilation process seems to be much less active. Thus, after all non-tensed plosives, -*hi*- is suffixed without exception.

[6] Note that /l/ palatalizes in this environment when it geminates. Otherwise, it would come out as [r].

(16) a. /pulu-/ [puri-] + /-i/ 'call'
pul i *u* [i-]-deletion
pull i *l*-gemination

b. /ttwulh-/ + /-i/ 'penetrate'
ttwul i *h*-deletion
ttwull i *l*-gemination

3. Causative Suffixation and Dissimilation

Considering the earlier analyses and observations, I will attempt to show the possibility of deriving the surface variants from a single underlying representation by consonantal dissimilation. In other words, it will be shown that the underlying representation of the suffix-initial consonant should be underspecified for its manner and laryngeal properties and that the stem-final consonant is the trigger of dissimilatory feature specification for the suffix consonant. For this purpose, I will adopt the basic insights made by K-M. Lee (1972), C-W. Kim (1973) and Bak (1982). As for the model of Feature Geometry, I will use a simplified version of feature representation since taking any specific version in featural representation is not our major concern. Nevertheless, the version used here is close to those of McCarthy (1988) and Clements & Hume (1993) in which the root node is reserved for manner specification.

3.1. Specification by Consonantal Dissimilation

In order to describe the dissimilatory process in causative specification, I will adopt the basic insights of K-M. Lee's *yi. As the velar fricative can be attested only historically, however, I will propose that the causative suffix /-Ci-/ has the following consonantal representation underlyingly. Here we see that the root and the laryngeal nodes are not specified for their feature values.

(17)
$$\begin{bmatrix} +\text{cons} \\ [\ \ ] \end{bmatrix}$$
/ \
L   P
|
[+bk]

Given the underlying representation shown above, we can now deal with the three major variants, -*ki*, -*hi* and -*i*. Here it is assumed that we specify both values for the [continuant] feature, while only the positive values are specified for other features.

First, as already shown in (12), *-ki* is suffixed after an /s/-final verb stem (e.g. *wus-ki-(ta), as-ki-(ta), ssis-ki-(ta)*, etc.). Consider that /s/ has the continuancy which /k/ lacks. Thus we may posit that the underspecified consonantal manner specification will be realized as [-continuant], opposite to the manner feature of /s/. This dissimilatory process can be illustrated as follows.

(18)

$$\begin{bmatrix} +\text{cons} \\ +\text{cont} \end{bmatrix} \quad \begin{bmatrix} +\text{cons} \\ [\ ] \end{bmatrix} \longrightarrow \text{tier of scansion: } [\ ] \longrightarrow [-\text{cont}]$$

```
    / \           / \
   L  ...        L   PL
   |             |
  [+ s.g.]      [+ bk]
```

Here we see that since the manner of the suffix-initial consonant is specified as [-cont], the consonant should be realized as a *k*, because the place node already has [+bk] specification underlyingly.

From a synchronic point of view, however, there are several possible exceptions, as shown below.

(19) tut-ki-ta [tɨtkida]   'make someone hear'
      ttut-ki-ta [t'ɨtkida]   'make someone take off something'
      math-ki-ta [matkida]   'leave something in one's charge'

These examples have roots ending with /t/ or /tʰ/, which would normally lead us to affix *-hi* or *-i*. Consequently, those cases in (19) are syncronically deviant forms, and we must treat them as exceptions.

The second variant is *-hi*. It occurs after a plain consonant which can be aspirated (e.g. *kwup-hi-ta, kwut-hi-ta, ik-hi-ta, sik-hi-ta, ilk-hi-ta, palk-hi-ta, nulk-hi-ta* [nɨlkʰida], etc.). Here it is assumed that /h/, like /s/, is a fricative which is specified as [+continuant]. (Of course, /s/ is specified further for [spread glottis].) Thus, this feature specification is also assigned by the dissimilatory process.[7]

(21) $\begin{bmatrix} + \text{cont} \\ - \text{cont} \end{bmatrix}$ $\begin{bmatrix} + \text{cont} \\ [\ ] \end{bmatrix}$ =>   [ ] --> [+ cont]
       / \   / \
       ... L   L PL
                                 |
                               [+ bk]

In (21), the negative value [-continuant] appears in the underlying representation. Therefore, since the suffix consonant takes the value [+cont] by dissimilation, it is realized as an /h/ because there is no specified feature for the laryngeal node. (As for the place specification [+back], I tentatively assume that it is delinked after the specification of the laryngeal node, since /h/ should not have any place specification.[8])

As mentioned in the previous section, however, there is a series of exceptional cases which take the unexpected -i suffixation as shown in (22a), rather than the expected -hi suffixation as in (22b).[9]

---

[7] Iverson (1989) proposed the following representation for Korean /h/, in which place specification is not specified.

         Root
         / |
   [+cont] L
            |
          [+s.g]

In this paper, however, I follow Iverson (p.c.) in that /h/ is specified simply as [+continuant], while /s/ and /ss/ [s'] are further specified as [+spread glottis] and [+constricted glottis], respectively.

       /h/   /s/   /ss/
      [cont]   [cont, s.g.]   [cont, c.g.]

[8] As /h/ is not specified for the place node, the prelinking of [+back] is not in conflict. Due to the well-formedness condition, this already linked [+back] is simply delinked after the laryngeal specification of /h/. However, since /s/ needs its own coronal place specification (even though it may be underspecified), the suffix-initial consonant cannot be realized as an /s/.

(22)   a. mek-i-ta [məgida], cwuk-i-ta, sak-i-ta, sek-i-ta [səgida],
       ssek-i-ta [ssəgida], sok-i-ta, swuk-i-ta, nok-i-ta, nwuk-i-ta, etc.
       b. ik-hi-ta, sik-hi-ta, etc.

Again note that the exceptional verbs have back vowels and they end with the velar consonant /k/, also specified as [+back]. Thus, in order to avoid this ill-formed triple [+back] sequence, the expected suffix-initial consonant does not surface. In other words, due to the backness of the verb-final segments, the suffix-initial consonant gets deleted because a sequence of three consecutive [+back] segments is prohibited. I conjecture that this aspect is another case of dissimilation.[10]

(23)
$$\begin{bmatrix} [-\text{cons}] & [+\text{cons}] & [+\text{cons}] & [-\text{cons}] \\ | & | & | & | \\ \text{PL} & \text{PL} & \text{PL} & \text{PL} \\ | & | & | & | \\ [+\text{bk}] & [+\text{bk}] & [+\text{bk}] & \\ & & | & \\ & & \emptyset & \end{bmatrix} \text{caus}$$

On the contrary, as for the regular cases in (22a), this further dissimilatory process does not apply since the verbs have front vowels which do not generate the triple [+back] sequence. Thus, after the regular -hi suffixation, the causative verbs undergo aspiration.

This dissimilatory process is unique for causative suffixation, not for passive suffixation. In fact, the passive counterpart for mek-ta takes -hi suffixation as expected, i.e. mek-hi-ta. Moreover, causative -hi and -i suffixes often alternate for several verbs, although they are regarded as substandard.

(24)   sak-i-ta ~ sak-hi-ta, ssek-i-ta ~ ssek-hi-ta, nok-i-ta ~ nok-hi-ta,
       nwuk-i-ta ~ nwuk-hi-ta, mwuk-i-ta ~ mwuk-hi-ta

---

[9] In those cases with root-final double consonants, -hi is always used.
   E.g. ilk-hi-ta, palk-hi-ta, nulk-hi-ta [nɨlkʰida], etc.
This might be due to the resyllabification process which changes the final coda consonant to an aspirated onset consonant.

[10] Note that it is not specified whether the would-be suffix initial consonant is /k/ or /h/. Because it is simply discarded in order to avoid the ill-formed triple [+back] sequence, we need not worry about the status of this consonant.

These cases show that the further dissimilatory process is still active syncronically, changing the place property. This further dissimilation process is also found in the *-wu* and *-chwu* suffixation, which will be discussed below in 3.3.

Finally, we get *-i* suffixation after a plosive with [+spread glottis] or [+constricted glottis] (e.g. *teph-i-ta* [təpʰida], *kkakk-i-ta*, etc). In other words, *-hi* cannot occur after a [+tense] consonant. In order to explain this process, we need to scan two different tiers in the feature tree.

(25)   [+ cons, - cont]   [+ cons, [ ]]   => [ ] -> [+cont]
         /   \   /   \
        PL   L   L   PL
              | | |
         $\begin{bmatrix} +c.g \\ +s.g \end{bmatrix}$ [ ] [+bk]   => [ ] -> [-tense]

This figure shows that the suffix-initial consonant takes its manner feature as [+cont], opposite to that of the root-final consonant. Moreover, since the laryngeal property ([spread glottis]/[constricted glottis]) of the verb-final consonant is already specified underlyingly, [-s.g] or [-c.g] is filled in for the laryngeal node of the suffix consonant. This two-way dissimilatory process leads to the segmental deletion of the consonant. In other words, if the initial segment is [+cont], it should be an /s/ or an /h/, both of which have [+s.g] feature specification. Neither segment, however, can surface; the second feature specification [-s.g]/[-c.g] prohibits the surface realization of the aspirated /s/ and /h/. (Here I will assume that Korean /s/ is underlyingly (and phonetically) [+spread glottis]. (Kagaya 1974; See Iverson (1983) for a different proposal.) There remains, however, the problem of how to derive *-i* after a vowel-final stem. That is, there seems to be no explanation why the suffix-initial consonant gets deleted after a vowel. At present, the only possibility might be to say that the feature specification of the suffix-initial consonant is filled in by consonantal dissimilation. Therefore, if there is no consonant to trigger dissimilation, the underspecified suffix-initial consonant cannot surface since there is no way to assign dissimilatory values to the underspecified slots.[11] This

---

[11] In other words, rather than delete it, we can simply leave the suffix-initial consonant so underspecified that it is not pronounced, like the French *h*-aspiré. This suggestion was made by Iverson (p.c.).

description might be a mere conjecture and thus remains open to further discussion and criticism.

3.2. Derivation of -li

I also assume that we can derive the -*li* suffixation in a similar way. In order to postulate the description shown below, it is crucial to assume the noncontinuancy of the lateral /l/. Thus, I will refer to Chomsky & Halle (1968:318) for this issue. (The emphasis is mine.)

(26)   The characterization of the liquid [l] in terms of the continuant-noncontinuant scale is even more complicated. If the defining characteristic of the stop is taken as total blockage of air flow, then [l] must be viewed as a continuant and must be distinguished from [r] by the feature "laterality". If, on the other hand, the defining characteristic of stops is taken to be blockage of air flow past the primary stricture, then [l] *must be included among the stops*. The phonological behavior of [l] in some languages supports the latter interpretation.

(27)
$$\begin{bmatrix} + \text{cons} \\ - \text{cont} \\ | \\ \text{LAT} \end{bmatrix} \begin{bmatrix} + \text{cons} \\ [\ ] \\ / \ \backslash \\ \text{L} \ \ \text{PL} \\ | \\ [+ \text{bk}] \end{bmatrix} \Rightarrow [\ ] \longrightarrow [+ \text{cont}]$$

-*hi* is derived by (27) and the initial-*h* undergoes intersonorant *h*-deletion, a very productive rule in Korean phonology (Kim-Renaud 1974). Because *h*-deletion leaves the skeletal slot unattended, the root-final /l/ spreads to this empty slot, producing a geminate -*ll*.

(28)

```
X + X X  =>  X + X X  =>  X X X  =>      X X X
|   | |      |   | |      | † |         | / |
l  [ ] i     l   h i      l h i         l   i
Causative    Rule (27)    h-deletion    l-spreading
suffixation
```

In earlier studies such as Bak (1982), it was not explained why the *l*-gemination had to be enforced for those verbs ending with an /l/. Following this approach, however, it is quite natural to explain the subsequent *l*-gemination as a consequence of *h*-deletion and the subsequent *l*-spreading.[12] An additional advantage of this approach can be found in the derivation of *sil-li-ta*, the causative of the *t*-irregular verb /sit-ta/ 'load'.[13] As shown in the following derivation, a stop is the trigger for dissimilation, which assigns a dissimilatory manner feature [-cont], as in other stop-final verbs. The suffix-initial consonant surfaces as [h] due to this dissimilation. Then the stem-final *t* is weakened to *l* by *t*-irregular conjugation. After the *t* -> *l* change, we have the same environment for *l*-gemination as the one shown above. In other words, as the suffix-initial *h* is deleted between *l* and *i*, the spreading of *l* produces -*li* allomorph in a similar way.

(29)

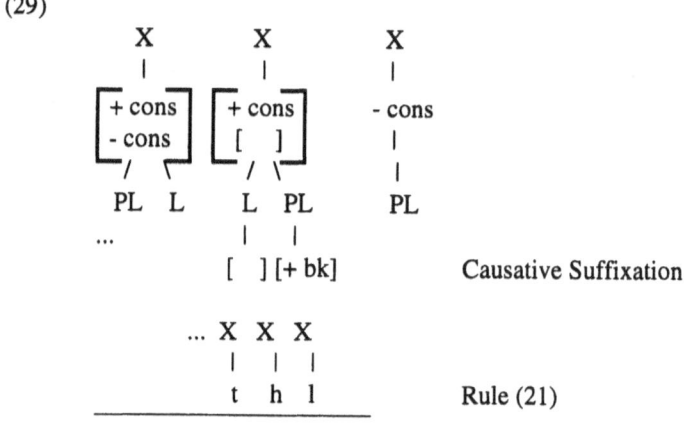

[12] Iverson (p.c.) suggested that it might be better to let the liquid spread into the empty C-slot directly, without going through the /h/ specification and deletion stages. And this way of derivation looks plausible.

```
   X X X
   |/ | |
   l [] i
```

This suggestion, however, faces a problem in explaining certain cases. In other words, without going through the /h/ specification stage by (27), we would need another way to explain why the underspecified suffix initial consonant does not surface, as in other cases discussed already. By applying the /h/ specification rule (27) and taking a free-ride on the already existing intersonorant *h*-deletion rule, it is easier to explain why the suffix-initial consonant does not surface.

[13] The causative form of /ssis-ta/ 'wash' is *ssis-ki-ta*.

```
... X  X  X
    |  |  |
    l  h  i           t-irregular conjugation
... X  X  X
    |/ |  |
    l  h  i           h-deletion and l-spreading
```

Notice that what triggers *h*-deletion and *l*-spreading is *t*-irregular conjugation which changes the stem-final *t* to an *l*. Therefore, the environment for this change should be 'V___+ (h) V' in which the suffix-initial *h* is optional. Then we apply the already existing rules of *h*-deletion and *l*-spreading. In other words, we do not need any special stipulation for the causative case of the irregular conjugation. (All we need to do is a slight modification of *t*-irregular conjugation.) Furthermore, while there was no explanation for motivating *l*-gemination in -*li* suffixation, *l*-gemination is now viewed as a natural consequence of *h*-deletion and subsequent *l*-spreading under our approach.

3.3. Further Evidence for Dissimilation

The dissimilation approach gains further support from -*wu* suffixation. As proposed in an earlier approach, -*wu* is suffixed after a front vowel; e.g. *kki-wu-ta*, *cci-wu-ta*, *chi-wu-ta*, *pi-wu-ta*, *phi-wu-ta*, *i-wu-ta*, *mey-wu-ta*, *kkay-wu-ta*, *sey-wu-ta*, etc. In order to account for this, the following type of dissimilation rule can be proposed.[14]

(30)   i -> wu [u] / V + ___]caus
              [-bk]

As previously mentioned, this is a process prohibiting a sequence of two back vowels in causative formation, which can be formalized as follows.

---

[14] There is a set of examples specifically similar to this pattern, i.e. *chay-wu-ta* [cʰɛuda] 'fill', *sey-wu-ta* [seuda] 'establish', *cay-wu-ta* [cɛuda] 'help someone to sleep'. These are, however, considered to be the cases of double causatives with both causative suffixes -*i* and -*wu*-. (S-O. Lee 1980) There is also one possible exception to this rule, i.e. *tot-wu-ta* 'encourage'. However, this is not a genuine counterexample since there is an alternative form, *tot-kwu-ta*.

(31)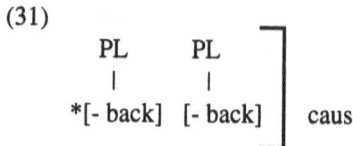

In other words, just as the process of consonantal dissimilation determines the suffix-initial consonant, so a similar process of vocalic dissimilation may change the value of the causative vowel *-i*. The only difference is that the consonantal dissimilation affects the values of both manner and laryngeal properties, while the vocalic dissimilation changes the place value only.[15]

There is another case of dissimilation in which consonantal and vocalic place features interact. As shown below, *-chwu-* is suffixed only to certain verb stems.

(32) nac-chwu-ta [natcʰuda]   'make it lower'
      kac-chwu-ta [katcʰuda]   'make it prepared'
      nuc-chwu-ta [nɨtcʰuda]   'make it slow down'

In an earlier allomorphy approach (Ahn 1989), no formalized rule was proposed for these cases since the distribution is so limited. Therefore, Ahn (1989) suggested to mark them in the lexicon. In our current dissimilation approach, however, this process can be regarded as another case of dissimilation in which the suffix vowel *-i* is changed to *-wu* in order to avoid a [-back][-back] sequence. Note that all the verbs in this category have the coronal root-consonant /c/, specified as [-back]. After aspiration, we have two front segments in a row, i.e. *ch + i*. Then the latter vowel is changed to *wu* [u] by place dissimilation.

---

[15] Of course, this process applies only to causatives, not to passives. For example, *kki-* 'to insert', *mey-* 'to cover', and *kkay-* 'to wake up' take *-i* for passives but *-wu* for causatives as shown below.

Root	Passive	Causative
kki-	kki-i	kki-wu
mey-	mey-i	mey-wu
kkay-	kkay--i	kkay-wu

(33)
```
    X X X     X X   X      X X X       X X X
    | + |     |  -->|  |    |  --> |  | |   -->   | | |
    ...c [ ] i...    c  h   i       c  h i         c h wu
    Causative        Rule (21)       Aspiration    Dissimilation
```

For aspiration, the stem consonant c spreads to the next X slot associated with h, producing a palatal ch [c^h]. Then the palatal [c^h] dissimilates the following front vowel i [i] to wu [u]. Here we also note that after the consonantal spreading for aspiration, it is not obligatory to delink the spreading segment from the original timing slot. Therefore, we may get one palatal segment phonetically in casual speech, as in /machwuta/ [mac^{h}uda], but we can also get *mac-chwu-ta* [matc^{h}uda] in careful speech. The orthographic representation reflects the latter, obeying the same constraint (31) for dissimilation.

Evidence for deriving *-chwu* from *-hi* is easily found. For example, there is a couple of cases in which both *-hi* and *-chwu* are possible, even though the variants might be dialectal.

(34)   mac-hi-ta ~ mac-chwuta   'make it hit'
       cac-hi-ta ~ cac-chwu-ta   'boil dry'

In this section, we have observed that it is prohibited to have a sequence of two segments with identical frontness. Now let us recall our earlier observation on causatives with a stem-final /k/. As already illustrated in (23), the expected suffix form *-hi* undergoes a further dissimilatory process, resulting in the deletion of h. Due to the backness of the preceding segments and a prohibition against three consecutive [+back] segments, the suffix-initial consonant /h/ is deleted. Therefore, the earlier constraint (31) can be modified in the following form.

(35)
$$\begin{bmatrix} * & \text{PL} & \text{PL} \\ & | & | \\ & [\alpha\text{back}] & [\alpha\text{back}] \end{bmatrix} \text{caus}$$

Consequently, (36) suggests that causative suffixation can undergo a further dissimilatory process, i.e. place dissimilation. This is precisely where we can observe a consonant-vowel interaction.

3.4. A Residual Problem

There remains one problem to be resolved, namely the explanation of the *-ki* suffixation after nasal-final stems.

(36)   nam-ki-ta 'leave it',   swum-ki-ta 'hide it',
       olm-ki-ta 'move it'   an-ki-ta 'cause to hug',
       sin-ki-ta 'cause to wear shoes'

As nasals are specified as [-cont], our current dissimilation approach would predict *-hi*, rather than *-ki*. Thus there seems to be no explanation for the unexpected appearance of *-ki*. However, there might be a possible explanation at this stage. The second possible explanation is to assume that nasals are not specified for [continuant] since the unmarked [-continuant] value can be obtained later from the suffix. That is, since there is no manner feature on the stem-final segment, the suffix-initial consonant takes [-continuant] by default. Hence we get *-ki*. Or we can conjecture that there might be a sonority dissimilation at play between the stem-final consonant and the suffix-initial consonant.[16] However, this possibility needs to be examined and tested in depth.[17]

4. Conclusion

We have observed that the various forms of the Korean causative suffix can be interpreted as the consequences of dissimilation. By taking this approach, all the variants of the causative suffix can be described in a natural way. Moreover, in the case of *-li* suffixation, we

---

[16] I owe the basic insight to Iverson (p.c.).

[17] Another possibility might be to conjecture that the appearance of *k* is the consequence of analogy. In Middle Korean, for example, many nouns ending with a nasal took an additional segment *-k* (as in *-ki, -kol/kul* [-kʌl, -kɨl], *-kuy* [-kɨy] in case marking.

(38)   namk   --> namk-i (subject), namk-ol [namgʌl] (object) 'tree'
       kwumwu   --> kwumk-i (subject) 'hole'
       nyenu [nyəni] --> nyenk-i (subject), nyenk-ul [nyəngil]] (object) 'anyone'
       pwulmwu-cil   --> pwulmk-uy [pulmgɨy] (possessive) 'bellows'

The appearance of *k* in the case-marked forms suggests that /k/ was a part of the underlying representation of each noun. Thus, in the process of causative suffixation in nasal-final stems, *-k-* might have been added to the stem, resulting in *-ki* suffixation.

can achieve an additional advantage by accounting for the formerly mysterious *l*-gemination process as a consequence of *h*-deletion and *l*-spreading.

References

Ahn, Sang-Cheol. On the derivation of causative/passive suffixes in Korean. A In *Festschrift to Professor Lee Hei-Sook*, Seoul: Hanshin Publishing Co, 139-189, 1989.

Bak, Sung-Yun. Causatives in Korean. *Linguistic Journal of Korea* 7.2, 332-342, 1982.

Cho, Euiyon. On the morphology of morphological causatives in Korean: an argument against Lieber's morpheme-based lexicon. *Studies in the Linguistic Sciences* 16.2, 27-43, 1986.

Chomsky, Noam and Morris Halle. *The Sound Pattern of English*. New York: Harper & Row, 1968.

Choy, Hyenpay. *Wuli Malpon* (The Grammar of Our Language). Seoul: Cengumsa, 1937.

Clements, George N. and Samuel J. Keyser. *CV Phonology*. Cambridge, MA: MIT Press, 1983.

Clements, G. N. and Elizabeth Hume. The internal organization of speech sounds. Ms, 1993.

Iverson, Gregory K. 1983. Korean *s*. *Journal of Phonetics* 11, 191-200. On the category Supralaryngeal. *Phonology* 6.2, 285-303, 1989.

Han, Jung-Kill. *Analyse des Constructions des Verbes Causatifs en Coréen Contemporain*, Ph.D. dissertation, Université de Paris VII, 1984.

_____. On the determination of a causative verb and a causative construction. *Language Research* 21.2, 179-197, 1985.

He Wung. *Kwuke Umwunhak* (Korean Phonology). Seoul: Cengumsa, 1968.

Kagaya, Ryohei. A fiberscopic and acoustic study of the Korean stops, affricates and fricatives. *Journal of Phonetics* 2, 161-180, 1974.

Kim, Chin-W. Adjustment rules in phonology. *Issues in Phonological Theory*, edited by M. J. Kenstowicz & C.W. Kisseberth, The Hague: Mouton Publishers, 130-144, 1973.

Kim, Young-Seok. *Aspects of Korean Morphology*. Ph.D. dissertation, University of Texas at Austin, 1984.

Kim-Renaud, Young-Key. *Korean Consonantal Phonology*. Ph.D. dissertation, University of Hawaii, 1974.

Kiparsky, Paul. How abstract is phonology? In *Three Dimensions in Linguistic Theory*, edited by O. Fujimura, Tokyo: TEC, 5-56, 1973.

_____. Lexical morphology and phonology. In *Linguistics in the Morning Calm*, edited by I.-S. Yang, Seoul: Hanshin Publishing Co, 3-91, 1982.
Lee, Ki-Moon. See Yi Kimun.
Lee, Sangek. See Yi Sangek.
Levin, Juliette. *The Metrical Theory of Syllabicity.* PhD. dissertation, MIT, 1985.
Lieber, Rochelle. *On the Organization of the Lexicon.* PhD. dissertation, MIT. Distributed by Indiana University Linguistics Club, 1980.
McCarthy, John. OCP effects: Gemination and antigemination. *Linguistic Inquiry* 17, 207-63, 1986.
McCarthy, John. Feature geometry and dependency: a review. *Phonetica* 45, 84-108, 1988.
Scalise, Sergio. *Generative Morphology.* Dordrecht, Holland: Foris Publications, 1984.
Song, Cheluy. *Kwuke uy Phasaynge Hyengseng Yenkwu* (A Study of Derivation in Korean). Doctoral Dissertation, Seoul National University, 1989.
Yi, Kimun [Lee, Ki-Moon]. *Kwuke Umwunsa Yenkwu* (A Study of Korean Historical Phonology). Seoul: Tower press, 1972.
Yi, Sangek. [Lee, Sang-Oak]. *Kwuke uy Satong-PhitongKwumwun Yenkwu* (A Study on causative-passive sentences in Korean). M.A. thesis, Seoul National University, 1970.
_____. Satong-phitong Ekan Hyengseng Cepmisa ey tayhan Takakcek Kochal (Diversified studies on the causative-passive suffixes). *Emwunnoncip* 21, 121-138, 1980.
Yu, Changton. *Icoe Sacen* (*A Dictionary of Yi Dynasty Korean*). Seoul: Yonsei University Press, 1964.

SYNTAX

5
Negative Polarity Items in Korean and English

Susumu Kuno[1]

1. Negative Polarity Items (NPIs) in Korean

1.1. Neg-NPI Clause Mate Constraint Cannot Be a D-structure Constraint

The following examples seem to indicate that Korean Negative Polarity Items (NPIs) observe some kind of a clause mate constraint:

(1.1) a. Hwanca-nun [caki-ka mwul-**pakk-ey** masi-ci
 patient-Top self-Nom water only drink

 mos hanun] kes-ul hanthanhayssta.
 not-can Comp-Acc resented
 'The patient resented that (s)he could drink only water.'

---

[1] This paper is based on my "Negative Polarity Items in Japanese and English," which was presented at the Third Nanzan University International Symposium on Japanese Language Pedagogy and Japanese Linguistics, June 18-19, 1994. I am deeply indebted to Nobuaki Nishioka and Ken-ichi Takami, with whom I have discussed the ideas presented in this paper at various stages of their formulation. I have benefited enormously from these discussions. They have also given me invaluable comments on several preliminary drafts of the paper. Without help from them, the paper would not have reached the state that it is in now. I have also benefited greatly from comments I have received from Keiji Konomi, Masako Tsuzuki, Soo-Yeon Kim, Youngjun Jang, Yunsun Jung, Chong-Kon Shi, and Ik-Hwan Lee, with whom I have discussed the behavior of Japanese and Korean NPIs. I have relied primarily on Alisa Kuno, Karen Courtenay, Dan Parmenter and Nan Decker for the native speaker judgments of the crucial English sentences. I want to thank them for their assistance.

b. *Hwanca-nun [caki-ka mwul-**pakk-ey** masi-l-
patient-Top self-Nom water only drink

swu issnun] kes-ul hanthanha-ci **anh**-assta.
can Comp-Acc resent not-Past
'The patient didn't resent the fact that (s)he could drink only water.'

(1.2) a. Hwanca-nun [caki-ka **amwukes-to** mek-ul-swu
patient-Top self-Nom anything eat-can

eps-nun] kes-ul hanthanhayssta.
not Comp-Acc resented
'The patient resented that (s)he couldn't eat anything.'

b. *Hwanca-nun [caki-ka **amwukes-to** mek-ul-swu
patient-Top self-Nom anything eat-can

issnun] kes-ul hanthanha-ci **anh**-assta.
Comp-Acc resent not-Past
'(Lit.) The patient didn't resent the fact that (s)he could eat anything.'

In (1.1a), which is acceptable, the negative morpheme *mos* 'cannot' and the negative polarity item *mwul pakk-ey* 'only water' are clause mates. In contrast, in (1.1b), which is unacceptable, *mos* is in the main clause while *mwul pakk-ey* is in the embedded clause. Likewise, in (1.2a), which is acceptable, the negative morpheme *anh-* 'not' and the negative polarity item *mwul pakk-ey* 'only water' are clause mates. In contrast, in (1.2b), which is unacceptable, the two are not clause mates. These contrasts show that Korean NPIs must find a licensing negative morpheme in the same clause. I will refer to this constraint as the Neg-NPI Clause Mate Constraint.

Konomi (1989) argues that complex NPs of the pattern of "NP + Relative Clause" are islands in Japanese, and that, therefore, it would not be plausible to derive (1.3) by extracting the NPI *kono hon sika* 'only this book' from the complex NP. He proposes that NPIs in sentences such as (1.3) be base-generated as main-clause elements. I give an analogous example in Korean in (1.4).

(1.3) Japanese
Watakusi wa kono hon **sika** [$_{\text{Complex NP}}$ kaita hito] o oboe-te
I this book only wrote person remember

i-**na**-i. (Konomi 1989)
is-NEG
'Only (with respect to) this book do I remember the person who wrote (it).'

(1.4) Korean
Speaker A: Nwu-ka i chayk-tul-ul ssessnun-ci
who-Nom these book-Pl-Acc wrote-Q

kiekha-ni?
remember
'Do you remember who wrote these books?'

Speaker B: Na-nun i chayk-**pakk-ey** [$_{\text{Complex NP}}$ ssun
I-Top this book only wrote

salam]-ul kiekha-ci **mos** hay.
person-Acc remember not-Pr
'Only (with respect to) this book do I remember the person who wrote (it).'

It is plausible to assume, as argued by Konomi, that the NPIs in (1.3, 1.4) are base-generated as main-clause elements. However, there are many speakers who consider sentences such as (1.5b) and (1.6b) acceptable. In the grammar of those speakers, the Neg-NPI Clause Mate Constraint cannot be stated at D-structure:

(1.5) a. *Na-nun [tayphyo-ka taytosi-**eyse-pakk-ey**
I-Top representative-Nom big-city-from only

wassta]-ko sayngkakha-ci **anh**-nunta.
came that think not-Pr
Intended Meaning: 'I think that representatives came only from big cities.'

b. Taytosi-**eyse-pakk-ey** na-nun [tayphyo-ka
big-city-from only I-Top representative

wassta]-ko sayngkakha-ci **anh**-nunta.
came   that think   not-Pr
'Only from big cities do I think that representatives came e.'

(1.6) a. *Na-nun [hoy-lul hoys-cip-**eyse-pakk-ey** mekko
           I-Top   sushi-Acc sushi-shop-Loc only eat

   siphta]-ko sayngkakha-ci **anh**-nunta.
   want   that think   not-Pr
   Intended Meaning: 'I think that [I want to eat sushi only at a sushi shop].'

b. ok/?Hoys-cip-**eyse-pakk-ey** na-nun [hoy-lul mekko
   sushi-shop-Loc only   I-Top   sushi-Acc eat

   siphta]-ko sayngkakha-ci **anh**-nunta.
   want   that think   not-Pr
   'Only at a sushi shop do I think that I want to eat sushi e.'[2]

The above sentences are different from those discussed by Konomi in that the NPIs show connectivity with embedded clauses. The oblique case marker *-eyse* 'from' in (1.5b) and (1.6b) can be justified only with respect to the propositions in the embedded clauses. Therefore, it must be assumed that these sentences are derived by extracting the NPIs out of the embedded clauses into the main clauses. The acceptability of these sentences for the speakers under discussion shows that the Neg-NPI Clause Mate Constraint in Korean must be stated after syntactic movement, and cannot be stated at D-structure. In contrast, for those speakers to whom the above (b) sentences are unacceptable, it must be the case that the Neg-NPI Clause Mate Constraint

---

[2] Sentence (1.6b) has another interpretation, in which *Hoys-cip-eyse-pakk-ey* modifies *sayngkakha-* 'think':

(1.6) b. ok/?Hoys-cip-**eyse-pakk-ey** na-nun [hoy-lul mekko
            sushi-shop-Loc only   I-Top   sushi-Acc eat want

   siphta]-ko sayngkakha-ci **anh**-nunta.
               that think   not-Pr

(ii) 'Only at a sushi shop do I think that I want to eat sushi; It is only when I am at a sushi shop that I have the urge that I want to eat sushi.'

In the above interpretation, the NPI is base-generated as a clause mate of the negative morpheme.

applies at D-structure. In the rest of this paper, I will limit my discussion to the idiolects of the speakers who consider the (b) sentences acceptable.

The acceptability of sentences such as the following might appear to be a problem for the extraction analysis of NPIs:

(1.7) a. Nan-un phathi-ey **amwu-to** chotay ha-lye-ko
I-Top party-to anyone invitation do-to

sayngkakha-ci **anh**-nunta.
think-ing not-Pr.
'I don't think that I will invite anyone to the party.'

b. Na-nun ne-wa hamkkey **eti-ey-to** ka-lye-ko
I-Top you-with together anywhere go-to

sayngkakha-ci **anh**-nunta.
thinking not-Pr.
'I don't think that I will go anywhere with you.'

For the clause-mate constraint to hold, it must be assumed that *phathi-ey* 'to the party' and *ne-wa hamkkey* 'together with you', too, have been extracted out of the embedded clause. There does not seem anything wrong with this assumption because these expressions are readily extractable from reportive clauses:

(1.8) a. Na-nun [Inswu-lul phathi-ey chotay ha-lye]-ko
I-Top party-to invitation do-to

sayngkakha-nta.
think-Pr.
'I think that I will invite Inswu to the party.'

b. Phathi-ey$_i$ na-nun [Inswu-lul e$_i$ chotay halye]-ko
party-to I-Top invitation do-to

sayngkakha-nta.
think-Pr.
'To the party$_i$, I think that I will invite Inswu e$_i$.'

(1.9) a. Na-nun [Sewul-ey ne-wa hamkkey ka-lye]-ko
I-Top to you-with together go-to

sayngkakha-nta.
think-Pr.
'I think that I will go to Seoul with you.'

b. Ne-wa hamkkey$_i$, na-nun [Sewul-ey e$_i$ ka-lye]-ko
    I-Top you-with together   to   go-to

sayngkakha-nta.
think-Pr.
'With you$_i$, I think that I will go to Seoul e$_i$.'

Therefore, it is plausible to assume that (1.7a, b) have the following S-structures:

(1.10) a. Na-nun phathi-ey$_i$ **amwu-to**$_j$ [e$_i$ e$_j$ chotay ha-lye]-ko
            sayngkakha-ci **anh**-nunta.

        b. Na-nun ne-wa hamkkey$_i$ **eti-ey-to**$_j$ [e$_i$ e$_j$ ka-lye]-ko
            sayngkakha-ci **anh**-nunta.

In the above structures, the NPI and its licensing negation are clause mates, and hence, the acceptability of (1.7a, b).

Now, compare (1.7a, b) with (1.1b) and (1.2b), in which the NPIs are preceded by the embedded clause subject NPs. As is well known, it is extremely difficult, if not impossible, to extract the nominative subject of an embedded clause. Therefore, it is most likely that the *ka*-marked NPs in (1.1b) and (1.2b) are elements of the embedded clauses. This leads to the conclusion that the NPIs in (1.1b) and (1.2b) are downstairs elements, not licensed by a clause mate Neg. Hence the total unacceptability of these sentences.

The Neg-NPI Clause Mate Constraint, with the proviso that NPIs can undergo extraction, can account for the fact that the following sentences are both acceptable:

(1.11) a. Na-nun Inswu-**pakk-ey** i kes-ul ha-l-swu **eps**-ta-ko
            I-Top   only   this thing-Acc do-can

            sayngkakha-nta.
            not-that think-Pr
        'I think that only Inswu can do this.'

b. Na-nun Inswu-**pakk-ey** i kes-ul ha-l-swu issta-ko
I-Top only this thing-Acc do-can-that

sayngkakha-ci **anh**-nunta.
think not-Pr
'It is only Inswu that I think can do this.'

The acceptability of (1.11a) is unproblematic. There is a derivation of the sentence in which *Inswu-pakk-ey* and the negative *eps-* are clause mates from D-structure to S-structure.

(1.12) [Na-nun [Inswu-**pakk-ey** i-kes-ul ha-l-swu **eps**-ta]-ko sayngkakhanta]

Hence the acceptability of (1.11a).
There can be two derivations of (1.11b):

(1.13) a. Base Generation of *Inswu-pakk-ey* as a matrix clause element:
Na-nun Inswu$_i$-**pakk-ey** [pro$_i$ i kes-ul ha-l-swu iss-ta]-ko sayngkakha-ci **anh**-nunta

b. Base Generation of *Inswu-pakk-ey* as an embedded clause element:
Na-nun [Inswu-**pakk-ey** i kes-ul ha-l-swu iss-ta]-ko sayngkakha-ci **anh**-nunta

Extraction:
Na-nun Inswu-**pakk-ey**$_i$ [e$_i$ i kes-ul ha-l-swu issta-ko sayngkakha-ci **anh**-nunta.

Both derivations satisfy the Neg-NPI Clause Mate Constraint at S-structure. Hence the acceptability of (1.11b).[3]

---

[3] In order to explain the acceptability of (1.11b), it is necessary to show that there is at least one derivation of the sentence that does not violate any constraints under discussion. Therefore, the argument here goes through even if it is assumed, in a given analytical framework, that there is only a base generation of *Inswu-pakk-ey* as a main clause element, or alternatively, that there is only an extraction generation of the NPI.

1.2. NPIs Can Be Scrambled Out of the Neg Clause

It is widely assumed by scholars in Japanese and Korean syntax that a constraint on the Neg-NPI relationship is observed at S-structure. For example, see Muraki (1978), Kato (1985), and Takahashi (1990 - *"sika* is lexically required to be bound by *na* at S-structure."). However, as noted by Kato (1991), an NPI can be scrambled out of the clause that contains its licenser.

(1.14) a.   Boku wa [Hanako ga **nani mo** wakat-te i-**na**-i]
            I   anything understand-ing

          to omo-u.
          is-NEG that think-Pr.
  'I think that Hanako doesn't understand anything.'

      b.   **Nani mo**$_i$ boku wa [Hanako ga e$_i$ wakat-te
             anything I   understand-

          i-**na**-i] to omo-u.
          ing is-NEG that think-Pr.
  '(Lit.) Anything$_i$, I think that Hanako doesn't understand e$_i$.'

(1.15) a.   Boku wa [Hanako ga **dare ni mo** sono himitu o
            I   anybody to the secret

          akasi-te i-**na**-i] to omo-u.
          reveal-ing is-NEG that think-Pr.
  'I think that Hanako hasn't revealed that secret to anybody.'

      b.   **Dare ni mo**$_i$, boku wa [Hanako ga e$_i$ sono himitu o
             anyone to   I   the   secret

          akasi-te i-**na**-i] to omo-u.
          reveal-ing is-NEG that think-Pr.
  '(Lit.) To anyone$_i$, I think that Hanako hasn't revealed that secret e$_i$.'

As observed by Kato (1991), the acceptability of sentences of the pattern of (1.14b) and (1.15b) shows that if the Neg-NPI Clause Mate Constraint in Japanese is to be applied at S-structure, the trace of an NPI must be allowed to satisfy the constraint.

The following examples show that Korean NPIs, like Japanese NPIs, can be scrambled out of the clauses that contain their licensers:

(1.16) a. Na-nun [Inswu-ka **amwukes-to** al-ci **mos** hanta]-ko
            I-Top   Nom anything   know-not-Pr -that

   sayngkakha-nta.
   think-Pr
   'I think that Inswu doesn't know anything.'

   b. **Amwukes-to**$_i$ na-nun [Inswu-ka e$_i$ al-ci **mos** hanta]-
       anything   I-Top   Nom   know-not-Pr-

   ko sayngkakha-nta.
   that think-Pr
   '(Lit.) Anything$_i$, I think that Inswu doesn't understand e$_i$.'

(1.17) a. Na-nun [Inswu-ka **nwukwu-eykey-to** pimil-ul
            I-Top   Nom anyone-to   secret-Acc

   nwuselha-ci **anh**-assta]-ko sayngkakha-nta.
   leak   not-Past that   think-Pr
   'I think that Insu hasn't revealed the secret to anybody.'

   b. **Nwukwu-eykey-to**$_i$, na-nun [Inswu-ka e$_i$ ku pimil-
       anybody-to   I-Top   Nom   the secret-

   ul nwuselha-ci **anh**-assta]-ko   sayngkakha-nta.
   Acc leak   not-Past - that   think-Pr
   '(Lit.) To anyone$_i$, I think that Inswu hasn't revealed that secret e$_i$.'

The acceptability of (1.14b - 1.17b) stands in marked contrast with the unacceptability of (1.18b):

(1.18) a. He didn't meet **any** of his former roommates at the reunion.
        b. *Any of his former roommates$_i$, he didn't meet e$_i$ at the
           reunion.

One might be tempted to conclude from the unacceptability of (1.18b) that NPIs in English cannot be extracted out of the domain, however it is to be defined, of the Neg that licenses them. I will show in Section 2 that such a ban cannot be maintained.

1.3. NPIs Do Not Have to Have an Overt Negative Element in Surface Sentences

It is widely assumed by scholars who have worked on NPIs in Korean that NPIs require the presence of an overt licenser in surface sentences. The following examples show that this assumption is incorrect:

(1.19) Speaker A: Ne, mwuenka mek-ess-ni?
you something eat-Past
'Did you eat something?'

Speaker B: (i) Ani, **amwukes-to an** mek-ess-e.
no anything not eat-Past
'No, I didn't eat anything.'
(ii) Ani, **amwukes-to** Ø.
no anything
'(Lit.) No, anything.'
(iii) Ani, **an** mek-ess-e, **amwukes-to**.
no not eat-Past anything
'(Lit.) No, I didn't eat – anything.'

(1.20) Speaker A: Ne, peythunam-ey yelepen ka-ss-ci?
you Vietnam-to many-times went
'Did you go to Vietnam many times?'

Speaker B: (i) Ani, hanpen-**pakk-ey an** ka-ss-e.
no once-only not go-Past
'No, I went only once.'
(ii) Ani, hanpen-**pakk-ey** Ø.
no once-only
'No, only once.'
(iii) Ani, **an** ka-ss-e, hanpen-**pakk-ey**.
no not go-Past once-only
'(Lit.) No, I didn't go -- only once.'

In informal speech, the licensing negative morpheme *an(h)* does not even have to be present in the sentence, as shown by the acceptability of (Bii). In (Biii), the NPIs are clearly outside the clause that contains the negative morpheme.

The acceptability of the (Bii) and (Biii) sentences above stands in marked contrast with the fact that discourse (1.20A - Bii) in English is totally unacceptable:

(1.21) Speaker A: Haven't you eaten?
        Speaker B: (i)   No, I haven't eaten **anything**.
                    (ii) *No, Ø **anything**.

For reasons that will become clear later in this paper, the unacceptability of (1.21Bii) cannot be attributed to a constraint to the effect that NPIs in English require the presence of an overt negative element in S-structure. Such a constraint does not exist in English, either.

I attribute the unacceptability of (1.21Bii) to the same discourse factor that makes (1.22Bii) unacceptable:

(1.22) Speaker A: Haven't you seen John?
        Speaker B: (i)   No, I haven't seen John.
                    (ii) *No, Ø John.

Across-the-Board Discourse Deletion is responsible for creating sentences such as (Bii). This rule leaves behind only the focus information, and deletes all the discourse-presupposed information. The unacceptability of (Bii) is due to the fact that *John*, which is not the focus of the answer, has been retained, and *I haven't seen*, which is not discourse-predictable, has been deleted.[4]

Likewise, the following exchange is unacceptable:

(1.23) Speaker A: What did you eat?
        Speaker B: (i)   I didn't eat **anything**.
                    (ii) *Ø **Anything**.

(1.23Bii) is unacceptable because the deleted string *I didn't eat* is not discourse-predictable--that is, I attribute the unacceptability of (1.23Bii) not

---

[4] Note that (1.21A) has the expectation on the part of the speaker that the answer will be in the affirmative. This fact makes *I haven't seen* in Speaker B's answer discourse-unpredictable. Observe that the following exchange is acceptable:

(i) Speaker A: Haven't you seen John?
     Speaker B: (i)   Yes, I have seen John, also.
                 (ii) Yes, Ø John, also.

In the above discourse, it is clear that the focus of the answer is on *John, also*, and that *I have seen* is discourse predictable.

to the lack of an overt NPI licenser, but to the fact that discourse deletion has applied incorrectly to delete focus information. The question then is why (1.19Bii), the Korean counterpart of (1.23Bii), is acceptable. It seems that this is due to the fact that Korean NPIs are unambiguous negative polarity items--they, even in isolation, imply negation--in that sense, they are like *nobody* and *nothing* in English. In contrast, English NPIs are not pure NPIs--they are ambiguous between the negative polarity interpretation and the "free-choice" interpretation, and furthermore, even as NPIs, they can show up in questions, *if* and *than* clauses, and so on. Therefore, *anything* in (1.23Bii), in isolation, cannot convey the negative nature of the answer. In other words, given an NPI and a Neg, in English, the Neg represents focus information, while in Korean, the NPI represents as much negation information as the negative morpheme:

(1.24) a. Korean
Speaker A: Ne, mwuenka mek-ess-ni?
you something eat-Past
'Have you eaten anything?'
Speaker B: (i) **Amwukes-to an** mek-ess-e.
  Focs   Focus
(ii) Ø   **an** mek-ess-e.
(iii) **Amwukes-to**.

b. English:
Speaker A: Haven't you eaten?
Speaker B: (i) No, I have**n't** eaten **anything**.
            Focus   Lesser Focus
(ii) No, I have**n't** Ø.
(iii) *No, Ø   **anything**.

Discourse Deletion of recoverable information applies subject to the following constraint:

(1.25) **Pecking Order of Deletion Principle**: Delete less important information first, and more important information last. (Kuno 1982, 1983)

In (1.24aBi), *amwukes-to* and *an* are of equal degree of importance, and therefore, either can be deleted without violating the Pecking Order of Deletion Principle. This accounts for the fact that both (1.24aBii) and (1.24aBiii) are acceptable. In contrast, in (1.24bBi), the negative morpheme represents more important information than the NPI. (1.24bBii) is acceptable because the less important *anything* has been deleted and the more important *not* has been retained. On the other hand, (1.24bBiii) is unacceptable because the more important *not* has been deleted, and the less important information *anything* has been retained.

The above explanation for the contrast between Korean and English predicts that it should be possible to have NPIs in English without an overt Neg in surface sentences in case the Neg is discourse-predictable. I will show in Section 3.2 that this is indeed the case.

The above explanation for the contrast between Korean and English is also supported by the NPI facts in Spanish. In Spanish, negative polarity items such as *nadie* 'nobody/anybody' and *nada* 'nothing/anything' can appear in postverbal position only in sentences that contain a negative element (*no* 'not' or an NPI) in preverbal position.

(1.26) a. Yo **no** quiero **nada**.
I not want anything.
'I don't want anything.'

b. **Nadie** quiere **nada**.
nobody wants nothing
'Nobody wants anything.'

c. *Yo quiero **nada**.
I want anything
'(Lit.) I want anything.'

Sentence (1.26a) is acceptable because the postverbal *nada* is licensed by the preverbal *no*. Likewise, (1.26b) is acceptable because the postverbal *nada* is licensed by the preverbal NPI *nadie*. In contrast, (1.26c) is unacceptable because the postverbal NPI lacks a preverbal licenser and because *nada* does not have a "free-choice" quantifier interpretation. Now, note that Spanish allows the discourse deletion pattern of the type of (1.19A-Bii):

(1.27) Speaker A: ¿Viste a alguien?
saw someone
'Did you see someone?'

100 • *Susumu Kuno*

Speaker B: (i) No, **no** vi a **nadie**.
no not saw anyone
'I didn't see anyone.'
(ii) No, Ø a **nadie**.
(iii) Ø A **nadie**.

Since *nadie* 'anybody/nobody' signals as much negation information as *no vie* does, the latter can undergo discourse deletion without violating the Pecking Order of Deletion Principle, yielding acceptable sentences (Bii) and (Biii).

1.4. The Mode of Application of the Neg-NPI Clause Mate Constraint

The task before us is how to reconcile the three factors in Korean that have been discussed above—(i) the Neg-NPI Clause Mate Constraint must apply after syntactic movement, (ii) NPIs can be scrambled out of the Neg Clause, and (iii) NPIs do not have to have an overt Neg in surface sentences. Let us assume that all the elements that undergo discourse deletion are still present at S-structure when the Neg-NPI Clause Mate Constraint applies. Thus, when the Neg-NPI Clause Mate Constraint applies to (1.19Bii), for example, it still has *an mek-ess-e* 'have not eaten' undeleted. This structure does not violate the Constraint, and hence, the acceptability of the sentence.

As noted by Kato (1991), the Neg-NPI Clause Mate Constraint can be fulfilled by the trace of a syntactically moved NPI. This is illustrated in (1.14b) - (1.17b). I assume that sentences involving Right Dislocation of the pattern of (1.19Biii) are derived from bi-clausal D-structures, as shown in (1.28): the Neg and the NPI in the second clause satisfy the Neg-NPI Clause Mate Constraint:

(1.28) S-structure of (1.19Biii) (bi-clausal derivation):
[**an** mek-ess-e] , [**amwukes-to an** mek-ess-e]
not eat-Past anything not eat-Past
'(Lit.) I haven't eaten; I haven't eaten anything.'

The underlined portion of the second clause, since it is recoverable from the corresponding portion in the first clause, undergoes discourse deletion in PF.

The acceptability of (1.20Biii) requires explanation. I assume that the sentence has the following bi-clausal S-structure, with irrelevant details ignored, at the time of application of the Neg-NPI Clause Mate Constraint:

(1.29)   S-structure of (1.20Biii) (bi-clausal derivation):
[yelepen **an** ka-ss-e] ,   [hanpen-**pakk-ey** **an** ka-ss-e]
many-times not go-Pas   only-once   not go-Past

The Neg and the NPI in the second clause satisfies the Neg-NPI Clause Mate Constraint. The underlined portion of the second clause undergoes discourse deletion in PF because it is recoverable from the underlined portion of the first clause of the structure. *Yelepen* 'many times' in the first clause undergoes discourse deletion because it is recoverable from the same expression in Speaker A's question.

The acceptability of discourse (1.20A-Biii) shows a marked contrast with the unacceptability of discourse (1.30A-B):

(1.30)   Speaker A: Ne peythunam-ey ka-ss-ci?
                      you Vietnam-to went
                      'Did you go to Vietnam?'

         Speaker B: *Ani, **an** ka-ss-e, hanpen-**pakk-ey**.
                      no   not go-Past   once-only
                      '(Lit.) No, I didn't go -- only once.'

In the analytical framework being proposed here, (1.30B) is assumed to have the following bi-clausal S-structure:

(1.31)   [peythunam-ey **an** ka-ss-e] [hanpen-**pakk-ey** peythunam-
         Vietnam   to not went   once   only   Vietnam

ey **an** ka-ss-e]
to not went.
'*I didn't go to Vietnam; I went to Vietnam only once.'

The second clause satisfies the Neg-NPI Clause Mate Constraint. However, (1.30B) is judged unacceptable as an answer to (1.30A) because the above S-structure is derived from a D-structure, shown in (1.31), that consists of two clauses that represent contradictory propositions.

2.   Subject-Object Asymmetry in NPI Licensing in English
2.1.   Past Research in NPIs

It is well known that the NPI licensing displays subject-object asymmetry in English, but it does not in Japanese or Korean. For example, observe the following sentences:

(2.1) a. John doesn't know **anyone**.
       b. ***Anyone** doesn't know John.

(2.2) a. John wa **dare mo** sir-**ana**-i.
                     anyone   know-NEG-Pr.
          'John doesn't know anyone.'

     b. **Dare mo** John o sir-**ana**-i.
        anyone   know-NEG-Pr.
        '(Lit.) Anyone doesn't know John.'

(2.3) a. Inswu-nun **nwukwu-to** kiekha-ci   **mos** hanta.
                 Topic anyone   remember-ing not-do-Pr.
          'Inswu doesn't remember anyone.'

     b. **Nwukwu-to** Inswu-lul kiekha-ci   **mos** hanta.
        anyone   Acc remember-ing not-do-Pr.
        '(Lit.) Anyone doesn't remember Inswu.'

Since Klima (1964), it has been widely assumed in the framework of generative grammar that NPIs in the two languages are subject to a c-command licensing condition that can be informally stated as follows:

(2.3)   C-command Condition for NPI Licensing: An NPI must be licensed by a c-commanding negation at S-structure.

       N.B. Node α c-commands node β if the first branching node that dominates α dominates β, and α does not dominate β.

The contrast between English and Japanese/Korean has been attributed to differences in phrase structure configurations at the time of application of the C-command Condition.

(2.4) Structure of a Negative Sentence in English (from Takahashi 1990)

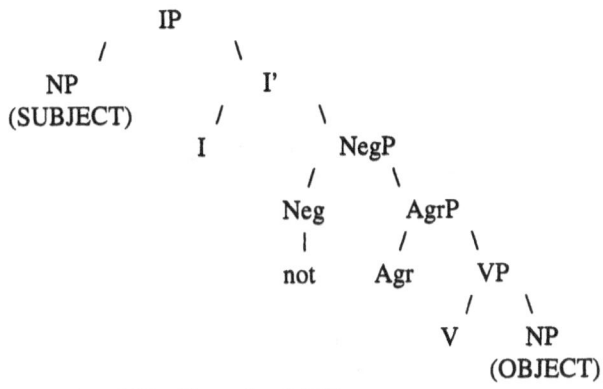

cf. Pollock (1989), Chomsky (1991)

(2.5) Structure of a Negative Sentence in Japanese (from Takahashi 1990)

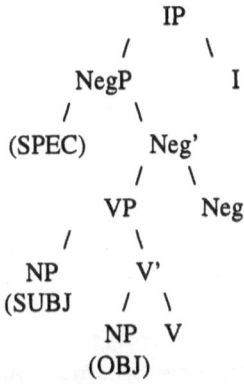

cf. Fukui (1986), Kitagawa (1986), Kuroda (1986), Lasnik and Saito (1992)

It is assumed above that in English the subject NP is base-generated in IP Specifier position, while in Japanese and Korean, the subject NP is base-generated as VP-internal subject and remains *in situ* at S-structure.[5]

In the negative sentence structure of English shown in (2.4), Neg c-commands the object NP, but it does not c-command the subject NP. Hence, the acceptability of (2.1a) and the unacceptability of (2.1b). In contrast, in the negative sentence structure of Japanese and Korean shown in (2.5), Neg c-commands both the subject and object NPs. Hence the acceptability of both (2.2a) and (2.2b).[6]

It is well recognized that the C-command Condition for NPI Licensing given in (2.3) cannot be made to apply to D-structure. Observe, for example, the following sentences:

(2.6) a. They have**n't** said **anything**.
b. *****Anything** has**n't** been said.

(2.7) a. *****Anybody** hasn't noticed this.
b. This has**n't** been noticed by **anybody**.

The unacceptability of (2.6b) and the acceptability of (2.7b) show that what is crucial is whether the C-command Condition is satisfied at S-structure.

Likewise, observe the following sentences:

(2.8) a. It is **not** likely that **anything** will happen.
b. *****Anything** is **not** likely to happen.

---

[5] In a theoretical framework in which the surface subject in English starts out as VP-internal subject, it is clear that the C-command Condition for NPI Licensing cannot be made to apply to the trace of syntactically moved NPs. Otherwise, the trace of the moved subject (*anyone* in (2.1b)) would satisfy the C-command Condition and there would not be any subject-object asymmetry in English.

[6] In GB Theory, there are various variations in proposed conditions for NPI licensing, but they are invariably rooted in the assumption that NPIs must be c-commanded by a licensing Neg. See, for example, Mahajan (1990):

(i)   A negative polarity item X must be c-commanded by a negative polarity licenser Y.

He claims that this constraint is universal, and that it applies at S-structure and at LF in English, and at LF alone in Hindi.

Progovac (1994) claims that NPIs are subject to Binding Condition A, thus adhering to the assumption that NPIs must be c-commanded by their licensers.

The C-command Condition on NPI Licensing is taken so much for granted that Kayne (1994), in order to account for acceptable NPI sentences that violate a c-command condition of the type defined in (2.3), has been led to propose a major change (which he is aware creates difficulties elsewhere) in the notion of "c-command", coupled with the assumption that a Specifier is necessarily to be taken as an adjoined phrase. See footnote 13 on Kayne's proposal.

In the framework under review, it must be assumed that the D-structure status of these sentences is irrelevant.

The C-command Condition as it applies to S-structure alone or to LF-representation alone (or to S-structure and LF-representation alone) begins to look less attractive in the face of the acceptability of sentences such as the following:

(2.9)   That **anyone** has finished yet is **not** likely.

The NPI in (2.9) is not c-commanded by Neg in S-structure, and therefore, the C-command Condition predicts that the sentence should be as unacceptable as (2.1b) is. Contrary to this prediction, the sentence is perfectly acceptable. Laka (1990), in discussing sentences of this pattern, proposes that what licenses the NPI in (2.9) is not *not*, but rather the negative complementizer *that* that heads the embedded clause. In arguing for this analysis, she discusses exchanges of the following kind:

(2.10) Speaker A: What is not likely (to be the case)?
        Speaker B: That **anyone** has finished yet.

Laka assumes that the S-structure of elliptical sentences of the pattern of (2.10B) does not have a substructure corresponding to the elided string. On that basis, she argues that the NPI in (2.10B) would not have a licensing Neg unless it is assumed that the complementizer *that* contains a negative element. I will show in the next section that Laka's [+Neg] complementizer analysis does not capture the true nature of the status of sentences such as (2.9) and (2.10B).

In the framework of checking theory proposed by Chomsky and Lasnik (1993) and Chomsky (1993), attempts have been made to account for the subject-object asymmetry in English and the subject-object symmetry in Japanese and Korean on the basis of Binding Condition C violations (due to A-to-A' (Neg)-to-A movement of the NPI in subject position) (Lee 1992, Kawashima and Kitahara 1992) and on the basis of the acceptable and unacceptable chains (Nishioka 1994). These approaches crucially assume that an NPI should have a licensing Neg that c-commands it either at S-structure, or at LF (or at both S-structure and LF).

2.2. Problems with the C-command Formulation

Although Laka's account of the acceptability of (2.9) and (2.10) might appear to make sense, it cannot account for the fact that many speakers consider sentences such as the following acceptable:[7]

(2.11)   a. ok/?/??The names of **any** potential nominees have **not** yet been forwarded to the FBI for background checking. (Therefore, it seems that they don't yet have a short list.)

        b. ok/?/??The existence of **any** willful wrongdoing on the part of the Senator has **not** been proved.

While all speakers consider (2.1b) unacceptable, there is a great deal of idiolectal variation in the acceptability judgments for (2.11a, b). To many speakers, the sentences are fully acceptable, while to some others, they are marginal. To most speakers, (2.11a, b), if not perfect, are considerably better than (2.1b). Constraints on NPIs must be formulated in such a way as to be able to account for these facts. It goes without saying that Laka's negative complementizer analysis of (2.9) and (2.10) is not applicable to (2.11a, b), and therefore, her analysis predicts that these sentences should all be as unacceptable as (2.1b) because of their violation of the C-command Condition on NPIs.

---

[7] Lee (1992), in a footnote, gives (ia-e) as sentences that cannot be accounted for by the c-command based condition on NPI licensing:

(i)   a. ?Students of any philosophical professor do not take this course.

           (Enc 1990 -class lecture)

        b. ?Pictures of anybody were not bought by the visitor. (Lasnik p.c.)

        c. ?Pictures of anybody did not seem to be on sale. (Lasnik p.c.)

        d. ?Pictures of anybody did not amuse the visitor. (Lasnik p.c.)

        e. ?Pictures of anybody did not arrive in the gallery at that time. (Lasnik p.c.)

Lee does not offer any explanation of the fact that these sentences are considerably better than (2.1b). Incidentally, for reasons that are not clear to me, Lee's sentences are not as acceptable as my examples given in (2.11).

2.3. Problems with the Assumption that NPI Licensing in English Takes Place at S-Structure

There is, however, a more fundamental problem with the approaches that have been outlined in Section 2.1. They have all assumed that the position of Neg (or *not*) in S-structure or in LF-representation is crucial. I will show below that this assumption is incorrect.

First, observe the following sentences:

(2.12) a. I didn't give **anyone anything**.
b. I gave **nobody anything**.
c. *I gave **anybody nothing**.

The contrast between (2.12b) and (2.12c) shows that what is crucial for these sentences is not a Neg that might exist under NegP in S-structure or LF-representation (cf. 2.4, 2.5), but where the negative morpheme *nobody/nothing* stands in the structure vis-à-vis the NPI *anything/anybody*. Therefore, in the c-command formulation, it must be assumed that it is *nobody/nothing* that is a potential licenser for NPIs in these sentences. In checking theory, it must be assumed that *nobody/nothing* is dominated by a node, call it NegNP, which has a Specifier position that is marked as [+Neg].

Now, observe the following sentences:

(2.13) a. *That **anything** serious would happen seemed to everybody to be likely.
b. That **anything** serious would happen seemed to **nobody** to be likely.

While (2.13a) is unacceptable, indicating that *anything* is not a "free-choice" quantifier, (2.13b) is perfectly acceptable in spite of the fact that the negative element *nobody* does not c-command *anything* in any sense of c-command, and in spite of the fact that there is no available checking position for the NPI. Even in Laka's framework, the complementizer *that* at the beginning of the sentence is not marked as [+Neg]. In order to see this, let us first follow the derivation of (2.14a):

(2.14) a. John seemed to Mary to be sick.
b. Intermediate Structure:
[(It) seemed to Mary for [[$_{NP}$ John] to be sick]
c. Subject-to-Subject Raising:
[[$_{NP}$ John] seemed to Mary (for) to be sick]

Subject-to-Subject Raising applies to the subject NP of the *for-to* clause in (2.14b), and raises it to the matrix-clause subject position. The derivation of (2.13b) follows the same steps, except that it has [$_{NP}$ that anything serious would happen], instead of [$_{NP}$ John], as the subject of the embedded *for-to* clause:

(2.15) a. Intermediate Structure of (2.13b):
[(It) seemed to nobody for [$_{NP}$ that anything serious
[+Neg]
would happen] to be likely]

b. Subject-to-Subject Raising:
[[$_{NP}$ That anything serious would happen] seemed to nobody (for) to be likely]
[+Neg]

Note that in Laka's framework, what could be marked as [+Neg] in (2.15a) is complementizer *for*, and not the complementizer *that* that heads the subject of *to be likely*. Therefore, *anything* would be left without a licenser either at S-structure or at LF, incorrectly predicting that (2.13b) should be unacceptable.
Likewise, observe the following sentences:

(2.16) a. It is likely that the destruction of **some** cities has taken place.
b. *It is likely that the destruction of **any** cities has taken place.
c. It is **not** likely that the destruction of **any** cities has taken place.
d. ok/?/??The destruction of **any** cities is **not** likely to have taken place.

The unacceptability of (2.16b) and the acceptability of (2.16c) makes clear that *any* in these sentences is an NPI, and not a "free-choice" quantifier. Observe that (2.16d), in which there is no c-command relationship between *not* and *any*, is acceptable to many speakers. There are many speakers who consider the sentence awkward or marginal, but even to those speakers, it is considerably better than (2.1b). Since the complementizer *for* does not c-command the NPI either at S-structure or at LF, Laka's analysis cannot account for this fact.
It might be argued that NPI Licensing takes place not at S-structure, but at LF, where moved elements are placed back to their original site. Such an argument is contrary to the generally held assumption that LF reconstruction applies to elements that have undergone A'-movement, but

not to those that have undergone A-movement. Observe that Subject-to-Subject Raising is an A-movement rule, and therefore, LF reconstruction should not be allowed to apply to the subject that-clause in (2.13b) and the subject NP in (2.16d). Furthermore, even if LF reconstruction were allowed to apply, it is easy to see that it would not account for the acceptability status of sentences of the type under discussion. LF reconstruction applied to NPs that have undergone A-movement would incorrectly predict that (2.6b) should be acceptable. Likewise, it would incorrectly predict that (2.17d) should be acceptable:

(2.17) a. It is likely that **some** cities have been destroyed.
        b. *It is likely that **any** cities have been destroyed.
        c. It is not likely that **any** cities have been destroyed.
        d. ***Any** cities are not likely to have been destroyed.

Therefore, the assumption that constraints on NPIs can be stated either at S-structure, at LF, or at S-structure and LF, must be abandoned.

Observe, also, the following sentences:

(2.18) a. They haven't yet forwarded the names of **any** potential nominees to the Supreme Court to the FBI for background checking.
        b. ok/?/??The names of **any** potential nominees to the Supreme Court, they haven't yet forwarded to the FBI for background checking.

(2.19) a. He couldn't remember the names of **any** of his former roommates.
        b. ok/?/??The names of **any** of his former roommates, he couldn't remember.
        c. He was full of nostalgia for the Yard and certain laboratories and classrooms he had frequented during his college years, but ok/?/??the names of **any** of his former roommates, he couldn't remember.[8]

---

[8] I am indebted to Karen Courtenay (p.c.) for this sentence.

(2.20) a. Jane **isn't** really fond of **anyone**.
   b. (She certainly seems to have thousands of acquaintances, but) ok/?/??really fond of **anyone** she **isn't**.[9]
   c. ***Anyone**, she **isn't** really fond of.

While (2.20c) is unacceptable to all speakers, (2.18b, 2.19b, 2.19c, 2.20b) are acceptable to many speakers, awkward to some, and marginal to others. Here again, most speakers consider these sentences considerably better than (2.20c). The NPIs in these sentences are not c-commanded by a Neg in any definition of c-command.

2.4. Problems with the Assumption that NPIs in English Require the Presence of Overt Neg in Surface Sentences

As stated in the C-command Condition for NPI Licensing given in (2.3), it is nearly universally assumed that the condition applies at S-structure in English, with an overt [+Neg] marked morpheme present, be it (i) *not*, (ii) *nobody*, *nothing*, etc., or (iii) the putative negative complementizer *that*. Likewise, in the framework of checking theory, the LF presence of the analog of the S-structure [+Neg]-marked licenser is assumed. The following exchanges show that this assumption is incorrect:

(2.21) Speaker B: The White House has been giving out tons of useless information, but they have been rather secretive about important things.
    Speaker A: What kind of information haven't they released?
    Speaker B: (i) They **haven't** released the names of **any** potential nominees to the Supreme Court.
        (ii) ok/?The names of **any** potential nominees to the Supreme Court.

(2.22) Speaker A: Who **didn't** you see at the reunion?
    Speaker B: (i) I **didn't** see **any** of my former roommates.
        (ii) ok/?**Any** of my former roommates.

To many speakers, (2.21Bii) and (2.22Bii) are each acceptable answers to (2.21A) and (2.22A), respectively. But in these sentences, the NPIs are not c-commanded by any *overt* negative element. The fact that these sentences are acceptable makes Laka's argument concerning (2.10B) a nonargument.

---

[9] I am indebted to Karen Courtenay (p.c.) for this sentence.

(2.11), (2.18-19), and (2.21-22) put together make English look very much like Japanese and Korean.

3. Reanalysis of NPI Licensing Conditions
3.1. Anti-Superiority Condition on Licensees

In the preceding section, I have shown that NPIs in English have what appear to be conflicting characteristics. On one hand, sentences such as those given in (3.1) suggest that NPI licensing takes place in D-structure. On the other hand, sentences such as those given in (3.2) suggest that it takes place at S-structure:

(3.1) a. That **anything** serious would happen seemed to **nobody** to be likely. (=2.13)
b. ok/?/??The destruction of **any** cities is **not** likely to have taken place. (=2.16d)
c. ok/?/??The names of **any** potential nominees to the Supreme Court, they **haven't** yet forwarded to the FBI for background checking. (=2.16b)
d. (She certainly seems to have thousands of acquaintances, but) ok/?/??really fond of **anyone** she **isn't**. (=2.18b)

(3.2) a.   ***Anyone** doesn't know John. (=2.1b)
b.   *I gave **anybody** nothing. (=2.12c)
c.   *Any cities are not likely to have been destroyed.

The above facts make it implausible that constraints on NPI licensing could be stated at a single level, be it D-structure, S-structure, or LF.

The striking difference between (3.1) and (3.2) is that in the latter, NPIs both precede and c-command the negative elements that should have been their licensers. I am assuming here the following extension of the concept of NPIs:

(3.3) a.   If an NPI is not an NP, then the smallest NP that contains it is also an NPI.
e.g.   the names [$_{PP}$ of [$_{+NPI}$ [$_{+NPI}$ **any**] potential nominees]]]
b.   Given a constituent that is marked as [+NPI], the feature percolates to the maximum projection of the constituent.
e.g.   [$_{+NPI}$ [$_{+NPI}$ **anything**] serious]
e.g.   [$_{+NPI}$ [$_{+NPI}$ **any**] of his former roommates]

In (3.3a) since *any* is not an NP, *any potential nominees* as a whole acquires an NPI status. But *the names of any potential nominees* is not an NPI because the PP node that dominates *any potential nominees* blocks the [+NPI] feature percolation.[10] In (3.3b), the NP node dominating *any of his former roommates* as a whole acquires an NPI status because it is the maximum projection of [$_{NP}$ *any*].

Let us assume that the following constraint holds:

(3.4) **Anti-Superiority Condition on Licensees**:
A licensee must not be syntactically superior to its licenser.
N.B. (i) Violation results in English if an NPI is superior to its licensing negative morpheme at S-structure in English.
(ii) Violation results in Korean if all of {NPI, NPI's trace(s)} are superior to the licensing Neg at S-structure.

Syntactic Superiority:
a. The Specifier of a given phrase is not superior to the Head of that phrase (e.g., a *wh*-expression in Specifier position is not superior to the Q that licenses it); otherwise
b. α is superior to β if it both precedes and PP-invisible-c-commands β.

N.B. **PP-invisible-c-command**: Node α PP-invisible-c-commands node β if the first non-PP branching node that dominates α dominates β, and α does not dominate β.

The NPI in each of (3.2a, b, c) both precedes and PP-invisible-c-commands the Neg that licenses it. That is, it is superior to the licensing Neg. Thus, the unacceptability of these sentences can be attributed to their violation of the Anti-Superiority Condition on Licensees. I have yet to present an explanation as to why (3.1a) is acceptable, and (3.1b, c, d) acceptable, awkward or marginal depending upon the speaker.

It is easy to see why Korean does not display subject-object asymmetry in NPIs. In the framework in which subject NPs in Korean are VP-internal at S-structure as well as at D-structure, and in which the presence of a NegP, with Neg as its head, is hypothesized, as in the structure shown in

---

[10] In Section 4, I hypothesize that there are speakers in whose idiolects the NPI status of *any potential nominees* in (3.3a) percolates to the higher NP via PP.

(2.5), an NPI *in situ* cannot be superior to the Neg that licenses it because the latter PP-invisible-c-commands the former. This explains the acceptability of (2.3b), as well as of (2.3a).

(2.3) a. Inswu-nun **nwukwu-to** kiekha-ci **mos** hanta.
Topic anyone   remember-ing not-do-Pr.
'Inswu doesn't remember anyone.'

       b. **Nwukwu-to** Inswu-lul kiekha-ci **mos** hanta.
anyone   Acc remember-ing not-do-Pr.
'(Lit.) Anyone doesn't remember Inswu.'

As observed in Section 1.2, Korean allows extraction of NPIs out of the Neg clause:

(1.16) a. Na-nun [Inswu-ka **amwukes-to** al-ci **mos** hanta]-ko
I-Top   Nom anything know-not-Pr -that

sayngkakha-nta.
think-Pr
'I think that Inswu doesn't know anything.'

       b. **Amwukes-to**$_i$ na-nun [Inswu-ka e$_i$ al-ci **mos**
anything   I-Top Nom know-not-Pr-

hanta]-ko sayngkakha-nta.
that   think-Pr
'(Lit.) Anything$_i$, I think that Inswu doesn't understand e$_i$.'

(1.17) a. Na-nun [Inswu-ka **nwukwu-eykey-to** pimil-ul
I-Top   Nom anyone-to   secret-Acc

nwuselha-ci **anh**-assta]-ko sayngkaha-nta.
leak   not-Past   that think-Pr
'I think that Inswu hasn't revealed that secret to anybody.'

       b. **Nwukwu-eykey-to**$_i$, na-nun [Inswu-ka e$_i$ ku
anybody-to   I-Top   Nom the

pimil-ul nwuselha-ci **anh**-assta]-ko sayngkakh-nta
secret-Acc leak   not-Past -that think-Pr
'(Lit.) To anyone$_i$, I think that Inswu hasn't revealed that secret e$_i$.'

The acceptability of (1.16b, 1,17b) necessitates the stipulation, given in (3.4ii), that the Anti-Superiority Condition on Licensees does not apply in Korean if the NPI or its trace is not superior to the NPI's licenser.

Returning to NPIs in English, the Anti-Superiority Condition can also account for the unacceptability of (3.5b):

(3.5)   a.   I don't remember what Inswu bought at that store.
        b.   Extraction of *what*:
           *****What**$_i$ I don't remember e$_i$ Inswu bought at that store.

It has been taken for granted that *wh*-expressions that have been fronted cannot undergo extraction from their final landing site. We must ask why this is the case. The obligatoriness of their fronting to the Specifier position of CP cannot provide an explanation for their inextractability because the following examples show that a constituent that has been obligatorily fronted can further undergo extraction:

(3.6)   a.   I expect Mary to be found innocent.
        b.   Mary$_i$, I expect e$_i$ to be found innocent.

The derived subject of a passive sentence undergoes obligatory movement, but as shown by the acceptability of (3.6b), the subject can further undergo extraction.

The Anti-Superiority Condition can now explain why (3.5b) is unacceptable: the structure that would result from the extraction of *wh*-expressions would violate the constraint:

(3.7)   *[what$_i$ [I don't remember [e$_i$ Q [Inswu bought at the store]]]]

In the above structure, the licensee *what* is superior to the licenser *Q*.

In Korean, the licenser Q is always to the right of *wh*-expressions which it licenses, but it is in S' position, and PP-invisible-c-commands the *wh*-expression. Therefore, *wh*-expressions *in situ* are never superior to the licensing *kka*. Furthermore, sentences such as (3.8Ab) and (3.9b) do not violate the Anti-Superiority Condition because the trace of the fronted *wh*-expression is not superior to its licenser:

(3.8) Speaker Aa: Ne-nun [Inswu-ka ku kakey-eyse **mwues-**
you that store at what

ul sa-ss-nun-**ci**] kiekha-ni?
buy-Past-Q remember-Q
'Do you remember what Insu bought at that store?"

Speaker Ab: **Mwues-ul**$_i$ ne-nun [Inswu-ka ku kakey-
what you that sore

eyse e$_i$ sa-ss-nun-**ci**] kiekha-ni?
at buy-Past-Q remember-Q
'Do you remember what Inswu bought at that store?"

Speaker B: Ung, kiekhay.
yes, remember
'Yes, I remember.'

(3.9) a. Na-nun [Inswu-ka ku kakey-eyese **mwues-ul**
I that store at what

sa-ss-nun-**ci**] kiekha-ci mos ha-nta.
buy-Past-Q remember-ing not-Pr.
'I don't remember what Insu bought at that store.'

b. **Mwues-ul**$_i$ na-nun [Inswu-ka ku kakey-eyse e$_i$
what I that store at

sa-ss-nun-**ci**] kiekha-ci mos ha-nta..
buy-Past-Q remember-ing not-Pr.
'I don't remember what Insu bought at that store.'

Now observe the following sentences:

(3.10) a. John introduced **Mary**$_i$ to a clone of **herself**$_i$.
b. John introduced a clone of **herself**$_i$ to **Mary**$_i$.
(3.11) a. John showed **Mary**$_i$ to a clone of **herself**$_i$.
b. John showed a clone of **herself**$_i$ to **Mary**$_i$.

The fact that both (3.10a, 11a) and (3.10b, 11b) are acceptable shows that given 'introduce x to y' and 'show x to y', it is necessary to assume that x and y PP-invisible-c-command each other in the representation to which Binding Condition A (an anaphor rule) applies. But once that assumption is made, the unacceptability of (3.12b, 3.13b) becomes a problem:

(3.12) a. John ended up introducing **Mary**$_i$ to **herself**$_i$.
 b. *John ended up introducing **herself**$_i$ to **Mary**$_i$.

(3.13) a. John (took Mary to the mirror, and) showed **Mary**$_i$ to **herself**$_i$.
 b. *John (took Mary to the mirror, and) showed **herself**$_i$ to **Mary**$_i$.
 (cf. Kuno 1987)

According to the assumption made for (3.10, 11), the reflexive *herself* is PP-invisible-c-commanded by *Mary* in (3.12b, 13b), and therefore, (3.12b, 13b) should be acceptable. It is not plausible to attribute the unacceptability of the sentences to the fact that *Mary* is PP-invisible-c-commanded by *herself* because the same PP-invisible-c-command relationship holds between *Mary* and *herself* in (3.12a, 13a), which are acceptable.

The Anti-Superiority Condition on Licensees can account for the contrast between (3.12a, 13a) and (3.12b, 13b). If we assume that a reflexive pronoun is a licensee, and its antecedent a licenser, then (3.12b, 13b), but not (3.12a, 13a), violate the Anti-Superiority Condition. Note that the licensee *herself* both precedes and PP-invisible-c-commands the licenser *Mary* in (3.12b, 13b).

The following examples show that the same phenomenon exists in Korean:

(3.14) a. **Inswu**$_i$-ka **caki**$_i$-uy pumo-nim-ul silmang sikhi-essta.
    self's parents disappointment make-Past
    '(Lit.) Inswu disappointed self's parents.'

 b. **Caki**$_i$ uyci-uy yakham-i Inswu-lul silmang sikhi-essta.
    self will's weakness   disappointment make-Past
    '(Lit.) The weakness of self's will disappointed Inswu.'

(3.15) a. **Inswu**$_i$-ka **caki**$_i$-lul silmang sikhi-essta.
    self disappointment make-Past
    '(Lit.) Inswu disappointed self.'

b. *Caki$_i$-ka Inswu$_i$-lul silmang sikhi-essta.
    self   disappointment make-Past
    '(Lit.) Self disappointed Inswu.'

The acceptability of both (3.14a) and (3.14b) shows that backward reflexivization from the object into the subject position must be allowed for psychological verbs in Korean. But this incorrectly predicts that (3.15b) should be acceptable. Here again, the Anti-Superiority Condition can mark (3.15b) unacceptable because at the time that Binding Condition A applies, the reflexive pronoun, a licensee, both precedes and c-commands *Inswu*, a licenser, in the sentence.[11]

3.2. NPI Licensing as a D-Structure Constraint

It is clear that the Anti-Superiority Condition alone is not sufficient to constrain NPIs. For example, observe the following sentence, which does not violate the Anti-Superiority Condition:

(3.16)   *That John didn't come means that **anything** serious happened.

It is clear why the sentence is unacceptable. The NPI in the sentence does not have a licensing Neg. We still need a command-based constraint of the kind that we have been assuming all along. The task before us is to determine when the above constraint applies in English, and what kind of structure it applies to. It has been argued that the constraint must apply after syntactic movement because of the unacceptability of sentences such as (3.17b):

(3.17)   a. The White House hasn't interviewed **any** of the potential nominees to the Supreme Court.
         b. ***Any** of the potential nominees to the Supreme Court, the White House hasn't interviewed.

However, since the Anti-Superiority Condition, which is an S-structure constraint, can mark the sentence unacceptable, it does not provide any proof that the NPI Licensing constraint must be an S-structure or LF constraint. As a matter of fact, as has already been pointed out, the acceptability of sentences such as those given in (3.1) shows that the NPI licensing constraint cannot be applied at S-structure or at LF.

---

[11] I am assuming that Binding Condition A applies cyclically both in English and Korean. See Kuno (1986, 1987) and Kuno and Kim (1994).

Now observe the following exchanges:

(3.18) Speaker A: Who didn't show up at the reunion?
        Speaker B: (i) *__Any__ of my former roommates did__n't__
                        show up.
                    (ii) ok/?__Any__ of my former roommates.

Unexpectedly, for many speakers, (3.18Bii) is perfectly acceptable in the given context. Some speakers find the sentence awkward or marginal, but they still find it far better than (3.18Bi). This shows that the NPI licensing takes place before Neg is incorporated into the VP-internal position:

(3.19) [__Neg__ [__any__ of my former roommates (did show up)]]

This leads us to the conclusion that the NPI licensing takes place at D-structure:

(3.20) **NPI Licensing (D-Structure Constraint):**
        An NPI must be licensed in D-structure by a c-commanding Neg.

In the above statement of the NPI licensing condition, I have used c-command rather than PP-invisible-c-command because there is no relevant difference between the two command concepts when the licenser is in sentence-initial A' position.[12]
    We have evidence that there is a Neg-initial derivation of negative sentences. Observe the following sentences:

(3.21) a. *And anyone couldn't tell where Mary was.
        b. **Nor** could **anyone** tell where Mary was.

(3.22) a. John doesn't like fish, and Bill doesn't like pork.
        b. *John doesn't like fish, and Bill Ø pork. (Gapping)
        c. John doesn't like fish, **nor** Bill Ø pork. (Gapping)

(3.21b) and (3.22c) would be underivable unless we assume that there are Neg-initial derivations of negative sentences.
    The D-structure A'-position Neg undergoes Neg Incorporation:

(3.23) D-Structure: [Neg [John has saved money]]
        Neg-Incorporation
                a. John hasn't saved money.
                c. John has saved no money.

Where Neg can land and where it cannot is a matter that is not well understood. For example, observe the following sentences, in which Neg has landed on an NP that is embedded in the subject NP:

(3.24) a. The dictator of a terrorist country should **not** be allowed to enter the United States.
b. ok/?The dictator of **no** terrorist country should **ever** be allowed to enter the United States. (Sherman 1984)

(3.25) a. The first section of the first chapter of all of the books written by him does**n't** contain **any** mention of what he is going to say in those books.
b. ok/?The first section of the first chapter of **none** of the books written by him contains **any** mention of what he is going to say in those books. (Kuno and Takami 1993)

(3.26) a. Visitors from ethnic groups, no matter how unpopular, should**n't ever** be subjected to this kind of discourteous treatment.
b. ok/?Visitors from **no** ethnic groups, no matter how unpopular, should **ever** be subjected to this kind of discourteous treatment.

---

[12] I am not concerned here with the so-called "island" constraint on NPI licensing, as illustrated below:

(i) a. NPI in a Complex NP:

*I don't accept the claim that I have done **anything** wrong.

b. NPI in an Adverbial Clause:

*He didn't publish any more papers after he had read **any** negative reviews of his first paper.

Nor am I concerned with NPIs licensed in the interrogative contexts, conditional and comparative clauses, and in semantically (but not syntactically) negative contexts:

(ii) a. Do you have **any** money?
b. If you have **any** money, let me know.
c. Mary is brighter than **anyone** I know.
d. I doubt that he has done **anything** wrong.

There is a great deal of idiolectal variation with respect to the acceptability status of sentences of the pattern under discussion, but most speakers consider (3.24b, 3.25b, 3.26b) acceptable, or nearly so. In contrast, many of the same speakers consider the following sentences marginal or unacceptable:

(3.27) a. ?/??/*Papers about **no** current domestic issues were presented.
b. ?/??/*Articles by **nobody** get published fast enough.[13]

The general rule seems to be that the richer the semantics of the preposition in the pattern under discussion, the less acceptable the sentence is. I have to leave a more accurate characterization of the controlling factors to future research.

Let us now see how NPIs fit into the framework introduced above, with Neg-initial D-structure to which NPI Licensing applies, and with the Anti-Superiority Condition on Licensees applying to the derived S-structure. First, observe the following:

(3.28) a. *That John did**n't** leave surprised **any** people.
D-structure: *any* is not licensed
b. *The man who did**n't** eat dinner paid **anything**.
D-structure: *anything* is not licensed

(3.28a, b) are unacceptable because the NPIs are not licensed by a c-commanding Neg in D-structure:
Observe, next, the following sentences:

(3.29) a. John does**n't** know **anyone**.
D-structure: *anyone* licensed by sentence-initial Neg
S-structure: Anti-Superiority Condition not violated

b. ***Anyone** doesn't know John.
D-structure: *anyone* licensed by sentence-initial Neg
S-structure: Anti-Superiority Condition violated

(3.29a) observes the NPI Licensing Condition at D-structure, and does not violate the Anti-Superiority Condition at S-structure. Hence the acceptability of the sentence. In contrast, (3.29b) violates the Anti-Superiority Condition at S-structure, although the NPI is licensed at D-structure. Hence the unacceptability of the sentence.

Likewise, observe the next sentences:

Negative Polarity Items in Korean and English • 121

---

[13] Kayne (1994), on the basis of the contrast illustrated by the following two sentences, has proposed a unique notion of "c-command":

(i)   a.   Nobody's articles **ever** get published fast enough.
         b.   *Articles by **nobody ever** get published fast enough.

Kayne defines the notion of c-command in such a way that *nobody* should c-command the NPI *ever* in (ia), but not in (ib):

(ii)   Kayne's Definition of C-command: X c-commands Y iff X and Y are categories and X excludes Y and every category that dominates X dominates Y.

Kayne hypothesizes the following phrase structure configuration for (ia):

(iii)

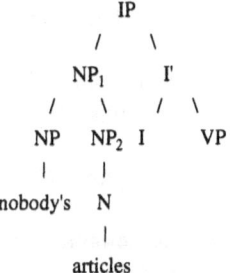

In the above structure, the sequence of segments NP_1 and NP_2 forms a category, and therefore, NP_1 is not a category by itself. Hence, it does not play any role in delimiting the c-command domain of the NP that dominates *nobody's*. Thus, in (iii), [$_{NP}$ nobody's] c-commands node I' and all the nodes that it dominates.

As Kayne himself is aware, this notion of c-command creates difficulties accounting for the acceptability of sentences such as the following:

(iv)   His$_i$ mother adores John$_i$.

The above Binding Condition C problem has led Kayne to stipulate a special phrase structure configuration for (iv) so as to block application of Condition C to *John*, with *his* as a binder. But Kayne leaves unresolved the contrast of the following type:

(v)   a.   ?John$_i$'s children consider John$_i$ strange.
        b.   *John$_i$ considers John$_i$'s children strange.

(3.30) a. I gave **nobody anything**. (=2.12b)
          D-structure: [Neg [I gave anybody anything]]
                             - *anything* licensed
          S-structure: Anti-Superiority Condition not violated

      b. *I gave **anybody nothing**. (=2.12c)
          D-structure: [Neg [I gave anybody anything]]
                             - *anybody* licensed
          S-structure: Anti-Superiority Condition violated

(3.30a) and (3.30b) both observe the NPI Licensing Condition at D-structure. (3.30a) also observes the Anti-Superiority Condition at S-structure, and hence the acceptability of the sentence. In contrast, (3.30b) violates the Anti-Superiority Condition at S-structure. Hence the unacceptability of the sentence.[14]

Observe, next, the following sentences:

(3.31) a. The White House has**n't** interviewed **any** of the potential nominees to the Supreme Court.
        D-structure: *any* is licensed by sentence-initial Neg.
        S-structure: does not violate the Anti-Superiority Condition

      b. ***Any** of the potential nominees to the Supreme Court, the White House has**n't** interviewed.
        D-structure: *any* is licensed by sentence-initial Neg.
        S-structure: violates the Anti-Superiority Condition.

(3.31a) observes the NPI Licensing Condition at D-structure, and it also observes the Anti-Superiority Condition at S-structure. Hence the

---

According to Kayne's definition of the notion of "c-command", the left-hand *John* c-commands the right-hand *John* in (va) as well as in (vb).

But more importantly, Kayne's notion of c-command, when applied to (3.24b) - (3.26b), would incorrectly predict that they should be unacceptable. Also, observe that (3.27b), which does not involve any NPI, is marginal or unacceptable for many speakers. Therefore, contrary to Kayne's claim, the unacceptability of (ib) seems to have more to do with where a sentence-initial Neg can land, than with NPI licensing. That is, in the framework of the analysis I am proposing in this paper, the NPI *ever* in both (ia) and (ib) is licensed by the sentence-initial Neg at D-structure, and it is not superior to *nobody* at S-structure. Therefore, there is nothing wrong with the use of the NPI in these sentences. Speakers who consider (ib) marginal are speakers who consider (3.27b) marginal.

acceptability of the sentence. In contrast, while (3.31b) observes the NPI Licensing Condition at D-structure, it violates the Anti-Superiority Condition at S-structure. Hence the unacceptability of the sentence.

Observe, next, the following sentences:

(3.32) a. *That **anything** serious will happen, I believe to be likely.
D-structure: *anything* not licensed.

---

[14] In the above discussions of how NPI Licensing at D-structure and the Anti-Superiority Condition on Licensees at S-structure interact to predict the acceptability status of (3.29a, b) and (3.30a, b), I have assumed that expressions such as *nobody* and *nothing* are not in D-structure, but are derived from the incorporation of Neg into D-structure *anybody* and *anything*. It will not be amiss here to examine whether conditions on NPIs can adequately be stated in a framework in which *nobody* and *nothing* are base-generated:

(i)   a.   I gave **nobody anything**. (=2.12b)

              D-structure: [I gave nobody anything] - *anything* licensed

      b.   *I gave **anybody nothing**. (=2.12c)

              D-structure: [I gave anybody nothing] - *anybody* not licensed

(ii) a.   I gave **nothing** to **anybody**.

              D-structure: [I gave nothing to anybody] - *anybody* licensed

      b.   *I gave **anything** to **nobody**.

              D-structure: [I gave anything to nobody] - *anything* not licensed

The problem here is that in the following sentences, whose D-structures contain the D-structures of (iia, b), the acceptability judgments are reversed:

(iii) a.   ***Anybody** was given **nothing**.
      b.   **Nobody** was given **anything**.

This implies that the c-command relationship between a negative word (e.g., *nothing*, *nobody*) and an NPI in D-structure would be irrelevant, and that NPI licensing would take place after movement. But then, the acceptability judgments of sentences in (3.1) would become inexplicable. This shows that conditions on the use of NPIs cannot be stated adequately in a framework in which *nobody* and *nothing* are base-generated.

b. That **anything** serious will happen, I believe **not** to be likely.
D-structure: [I believe [Neg [[that anything serious will happen] to be likely]]] -- *anything* licensed
S-structure: Anti-Superiority Condition not violated

(3.32a) is marked unacceptable at D-structure because there is no Neg that licenses the NPI. In contrast, the NPI *anything* in (3.32b) is licensed at D-structure, and the sentence does not violate the Anti-Superiority Condition at S-structure. Hence the acceptability of the sentence.

Likewise, observe the following sentences:

(3.33) Speaker A: What is not likely (to be the case)?

Speaker B: (i) That **anyone** has finished yet is **not** likely.
D-structure: *anyone* licensed.
S-structure: Anti-Superiority Condition not violated

(ii) That **anyone** has finished yet Ø.
D-structure: *anyone* licensed
S-structure: Anti-Superiority Condition not violated
PF: Discourse Deletion of *is not likely*.

In both (3.33Bi) and (3.33Bii), the NPI *anyone* is licensed in D-structure by the sentence-initial Neg. Both sentences are acceptable because they do not violate the Anti-Superiority Condition at S-structure.

Finally, observe the following sentences:

(3.34) Speaker A: Who didn't show up at the reunion?

Speaker B: (i) ***Any** of my former roommates did**n't** show up.
D-structure: *any* licensed by sentence-initial Neg
S-structure: Anti-Superiority Condition violated

(ii)   ok/? **Any** of my former roommates.
D-structure: [Neg [any of my former roommates did show up]]
               - *any* licensed
S-structure: [Neg [any of my former roommates did show up]]
               Anti-Superiority Condition not violated
PF: Discourse Deletion of *Neg did show up*

(3.34Bi) observes the NPI Licensing Condition at D-structure, but it violates the Anti-Superiority Condition at S-structure. Hence the unacceptability of the sentence. For (3.34Bii), I assume that Neg is present in sentence-initial position at D-structure, and this satisfies the NPI Licensing Condition. In the S-structure shown in (ii), it is assumed that Neg has not been incorporated into the VP.[15] This structure does not violate the Anti-Superiority Condition. Discourse Deletion applies to *Neg did show up*, yielding the acceptable sentence (3.34Bii).

---

[15] There are speakers for whom the next discourse is acceptable:

(3.34)   Speaker A: Who didn't show up at the reunion?

         Speaker B: (iii)   **None** of my former roommate.

(Biii) is derived from the S-structure in which Neg has been incorporated into the subject NP. Discourse Deletion applies in PF to *did show up at the reunion*, yielding Speaker B's elliptical answer. To many speakers, however, (iii) is unacceptable because they interpret the sentence as semantically involving double negation: "None of my former roommate didn't show up at the reunion." For those speakers who do not accept (Biii), it must be assumed that across-the-board Discourse Deletion cannot apply to the affirmative *did show up at the reunion* with the negative *didn't show up at the reunion* as trigger.

4. Conclusion

In Section 1 of this paper, I have proposed the following generalizations for NPIs in Korean:

(4.1) a. In the grammar of many speakers of Korean, the Neg-NPI Clause Mate Constraint cannot be stated at the D-structure level. It must be assumed to apply at S-structure.
b. An NPI can be scrambled out of the Neg clause that licenses it. (cf. Kato 1991) It must be assumed that the trace of an extracted NPI can be used to satisfy the Neg-NPI Clause Mate Constraint.
c. An NPI does not have to have an overt negative licenser in surface sentences. It must be assumed that the negative licenser is present at S-structure, and undergoes discourse deletion in PF.

In Section 2, I have shown that there are serious problems with the generally held assumption that the NPI licensing condition in English can be stated at S-structure alone, at LF alone, or at S-structure and LF alone. There are sentences such as (2.13b) which are acceptable to all speakers, but in which NPIs are not c-commanded by their licensers either at S-structure or at LF:

(2.13) b. That **anything** serious would happen seemed to **nobody** to be likely.

There are also numerous sentences such as (2.11a) and (2.16d) which the generally held c-command licensing condition predicts to be unacceptable but which are perfectly acceptable to many speakers, awkward to some, and marginal to others:

(2.11) a. ok/?/??The names of **any** potential nominees have **not** yet been forwarded to the FBI for background checking. (Therefore, it seems that they don't yet have a short list.)
(2.16) d. ok/?/??The destruction of **any** cities is **not** likely to have taken place.

In Section 3, I have proposed a new two-step approach to NPI licensing: NPI Licensing at D-structure, and the Anti-Superiority Condition on Licensees at S-structure:

(4.2)   **NPI Licensing (D-Structure Constraint)**
An NPI must be licensed in D-structure by a c-commanding Neg.
(=3.20)
N.B. It is assumed that Neg is base-generated in S'-initial position, and undergoes Neg Incorporation.

(4.3)   **Anti-Superiority Condition on Licensees:**
A licensee must not be syntactically superior to its licenser. That is, a licensee cannot both precede and PP-invisible-c-command its licenser. (cf. (3.4))

According to the above approach, the NPIs in (2.13b), (2.11a) and (2.16d) are licensed by the c-commanding Neg in D-structure, and the sentences are acceptable because the NPIs do not violate the Anti-Superiority Condition at S-structure. In contrast, sentences such as

(2.1)   b.   *Anyone doesn't know John.
(3.2)   c.   *Any cities are not likely to have been destroyed.

observe NPI Licensing at D-structure, but violate the Anti-Superiority Condition at S-structure.

What remains to be explained is why there are wide idiolectal variations in the acceptability status of sentences such as (2.11a) and (2.16d). I speculate that this is due to idiolectal variations with respect to what constitutes an NPI. In (3.3), I have assumed that NP constructions such as:

(4.4)   a.   [$_{+NPI}$ **any** [$_{PP}$ of his former roommates]]
            b.   [$_{+NPI}$ **any** potential nominees]

are NPIs for all speakers. I assume that there are idiolectal differences with respect to the NPI status of the NP constructions such as

(4.5)   a.   [$_{NP}$ the names [$_{PP}$ of [$_{+NPI}$ **any potential nominees**]]]
            b.   [$_{NP}$ the destruction [$_{PP}$ of [$_{+NPI}$ **any cities**]]]

It seems that those speakers who consider (2.11a) and (2.16d) marginal are speakers for whom the NPI status of the embedded NP percolates to PP to the larger NP.[16] For those speakers, (2.11a) and (2.16d) are marginal because

---

[16] See Martín-Gonzáles (1994) for the notion of NPI percolation from NP to PP to NP in Spanish.

the names of any potential nominees and *the destruction of any cities*, NPIs via NP-to-PP-to-NP percolation, both precede and PP-invisible-c-command their licensing Neg at S-structure. In contrast, those speakers who consider (2.11a) and (2.16d) perfectly acceptable are speakers for whom there is no percolation of the embedded NPI to PP to the larger NP. For these speakers, *any potential nominees* in (2.11a) and *any cities* in (2.16d) are NPIs, but *the names of any potential nominee* and *the destruction of any cities* are not. Since the NPIs do not PP-invisible-c-command the licensing Neg, the sentences do not violate the Anti-Superiority Condition. For some speakers, NPIs via NP-to-PP-to-NP percolation constitute only weak NPIs. The violation of the Anti-Superiority Condition does not yield heavy penalty when weak NPIs are involved. Those speakers judge (2.11a, b) not perfect, but considerably better than (2.1b).

Now we have an explanation why (2.13b) is acceptable for all speakers. NPI percolation takes place from NP to PP to NP, but not from NP or PP to S. Therefore, the *that*-clause in the sentence is a nonNPI for all speakers. The NPI of the sentence (i.e., *anything serious*) does not PP-invisible-c-command the licensing Neg, and hence, it does not violate the Anti-Superiority Condition in any speaker's idiolect.

There is one unresolved issue that I will have to leave for future research. Observe the following sentences:

(2.20) c.   ***Anyone**, she is**n't** really fond of.
(4.6)   a.   John$_i$ considers himself$_i$ first-rate.
        b.   Himself$_i$, John$_i$ considers e$_i$ first-rate.

If a reflexive and its antecedent have an licensee-licenser relationship, as I have assumed in Section 3.1, (4.6b) violates the Anti-Superiority Condition on Licensees as much as (2.20c) does, and should therefore be as unacceptable as (2.20c) is. Contrary to this prediction, (4.6b) is perfectly acceptable. I cannot at present propose a principled way to exclude a fronted reflexive from application of the Anti-Superiority Condition. One approach to resolve this dilemma is to assume that the Anti-Superiority Condition applies not to S-structure, but to the representation prior to the application of stylistic fronting (Yiddish Movement) and to assume that sentences such as (2.20c) are unacceptable due to a general ban on fronting nonanaphoric NPs:[17]

---

[17] As discussed in Kuno (1987), stylistic fronting changes quantifier scope and coreference possibilities. Therefore, it cannot be assumed to take place at PF. It must be assumed to apply before S-structure.

(4.7) a. John wrote several letters yesterday.
 b. *Several letters, John wrote yesterday.

According to this approach, the Anti-Superiority Condition is not applicable either to (2.20c) or to (4.6b). (4.6b) is acceptable because the fronted NP *himself* is anaphoric, but (2.20c) is unacceptable because the fronted NP *anyone* is nonanaphoric. It might also explain why an NPI in Korean can be extracted out of the clause that contains its licensing Neg--the ban on fronting nonanaphoric NPs, if it ever exists in Korean, is a weak constraint, and its violation does not result in clear-cut unacceptability:

(4.8) a. Nay-ka [Inswu-ka phyenci hancang-ul ssu-nun-kes-ul
 I   letter one-Class. write-ing

  po-assta.
  see-Past
  'I saw Inswu writing one letter.'

 b. ok/?Phyenci hancang-ul$_i$, nay-ka, [Inswu-ka e$_i$ ssu-
  letter one I   write-to

  nun-kes-ul po-assta.
    see-Past
  '(Lit.) One letter$_i$, I saw Inswu writing e$_i$.'

I will have to leave a fuller development of this approach to future research.

References

Chomsky, N. Some Notes on Economy of Derivation and Representation. In *Principles and Parameters in Comparative Grammar*, edited by Freidin, R., MIT Press, Cambridge, MA, 417-454, 1991.

Chomsky, N. A Minimalist Program for Linguistic Theory. In, *The View from Building 20*, edited by K. Hale and S. J. Keyser, MIT Press, Cambridge, MA, 1-52, 1993.

Chomsky, N. and H. Lasnik, The Theory of Principles and Parameters. In *Syntax: An International Handbook of Contemporary Research Vol. 1*, edited by J. Jacobs, A. van Stechow, W. Sternefeld, and T. Vennemann, Walter de Gruyter, Berlin, 506-569, 1993.

Fukui, N., *A Theory of Category Projection and Its Applications*, MIT Dissertation, 1986.

Kato, Y. Negative Sentences in Japanese. *Sophia Linguistica 19* (Monograph), Sophia University, Tokyo, 1985.

Kato, Y. Negative Polarity in Japanese and the Levels of Representation,. *The Tsuda Review 36*, 151-179, 1991.

Kayne, R. *Antisymmetry of Syntax.* Linguistic Inquiry Monograph Series, MIT Press, Cambridge, MA, 1994.

Kawashima, R. and H. Kitahara Licensing of Negative Polarity Item and Checking Theory: A Comparative Study of English and Japanese, *Proceedings of Formal Linguistic Society of Mid-America 3*, 1992.

Kitagawa, Y. *Subjects in Japanese and English*, UMass Dissertation, 1986.

Klima, E. E. Negation in English, In *The Structure of Language, edited by* J. A. Fodor and J. Katz, Prentice-Hall Inc., Englewood Cliffs, N.J., 246-323, 1964.

Konomi, K. 'Sika~Nai' Koobun no Koozoo. In, *Eigogaku no Siten*, edited by Ohye Saburo Sensei Tuitoo Ronbunsyuu Hensyuu-iinkai Kyusyu Daigaku Syuppankai, 369-392, 1989.

Kuno, S. *Danwa no Bunpoo (Grammar of Discourse).* Taishukan Publ. Co., Tokyo, 1978.

Kuno, S. Discourse Deletion: Case Studies from English, Russian, and Japanese. *Journal of Semantics*, Vol. 1, pp. 61-93, 1982.

Kuno, S. Principles of Discourse Deletion. *Proceedings of the XIIIth International Congress of Linguists (Tokyo 1982)*, Tokyo, pp. 30-41, 1983.

Kuno, S. Anaphora in Japanese, In *Working Papers from the First SDF Workshop in Japanese Syntax*, edited by Kuroda, S.-Y. , Department of Linguistics, University of California, San Diego, La Jolla, CA, l986, pp. 11-70, 1986.

Kuno, S. *Functional Syntax.* the University of Chicago Press, 1987.

Kuno, S. and S.Y. Kim The Weak Crossover Phenomena in Japanese and Korean, In *Japanese/Korean Linguistics 4*, edited by Akatsuka, N.,CSLI Publications, pp. 1-38, 1994.

Kuno, S. and K. Takami. Negation and Extraction. *CLS 28*, Vol. 1, 297-317, 1993.

Kuroda, S.-Y. Whether We Agree Or Not (manuscript). UCSD, 1986.

Laka, I. M. *Negation in Syntax: On the Nature of Functional Categories and Projections.* MIT Dissertation, 1990.

Lasnik, H. Remarks on Coreference. *Linguistic Analysis 2 (1)*, 1-22, 1976.

Lasnik, H. and M. Saito *Move α: Conditions on Its Application and Output.* MIT Press, Cambridge, MA, (1992).

Lee, K. R. Y. Negative Polarity Items Licensing and the Nature of Neg Projection (manuscript). University of Connecticut, Storrs, 1992.

Mahajan, A. K. LF Conditions on Negative Polarity Licensing. *Lingua 80*, pp. 333-348, 1990.

Martín-Gonzáles, Javier NEG Incorporation and NPIs in Spanish. In *Harvard Working Papers in Linguistics 4*, edited by Epstein, E. D., H. Thraínsson, and S. Kuno, Department of Linguistics, Harvard University, Cambridge, MA, pp. 114-132,1994.

Muraki, M. The *sika nai* Construction and Predicate Restructuring. In *Problems in Japanese Syntax and Semantics*, edited by J. Hinds and I. Howard, Kaitakusha, Tokyo, pp. 155-177, 1978.

Nishioka, N. On Negative Polarity Items in English and Japanese: An Analysis in Terms of Movement for Feature Checking. In *Harvard Working Papers in Linguistics 4*, edited by H. Thrainsson, et al., Department of Linguistics, Harvard University, Cambridge, MA., pp. 141-162, 1994.

Pollock, J.-Y. Verb-Movement, Universal Grammar and the Structure of IP. *Linguistic Inquiry 20*, pp. 365-424, 1989.

Progovac, L. *Negative and Positive Polarity: A Binding Approach*. Cambridge University Press. 1994.

Saito, M. *Some Asymmetries in Japanese and Their Theoretical Implications.* MIT Dissertation, 1985.

Sherman, D. Negation and Inversion. Unpublished Manuscript, Department of Psychology, Harvard University, 1984.

Takahashi, D. Negative Polarity, Phrase Structure, and the ECP. *English Linguistics 7*, pp. 129-146, 1990.

6
Case Assignment in the *siphta* Construction and Its Implications for Case on Adverbials

Soowon Kim and *Joan Maling*

1. Introduction[1]

Adverbial expressions typically belong to the category PP; but some languages have adverbial NPs (that is, adverbials not overtly marked by a preposition or postposition). Although adverbial NPs have frequently been analyzed as covert PPs with a null P, there is good reason to assume that they can indeed be ordinary "bare" NPs in some languages. Cross-linguistically, such adverbial NPs are case-marked in two distinct ways. In languages like Icelandic and Russian, duration adverbs like *all day* or *an hour* receive a certain morphological case (m-case), typically accusative, and that m-case is invariant–that is, it does not alternate with any other morphological cases, nor is it subject to the syntactic (or grammatical) conditions that affect case-marking of argument NPs. Hence such instances of "adverbial accusatives" are often referred to as semantic case-marking. It is somewhat surprising, perhaps, that there are languages in which certain adverbials seem to bear structural Case (nominative or accusative) just like argument NPs. In Finnish, for example, duration adverbs show the case alternations characteristic of verbal objects, and exhibit case alternations under exactly the same syntactic conditions (Karlsson 1987, Maling 1993). This is illustrated in (1): the durative NP receives ACC or NOM depending on the voice of the sentence (taken from Hakulinen & Karlsson 1979).

---

[1] We are grateful to Peter Sells, James Hye-Suk Yoon, and Ray Jackendoff for comments and discussion. We also would like to thank an anonymous ICKL reviewer whose criticisms and comments contributed greatly to the form and content of this paper, and Ross King as well for his editorial advice and patience. The second author gratefully acknowledges the support of the M. W. Keck Foundation.

(1) a. (Minä) viivyin matkalla viikon.
         (I-NOM) stay-1sg trip-ADE week-ACC
         'I stayed on the trip for a week.'
     Siellä   viivyttiin kokonainen viikko.
     there-ADE stayed-PASS whole   week-NOM
     'We/they/one stayed there a whole week.'

Furthermore, it has been argued that in Chinese, a language with no morphological evidence for Case, duration and frequency adverbs compete with object NPs for a single structural objective Case, presumably abstract ACC (Li 1990). It is surely no accident that in language after language, it is precisely the class of duration and frequency or count (D/F) adverbs that can be bare NPs (see Wechsler & Lee 1994 for an important first step in attempting to account for this fact).
    Where does Korean fit into this picture? Maling (1989) provides evidence that in Korean, D/F adverbials exhibit the case alternation characteristic of structural Case. Subsequent work has uncovered two important generalizations regarding case marking of adverbials in Korean (Bratt 1993, Y.-S. Kang 1991, Y.-J. Kim 1990, Kim & Maling 1993, J.-S. Lee 1992), which can be recapitulated as follows. First, D/F adverbials do participate in the domain of structural Case, but such adverbials as event-setting locatives and time adverbials do not. Second, frequency adverbials and argument NPs behave alike with respect to Case, and they show the expected NOM-ACC case alternation in exactly the same syntactic environments. But duration adverbials behave rather differently, and can still bear ACC case even when ACC case is unavailable for argument NPs or frequency adverbials. These facts are illustrated in (2).

(2) a. Soy-ka   han sikan-ul/*i   pul-eyse talkwu-eci-ess-ta.
        metal-NOM one hour-ACC/*NOM fire-in heat-Pass-Pst-Ind
        'The metal was heated in the fire for two hours.'
    b. Ku-ka   chongli-ka   twu pen-i/*ul
        he-NOM prime.minister-NOM two times-NOM/*ACC
        toy-ess-ta.
        become-Pst-Ind
        'He became/was elected a prime minister twice.'

c. Swuni-nun phyengsayng-ul/*i pulkwuca-ka
    Swuni-TOP life.time-ACC/*NOM disabled.man-NOM

   toy-ess-ta.
   become-Pst-Ind
   'Swuni became/lived disabled for life.'

(2a) is a passive sentence (*ci*-passive), where accusative case is unavailable to argument NPs as well as frequency adverbials (see Kim & Maling 1993); in (2b,c), the predicate complement NPs bear only NOM case; (2b) shows that a frequency adverbial must also bear NOM case when it occurs in the predicate complement construction. In all of these cases, however, a durational adverbial bears ACC case (and only accusative) as indicated above. But notice that accusative is not the only case durational adverbials can bear. Under certain as yet poorly-understood circumstances, adverbials of duration can bear only NOM case. Consider the contrasts in (3).

(3) a. Swuni-nun *phyengsayng-ul* emeni-ka/*lul kuliw-ess-ta.
        Swuni-TOP life.time-ACC mother-NOM/*ACC miss-Pst-Ind
        'Swuni missed her mother for life.'

   b. Mulken-ul ta nalu-camyen van-i *twusikan-i/*ul*
       stuff-ACC all carry-PURP van-NOM 2hours-NOM/*ACC

       philyoha-ta
       need-Ind
       'To carry all the stuff, one needs a van for two hours.'

Duration adverbials are typically marked ACC in Korean, but for some predicates, they must instead be marked NOM, as illustrated in (3b). It seems unlikely therefore that D/F adverbials both get structural Case from the same Case-assigner, namely the Verb.[2]

We thus have two outstanding research questions. First, what is the source for the accusative case on durational adverbials when the Verb does not itself govern accusative on its object? Second, under what circumstances can they not get accusative? To the extent that durational adverbials in Korean sometimes bear nominative, the accusative case they usually bear cannot be analyzed as "adverbial accusative" or "semantic case" of the sort found in languages like Icelandic and Russian.

---

[2] Interestingly, the observed case patterns on adverbials in Korean seems just the opposite of the case patterns that duratives and frequency adverbials in Finnish show.

In this paper, we suggest that durational adverbials get ACC from Aspect because like verbal objects, they delimit the event of the clause they occur in. We provide evidence that Aspect in Korean is a functional category heading its own projection above VP. We then show that in the *siphta* construction, D/F adverbials exhibit fundamentally the same case patterns as argument NPs, which is in fact expected if they both get structural Case. We discuss the relevance of Aspect to the case marking of both duratives and verbal objects, and some of the theoretical implications.

2. Case Alternation in the *siphta* Construction

Kim & Maling (1993) show that in Korean, voice is responsible for the NOM-ACC case alternations on frequency adverbials. But since voice appears to bear little on case-marking of adverbials of duration, we have to find out the syntactic environment in which duratives show case alternations. The *siphta* construction appears to be the right kind of syntactic environment that tells us how duration adverbials can be case-marked. We will therefore discuss the syntax of this construction in some detail.

2.1 Case Alternations on Verbal Complements

The *siphta* construction, famous for unexpected nominative-accusative case alternations on verbal complements, has many intriguing and peculiar properties still in need of satisfactory explanations (see Appendix for relevant discussion). One salient property of it is that argument NPs/DPs in this construction show NOM-ACC alternations that are otherwise impossible. This is illustrated by the contrasts in (4).[3]

(4) a.   Cheli-nun kwaca-lul/*ka   mek-ess-ta.
         Cheli-TOP cookie-ACC/*NOM eat-Pst-Ind
         'Cheli ate cookies.'

    b.   Cheli-nun kwaca-lul/ka   mek-ko siph-ess-ta.
         Cheli-TOP cookie-ACC/NOM eat-KO want-Pst-Ind
         'Cheli wanted to eat cookies.'

The verb *mek-* 'eat' is an ACC case-assigner, hence NOM is impossible for the object NP, as shown in (4a). But when this verb occurs in the *siphta* construction, as in (4b), the same internal argument NP can occur either in the accusative or in the nominative. It is obvious that in (4b), the verb *mek-* must be responsible for the ACC case on the object NP. This is confirmed by the fact that if the verb in this construction is not an ACC case-assigner, accusative is not available to the complement NP:

[3] But there are cases where NOM-ACC case alternations are not permitted in the *siphta* construction. Consider the case-marking of objective complements illustrated in (ia-d).

(i) a.　　Swuni-nun atul-ul uysa-lul　mantul-ko siph-ess-ta.　　　　ACC-ACC

　　　　　Swuni-TOP son-ACC doctor-ACC make-ASP want-Pst-Ind

　　　　　'Swuni wanted to make his son a doctor.'

　b.　　*Swuni-nun atul-i　uysa-ka　mantul-ko siph-ess-ta.　　　　*NOM-NOM

　c.　　*Swuni-nun atul-ul uysa-ka　mantul-ko siph-ess-ta.　　　　*ACC-NOM

　d.　　*Swuni-nun atul-i　uysa-lul　mantul-ko siph-ess-ta.　　　　*NOM-ACC

The unacceptability of (ic,d) may be accounted for if the objective complement gets its case via case agreement with the object NP it is predicated of. Given that NOM-ACC alternations should be possible in the *siphta* construction, the unacceptability of (ib) however comes as a surprise. Maling & Kim (1992) argue that objective complements in Korean are not case-marked via case agreement. The unacceptability of (ib) is obviously related to the fact that objective complements can never bear NOM even when the object NPs they are predicated of bear NOM in passives (Maling & Kim 1992:54-57). Moreover, as shown by Maling & Kim (1992), objective complements in Korean typically bear an instrumental case, and only in a few instances can they bear ACC. Below are more examples:

(ii) a.　　pro ku.ay-lul　yangca-lo/lul　sam-ko　siph-ess-ta.

　　　　　the.child-ACC stepson-INST/ACC take-ASP want-Pst-Ind

　　　　　'(They) wanted to take the child as (their) stepson.'

　b.　　?pro ku.ay-ka　yangca-lo sam-ko siph-ess-ta.　　　　NOM-INST

　c.　　*pro ku.ay-ka　yangca-ka sam-ko siph-ess-ta.　　　　*NOM-NOM

As shown in (iib), when the case pattern on the NPs at hand is NOM-INST rather than NOM-NOM, the sentence improves significantly.

Notice that the impossibility of the NOM-NOM patterns in the *siphta* construction is clearly related to the fact that the passive of a small clause does not allow NOM-NOM patterns, either:

(iii) a.　　Cheli-nun ku.ay-ul　yangca-lo/lul　sam-ass-ta.

　　　　　Cheli-TOP the.child-ACC stepson-INST/ACC make-Pst-Ind

(5) a. Cheli-nun uysa-ka/*lul   toy-ess-ta.
        Cheli-TOP doctor-NOM/*ACC become-Pst-Ind
        'Cheli became a doctor.'

   b.   Cheli-nun uysa-ka/*lul   toy-ko   siph-ess-ta.
        Cheli-TOP doctor-NOM/*ACC become-KO want-Pst-Ind
        'Cheli wanted to become/be a doctor.'

As shown by (5a), the verb *toy-* 'become' is not an accusative case-assigner. This then explains why accusative is not possible for the predicate complement NP in the siphta construction in (5b).

The question then is, How can the object NP of the accusative case-assigning verb in (4b) get nominative? More generally, how can (VP-internal) complement NPs be assigned nominative in the *siphta* construction? The answer must be that the verb *siph-* 'to wish/want' is primarily (but not ultimately) responsible for the assignment of nominative to VP-internal complement NPs: simply, *siph-* is not an accusative assigner. The unavailability of accusative in (5b) is now fully explained since neither verb is an accusative assigner. The NOM-ACC alternation in (4b) is also accounted for since one of the verbs is an accusative-assigner and the other is not.

The obvious analysis to pursue is, then, to assume that this construction may involve a complex predicate, whereby the two verbs combine to yield one complex verb in the form of V-*ko siph-*, perhaps via head-movement. On this analysis, it must be ensured that the resulting complex verb inherits the case-assigning property of the verb *siph-*, not that of the other verb. This follows if we assume the verb *siph-* to be the head of the resulting complex verb.[4]

Since we assume, as standardly viewed, that nominative is not a lexical or inherent case assigned by V, but is a syntactic case, the next question then is, What can assign nominative to complement NPs? While various proposals have been made to account for the NOM-marking on

        'Cheli took the child as his stepson.'

   b.   Ku.ay-ka   yangca-lo/*ka   sam-aci-ess-ta.

        the.child-NOM stepson-INST/*NOM make-Pass-Pst-Ind

        'The child was taken as his stepson.'

It thus appears that the impossibility of the NOM-NOM pattern shown in (ib) and (iic) must be accounted for independently of the *siphta* construction. The remaining question then is what makes the agreeing NOM-NOM pattern in (iiib) impossible, for which we have no answer.

complement NPs (see Dubinsky 1993, Han 1991, Sells 1993, Tada 1992, to cite some of the more recent ones), we will assume that if an accusative-assigner is absent, nominative can be assigned to VP-internal NPs by Infl, due to the absence of barrierhood of VP (see Emonds 1989 for Finnish, J.-S. Lee 1992 for Korean, Sigurdsson 1989 for Icelandic, and Takezawa 1987 for Japanese).

2.2 Case Alternations on Duration Adverbials

As noted earlier, adverbials of duration are usually marked ACC even when the complement verb governs NOM on its complement. Consider now the case patterns illustrated in (6), where the durational adverbial follows rather than precedes the verbal object.

(6) a. Na-nun cacenke-lul hansikan-ul   **ACC-ACC**
I-TOP bicycle-ACC one.hour-ACC

tha-ko siph-ess-ta.
ride-KO want-Pst-Ind
'I wanted to ride a bicycle for an hour.'

b. Na-nun cacenke-ka hansikan-i   **NOM-NOM**
tha-ko siph-ess-ta.

c. *Na-nun cacenke-ka hansikan-ul   ***NOM-ACC**
tha-ko siph-ess-ta.

d. *Na-nun cacenke-lul hansikan-i   ***ACC-NOM**
tha-ko siph-ess-ta.

Notice that in each of the sentences in (6), the durative could in principle modify either of the two predicates, *tha-* and *siph-*. But in the above paradigm, the durative is intended to delimit only the act of riding a bicycle, and the judgments indicate whether or not this intended reading is possible in each case. The paradigm shows that when the lower V in the *siphta* construction, is an accusative case assigner, then the complement NP and

---

[4] It has been a matter of debate whether or not Korean has the syntactic category Adjective distinct from Verb. We will assume that traditionally-labelled adjectives in Korean can be reanalyzed or re-categorized as members of Verb, arguably as stative verbs, which now seems to be standard practice in the generative literature on Korean syntax. But nothing that follows will hinge on this.

the durational adverbial must bear the same case, either ACC-ACC or NOM-NOM, and the non-matching case patterns are excluded; in particular, nominative is impossible for the durative when the verbal object bears accusative. Note that independently of the *siphta* construction, if the durative adverbial is marked nominative, then it cannot precede the object. In sum, this paradigm is quite reminiscent of the case-marking properties of frequency adverbials discussed by Kim & Maling (1993), which is what ought to be expected if D/F adverbials bear syntactic Case (Maling 1989). We will return to this paradigm in Section 3.3.

2.3 Syntactic Correlations

We will start from the assumption that the case alternations on the verbal object should not be interpreted as optionality of accusative case assignment; rather they must reflect a structural difference of some kind. We first point out that the observed case alternations are correlated with a cluster of syntactic differences. We will discuss (i) coordination/gapping and (ii) scope ambiguity of aspect/time adverbials in this section and other syntactic differences in section 3.4.

2.3.1 Coordination/Gapping. Consider the examples in (7) that involve coordination or gapping.

(7) a. Cheli-nun pap-ul cis-ko ppallay-lul
Cheli-TOP rice-ACC cook-CONJ laundry-ACC

ha-ko siph-ess-ta.
do-KOwant-Pst-Ind
'Cheli wanted to cook rice and do the laundry.'

b. *Cheli-nun pap-i cis-ko ppallay-ka
Cheli-TOP rice-NOM cook-CONJ laundry-NOM

ha-ko siph-ess-ta.
do-KO want-Pst-Ind

c. Cheli-nun Ford-lul sa-ko, Swuni-nun BMW-lul
Cheli-TOP Ford-ACC buy-KO Swuni-TOP BMW- ACC

sa-ko siph-ess-ta.
buy-KO want-Pst-Ind
'Cheli wanted to buy a Ford, and Swuni a BMW.'

d. *Cheli-nun Ford-ka sa-ko, Swuni-nun BMW-ka
Cheli-TOP Ford-NOM buy-KO Swuni-TOP BMW-NOM

sa-ko siph-ess-ta.
buy-KO want-Pst-Ind

When the verbal object bears accusative case, coordination of the complement VPs or gapping is perfect, as illustrated in (7a,c). The phrasal coordination in (7a) or gapping in (7c) indicates that the complement of *siph-* cannot be V⁰, but must be a maximal projection of some kind, minimally a VP (see Sells & Cho 1991 for discussion). In contrast, when the verbal object is marked NOM, neither coordination nor gapping is possible, as illustrated in (7b,d). This shows that when the verbal object bears nominative case, V-*ko siph-* behaves like one complex predicate, hence it resists linear separation. We thus have very strong evidence to suggest that two different structures in fact underlie case licensing of the verbal object in the *siphta* construction.

2.3.2 Scope Ambiguity of Aspect/Time Adverbials. Another syntactic difference correlated with the case alternation in the *siphta* construction lies in the scope of aspect/time adverbials. The normal word order is for the durational adverb to precede the verbal object. Consider the interpretation of sentence (8).

(8) Na-nun pamsay swul-ul masi-ko siph-ess-ta.
I-TOP all.night liquor-ACC drink-KO want-Pst-Ind
a. To drink all night was my desire
b. All night long, I had a desire to drink

The time-span adverb *all night long* can delimit either the event of drinking or the time span for which the desire to drink holds. The sentence is thus ambiguous as paraphrased above, and it is clearly a scope ambiguity. Consider next the interpretation of sentence (9) when the complement of *masi-* 'to drink' bears nominative case.

(9) Na-nun pamsay swul-i masi-ko siph-ess-ta.
I-TOP all.night liquor-NOM drink-KO want-Pst-Ind
a. All night long, I had a desire to drink
b. ?*To drink all night was my desire

Unlike (8), (9) is not ambiguous; the reading in (9b) in which the durative delimits the event of drinking is very difficult to get without changing the word order. Notice that (8) and (9) differ only in the case marking of the object NP: when the object NP bears NOM, the time-span adverb appears not to delimit the act of drinking. The scope properties of duratives are shown more clearly in the sentence in (10), in which the object NP *kimchi* is marked with nominative.

(10)   Ku-nun mikwuk-ey iss-nun tongan naynay kimchi-ka
        he-TOP States-DAT stay-COMP period all   kimchi-NOM

        mek-ko   siph-ess-ta.
        eat-KO   want-Pst-Ind
        'He wanted to eat kimchi for the entire period of his stay in the US.'

The durative phrase *during the entire period of his stay in the U.S.* is coextensive with the period of time that his desire to eat *kimchi* holds for. Hence, (10) implies that he failed to eat *kimchi* at any time despite his strong desire to do so. This Gicean implicature falls out naturally from the scope property of a durative phrase in connection with case marking, in support of our analysis that when the verbal object bears NOM, V-*ko siph-* behaves like a single complex predicate (of which *siph-* is the head). From this, the failure of modification of the complement V by the durative adverbial follows. Note that when the NP *kimchi* in (10) bears ACC case instead of NOM, then the sentence becomes ambiguous just like (8); the implication can then be that he did eat *kimchi* at some point, but not for the entire period specified. Similar scope facts are obtained when the VP eat *kimchi* is replaced by *study Korean:*

(10')   Ku-nun mikwuk-ey iss-nun tongan naynay
        he-TOP States-DAT stay-COMP period all

        hankwukmal-ul kongpuha-ko siph-ess-ta.
        Korean-ACC   study-KO   want-Pst-Ind
        'He wanted to study Korean during the entire period of his stay in the US.'

With ACC on object, implication is that he did study Korean for some period, but not for all of the intended period. We thus obtain the following generalization: if the verbal object is marked ACC, then the scope of the duration adverbial is ambiguous; if the verbal object is marked NOM, then the scope is unambiguously wide scope.

From the semantic/pragmatic side, it is noteworthy that native speakers have a strong intuition that the complement with NOM-marked object is used more naturally in contexts in which the event denoted by the complement VP is unlikely to be realized. In other words, NOM case marking on the object tends to yield a reading in which the event denoted by the complement verb has the flavor of a mere wish, rather than an actual event that could easily be carried out. For example, given a sentence like *I wish to drink water*, NOM case on the object is more natural than ACC if the sentence is uttered by someone who is dying of thirst in the desert. Put differently, when the object is marked ACC, the event denoted by the complement VP receives an activity-like interpretation; but when the object bears NOM, then the *siphta* construction behaves like one of the familiar psych predicates, both in terms of the case-marking (NOM on the object), and the intuition that the entire sentence is felt to express a psychological state rather than a process that can be acted upon. This means that when the object is marked NOM, the VP-complement is understood as unrealized, which would follow if the complement has no independent aspect, so that it is impossible to say whether the action is completed or not. We will return to the role of Aspect in Section 3.

In sum, the coordination and scope facts together suggest that the *siphta* construction has two possible syntactic structures, which are reflected in the case marking difference. When the object of the complement verb bears ACC, the construction exhibits a full range of properties of VP-complementation; on the other hand, when the object NP bears NOM case, the construction shows none of the properties of VP-complementation. These properties are summarized in Table I.

TABLE I

full VP-complement (VP2)	complex predicate V-*ko siph*-
ACC case on verbal object	unexpected NOM case on verbal object
coordinated VP-complements ok gapping allowed for V-*ko siph*-	*coordinated VP-complements *gapping for V-*ko siph*-
no NOM case on duratives	NOM case only on narrow scope duratives
independent aspect in VP2	no independent aspect

A *caveat* is in order: the distinction cannot be defined in terms of surface morphological nominative alone. The key word in the right column of Table I is unexpected NOM (since the complement verb would normally govern ACC case).

Note that if the lower verb is one which normally governs NOM case on its complement, then it may have the properties of the full VP-complement version in the left-hand column. For example, should the complement verb normally govern NOM, coordination of complement VPs with NOM objects or gapping is fine, as illustrated in (11a). In (11a), the NOM case on the predicate complement NPs is crucially not the "unexpected" NOM peculiar to the *siphta* construction, but is just an "ordinary" NOM case. It is even possible to coordinate a VP with NOM object and another VP with ACC object, as shown in (11b).

(11) a. Cheli-nun wang-i   toy-ko, Swuni-nun
        Cheli-TOP king-NOM become-KO Swuni-TOP

   yewang-i   toy-ko   siph-ess-ta.
   queen-NOM become-KO want-Pst-Ind
   'Cheli wanted to be a king, and Swuni wanted to be a queen.'

b. Na-nun canglo-ka toy-ko   answu-lul   pat-ko
    I-TOP elder-NOM become-CONJ ordination-ACC get-KO

    siph-ta.
    want-Ind
    'I want to become an elder and get ordained.'

In such examples of ordinary NOM complements, durational adverbials also exhibit ordinary case patterns, as illustrated in (12).

(12) a. Cheli-nun halustongan-ul wang-i
         Cheli-TOP one.day-ACC king-NOM

    toy-ko   siph-ess-ta.
    become-KO want-Past-Ind
    'Cheli wanted to become/be a king for a day.'

b. Phyengsayng-ul, ku-nun halustongan-ul wang-i
    all.life-ACC   he-TOP one.day-ACC   king-NOM

    toy-ko siph-ess-ta.
    become-KO want-Pst-Ind
    'All his life, he wanted to be a king for a day.'

In (12a), the duration adverbial clearly has narrow scope; but it must be marked ACC and cannot be NOM, even though the complement V *toy*- takes only nominative complements. Furthermore, the two verbs can be independently modified by a durative, as shown in (12b), and they must each be ACC. To summarize, the examples in (11) and (12) have the properties of the full VP-complement version of the *siphta* construction listed in the left-hand column of Table I, despite the NOM case on the complement NP.

3. The Analysis

Now that we have established that the *siphta* construction exhibits two different structural properties, the next question is, What kind of complement does the matrix verb *siph-* take? Note that, as is well known, the complement V cannot occur with its own tense, regardless of the case marking on the verbal object. We conclude that *siph-* takes a VP complement rather than TP or IP or CP; but the presence of *-ko* indicates that there is at least one functional projection above VP. What functional category does *-ko* belong to? How and why is the verbal complex V-*ko siph-* created? How does this result in NOM case on the verbal object?

We suggest (i) that *-ko* heads an Aspect Phrase with the feature [-complete], as selected for by the matrix verb *siph-*, (ii) that head movement creates the amalgamated verbal complex V-*ko siph-* in syntax, which projects the properties of *siph-*, not those of the moved V, and (iii) that head movement helps remove the barrierhood of VP, due to the Government Transparency Corollary (Baker 1988:64), which results in NOM case assignment to the verbal object. Below, we will turn to the details of our proposed analysis.

3.1 Complementation: Aspect Phrase

We argue that the verb *siph-* selects for [-complete] complements that are headed by the functional category *-ko* (see Section 4 for relevant details). We assume that this must be stated in the lexicon as part of the selectional restrictions for *siph-*. The relevant structure can be (schematically) represented as in the partial tree shown in (13) (for a syntactic projection of Mood, see Ahn & Yoon 1989, Whitman 1989, among many others).

(13)
```
                    MoodP
                   /    \
                  TP    Mood
                 /  \
                AspP  T
               /   \
             VP₁   Asp
            /   \
          AspP   V₁
          / \   siph-
        VP₂  Asp
        / \   -ko [-complete] or [0complete]
       NP  V₂
```

When the object NP bears ACC case, the *siphta* construction exhibits the usual properties of a biclausal sentence with respect to case marking, quantifier scope, and aspect.

The problem is to account for the monoclausal properties of this construction when the object NP bears unexpected NOM case. As discussed above, the construction behaves as if it has only one tense and one aspect, namely, the tense and aspect associated with the matrix predicate *siph-*. To account for this, we suggest that in addition to the feature value [-complete], *-ko* can be underspecified, with value 0. That is, *-ko* denotes either an incompleted event (i.e. [-complete]), or an unrealized event (i.e. [0complete]), presumably irrealis, similar to an infinitival complement in English. This, then, means that -*ko* indicates incompleteness in two different senses (essentially along the lines of Travis 1992); and in either case, the aspectual property of -*ko* will be compatible with the semantic property of *siph-*, namely, the act of wishing. Although the term irrealis may be a bit misleading, it is consistent with the native speaker intuition concerning the interpretation of NOM case-marking in the *siphta* construction mentioned earlier.

3.2 Head Movement

When -*ko* is underspecified with feature value 0, the VP-complement, then, is defective in some sense, and this defectiveness needs to be remedied in one way or another. We assume head movement is forced to produce the verbal complex V-*ko* *siph-* (for reasons to be discussed shortly): V movement will first produce the amalgamated form V_2-*ko*, which further moves up to the position of V_1, yielding the verbal complex V-*ko* *siph-*. But the head of this verbal complex is *siph-*, not the V_2 that undergoes head movement, which means that this verbal complex inherits the case-assigning property of the head *siph-*. This explains why the object of V_2 can (and in fact must) bear nominative, since like other similar psych predicates of its class, the head of this amalgamated verbal complex, *siph-*, is not an ACC-assigner. This head movement in effect removes barrierhood of VP_2, making the object NP susceptible to NOM case-assignment from matrix Infl, due to the Government Transparency Corollary (Baker 1988:64).

Notice that there are two separate Aspect Phrases in the tree in (13), each of which is associated with a different verb. If, as we assume here, the amalgamated verbal complex V-*ko* moves up to the position of the matrix verb and gets incorporated into it, it must be guaranteed that the entire verbal complex V-*ko* *siph-* can only have one aspectual property associated with it. Provided that the matrix verb *siph-* has its own Aspect Phrase to combine, the verbal complex V-*ko* that gets incorporated should have no aspectual property of its own; otherwise, there would be no meaningful interpretation for a verbal complex that has two different aspectual properties. This can explain why the lower Aspect is underspecified, with value 0.

The question yet to be answered then is, Why can't the lower verb V_2 assign accusative to its object NP in the structure (13), given that it is otherwise an accusative-assigner? We tentatively suggest, without much discussion, that Aspect plays a licensing role in syntax: Verb can realize its Case capacity fully in syntax only when it combines with Aspect. This is not to say that Aspect is the source of accusative Case on verbal arguments. No doubt the capacity of assigning Case is the lexical property of Verb. Rather, what we are suggesting is that association with Aspect (with adequate value) is a prerequisite for Verb to properly discharge its Case. But if

Aspect is underspecified, Verb may not be licensed to discharge its Case in syntax. The Last Resort Condition (not in the sense of Greed in Chomsky (1993), but in the sense of Lasnik's (in press) Enlightened Self-Interest) then dictates head movement: movement of V_1 to V_2 via Aspect enables Infl to assign NOM case all the way down into VP_1.[5]

3.3 Case Assignment to Adverbials

We are now ready to account for the case patterns illustrated in (6) above, repeated here as (14). (Note that -*ko* is now glossed as ASP.)

(14) a. Na-nun *cacenke-lul hansikan-ul*   **ACC-ACC**
I-TOP bicycle-ACC one.hour-ACC

tha-ko   siph-ess-ta.
ride-ASP want-Pst-Ind
'I wanted to ride a bicycle for an hour.'

b. Na-nun *cacenke-ka hansikan-i*   **NOM-NOM**
tha-ko siph-ess-ta.

c. *Na-nun *cacenke-ka hansikan-ul*   ***NOM-ACC**
tha-ko siph-ess-ta.

d. *Na-nun *cacenke-lul hansikan-i*   ***ACC-NOM**
tha-ko siph-ess-ta.

The paradigm shows that in the *siphta* construction, when the lower V is an accusative case-assigner, then the complement NP and the durational adverbial must bear the same case, either ACC-ACC or NOM-NOM, and the non-matching case patterns are excluded.[6] The important point to be emphasized here is that as shown by the contrast between in (14b) and (14d), the occurrence of NOM on the adverbial, which is otherwise impossible, must be due to the fact that the complement NP also bears NOM.

Recall that complement NPs and duration adverbials generally do not show matching case patterns. Why, then, do the "unexpected" matching case patterns arise here? Our answer is this. The case on the duration adverbial and that on the complement NP must come from the same source (given the word order with the durational adverbial following the object

---

[5] The mechanism of case marking assumed in much recent work, including Minimalist Theory, is case checking, not case assignment. If adverbial NPs bear structural Case, as argued here and elsewhere, it is quite unclear how the checking theory should extend to case marking of adverbials, since case checking involves only Spec-Head relations.

NP). When the complement NP gets accusative, there is a projection of Aspect above VP, which is responsible for assigning accusative to the adverbial NP. But when the complement NP gets nominative, the verb that subcategorizes for it projects without independent Aspect (i.e. -*ko* is underspecified). Hence, the durational adverbial that modifies the complement verb may not get accusative. Since the adverbial occurs within the projection of the complement verb (namely, VP_2), it is assigned nominative by the same case-assigner that assigns NOM to the object NP. Crucially, then, the matching case patterns arise because they both occur within the same domain of case assignment. But in other environments (e.g. in (3a) above, repeated here), they do not show matching case patterns.

(3) a. Swuni-nun *phyengsayng-ul/*i* emeni-ka/*lul
Swuni-TOP life.time-ACC/*NOM mother-NOM/*ACC

kuliw-ess-ta.
miss-Pst-Ind
'Swuni missed her mother for life.'

In (3a), the complement NP gets nominative, whereas the durational adverbial bears accusative. This is because the duration adverbial gets its case assigned by Aspect, not the Verb (or Tense), as the adverbial is likely to be an argument that participates in the event structure, not the argument structure, of the Verb.

Recall that when the predicate is *philyoha-* 'need', as in (3b) above, the durative is marked NOM.

---

[6] Speakers find the distinction between (14a,b) on the one hand, and (14d) on the other, fairly clear: when the object NP bears ACC, NOM case on the duration adverbial ranges from quite odd to totally unacceptable. But it should be noted that some speakers find the contrasts in (14) not as sharp as indicated, especially the contrast between (14c) and (14d): those speakers find (14c) a bit better than (14d), and that (14c) may be marginally acceptable if the object NP bears a contrastive focus/stress (e.g. a bicycle as opposed to a car or motorcycle). We must admit that we do not yet understand why contrastive focus leads to improvement, and the instability or variability in judgments might undermine our argument concerning case assignment to adverbials. Nonetheless, the point remains that NOM case is possible for the duration adverbial only when the object NP also bears NOM.

(3) b. Mulken-ul ta nalu-camyen van-i *twusikan-i/*ul*
stuff-ACC all carry-PURP van-NOM 2.hours-NOM/*ACC

philyoha-ta
need-Ind
To carry all the stuff, one needs a van for two hours.'

Does this mean that there is no Aspect node to assign ACC case to the adverbial? Note that this predicate is not an accusative case-assigner, independently of case-marking on the duration adverbial.

In our present analysis, two different accounts seem possible: (3b) lacks (the grammatical marking of) Aspect altogether (as suggested by an anonymous reviewer), or as we would tentatively suggest here, its aspect indicates the "irrealis" status of the event denoted by the verb, in the sense that a van is not in one's possession for an intended period of time.[7] In the analysis of event structure of Pustejovsky (1988; 1991), the "eventual" property denoted by the verb *need* would correspond to the predicate opposition (i.e. 'van is not in one's possession') that is a simultaneous part of PROCESS rather than STATE (i.e. 'van is in one's possession'). It thus remains a research question to investigate how the event structure proposed by Pustejovsky can be projected syntactically if event structure is syntactic

---

[7] An anonymous reviewer pointed out to us that the past tense *ess* developed diachronically through a contraction of *-e isi-*, which marked 'completed aspect' in Middle Korean, and then the reviewer noted that there is a contrast between (i) (i.e. our (3b)) and (ii).

(i) *Swuni-nun twu sikan tongan-ul van-i philyoha-ta.

Swuni-TOP two hour period-ACC van-NOM need-Ind

(ii) ?Swuni-TOP twu sikan tongan-ul van-i philyoha-ess-ta.

Swuni-TOP two hour period-ACC van-NOM need-Pst-Ind

While (i) is downright unacceptable, (ii) is certainly better than (i), and the speakers we consulted agreed with the reviewer on the observed contrast. This observation raises an interesting question on the nature of such functional morphemes as *-nun* and *-ess-*, which are commonly viewed as simple tense markers. In the light of the idea hitherto suggested in the literature that these morphemes have more properties of aspectual marking rather than mere tense marking, the matter obviously merits further investigation. It is noteworthy in this regard that the morpheme *-nun* never cooccurs with stative verbs in Korean, and this fact can receive a nice explanation, should *-nun* indicate (non-past) PROCESS rather than the simple present, since it will be incompatible with STATE.

in nature, as Pustejovsky argues. We will not explore the relationship between Aspect and event structure any further here, leaving it for future research. Whether this approach proves tenable depends largely on our understanding of the syntactic relationship between Aspect and event structure or event types.

One question still remains to be answered. In sentence (14b), the duration adverbial bears nominative modifying the complement V. But in the structure assigned to it, the complement VP has an Aspect node underspecified for completeness. We assume that the durational adverbial can be licensed by the event structure of the complement verb, which is a process verb. It should be emphasized, therefore, that we do not construe Aspect with event types here. In fact, this distinction is made clear in work by Comrie (1976) and Lyons (1977), who argue that event types may denote (im)perfectivity since event types and aspects may share similar ontological properties. While event types (such as achievements and accomplishments) have "lexicalized or inherent" aspectual characters, the term Aspect is reserved for the grammaticalization of aspectual properties by means of explicit grammatical morphemes. Thus, verbs denoting event types have certain semantic/aspectual properties in common across languages, but Aspect is not a universal grammatical category in all languages.

The analysis makes a prediction. As mentioned earlier, the paradigm illustrated in (14) holds under the intended interpretation in which the duration adverbial modifies the event of the complement verb. But what happens if the duration adverbial should modify the matrix verb? Since the matrix verb has its own Aspect node (see the structure in (13)), we predict that the adverbial would get ACC case from its own Aspect. The prediction is correct, as shown in (15).

(15) a. Na-nun *hansikan-ul cacenke-lul*   **ACC-ACC**
I-TOP one.hour-ACC bicycle-ACC

tha-ko siph-ess-ta.
ride-ASP want-Pst-Ind
'For an hour, I wanted to ride a bicycle.'

b. Na-nun *hansikan-ul cacenke-ka*   **ACC-NOM**
tha-ko siph-ess-ta.

c. *Na-nun *hansikan-i cacenke-ka*   ***NOM-NOM**
tha-ko siph-ess-ta.

d. *Na-nun *hansikan-i cacenke-lul*   ***NOM-ACC**
tha-ko siph-ess-ta.

The sentences in (14) and (15) differ only in the relative order of the object NP and the duration adverbial. In (15a,b), the duration adverbial gets accusative, regardless of the case on the complement NP. (15c,d) are ruled out since the duration adverbial bears NOM; it cannot get nominative because it is a constituent of the matrix VP, which gets associated with the higher Aspect node in the tree in (13). Note, in passing, that sentence (14c) above may be acceptable when its intended reading is to have the adverbial modify the matrix verb, just like (15b) here.

3.4 Supporting Evidence

3.4.1 The Behavior of Temporal Adverbs. There is a further property to note. A point-in-time adverbial such as *yesterday* serves to provide a reference time at which an event is located in the universe of discourse. Consider sentence (16) for the behavior of the point-in-time adverbial.

(16) a. Na-nun myechilceney *phyenci-lul*
I-TOP a.few.days.ago letter-ACC

ssu-ko   siph-ess-ta.   ACC
write-ASP want-Pst-Ind
i) A few days ago, I wanted to write a letter.
ii) I wished I could write a letter a few days earlier.

b. Na-nun myechilceney *phyenci-ka*
I-TOP a.few.days.ago letter-NOM

ssu-ko   siph-ess-ta.   NOM
write-ASP want-Pst-Ind
i) A few days ago, I wanted to write a letter.
ii) I wished I could write a letter a few days earlier.

Again, (16a,b) differ only in the case-marking on the object NPs. As paraphrased above, they both have a wide scope reading in which the point-in-time adverbial marks the reference time at which the act of wishing had taken place. In addition, (16a) allows a narrow scope reading in which the adverbial serves to provide the reference time at which the act of writing was intended but failed to take place. The narrow scope reading can be easily detected when the adverbial occurs after the object NP:

(16) c. Na-nun phyenci-lul myechilceney ssu-ko   siph-ess-ta.
I-TOP letter-ACC a.few.days.ago write-ASP want-Pst-Ind

However, sentence (16b) in which the object NP bears NOM is for some speakers unambiguous, and disallows the narrow scope reading; other speakers find the ambiguity, but strongly prefer the broad scope reading.

When -*ko* has a feature value, it denotes an incompleted aspect of the complement verb, entailing that the event of writing had occurred, and this will account for the fact that the act of writing could have been completed but not at the specified reference time. We thus obtain the reading that the event had remained incompleted with respect to the reference time. When underspecified, on the other hand, -*ko* refers to an unrealized event, and this will account for the fact that the event of the complement verb in sentence (16b) cannot have its own reference time. In fact, when the narrow scope reading is forced for (16b) by the reversed order of the object NP and the adverbial, most speakers judge the sentence quite odd:

(16) d. ?*Na-nun phyenci-ka myechilceney   **NOM**
         I-TOP letter-NOM a.few.days.ago

   ssu-ko   siph-ess-ta.
   write-ASO want-Pst-Ind
   'I wished I could write a letter a few days earlier.'

The reason is that the tense of the event of the complement verb is specified for [irrealis], that is, [-realized], and therefore, an event that never occurs cannot have a reference time in the universe of discourse.

The proposed analysis predicts, then, that when the object of the complement verb occurs in the nominative, and the tense of the matrix clause is the present, a time-span adverbial like *in three days* would make the sentence ungrammatical. Consider the sentences in (17).

(17) a. Na-nun i cha-lul sahul   hwuey-nun
         I-TOP this car-ACC three.days in/after-TOP

   phalapeli-ko   siph-ta.
   sell.away-ASP   want-Ind
   'I want to sell this car in three days.'

   b. ??*Na-nun i cha-ka sahul   hwuey-nun
       I-TOP this car-NOM three.days in/after-TOP

   phalapeli-ko   siph-ta.
   sell.away-ASP   want-Ind

In both (17a) and (17b), the tense associated with *siph-* is the present. The reference time at which the act of wishing takes place must therefore be the present, too, which then excludes the reading in which *in three days* modifies the matrix verb *siph-*. In (17a), the time-span adverbial provides the reference time for the event of selling. But since *-ko* indicates incompleteness, the sentence cannot have any implications beyond the reference time with respect to the act of selling. Now the oddness of (17b) is exactly what is expected under the present account. (17b) is odd because the event of selling should be treated as an unrealized event, being unable to have its reference time specified, but the time-span adverbial forces this unrealized event to have a reference time nevertheless. Notice that the event of selling in fact remains an unrealized event also in the case of (17a), but this is due to the fact that its reference time is located in the future. Thus, (17a), unlike (17b), does not mean that the event of selling is unrealizable, but it isn't yet realized with respect to the utterance time (which is the present).

3.4.2 Availability of the DAT-NOM Case Pattern. The proposed analysis makes yet another prediction. When the object NP of the complement verb occurs in the nominative, the construction undergoes head movement, producing the verbal complex V-*ko siph-*. As the matrix verb *siph-* becomes the head of the resulting verb complex, the construction should behave like one of the familiar psych verb constructions: the DAT-NOM case property. This is indeed the case, as shown by (18a) and (18b).

(18) a. Swuni-eykey-nun ku   nal caki   **DAT-NOM**
         Swuni-DAT-TOP   that day her   ***DAT-ACC**

   emma-ka/*lul   po-ko   siph-ess-ta.
   mother-NOM/*ACC see-ASP want-Pst-Ind
   'Swuni wanted to see her mother on that day.'

   b. Swuni-eykey ku ttay po-ko   siph-ess-ten salam-un ...
       Swuni-DAT   that time see-ASP want-Pst-Comp person-TOP
       'the person that Swuni wanted to see at that time ...'

The DAT-NOM case pattern is never possible when the accusative case-assigning verb *po-* 'see' occurs as the matrix verb (as in *I saw her*), and the NOM-ACC pattern is the only possibility. But as shown by the contrast in (18a), DAT case can occur on the experiencer subject only when the object of the complement V occurs in the nominative. This striking case pattern (noted by Lim 1994) lends strong support to the present analysis.

3.4.3 Arguments Against an Alternate Lexical Account.

An anonymous reviewer raised the question of whether it is necessary to invoke head movement and AspectPhrase-complementation to account for the observed properties of the *siphta* construction, especially those in Table I. In further support of the proposed analysis, we need to address the issue and briefly discuss problems for the alternate lexical account that suggests that the verbal complex V-*ko siph*- can be generated in the lexicon by means of complex predicate formation, that is, that the construction can either involve VP-complementation in syntax or complex predicate formation in the lexicon. Certainly, such an alternate lexical account can also deal with the syntactic properties of the construction listed in Table I above. For example, VP-complementation will account for the biclausal properties in the left-hand column; complex predicate formation will account for the monoclausal properties in the right-hand column.

The problem, however, is that it cannot account for a certain significant property of the construction that our proposed syntactic account can immediately handle. Consider the paradigms illustrated in (14) and (15) above with respect to the scope and case-marking of duration adverbials, especially when the object of the complement V occurs in the nominative. We have observed that when the object NP bears nominative, the adverbial can occur either in the nominative or in the accusative, but then, the case on the duration adverbial must correlate with its scope interpretation: NOM case on the adverbial allows narrow scope only, while ACC case on the adverbial allows wide scope only. If the verbal complex V-*ko siph*- is driven in the lexicon, it must have only one event structure (and one argument structure), since it is implausible to think of a single predicate with two separate event structures simultaneously. This means that such a lexical account makes two incorrect predictions, contrary to fact: it predicts (i) that a duration adverbial can only delimit the event structure of the entire verbal complex (as there is only one, due to lexical integrity), and (ii) that the entire verbal complex can give the adverbial only one case (namely, ACC case). The former prediction is false: the adverbial can modify either the matrix verb or the complement verb, indicating that it should be associated with two different event structures separately. The latter prediction is also false: the fact that the duration adverbial, when the object of the complement verb that it modifies bears NOM, must also bear NOM cannot be accounted for, given that the adverbial occurs only in the accusative when it gets associated with the matrix verb *siph*-. Hence, the failure of a lexical account leaves us only one possibility: the ambivalent properties of the *siphta* construction must be accounted for in syntax, allowing for some kind of incorporation through head movement.

4. On Aspect
4.1 The Functional Category Aspect

We now turn to our suggestion that *-ko* belongs to the functional category Aspect, for which we will provide further justification. A longstanding problem in the generative analysis of Korean syntax is the fact that certain grammatical formatives have not been assigned identifiable syntactic categories. Consider the verbal morphemes in the minimal pair in (19) (that are glossed with a question mark).

(19) a. Elum-i   nok-a   iss-ta.   (V-*a/e iss*-)
         ice-NOM melt-?   AUX-Ind
         'The ice has melted.'

   b   Elum-i   nok-ko   iss-ta.   (V-*ko iss*-)
         ice-NOM melt-?   AUX-Ind
         'The ice is melting.'

(19a) can be paraphrased as *the ice has already melted and remains watery at the time of utterance*; (19b) as *the ice began melting and is still in the process of melting at the time of utterance*. What is the function of these verbal suffixes, and what syntactic category do they belong to?

We suggest that the suffix *-a/e* (the alternation is due to vowel harmony) or *-ko* on the verb root in (19a,b) is a morpheme that grammaticalizes aspect, providing some evidence for a syntactic projection of Aspect (see Y.-S. Lee (1994) for a similar suggestion based on a very different set of data). Notice that the two suffixes makes a crucial difference with respect to the aspectual property of completeness (or perfectivity): *-a/e* refers to completion of the act denoted by the verb, whereas *-ko* indicates its incompleteness. This observation is not at all new; and goes back at least as far as the pioneering work of Choy Hyenpay (1929) (for more recent discussions of aspectual properties in Korean, see also Se Cengswu (1976) and Ko Yengkun (1983)). Recent studies on syntactic projections of functional categories (Chomsky 1991, Mahajan 1990, Pollock 1989, Yoon 1989, *inter alia*) offer a natural place for this distinction. We suggest that the functional category Aspect has its syntactic projection above VP, in the manner depicted in (20), consisting of a binary feature with two values, [+complete] and [-complete] (where XP, WP, and ZP can be any constituents).

(20)   AspP
          /   \
         WP   Asp'
              /   \
             VP   Asp0
            / \
           ZP   V'
               / \
              XP   V°

Verb movement will then produce the verbal complex V-*ale* or V-*ko* in syntax.[8]

We assume the morpheme *iss-* to be an (aspectual) auxiliary verb with a durative/stative meaning, but nothing that follows hinges on this assumption. In (19a), this auxiliary verb indicates that the (resulting) state that ensues the completion of the event holds at the time of utterance; in (19b), the event still remains incompleted at the time of utterance, which then gives it an ongoing process or progressive reading. Hence, the sentences in (19) have the property of states as a whole.

The structure of verbal projections sketched in (20) gains independent support from coordination facts. Assuming the standard view that coordination applies only to syntactic constituents, the fact illustrated by the sentences in (21) that two coordinated VPs can share the same Aspect can be accounted for immediately by the proposed structure in (20).[9]

(21)a.   Cheli-nun nwup-ko iss-ess-ta.   [-complete]
         Cheli-TOP lie-ASP AUX-Pst-Ind
         'Cheli was in the process of lying down.'

---

[8] Recall the discussion of the aspectual property of *-ko* in the previous sections. In effect, then, we suggest that the Aspect node has three values, [+complete], [-complete], and [0].

[9] Note that the morpheme *-ko* has many meanings, all homophonous: it can be a conjunctive, a complementizer, or an aspectual morpheme. Note also that given the VP-Subject Hypothesis, the sentences in (21) are not necessarily examples of gapping.

b. Cheli-nun nwup-ko Swuni-nun
　　Cheli-TOP lie-CONJ Swuni-TOP　　[+complete]

　　anc-a　iss-ess-ta.
　　sit-ASP AUX-Pst-Ind
　　'Cheli was lying down, and Swuni was sitting.'

c. Cheli-nun ttwi-ko Swuni-nun　　[-complete]
　　Cheli-TOP run-CONJ Swuni-TOP

　　ket-ko　iss-ess-ta.
　　walk-ASP AUX-Pst-Ind
　　'Cheli was running, and Swuni was walking.'

In (21a), the event of lying down can only be understood to be an ongoing process (hence, its slight oddness from a pragmatic point of view), meaning that the act of lying down has already started but has not yet been finished; in (21b), in contrast, the act of lying down, just like the act of sitting, is interpreted as an achievement with its terminal point reached. This reading arises because (21b) has coordination of two VPs under the same Aspect node, hence Aspect governs both VPs. (For much relevant discussion of coordination in Korean, see Yoon (1989), Chapter 2.) The same holds true for (21c), which the reader can easily verify. These facts from coordination thus provide further evidence for a syntactic projection of Aspect.

　　The suggestion that there is a syntactic projection of Aspect makes a further prediction: that we can even coordinate two Aspect Phrases, as illustrated in (21d).[10]

---

[10] An anonymous reviewer claimed that it is the sequence -*ale iss*- or -*ko iss*-, not just -*ale* or -*ko*, that contributes to the aspectual interpretations under discussion, questioning seriously the idea that verbal suffixes of this class can have identifiable functions and/or meanings by themselves (cf. Cho & Sells 1995). It should be emphasized, therefore, that we do not intend to make any claim beyond what is actually suggested here, to the effect that all verbal affixes in Korean can be assigned a particular functional category along the same line. Nevertheless, we would like to point out that the coordination fact (or gapping, if one would like) shown in (21d) demonstrates that the sequence -*ale iss*- or -*ko iss*- must be able to have two separate syntactic constituents in it, lending strong support for our syntactic treatment of the morphemes at hand.

(21) d. (Cip-ey ka-ni) mul-un acikto kkulh-ko pap-un
(home-DAT arrive-NI) water-TOP still boil-ASP rice-TOP

imi toy-e iss-ess-ta.
already cook-ASP AUX-Pst-Ind
'(When I went home, I found that) the water was still boiling and the rice was already cooked.'

(21d) involves coordination of two Aspect Phrases (with different aspectual properties), hence each conjunct can receive a different aspectual interpretation, as expected.

4.2 Aspects and Event Types

A duration adverbial requires that the event that it delimits meet the subinterval condition (which says that if an event E occurs for a period of time P, then E also holds true for any proper parts of P). The property of (temporal) homogeneity is thus characteristic of atelic aspects such as states and processes. But telic events like achievements and accomplishments are heterogeneous with respect to the time that they occupy, being characterized by a transitional culmination (see Dowty 1979, Herweg 1994, Krifka 1987, Verkuyl 1972, and many others.) The distinction between telicity and non-telicity thus explains the behavior of duratives in the sentences in (22).

(22) a. John ran for an hour.
b. John stood on the lawn for ten minutes.
c. *John ran to the store for ten minutes.
d. *John reached the top for an hour.

In sentence (23), the durative can only be understood to delimit the aspect of the entire sentence, but not the verb *climb*.

(23) a. Cheli-nun hansikan-ul san-ul
Cheli-TOP one.hour-ACC mountain-ACC

oll-a iss-ess-ta
climb-ASP AUX-Pst-Ind
a. Cheli climbed the mountain and stayed on the top for an hour.
b. *Cheli climbed the mountain for an hour and finally reached the top.

(23a) is the only possible reading since the aspectual morpheme -*ale* (i.e. [+complete)] makes the act of climbing a telic event, which is incompatible with the durative, while the entire clause denotes a state (like (22b) above)).

This analysis, then, predicts that verbs whose event types are inherently states cannot cooccur with -*ale* or -*ko*, which is a correct prediction, as shown in (24).

(24) a. *Swuni-ka yeyppu-e/ko iss-ta.
Swuni-NOM be.pretty-ASP AUX-Ind

b. *Cheli-ka paym-i coh-a/ko iss-ta.
Cheli-NOM snakes-NOM like-ASP AUX-Ind

The aspectual property [±complete] entails that there is a beginning point of the event, the difference being whether the event is telic or atelic. Since states have no implication for a beginning point or an end point, the aspectual morphemes -*ale* and -*ko* can only occur with event-denoting verbs (such as achievements and accomplishments) and process-denoting verbs, but not with state-denoting verbs. Hence the ungrammaticality of (24a,b).

It is worth noting that while achievements and accomplishments can both occur with -*ale*, they appear to select different auxiliary verbs. This is illustrated by the contrasts in (25).[11]

(25) a. Swuni-ka uysa-ka toy-e iss-ess-ta /
Swuni-NOM doctor-NOM become-ASP AUX-Pst-Ind/

*noh-ass-ta.
AUX-Pst-Ind
'Swuni had become a doctor.'

---

[11] But the distinction does not obtain in all dialects; thus in some dialects, the auxiliary verb *iss*- can still occur with verbs that denote accomplishments:

(i) Swuni-ka entek-ey cip-ul han-chay ci-e iss-ess-ta.
Swuni-NOM hill-LOC house-ACC one-CL build-ASP AUX-Pst-Ind
'Swuni had built a house on the hill.'

b. Swuni-ka kulim-ul kuli-e noh-ass-ta/
   Swuni-NOM picture-ACC paint-ASP AUX-Pst-Ind/

   *iss-ess-ta.
   AUX-Pst-Ind
   'Swuni had painted a picture.'

This contrast seems to correlate with the difference in the event structure between achievements and accomplishments.

Pustejovsky (1987; 1991) argues that the conventional aspectual classes and event types can be structurally decomposed into two subeventual types, PROCESS and STATE. So the event structure of accomplishments can be represented as (26) (somewhat simplified).

(26)   EVENT
             /   \
         PROCESS   STATE
            | |
      (act(E1)&~(E2)) (E2)

The two subevents are temporally ordered such that STATE follows the end point of PROCESS, and thus, the whole event has a transitional culmination. For instance, *John built a house* comprises the act of building (namely, E1) and the resulting state (namely, E2) that the activity brings about (hence, the existence of a house). A predicate opposition (i.e. ~E2) then becomes a part of PROCESS simultaneously with E1, as it is entailed by the transition. Pustejovsky suggests that agentivity distinguishes accomplishments from achievements (see also Dowty (1979) for a similar view), hence there is no need to make any further distinctions between them in terms of event composition: that is, achievements are nonagentive transitions.

It then seems possible to suggest, following Pustejovsky, that the selection of an aspectual morpheme and an auxiliary verb noted here should correlate with the properties of verbs' event structures and argument structures. This would mean that the selected aspectual morpheme and auxiliary verb should both contribute to the aspectual interpretation of the sentence, as it appears that they each denote a particular aspectual property. Thus, we would suggest that while the auxiliary verb *iss-* serves to denote states, the auxiliary verb *noh-* serves to denote agentive events (i.e. accomplishments). This analysis will not only give an immediate account for the selectional properties at hand, but will also make many correct predictions. For example, it explains why the aspectual morpheme *-ko* and the auxiliary verb *noh-*

cannot cooccur, as illustrated in (27): a feature mismatch arises, as *-ko* indicates incompleteness, whereas *noh-* entails the end point of an activity.

(27) *Cheli-ka uyca-lul mantul-ko noh-ass-ta.
      Cheli-NOM chair-ACC make-ASP AUX-Pst-Ind
      'Cheli had made a chair.'

It also accounts for the fact that not only is the combination of *-ko* and *iss-* possible (see the example in (19b) above), but they together can denote progressiveness, progressiveness being a special subcase of states. Furthermore, as predicted, a time-span adverbial (like *in an hour*) can occur in the V-*a/e noh-* context, but a durative may not. Consider the contrasts illustrated in (23) above and (28) here.

(28) pro samnyen-hwuey/*-tongan cip-ul ci-e noh-ass-ta.
      three.year-after/for house-ACC build-ASP AUX-Pst-Ind
      'They had built a house in/*for three years.'

In sum, the basic facts discussed so far will then fall out from the present analysis. But an investigation of full details of aspectual (or eventual) properties of Korean goes far beyond the scope of this paper, and we will leave them to future research.

5. Conclusion

In this paper, we suggested that being a functional category, Aspect heads its own syntactic projection above VP. We then argued that the *siphta* construction involves Aspect Phrase-complementation, which yields two different structures depending on whether the complement Aspect Phrase is fully specified as [-complete], and that this structural difference is crucial for the nominative-accusative case alternations that the construction exhibits. The case behavior of durational adverbials in the *siphta* construction, we argue, provides the evidence that they in fact get their syntactic case (accusative) from Aspect, which will explain why they can bear accusative even in contexts where verbal arguments/complements may not bear accusative. If this conclusion is correct, this paper provides strong evidence for the view that adverbials are indeed assigned case syntactically, just like verbal arguments.

Appendix

The *siphta* construction does not allow a certain class of verbs to occur in its complement clause. In this appendix, we would like to discuss this puzzling restriction in some detail. But the discussion will remain largely descriptive as we do not have an explanation for it at the moment.

It appears that the class of psych verbs that take nominative objects (theme) and dative subjects (experiencer) is excluded in the *siphta* construction. This is illustrated in (29).

(29) a. *Na-nun paym-i (an) musep-ko siph-ta.
   I-TOP snake-NOM (not) fear-ASP want-Ind
   'I want (not) to fear snakes.'

   b. *Na-nun wuli cip-i calangsulep-ko siph-ta.
   I-TOP my/our family-NOM be.proud-ASP want-Ind
   'I want to be proud of my family.'

   c. *Na-nun ku-ka (mopsi) coh-ko siph-ta.
   I-TOP he-NOM (much) like-ASP want-Ind
   'I want to like him (a lot).'

However, it is obvious that the restriction has nothing to do with nominative objects *per se*, since other verbs that take nominative complements can surely occur in this construction. This was shown in (5b) above, repeated here as (30).

(30) Cheli-nun uysa-ka toy-ko siph-ess-ta.
   Cheli-TOP doctor-NOM become-ASP want-Pst-Ind
   'Cheli wanted to become/be a doctor.'

Note further that Korean has another class of psych predicates that is very similar in interpretation to, but behaves quite differently in case-marking from, the class of psych predicates in question. As illustrated by the sentences in (31), they all occur with the verb *ha-*, the so-called "light" verb, and assign accusative case to their objects like other well-behaved transitive verbs.

(31) a. Na-nun paym-ul (an) museweha-ko siph-ta.
   I-TOP snake-ACC (not) fear-ASP want-Ind
   'I want (not) to fear snakes.'

b. Na-nun wuli cip-ul   calangsuleweha-ko siph-ta.
   I-TOP my/our family-ACC be.proud-ASP   want-Ind
   'I want to be proud of my family.'

c. Na-nun ku-lul (mopsi) cohaha-ko siph-ta.
   I-TOP he-ACC (much) like-ASP want-Ind
   'I want to like him (a lot).'

Why should there be such contrasts? What will account for this sort of selectional restriction?

We suspect that the *musep*-class of psych predicates in (29) and their transitive counterparts in (31), the *museweha*-class of psych predicates, might differ in aspectual or eventual properties. In fact, unlike the former, the latter class of psych predicates seem to behave more or less like inchoative verbs. There is some evidence that suggests that this may be a relevant distinction. Consider the contrast illustrated in (32).

(32) a. Cheli-nun paym-ul   museweha-ko iss-ta.
        Cheli-TOP snake-ACC fear-ASP   AUX-Ind

    b. *Cheli-nun paym-i   musep-ko   iss-ta.
        Cheli-TOP snake-NOM fear-ASP AUX-Ind
        'Cheli fears snakes.'

Given our earlier discussion regarding the aspectual morphemes -*a/e* and -*ko*, (32b) is correctly predicted to be ruled out since the verb *musep*-, an inherently state-denoting predicate, is incompatible with the aspectual property of -*ko*. The grammaticality of (32a), on the other hand, indicates that the verb *museweha*-, unlike *musep*-, should denote inchoativeness (meaning *Cheli came to fear snakes, and his fear persists at the utterance time*).

What is left unexplained, however, is that fact that other state-denoting verbs differ from the *musep*-class of psych predicates in that although they cannot occur in the -*ko iss*- construction, they do occur in the *siphta* construction:

(33) a. *Na-nun kenkangha-ko   iss-ta.
        I-TOP be.healthy-ASP AUX-Ind

    b. Na-nun kenkangha(y)-ci-ko   iss-ta.
       I-TOP be.healthy-INCH-ASP AUX-Ind
       'I am recovering; I am getting well.'

c. Na-nun kenkangha-ko siph-ta.
   I-TOP be.healthy-ASP want-Ind
   'I want to be/become healthy.'

As shown in (33a,b), the *-ko iss-* construction does not allow state-denoting predicates like *kenkangha-* 'healthy', unless the inchoative morpheme *ci-* can be added. Although an inchoative reading is forced in (33c), the question is why the *musep-*class of psych predicates in (29) above cannot have this intended inchoative interpretation.

Furthermore, it is all the more mysterious that the *museweha-*class of psych predicates illustrated in (31) does not exhibit the NOM-ACC case alternations characteristic of the *siphta* construction:

(34) a. ?*Na-nun paym-i (an) museweha-ko siph-ta.
        I-TOP snake-NOM (not) fear-ASP want-Ind
        'I want (not) to fear snakes.'

   b. ?*Na-nun wuli cip-i calangsuleweha-ko siph-ta.
      I-TOP my/our family-NOM be.proud-ASP want-Ind
      'I want to be proud of my family.'

   c. ?*Na-nun ku-ka (mopsi) cohaha-ko siph-ta.
      I-TOP he-NOM (much) like-ASP want-Ind
      'I want to like him (a lot).'

What will prevent the object NPs in (34a-c) from being assigned NOM case, given that the "unexpected" NOM case should be available in the *siphta* construction?

At this point, then, it is not even clear how to characterize the restriction at hand. Nevertheless, what seems fairly clear from the discussion so far is that the selectional restriction has to do with some property of psych predicates as the class of predicates concerned here appears to be all psych predicates. Note that while *calangsuleweha-* pride oneself on in (31b) above is a psychological predicate with an experiencer subject, *calangha-* talk proudly about in (35a,b) is an ordinary transitive verb with an agent subject. As expected, the by now familiar ACC-NOM case alternation indeed takes place in (35a,b).

(35) a. Cheli-nun say moca-lul/ka calangha-ko siph-ess-ta.
        Cheli-TOP new hat-ACC/NOM show.off-ASP want-Pst-Ind
        Cheli wanted to show off/talk proudly about his new hat.'

b. Ne-nun mues-ul/i   calangha-ko siph-ni?
   you-TOP what-ACC/NOM show.off-ASP want-Q
   'What do you want to show off or talk proudly about?'

Taken at its face value, then the descriptive generalization appears to be the following: when the complement verb takes an experiencer subject, its theme object cannot bear nominative case in the *siphta* construction. Why this should be so remains unclear to us, however, and we will leave it for future research.

References

Ahn, Hee-Don and Hang-Jin Yoon. Functional Categories in Korean. *Harvard Studies in Korean Linguistics* 3, 79-88, 1989.

Baker, Mark. *Incorporation*. Chicago: The University of Chicago Press, 1988.

Bratt, Elizabeth Owen. Case Marking and Constituent Structure: Evidence from Korean, paper read at the Winter meeting of the LSA, January 9, 1993.

Cho, Young-Mee Yu and Peter Sells. A Lexical Account of Inflectional Suffixes in Korean. *Journal of East Asian Linguistics* 4, 119-174, 1995.

Choy, Hyenpay. *Wuli Malpon*. Seoul: Cengumsa, 1929.

Chomsky, Noam. Some Notes on Economy of Derivation and Representation. In *Principles and Parameters in Comparative Grammar*, edited by R. Freidin, Cambridge, Massachusetts: MIT Press, pp. 417-454, 1991.

Chomsky, Noam. A Minimalist Program for Linguistic Theory. In *The View from Building 20*, edited by Kenneth Hale and Samuel J. Keyser, Cambridge, Massachusetts: MIT Press, pp. 1-52, 1993.

Comrie, Bernard. *Aspect*. Cambridge: Cambridge University Press, 1976.

Dowty, David. *Word Meaning and Montague Grammar*. Dordrecht: Reidel, 1979.

Dubinsky, Stanley. Case-Motivated Movement to Non-Argument Positions: Evidence from Japanese. In *Japanese/Korean Linguistics* 2, edited by P. M. Clancy, Palo Alto, California: CSLI, Stanford University, pp. 338-354, 1993.

Emonds, Joseph. Timberlake's Nominative Objects in Finnish and Old Russian. Paper read at the Winter meeting of the LSA, 1989.

Hakulinen, Auli and Fred Karlsson. *Nykysuomen Lauseoppia*. Jyväskylä: Finnish Literature Society, 1979.

Han, Hak-Sung. The Case of Korean Adjectives and Passive Verbs. *Studies in Generative Grammar* 2, pp. 219-249, 1991.
Herweg, Michael. A Critical Examination of Two Classical Approaches to Aspect. *Journal of Semantics* 8, pp. 363-402, 1994.
Kang, Young-Se. Adverbial Nominals Case is Well-Explained by the Generalized Case Marking Principle. *Harvard Studies in Korean Linguistics* 4, pp. 295-303, 1991.
Karlsson, Fred. *Finnish Grammar.* Helsinki: Werner Soderstrom, 1987.
Kim, Soowon and Joan Maling. Syntactic Case and Frequency Adverbials in Korean. *Harvard Studies in Korean Linguistics* 5, pp. 368-378, 1993.
Kim, Young-Joo. *The Syntax and Semantics of Korean Case.* Doctoral dissertation, Harvard University, Cambridge, Massachusetts, 1990.
Ko, Yengkun. Kwuke cinhayngsang hyengthay uy chesoloncek haysek (A localistic interpretation of the progressive aspect in Korean). In *Kwuke uy Thongsa.uymilon*, edited by Yengkun Ko and Kisim Nam, Seoul: Tower Press, pp. 152-170, 1983.
Krifka, Manfred. Nominal Reference and Temporal Constitution: Towards a Semantics of Quantity, in J. Groenendijk. *Proceedings of the Sixth Amsterdam Colloquium*, edited by M. Stokhof, and F. Veltman, pp. 153-173, 1987.
Lasnik, Howard (in press) Case and Expletives Revisited: On Greed and Other Human Failings. *Linguistic Inquiry* 26.4.
Lee, Jeong-Shik. *Case Alternation in Korean: Case Minimality.* Doctoral dissertation, University of Connecticut, Storrs, 1992.
Lee, Young-Suk. Accusative Case Licensing and Aspect Phrase. Paper presented at ICKL 9, SOAS, London, July 22, 1994.
Li, Audrey Yen-hui. *Order and Constituency in Mandarin Chinese.* Dordrecht: Kluwer, 1990.
Lim, Jeeya. ACC/NOM Case Alternations on Objects: Externalization and Internalization of the Subject. Ms., University of Washington, Seattle.
Lyons, John. 1977. *Semantics 2.* Cambridge: Cambridge University Press, 1994.
Mahajan, Anoop. *The A/A-bar Distinction and Movement Theory.* Doctoral dissertation, MIT, Cambridge, Massachusetts, 1990.
Maling, Joan. Adverbials and Structural Case in Korean. *Harvard Studies in Korean Linguistics* 3, pp. 297-308, 1989.
Maling, Joan. Of Nominative and Accusative: The Hierarchical Assignment of Grammatical Case in Finnish. In *Case and Other Functional Categories in Finnish Syntax*, edited by A. Holmberg and U. Nikanne, The Hague: Mouton de Gruyter, pp. 51-76, 1993.

Maling, Joan and Soowon Kim. Case Assignment in the Inalienable Possession Construction in Korean. *Journal of East Asian Linguistics* 1, pp. 37-68, 1992.

Pollock, Jean-Ives. Verb Movement, Universal Grammar, and the Structure of IP. *Linguistic Inquiry* 20, pp. 365-424, 1989.

Pustejovsky, James. Event Semantic Structure, ms., Brandeis University, Waltham, Massachusetts, 1987.

Pustejovsky, James. The Syntax of Event Structure. *Cognition* 41, pp. 47-81, 1991.

Sells, Peter. Nominative Objects in Korean. Paper read at the Winter meeting of the LSA, January 9, 1993.

Sells, Peter and Young-Mee Yu Cho. On the Distribution of X0 Elements in Korean. Ms., Stanford University, Stanford, California. To appear in the *Proceedings of the Santa Cruz Workshop on Korean Syntax and Semantics*, 1991.

Sigurdsson, Halldór. *Verbal Syntax and Case in Icelandic*. Doctoral dissertation, University of Lund, 1989.

Se, Cengswu [Suh, Cheong-Soo]. Kwuke Sisanghyengthayso uy Uymipunsek (A semantic analysis of Korean aspectual morphemes). In *Munpep Yenkwu* 3, edited by Munpep Yenkwuhoy, 1976.

Tada, Hiroaki. On Nominative Objects in Japanese. *Journal of Japanese Linguistics* 14, pp. 91-108, 1992.

Takezawa, Koichi. *A Configurational Approach to Case-Marking in Japanese*. Doctoral dissertation, University of Washington, Seattle, 1987.

Travis, Lisa. Derived Objects, Inner Aspect and the Structure of VP. Unpublished paper presented at NELS 22, 1992.

Verkuyl, Henk J. *On the Compositional Nature of the Aspects*. Dordrecht: Reidel, 1972.

Wechsler, Steven and Yae-Sheik Lee. The Domain of Direct Case Assignment. Ms., University of Texas, Austin, 1994.

Whitman, John. Topic, Modality, and IP Structure. *Harvard Studies in Korean Linguistics* 3, pp. 341-356, 1989.

Yoon, James Hye-Suk. *A Restrictive Theory of Morphosyntactic Interaction and Its Consequences*. Doctoral dissertation, University of Illinois, Urbana-Champaign, 1989.

7
Anaphoric Dependencies and Predication

Hyunoo Lee

1. Introduction[1]

In this paper I will first support the claim that there is no universal principle that constrains the distribution of referentially dependent items (RDIs), ones interpreted as bound variables. I will then propose one axiom of semantic interpretation, called the Principle of Referential Autonomy (PRA). In distinction to Binding-Theoretic accounts, the PRA directly constrains the presence of a referentially autonomous NP in the "basic" sentences of a natural language. Together with certain mechanisms of language acquisition, the principle accounts for the fact that RDIs and their antecedents are "asymmetrically" distributed in the sentence.

As we shall see, the approach taken here enables us to infer the ungrammaticality of (1b) from a grammatical string like (1a).

---

[*] This paper is part of my doctoral dissertation, *Categories, structures, and principles of anaphoric dependencies*. I would like to thank Ed Keenan, Anna Szabolcsi, and Ed Stabler for their valuable comments and suggestions.

The following list contains the abbreviations used in the paper:

AA: anaphor-antecedent
A-position: argument position
ART: article
Dom(f): domain of a function f
MUCP: Maximal Uniformity Condition on Predication
NOM: nominative-marker
PST: past tense
TOP: topic-marker

ACC: accusative-marker
A'-position: nonargument position
DE: declarative ending
PRA: Principle of Referential Autonomy
RA: referentially autonomous
RAF_L: referential autonomy function in L
RDIs: referentially dependent items

(1) a. John$_i$ criticized himself$_i$.
    b. *Himself$_i$ criticized John$_i$.

This means that Universal Grammar allows only one of the two anaphoric relations illustrated above to be grammatical if both strings have the "same" structure, and that English chooses the form shown in (1a). Here one question naturally arises. Why is (1a), but not (1b), given as grammatical? In other words, why is it that many languages allow anaphors to be anteceded by the "subject" in minimal transitive sentences? To answer this question, I argue that there exists a correlation between the form of predication and the positioning of a possible antecedent of an anaphor.

2. The Asymmetry of Anaphor-Antecedent Relations

At the level of observable structures, different languages present different ways of coding anaphoric dependencies. Keenan (1991) claims that there is no common structural relation relating anaphors to their antecedents in the verb-initial languages he studied, and suggests that asymmetry, in the sense specified in (2), is the only descriptive generalization that universally characterizes the anaphor-antecedent (AA) relation.

(2) Anaphora Asymmetry Universal

Let an NP α antecede an anaphor β in a sentence S, and let a sentence S' be derived from S by replacing α with an anaphor β' and β with a referentially autonomous (RA) NP α'. Then S' is ungrammatical if α' is understood to antecede β' and S and S' have the "same" structure.

In section 2.1, I will review Keenan's claim with the illustration of the Toba Batak anaphora facts. Then, in section 2.2, I will show that certain anaphora patterns in Korean further support this claim.

2.1. Toba Batak

Consider the Batak sentences in (3).

(3) a. Mang-ida dirina$_i$ si Torus$_i$.
        sees   self-his ART
        'Torus sees himself.'

    b. Di-ida si Torus$_i$ dirina$_i$.
        saw   ART   self-his
        'Torus saw himself.'

a'. *Mang-ida si Torus$_i$ dirina$_i$.
   sees   ART   self-his
   'He-self sees Torus.'

b'. *Di-ida dirina$_i$ si Torus$_i$.
   saw   self-his   ART
   'He-self saw Torus.'

It has been pointed out by Schachter (1984), Keenan (1989), and Clark (1991) that whether the verb is prefixed with *mang-* or *di-*, the verb forms a constituent with the immediately following NP. That is, the Batak transitive sentences have the form in (4).

(4)   [[pref-V NP$_1$] NP$_2$]
    where pref- is *Mang-* or *Di-*

As we see below, the Standard binding theory (Chomsky 1981, 1986) is based on the C-Command Condition in (5).

(5)   C-Command Condition

Anaphors must be c-commanded by their antecedents.

(6)   Definitions
   a. α is bound by β iff α and β are co-indexed and β c-commands α.
   b. α is free iff α is not bound.

(7)   a. Principle A: An anaphor must be bound in its governing category.
   b. Principle C: An R-expression must be free (in the root clause).

Given the constituent structure in (4), Principles A and C make accurate predictions in the case of the *mang*-prefixed verb, but inaccurate ones in the case of the *di*-prefixed verb. In (3a) *dirina* 'himself' is asymmetrically c-commanded by *si Torus*, satisfying Principles A and C. In (3a') *dirina* asymmetrically c-commands its intended antecedent *si Torus*, violating both principles. As in (3a'), *dirina* asymmetrically c-commands *si Torus* in (3b). But the sentence is GRAMMATICAL. As in (3a), *dirina* is asymmetrically c-commanded by its intended antecedent *si Torus*. Nonetheless, the string is UNGRAMMATICAL.

In the above I have argued that the Batak anaphora paradigm in (3) cannot be accounted for by the Standard binding theory. This does not mean that no generalization holds of it. In fact, careful examination of (3) reveals one interesting fact. Assuming verbal affixation is crucial to the structure of the Batak sentences, we see that (3) conforms to the Anaphora Asymmetry Universal in (2). Compare (3a-b) with (3a'-b'), respectively.

2.2. Korean

In this section I will argue that certain data from Korean not only pose an empirical problem for current theories of anaphora but also support the claim that the Anaphor Asymmetry Universal is the strongest universal generalization that constrains anaphoric dependencies.

Consider now the following Korean sentences:

(8) a. John-hako Mary-nun   selo-lul   pinanhay-ss-ta.
        -and   - TOP   each other-ACC   criticize-PST-DE
       'As for John and Mary, they criticized each other.'

   b. John-hako Mary-nun   caki-lul   pinanhay-ss-ta.
        -and   -TOP   self-ACC   criticize-PST-DE
       'As for John and Mary, they criticized themselves.'

(9) a. John-hako Mary-nun   selo-ka   pinanhay-ss-ta.
        -and   -TOP   each other-NOM   criticize-PST-DE
       'As for John and Mary, each other criticized them.'

   b. John-hako Mary-nun   caki-ka   pinanhay-ss-ta.
        -and   -TOP   self-NOM   criticize-PST-DE
       'As for John and Mary, themselves criticized them.'

(8a) contains the accusative marked reciprocal *selo-lul*, and (8b), the accusative marked reflexive *caki-lul*. In (9), however, it is the nominative marked NPs that are referentially dependent. (8a) and (8b) are normal, unmarked ways of expressing reciprocality and reflexivity, respectively. These sentences are not only grammatical but also natural. (9a) and (9b) are alternative ways of expressing reciprocality and reflexivity, respectively. Although the sentences in (8) and their corresponding sentences in (9) have the same truth conditional meaning, there is a pragmatic difference between those sentences. The sentences in (9) convey a "contrastiveness" that is absent in the corresponding sentences in (8). We may paraphrase (9a) and (9b) as (10a) and (10b), respectively.[2]

(10) a. As for John and Mary, it is John that criticized Mary and it is Mary that criticized John.

   b. As for John and Mary, it is they themselves that criticized John and Mary.

Notice that the grammaticality of (9) poses a problem for Chomsky's binding theory. Since the theory requires that the antecedent of an RDI like a reflexive or reciprocal pronoun be in an A-position, and since topic-marked NPs are assumed by the theory to occur in an A'-position, the sentences in (9) would be incorrectly predicted to be ungrammatical.

The fact that the sentences in (9) are grammatical is also problematic for the approaches taken by Jackendoff (1972) and his advocates. Consider (11).

(11) Theta Role Hierarchy Condition

Anaphors may not outrank their local antecedents on the Theta Role Hierarchy:

Agent, Experiencer > Non-Agent

In (9a) and (9b), the RDIs bear the Agent role and their intended antecedents, the Theme role, violating (11). But the sentences are grammatical, and hence (11) makes an incorrect prediction in these cases.

Now consider the following contrast:

(12) a. Kutul-un caki-ka pinanhay-ss-ta.
      they-TOP self-NOM criticize-PST-DE
      'As for them, it is themselves that criticized them.'

   b. *Caki-nun kutul-i pinanhay-ss-ta.
      self-TOP
      they-NOM criticize-PST-DE
      'As for themselves, it is they that criticized them.'

The contrast between (12a) and (12b) further supports the Anaphora Asymmetry Universal in (2), since both strings would be considered to have the same structure if (12b) is to be assigned any structural analysis.

---

[2] Note that some speakers find (9b) marginal. However, even such speakers do not hesitate in accepting the grammaticality of (9a). I suspect that they perceive (9a) as expressing contrastiveness more easily than (9b).

3. The PRA and Deriving the Anaphora Asymmetry Universal

While one might consider taking the Anaphora Asymmetry Universal as a basic constraint on the form of natural language, I would prefer to derive it from independently motivated principles of grammar. Below I pursue the latter objective in terms of the approach to language structure and language invariants in Keenan and Stabler (1992).

3.1. The Principle of Referential Autonomy

Our explanation of the Anaphora Asymmetry Universal is based on an axiom of which the informal version is given in (13).

(13) Principle of Referential Autonomy (Informal)
For each language L,
   i. in each nuclear sentence S of L, at least one independent NP occurrence is referentially autonomous, and
   ii. L provides a structurally uniform way of identifying the required RA NP in each S. That is, whenever sentences S and T are isomorphic (= have the same structure) then the NP L identifies in T is the isomorphic image of the one it identifies in S. I.e., it makes the "same" choice for T as it does for S.

Before giving a somewhat more rigorous statement of the PRA, I should elaborate on some of the basic notions used above. Suppose XP is an arbitrary phrase. An XP occurrence is called INDEPENDENT iff it is not a proper subconstituent of another XP occurrence. For example, only *John* and *Bill's mother* are independent NP occurrences in *John criticized Bill's mother*. A sentence S is an N-ARY NUCLEAR sentence iff (i) S consists of n independent NP occurrences, an n-ary predicate, and nothing else, and (ii) S is independent. *John laughed* is a unary nuclear sentence, and *John criticized Bill*, a binary nuclear one. But neither *John thinks that Bill laughed* nor *John came early and Bill came late* is a nuclear sentence. By definition, the string *Mary laughed* cannot count as a nuclear sentence when it is embedded in a string like *John said Mary laughed*.

Now consider (14) and (15).

(14) a. [Most of John's students] criticized [Bill].
      b. [No student in LA] reads [every paper published in the USA].
(15) a. No student criticized [himself].
      b. Each student$_i$ criticized [his$_i$ teacher].
      c. John criticized [everyone but himself].

All the bracketed NPs in (14) are referentially autonomous. They do not depend on expressions outside of them for their contribution toward the truth conditional meaning of the sentences they occur in. Their contribution is determined solely by the interpretations of their parts. By contrast, all the bracketed NPs in (15) are referentially dependent. Unlike the RA NPs given in (14), they depend on expressions outside of them for their contribution toward the truth conditional meaning of the sentences they occur in.

Given the distinction between the two types of NPs, we are now able to substantiate the PRA given informally in (13) above. Now consider the paradigm shown in (16)-(18).

(16) *John* laughed.   one RA NP

(17) a. *John* criticized *Bill*.   two RA NPs
      b. *John* criticized himself.   one RA NP

(18) a. *John* introduced *Mary* to *Bill*.   three RA NPs
      b. *John* introduced *Mary* to himself.   two RA NPs
      c. *John* introduced *Mary* to herself.   two RA NPs
      d. *John* introduced himself to *Mary*.   two RA NPs
      e. *John* introduced himself to himself.   one RA NP

In a unary nuclear sentence like (16), there is only one independent NP occurrence, which is referentially autonomous. A binary nuclear sentence may present two independent RA NP occurrences, as in (17a), or just one, as in (17b). A ternary nuclear sentence may present three independent RA NP occurrences, as in (18a), or just two, as in (18b)-(18d), or just one, as in (18e). These data are consistent with the PRA. But consider (19).

(19) a. *Himself cried.
      b. *Himself criticized himself.

Given how *himself* is interpreted in Standard American English, these expressions lack an RA NP and thus are ungrammatical as sentences because they violate the PRA.

Furthermore, the sentences in (16)-(18) bear out the second part of the PRA, which says that all languages provide a uniform way of structurally identifying an NP in nuclear sentences as referentially autonomous. Cf. the italicized *John* in (16)-(18). It seems to be the case that in English nuclear sentences, there is always an NP (provably unique) which is higher in the syntactic analysis tree than the other NPs in the sentence. This NP, called the "subject", is always interpreted as RA in nuclear sentences. I, however, do not require that the identifying mechanisms be given in terms of syntactic hierarchy. The idea underlying UNIFORM IDENTIFIABILITY is that the structure of a sentence depends on the lexical items occurring in it and the way they are combined. But our approach allows that different languages may combine lexical items in different ways.

To implement our claim, I first introduce the notion of isomorphism invariance drawn from Keenan and Stabler (1992). Following them, I think of a language L as a set of categorized expressions built from a lexicon LEX and a set F of generating functions. Specifically, L is the closure of LEX with respect to the functions f in F. Then, two expressions, σ and τ, are (syntactically) isomorphic iff each can be mapped to the other by a structure-preserving map (a 'hom'). A map (function) h from the expressions of L to the expressions of L preserves structure iff h preserves the domains of the generating functions and h commutes with each of them. That is, whenever $f(\sigma) = \tau$ then $f(h(\sigma)) = h(\tau)$ [equivalently: $f(h(\sigma)) = h(f(\sigma))$]. Then, to say that a function f *is isomorphism invariant* is just to say that f treats isomorphic expressions in the same way. That is, (20).

(20) Whenever some σ is isomorphic to τ, then the value $f(\tau)$ of f at τ is the isomorphic image of $f(\sigma)$. Formally, f is isomorphism invariant iff whenever $<\sigma, \tau> \in$ f and $<\sigma, \tau>$ is isomorphic to $<\sigma', \tau'>$ then $<\sigma', \tau'> \in$ f.

And we say that an isomorphism invariant function (structurally) identifies its value, since what value f has at a given expression is determined by the structure of that expression--once the structure of S in Dom(f) is given, then the value of f at S is determined.

Given the notions introduced above, it is now possible to state the PRA more formally as in (21).

(21) Principle of Referential Autonomy (Formal)

For each natural language L, there is an isomorphism invariant function f_L such that (i) and (ii):
i. $\text{Dom}(f_L)$ includes all nuclear sentences of L, and
ii. For each nuclear sentence S, $f_L(S)$ is an independent RA NP occurring in S.

The domain of the function whose existence is guaranteed by the PRA includes all n-ary nuclear sentences. The PRA says that at least one of the independent NPs is structurally identifiable and RA in every nuclear sentence. Where the language is English, we are tempted to call the function referred to in the PRA "Subject$_L$" or "Nom$_L$", but this notation is misleading. It is in fact implausible to think that any pretheoretical notion of "subject" or "nominative" applies uniformly to languages with different structures. For this reason, I will call the function referred to in (21) RAF_L (for the referential autonomy function in L).

3.2. Explaining the Toba Batak Anaphora

Before we explain the Toba Batak Anaphora, it is necessary to recall that in this language, the verb forms a constituent with an adjacent NP whether it is prefixed with *mang-* or *di*, as in (4), repeated here as (22).

(22) [[pref-V NP$_1$] NP$_2$]
where pref is *Mang-* or *Di-*

Given (22), I propose that the referential autonomy function for Batak, $\text{RAF}_{\text{Batak}}$, be given by:

(23) For any binary nuclear sentence S, $\text{RAF}_{\text{Batak}}(S) = \text{NP}_2$ in (22) if S is headed by a *mang*-prefixed verb, or NP$_1$ in (22) if S is headed by a *di*-prefixed verb.

Notice that I treat the grammatical sentences in (3), repeated as (24a) and (24b), as having different structures.

(24) a. Mang-ida dirina$_i$ si Torus$_i$.
sees self-his ART
'Torus sees himself.'

b. Di-ida si Torus₁ dirina₁.
   saw ART   self-his
   'Torus saw himself.'

a'. *Mang-ida si Torus₁ dirina.
    sees   ART   self-his
    'He-self sees Torus.'

b'. *Di-ida dirina₁ si Torus₁.
    saw   self-his ART
    'He-self saw Torus.'

The constituency requirement in (22) might suggest that (24a) and (24b) have the same tree structure, but it DOES NOT guarantee that they are syntactically isomorphic. In relation to this, it is worth noting that Szabolcsi (1990) treats *mang-ida* as a verb of type (t/e)/e but *di-ida* as a verb of type (t/((t/e)\((t/e)/e)))/e, as in (25).

(25)
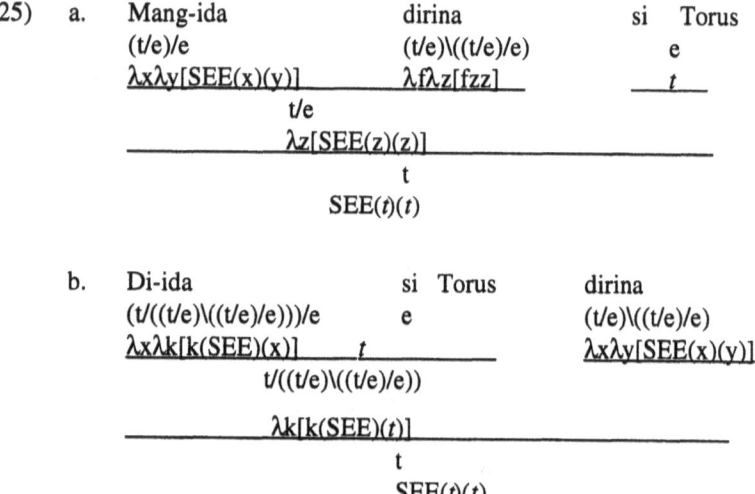

In addition to the derivational difference shown in (25), the fact that (24a') and (24b') are ungrammatical clearly shows that (24a) and (24b) are not isomorphic. If they are isomorphic, there is no reason that (24a') and (24b') are ungrammatical, and it will be incorrectly predicted that (24a') and (24b') are isomorphic to (24b) and (24a), respectively.

By virtue of (23), RAF$_{Batak}$ structurally identifies *si Torus* as an RA NP in both (24a) and (24b). We are now able to account for the ungrammaticality of (24a') and (24b'). Suppose, contrary to fact, that they are grammatical. Then RAF_{Batak} would incorrectly identify *dirina* 'self-his' as an RA NP in (24a') and (24b'), since RAF_{Batak} is isomorphism invariant and since (24a') and (24b') must be isomorphic to (24a) and (24b), respectively.[3] Since *dirina* is not RA, this would then result in a violation of the PRA. Since the PRA is inviolable, we must abandon the initial assumption that (24a') and (24b') are grammatical. Once we learn the AA relations coded by (24a) and (24b), we do not have any chance to generate sentences like (24a') and (24b'), without violating the PRA.

3.3. Explaining the Korean Anaphora

Suppose we define the referential autonomy function for Korean, RAF_{Korean}, as below:

(26) For any nuclear sentence S, $RAF_{Korean}(S)$ is
  i. the leftmost NP suffixed with *-ka/-i* if there is no NP suffixed with *-nun/-un* in S, or
  ii. the NP suffixed with *-nun/-un* if it is leftmost in S.

According to (26ii), RAF_{Korean} identifies the topic marked NPs in (9) as referentially autonomous. However, it does not constrain how RDIs are case marked or distributed, as desired. This also enables us to account for the contrast shown in (12), repeated as (27).

(27) a. Kutul-un caki-ka pinanhay-ss-ta.
    they-TOP self-NOM criticize-PST-DE
    'As for them, it is themselves that criticized them.'

---

[3] A few words are in order about one minor technical point. If the NP dominating *si Torus* branches, but the NP dominating *dirina* does not branch, there is no hom that maps the former to the latter, even though there may be a hom that maps the latter to the former. So, technically speaking, (24a) and (24b) cannot be isomorphic to (24a') and (24b'), respectively, even if we assume the latter strings are grammatical. To avoid this problem, one may assume that the NP dominating *dirina* also dominates the empty article corresponding to *si*. Then, the NP branches and thus is isomorphic to the NP dominating *si Torus*. Alternatively, one may hold that the NP dominating *si Torus* does not branch but that the article *si* is inserted by a lexical spell-out rule. On this view, the NP dominating *si Torus* is "syntactically" isomorphic to the non-branching NP dominating *dirina*. We will not pursue the exact mechanisms of guaranteeing the isomorphism between the two NPs. Instead we will simply assume that they are mapped to each other by a structure-preserving map.

b. *Caki-nun kutul-i   pinanhay-ss-ta.
    self-TOP
    they-NOM criticize-PST-DE
    'As for themselves, it is they that criticized them.'

Suppose, contrary to fact, that (27b) is grammatical. Then RAF_{Korean} would incorrectly identify *caki-nun* as an RA NP in (27b), since RAF_{Korean} is isomorphism invariant and since (27a) and (27b) must be isomorphic. But *caki-nun* is not RA, and this would lead to a contradiction. Since the PRA is inviolable, we must abandon the initial assumption that (27b) is grammatical.

4. Toward a Fully Explanatory Account of Anaphora

We have seen that the PRA enables us to infer the ungrammaticality of the strings that are in disharmony with the Anaphora Asymmetry Universal from their grammatical counterparts. It turns out that our approach gives an empirically better account of the AA relations which are asymmetric relative to the sentence types of language rather than language itself.

Yet, there remains one question that should be tackled on our account. To illustrate the point, let us consider (1), repeated as (28).

(28) a. $John_i$ criticized $himself_i$.
      b. *$Himself_i$ criticized $John_i$.

It is a fact that English and many other languages codify the AA relation shown in (28a), but not the one shown in (28b). Given that the PRA permits only one of the two types of AA relations from being realized in a language, this fact is mysterious within our approach.

Before we answer the question raised above, we should recall how reflexive pronouns are interpreted. Consider the following examples:

(29). a. $Mary_i$ criticized $herself_i$.
      b. *$Herself_i$ criticized $Mary_i$.
      c. SELF = $\lambda R \lambda x[x\ R\ x]$ for $x \in E$ (the set of objects), $R \subseteq E \times E$
      d. $I_m(SELF(CRITICIZE)) = I_m(\lambda x[x\ CRITICIZE\ x])$
         $= \lambda x[x\ CRITICIZE\ x](m)$
         $= m\ CRITICIZE\ m$

Reflexives are interpreted as the SELF function in (29c) that sends a binary relation R to a property $\lambda x[x\ R\ x]$. So SELF takes CRITICIZE, the denotation of *criticized* to a property $\lambda x[x\ CRITICIZE\ x]$. Then, I_m, the principal filter generated by the property of being *m*, applies to this property, as in (29d).

If (29b) were grammatical, it would be interpreted in the same way that (29a) is interpreted.
What is crucial to our discussion is the notion of "target" of predication. Let S be a binary nuclear sentence of the form:

(30) $[_S \text{NP}_1 \text{ V NP}_2]$
        (order irrelevant)

Then we say that for x = 1 or 2, NP_x is a target of predication in S iff the denotation of NP_x applies to the property denoted by the rest of S. The way we interpret the strings in (29a) and (29b) suggests that the antecedent of an RDI must be a target of predication in the binary nuclear sentence it occurs in. It is utterly implausible to say that the RDI occurring in the binary nuclear sentence denotes something that may apply to the property denoted by its antecedent and the transitive verb. Note that RDIs never occur in unary nuclear sentences unless they are used deictically. In interpreting binary nuclear sentences like (29a) and (29b), we must first combine an RDI with a transitive verb.

By contrast, in interpreting the binary nuclear sentence that contains no RDI, either of the independent NP occurrences can, in principle, be a target of predication in that sentence. As illustration, let us consider how we interpret (31a).

(31)   a. Mary criticized John.
        b. $\text{MARY}_{nom}(\text{JOHN}_{acc}(\text{CRITICIZE})) = \mathbf{I}_m(\lambda x[x \text{ CRITICIZE } j])$
        c. $\text{JOHN}_{acc}(\text{MARY}_{nom}(\text{CRITICIZE})) = \mathbf{I}_j(\lambda x[m \text{ CRITICIZE } x])$
        d. $\mathbf{I}_m(\lambda x[x \text{ CRITICIZE } j]) = \lambda x[x \text{ CRITICIZE } j](m)$
                $= m \text{ CRITICIZE } j$
                $= \lambda x[m \text{ CRITICIZE } x](j)$
                $= \mathbf{I}_j(\lambda x[m \text{ CRITICIZE } x])$

Whether we interpret the sentence as in (31b) or in (31c), we have the same truth condition, as the lambda abstraction and conversion in (31d) shows. In (31b) *Mary* is the target of predication, but in (31c) *John* is. Although it does not matter from the semantic point of view whether we interpret (31a) as in (31b) or as in (31c), only (31b) is compatible with the observed syntactic fact regarding English sentences. It has been assumed that a transitive verb forms a constituent with its object NP to the exclusion of its subject NP in a binary nuclear sentence like (31a). Since no syntactic operations are available that allow the transitive verb to form a constituent with its subject NP to the exclusion of its object NP, we are naturally led to conclude that only the occurrence of a subject NP can be a target of predication in a binary nuclear sentence like (31a).

The conclusion that (31b), but not (31c), is a legitimate way of interpreting (31a) suggests a functional explanation of why the antecedent of an RDI, required to be a target of predication, must be a subject in a binary nuclear sentence. I think that there is a correlation between the structure of predication and the pattern of anaphoric dependencies, and attribute the fact that English chooses, say, (29a) rather than (29b) to code the AA relation in a binary nuclear sentence to the Maximal Uniformity Condition on Predication in (32).

(32)   The Maximal Uniformity Condition on Predication (MUCP)

In every language the structure of predication should be maximally uniform, unless marked otherwise.

Since (29a) has the predication structure parallel to (31b), it satisfies the MUCP (32). As noted before, however, (29b) would have a predication structure which is quite different from (31b), and hence it does not conform to (32).

5. Conclusions

In this paper I provided supporting evidence for the claim that there is no universal structural relation that relates RDIs to their antecedent. Given that the Anaphora Asymmetry Universal is the strongest generalization that constrains the AA relations in natural languages, I proposed to derive it from the Principle of Referential Autonomy. In many languages where the notions of subject and object are well-understood, subject is a prime target of predication in the binary nuclear sentences containing no RDI, and the MUCP requires subject to be a target of predication also in the binary nuclear sentences that contain an RDI but are structurally similar to the binary nuclear sentences where no RDI occurs and subject is a target of predication. The Maximal Uniformity Condition on Predication, however, DOES NOT require that in such languages, subject must be a target of predication in all binary nuclear sentences.

References

Chomsky, Noam. *Lectures on government and binding.* Dordrecht: Foris, 1981.

Chomsky, Noam. *Knowledge of language: Its nature, origin and use.* New York: Praeger, 1986.

Clark, Robin. Towards a modular theory of coreference. In *Logical structure and linguistic structure*, ed. C.-T. James Huang and Robert May, Dordrecht: Kluwer, pp. 49-78, 1991.

Jackendoff, Ray. *Semantic interpretation in generative grammar.* Cambridge, Mass.: MIT Press, 1972.

Keenan, Edward L. Semantic case theory. In *Groningen-Amsterdam studies in semantics 11: Semantics and contextual expressions*, edited by Renate Bartsch, Johan van Benthem, and R. van Emde-BoasDordrecht: Foris, 1989.

Keenan, Edward L. Anaphora invariants and language universals. In *Proceedings of the West Coast Conference on Formal Linguistics* 10. Stanford Linguistics Association, Stanford University, Stanford, Calif, 1991.

Keenan, Edward L, and Edward P. Stabler. Language invariants. To appear in *Papers from the Eighth Amsterdam Colloquium.* Dordrecht: Foris, 1992.

Lee, Hyunoo. The Korean topic construction and the semantics of bare NPs. Ms., University of California, Los Angeles, 1991.

Lee, Hyunoo. Categories, structures, and principles of anaphoric dependencies. Doctoral dissertation, UCLA, 1993.

Lee, Hyunoo. Anaphora and the principle of referential autonomy. In *Proceedings of NELS 24*, Graduate Linguistic Student Association, Department of Linguistics, University of Massachusetts, Amherst, 1994.

Lee, Hyunoo. To appear. Binding theory and the principle of referential autonomy. In *Proceedings of the West Coast Conference on Formal Linguistics* 12. Stanford Linguistics Association, Stanford University, Stanford, Calif.

Schachter, Paul. Semantic role based syntax in Toba Batak. In *UCLA Occasional Papers in Linguistics*, No. 5. Department of Linguistics, UCLA, 1984.

Szabolcsi, Anna. Across-the-board binding meets verb second. In *Grammar in progress: GLOW essays for Henk van Riemsdijk*, ed. Joan Mascaró and Marina Nespor, Dordrecht: Foris, pp. 319-328, 1990.

8
A Minimalist Approach to Case Alternation in the Context of Korean Exceptional Case-Marking

Kwangho Lee

1. Introduction[1]

In standard GB theory, syntactic relations under which Case-marking occurs are inconsistent. Nominative Case-marking occurs in the SPEC-head relation, whereas Accusative Case-marking occurs in the head-complement relation. Exceptional Case-marking (ECM) occurs in a relation different from that for Nominative or ordinary Accusative Case-marking. To remove this inconsistency Chomsky (1993) proposed, in his recent minimalist program, that all Case-marking occurs with the Case-assigners and Case-assignees in a SPEC-head syntactic configuration, and that Case-marking be

---

[1] Earlier versions of material in this paper were presented at the Ninth International conference on Korean Linguistics held at the University of London and the Linguistics Colloquium of the University of Minnesota. I am grateful to audiences at these talks for their questions and comments, and especially grateful to Professors Nancy Stenson, Gerald Sanders, Jeanette Gundel, and Michael Hegarty for their valuable comments and suggestions. All errors are mine.

The Yale Romanization system is used for the transcription of Korean. The following abbreviations for grammatical terms are used in this paper:

Nom: Nominative	Acc: Accusative	Comp: Complementizer
Dat: Dative	Dec: Declarative	Foc: Focus
Hon: Honorific	Neg: Negator	Pass: Passive
Past: Past Tense	Pres: Present Tense	Top: Topic

dealt with in terms of morphological feature checking between Case-assigner and Case-assignee.

Under the Checking Theory (Chomsky 1993) lexical items are drawn from the lexicon with all morphological features such as Case and agreement features. The functional categories Tense and AGR are assumed to have such morphological features as V-features and NP-features. The V-features and NP-features of inflectional elements disappear when they check off against the corresponding features of V and NP (DP). Otherwise, they remain at LF, resulting in the crash of the derivation (ungrammaticality) (Chomsky 1994: 9). Strong features,[2] which trigger overt movement of a subject or a verb out of its original VP-internal position, must be checked off before SPELL-OUT[3] for a derivation to converge, since they are assumed to be ineliminable after SPELL-OUT (Chomsky 1994: 9).[4] Weak features, which do not trigger overt movement of a subject or a verb, must be checked off at LF for derivational convergence,[5] since they are assumed to be eliminable at LF.

Under the Checking Theory a subject NP raises to SPEC of AGRsP to have its Nominative Case and subject agreement features checked by the NP-features of Tense and AGRs, respectively. An object NP raises to SPEC of AGRoP to have its Accusative Case and object agreement features checked by the Case feature of a verb and the NP-features of AGRo, respectively.[6] Exceptional Case-marking (ECM) by V is interpreted as raising to SPEC of AGRoP. In this way Case-assignment is dealt with under the uniform SPEC-head relation in terms of the Checking Theory.

In this paper I seek to account for Korean ECM in terms of the SPEC-head relation by raising the Accusative Case-marked embedded subject to SPEC of the matrix AGRoP, as suggested by Chomsky. I discuss a problem that arises in this approach and suggest how to avoid it, using Watanabe's (1993) Three-Layered Case Theory in the framework of the minimalist approach. It is shown also that this approach can be extended to an account of Case alternation in Korean Periphrastic Causative constructions. I assume that in Korean Tense bears a Nominative Case feature,[7] following Jung (1992) and that the NP-features of Tense and AGR are weak. I also assume that Korean Tense has a strong V-feature which triggers overt verb movement, and that AGR has a weak V-feature.[8]

2. A Problem with Korean ECM Constructions

(1a) is a Korean ECM construction, where the embedded subject is assigned Accusative Case from the matrix verb, which is not a theta-role assigner for it.[9] The Korean ECM construction has an overt complementizer -*tako*,[10] and a tense morpheme in the embedded clause like the non-ECM construction (1b), where the embedded subject bears a Nominative Case marker.

---

[2] Features are divided into "strong" and "weak" features. The distinction between "strong" and "weak" features of functional categories is language-particular and determined by theory-internal considerations. As it turns out, "strong" (Case or agreement) features are (Case or agreement) features which motivate overt syntactic movement of a verb or an NP (DP). "Weak" (Case or agreement) features are (Case or agreement) features which do not motivate overt syntactic movement but only covert LF movement. For instance, AGR of French finite clauses is assumed to have a strong V-feature, which motivates verb raising over NEG in finite clauses, whereas AGR of French infinitival clauses is assumed to have a weak V-feature, which does not motivate verb raising over NEG in infinitival clauses. This distinction between "strong" and "weak" features is no more than a language-particular stipulation now. Chomsky (1993) argues that Tense in English has a strong NP-feature and AGR has weak V-features and NP-features (agreement features), since English subject DPs overtly raise to SPEC of AGRsP, whereas object DPs and main verbs do not overtly raise to SPEC of AGRoP and to AGRs, respectively, as shown in the following examples:

(i) The police have arrested John.
(ii) *The police have John$_i$ arrested t$_i$.
(iii) *has been arrested John.
(iv) John$_i$ has been arrested t$_i$.
(v) *The police arrested$_i$ often t$_i$ John.
(vi) The police have$_i$ often t$_i$ arrested John.

(i), where the object has not overtly moved out of its original object position, is grammatical. (ii) is, however, ungrammatical, since the object has wrongly moved out of the original position. This is taken to indicate that AGR in English has a weak NP-feature which, in fact, does not allow the overt movement of an NP out of its original position. (iii) is ungrammatical, since the subject *John* has not moved to SPEC of AGRsP over Tense. (iv) is grammatical, however, since the subject has overtly moved to SPEC of AGRsP over Tense. This is taken to indicate that Tense has a strong NP-feature which forces the overt movement of the subject out of the VP-internal position. (v) is ungrammatical, since the verb has moved over the adverb to AGRs. The ungrammaticality of (v) is assumed to indicate that AGRs has a weak V-feature, which does not motivate the overt movement of V over the adverb. In (vi) the main verb remains in the original position, but the auxiliary verb has overtly moved crossing the adverb to have its inflectional features checked off against the V-features of Tense and AGR, since auxiliary verbs, which lack semantically-relevant features, are assumed to be invisible to LF rules. If auxiliary verbs have not overtly raised, they will not be able to raise by LF rules and the derivation will crash, since their inflectional features and the V-features of Tense and AGR will remain unchecked.

(1)   a. Mary-ka [$_{CP}$[$_{C'}$ [$_{AGRsP}$ John-ul   cengikha-ess]-tako]]   mit-ess-ta.[11]
          -Nom   -Acc   honest-Past-Comp   believe-Past-Dec
       'Mary believed that John was honest.'

---

[3] SPELL-OUT is a branch point where a copy of a structure derived to that point is sent to PF and the other copy of the structure is sent to LF. No further syntactic operation occurs on the former, whereas further syntactic operations, i.e., movement or feature checking, occur on the latter.

[4] Chomsky (1993) assumed that if strong features are not checked off before SPELL-OUT, they remain at PF, causing the derivation to crash, since they are illegitimate objects at PF. Chomsky (1994), however, suggests that strong features that are not checked off before SPELL-OUT cause the derivation to crash at LF.

[5] Convergence" means "completion of a derivation".

[6] AGRs stands for subject agreement and AGRo, object agreement

[7] Han (1987), Choe (1988), J.-Y. Yoon (1990), and D.-W. Yang (1993) among others assume that Korean (honorific) AGR assigns Nominative Case.

[8] Unlike English, Korean does not show evidence for the overt movement of the subject and object out of their original positions as shown below:

(i)   John-i   cap-hi-ess-ta.
       -Nom   catch-Pass-Past-Dec
       'John was caught.'

(ii)   kyengchal-i   John-ul   cap-ass-ta.
       The police-Nom   -Acc   catch-Past-Dec
       'The police caught John.'

Therefore, I assume that Korean AGRs and AGRo have weak NP-features and that Korean subject and object NPs covertly raise to SPEC of AGRsP and AGRoP at LF, respectively. I assume, however, that Korean Tense has a strong V-feature, considering that Tense triggers overt verb movement across NEG as in the following example:

(iii) *Mary-ka   o-ass-ta   ani.
        -Nom   come-Past-Dec   Neg
       ' Mary did not come.'

(iv)   Mary-ka   ani   o-ass-ta.
       -Nom   Neg   come-Past-Dec
       'Mary did not come.'

b. Mary-ka [$_{CP}$[$_{C'}$ [$_{AGRsP}$ John-i   cengcikha-ess]-tako]] mit-ess-ta.
   -Nom   -Nom   honest-Past-Comp believe-Past-Dec
   'Mary believed that John was honest.'

If the embedded subject of the Korean ECM construction covertly raises to SPEC of the matrix AGRoP—a case of LF movement—to have its Accusative Case checked by the matrix verb, adjoined to the matrix AGRo, as in (2),[12] Korean ECM can be accounted for in terms of the general SPEC-head relation, as is the case with the English ECM construction (Chomsky 1993).

(2)   (LF)   CP
                          |
                          C'
                         / \
                      AGRsP C
                      / \ |
                    NP AGRs' mit-ess$_j$+AGRo+T+AGRs+ta [13]
                    | / \

---

[9] Example (i) shows that ECM is not possible when the embedded predicate is non-stative as observed by K.-H. Lee (1988) among others.

(i)   John-i   [Mary-*lul/ka   Tom-ul   manna-ss-tako]   mit-nun-ta.
      -Nom   -*Acc/Nom   -Acc   meet -Past-Comp believe-Pres-Dec
      'John believes that Mary met Tom.'

(ii) John-i   [Mary-lul/ka   yeyppu-ess-tako]   mit-nun-ta.
      -Nom   -Acc/Nom   pretty-Past-Comp   believe-Pres-Dec
      'John believes that Mary is pretty.'

J.-M. Yoon (1989; 1991) argued that ECM is possible only with stative predicates or with individual-level predicates (Carlson 1977; Diesing 1988; Kratzer 1989), which are associated with the non-temporary characteristic or habitual reading (cf. Yoon & Yoon 1991). I consider this predicate restriction a kind of semantic restriction holding at LF which can rule out even a syntactically convergent ECM construction if it violates the restriction (cf. J.-M. Yoon 1989; 1991). In (i) the embedded predicate is not an individual-level predicate but a stage-level predicate (Carlson 1977; Diesing 1988; Kratzer 1989), which is associated with a temporary event or happening reading. Therefore, it violates the semantic restriction for the ECM construction. Hence, the sentence is ruled out even though its derivation can converge.

[10] -*ko* is a connector and -*ta* is a declarative sentence ending marker, which is considered a mood marker. I consider -*ta-ko* a complex complementizer, following J.-M. Yoon (1991).

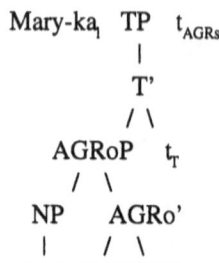

[11] E.-J. Lee (1990) argues against the Control (or Equi-NP deletion) analysis of a sentence like (1), where the Accusative Case-marked NP is base-generated as the matrix object and the embedded subject position is occupied by an empty category coindexed with the matrix object. E.-J. Lee provides the following facts as evidence against the Control analysis. First, passivization of the embedded clause does not change the basic sentence meaning of the ECM construction, whereas it changes the meaning of the Control construction. Second, *nwukwunka* 'someone' can have either a wide or narrow scope in the Korean ECM context, where it occurs as the embedded subject with Accusative Case as in the English ECM context, whereas in the non-ECM context, where *someone* occurs in the matrix clause as in the following example, *someone* has only a wide scope.

I believe of someone [that he was arrested].

Kuno (1976), too, argues against the Control (or Equi-NP deletion) analysis for ECM based on different syntactic behaviors between the Control and ECM Constructions in Japanese. One of his arguments is that the complement clause of the Control verb can be preposed before the NP controller, whereas that of the ECM verb cannot be preposed before the alleged NP controller (J.-S. Lee 1992). J.-S. Lee (1992) makes a similar argument against the Control analysis of the ECM construction. See E.-J. Lee (1990) and J.-S. Lee (1992) for the relevant data and a detailed discussion of the above evidence against the Control analysis of Korean ECM constructions.

[12] I assume that AGRsP dominates TP in Korean in the spirit of Jonas and Bobaljik (1993: 63), who argue that "the AGR heads do not represent the (overt or null) agreement morphemes of a particular language, but rather a collection of abstract morphological features. . .; the inflectional heads in the tree are ordered by UG and do not necessarily correspond to the order of overt "inflectional" morphemes on the lexical elements."

[13] Since the complementizer -*ta* is a verbal suffix, it must be attached to the end of the verb in order not to violate the morphological filter (Lasnik 1981), which bans an affix that is not lexically supported. It can be said that the affixation motivates raising of the verb and INFL complex to C in (2). However, in section 4, I suggest that the complementizer is lowered to be suffixed to the verb in the overt syntax and raises to its original C position for an [F] feature--a feature arising on AGR during the process of Case checking--to be checked off against the C. This will be discussed in more detail in section 4.

```
John-ul_k    VP         t_AGRo
            /  \
           NP   V'
           |   / \
           t_i CP  V
               |   |
               C'  t_j
              / \
         AGRsP   C
         /  \    |
        NP  AGRs'  cengcikha-ess_i+AGRo+T+AGRs+tako
        | / \
        t_k' TP   t_AGRs
             |
             T'
            / \
        AGRoP  t_T
        |
        AGRo'
        / \
       VP  t_AGRo
       / \
      NP  V
      |   |
      t_k t_i
```

However, there is a problem—the embedded subject NP of the Korean ECM construction (1a) cannot raise from SPEC of the embedded AGRsP to SPEC of the matrix AGRoP, because SPEC of the embedded AGRsP is a Case position, where Nominative Case is assigned by the embedded Tense. The covert movement of the embedded subject *John-ul* bearing Accusative Case to SPEC of the matrix AGRoP violates the Chain Condition (Chomsky 1981; 1986),[14] which requires that the tail of a maximal Chain occupy a unique theta position and that the head of the Chain occupy a unique Case-marked position, and violates the Last Resort Principle (Chomsky 1991; 1993; Chomsky and Lasnik 1993), which requires that every unary transformation be a necessary part of making the phrase convergent. When the embedded subject reaches SPEC of the embedded AGRsP, which is a

---

[14] The Chain Condition states:
If C=$(a_1, ---, a_n)$ is a maximal CHAIN, then a_n occupies its unique theta position and a_1 its unique Case-marked position.

Case position, it cannot move to SPEC of the matrix AGRoP, which is another Case position. Therefore, at LF the embedded subject NP must stay in SPEC of the embedded AGRsP. If the embedded subject cannot move to SPEC of the matrix AGRoP, but must stay in SPEC of the embedded AGRsP, the derivation is wrongly predicted to be ungrammatical, because the Accusative Case of the embedded subject does not match the NP-feature, or the Nominative Case feature of the embedded Tense and so cannot be licensed.[15]

A similar problem arises with the way Chomsky (1993) deals with the English ECM construction in (3) under the assumption that infinitival Tense bears a null Case feature, since the embedded subject position is a Case position where null Case is licensed by the infinitival Tense:[16]

(3)   Mary believes [$_{AGRsP}$ him to be honest]
(4)(=3) (Before SPELL-OUT)

   [$_{AGRsP}$ Mary [$_{TP}$ [$_{AGRoP}$ [$_{VP}$ believes [$_{AGRsP}$ him to be honest]]]]]

Due to the Chain Condition and the Last Resort Principle a DP cannot move from the embedded subject position, which is a Case position, to SPEC of the matrix AGRoP, which is another Case position. If the embedded subject DP cannot move to SPEC of the matrix AGRoP, the derivation of the English ECM construction (4)(=3) cannot converge at LF, since the embedded subject cannot have its Accusative Case feature licensed. Thus, Chomsky's (1993) Checking Theory wrongly predicts that the English ECM construction is ungrammatical, contrary to the facts.

To avoid this problem Chomsky (1995) assumes that raising infinitives do not assign null Case, whereas Control infinitives do, as in Martin (1992). Based on Stowell's (1981) distinction between English ECM/Raising constructions and Control constructions, Martin (1992) suggested that the embedded Tense of English ECM and Raising constructions is Tense$_{ECM/raising}$, which bears no null Case, whereas that of English Control constructions is Tense$_{Control}$, which bears null Case. Stowell claims that the embedded clause

---

[15] Ura (1994) claims that an NP can move from a Case position to another Case position. However, adopting this approach does not help, since even if the embedded subject moves to SPEC of the matrix AGRoP and has its Accusative Case feature checked by the matrix verb, the NP-feature of the embedded Tense remains unchecked, which causes the derivation to crash at LF according to the Checking Theory.

[16] Chomsky and Lasnik (1993) suggest that infinitival Tense bears a null Case feature and PRO receives null Case. See Chomsky and Lasnik (1993) for discussion of motivation for this suggestion.

of English Control constructions like (5a) has independent unrealized Tense, whereas the embedded clause of English ECM and Raising constructions like (5b) and (5c) lacks independent Tense and so its Tense interpretation is dependent on the matrix Tense.

(5) a. John convinced his friends [PRO to leave]
b. Bill considers [himself to be the smartest]
c. John appears [t to like poker]
(Watanabe 1993: 66)

This distinction is also linked to the presence or absence of COMP. According to Stowell COMP is assumed to serve as an operator position for Tense, which functions as a propositional operator, similar to a negation operator. Therefore, there is no COMP in the embedded clause of ECM and Raising constructions, since it has no independent Tense, whereas there is COMP in the embedded clause of Control constructions, since it has unrealized Tense.

One might suggest that the embedded Tense of Korean ECM constructions does not have a Nominative Case feature, whereas that of non-ECM constructions does, as in English. However, it is hard to justify that assumption, because no difference is found between Korean ECM and non-ECM constructions except the different Case markers on the embedded subjects. The embedded clause of Korean ECM constructions has finite Tense and (honorific) agreement morphemes as well as an overt complementizer like non-ECM constructions. Therefore, there are no grounds for making a Case feature distinction between the embedded Tense of the Korean ECM construction and that of the non-ECM construction.

If one simply assumes that the embedded Tense of Korean ECM constructions bears an optional Nominative Case feature, it will be hard to make sure that only the Tense of the complement to *mit*-type verbs has an optional Nominative Case feature, because it is unclear if the matrix verb can determine the Case feature of the Tense of the embedded clause.

Therefore, Case-marking on the embedded subject of Korean ECM constructions remains a problem under the Checking Theory.

3. Previous Analyses of Korean ECM Constructions

Yoon & Yoon (1991), J.-M. Yoon (1991), and J.-S. Lee (1992) have claimed that the embedded subject of the Korean ECM construction can raise from SPEC of IP to SPEC of CP to receive Accusative Case from the matrix verb as shown below.[17]

(6)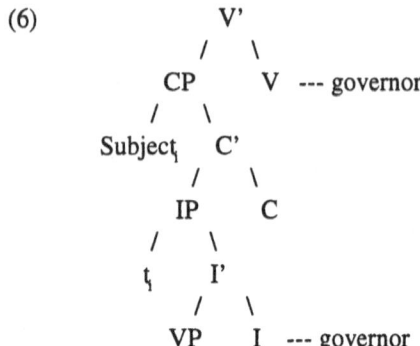

Under the Raising to SPEC of CP analyses suggested by Yoon & Yoon, J.-M. Yoon, and J.-S. Lee the Chain of the ECMed subject is assigned two Cases--Nominative Case from the INFL of the embedded clause and Accusative Case from the matrix verb after raising to SPEC of CP.

J.-S. Lee (1992:78) has argued that double Case-marking on the Chain is not a problem, since the Chain in question is an A'-Chain, which is not subject to the Chain Condition, which describes the property of A-Chains (cf. Massam 1985).

Yoon & Yoon (1991) and J.-M. Yoon (1991) have claimed that "while no single structural position (or link) in a Chain can be ambiguously Case-governed, the Chain as a whole can bear multiple Cases, as long as each link is uniquely governed (Yoon & Yoon 1991:422)." They take sentences like (7) and (8) to be data providing evidence for their claim.

(7) ?ku chayk$_i$-i (motun salam-ey uyhay) [Hemingway-ka t$_i$ ssu-ess-tako]
    that book-Nom all people-by   -Nom write-Past-Comp

sayngkak-toy-n-ta.
think-Pass-Pres-Dec
'*That book is thought (by everybody) that Hemingway wrote t.'

---

[17] Yoon & Yoon (1991) and J.-M. Yoon (1991) take a different position from J.-S. Lee (1992) on the nature of SPEC of CP in Korean. Yoon & Yoon and J.-M. Yoon take the position that SPEC of CP in Korean is an A-position, whereas J.-S. Lee takes the position that it is an A'-position. Thus, under J.-S. Lee's analysis, the ECM movement as in (6) is A'-movement, whereas under Yoon & Yoon and J.-M. Yoon's analyses, it is A-movement. See J.-M. Yoon (1991) for a detailed discussion of the view that SPEC of CP in Korean is an A-position.

(8) Chelswu-eykey-ka paym-i mwusep-ta.
    -Dat-Nom snake-Nom fearful-Dec
    'Chelswu is afraid of snakes.'

They claim that the Chain (*ku chayk*, t) in (7) bears two Cases: the trace of the NP bears Accusative Case assigned from the verb *sse-* 'write' and the head NP bears Nominative Case assigned from the matrix INFL. They assume that *Chelswu* in (8) bears two Cases: Dative Case *-eykey* and Nominative Case *-ka*.

However, there is evidence that A-Chains in Korean should not violate the Chain Condition and the Last Resort Principle (K. Lee 1996). Consider (9). According to Yoon & Yoon (1991) and J.-M. Yoon (1991) the Korean sentences in (9) should be grammatical.

(9) a. *chayk$_i$-i (motun salam-ey uyhay) [Hemingway-ka t$_i$ ssu-ess-tako]
       book-Nom all people-by   -Nom write-Past-Comp

    sayngkak-toy-n-ta.
    think-Pass-Pres-Dec
    '*A book is thought (by everybody) that Hemingway wrote t.'

    b. *chayk$_i$-i [Mary-ka t$_i$ ilhepeli-ess-tako]
       book-Nom   -Nom   lose-Past-Comp

    sayngkak-toy-n-ta.
    think-Pass-Pres-Dec
    '*A book is thought that Mary lost t.'

In (9) *chayk* 'book' is indefinite and the Chain (*chayk*, t) bears two Cases: overt Nominative Case *-i* and abstract Accusative Case. However, sentences like those in (9) are not actually well-formed. The ungrammaticality of these sentences constitutes evidence that A-Chains in Korean cannot bear multiple Cases, contrary to the claim by Yoon & Yoon (1991) and J.-M. Yoon (1991).

Yoon & Yoon (1991) and J.-M. Yoon (1991) assume that *-eykey* in sentences like (8) is a Dative Case marker and that the Dative Case marker can cooccur with Nominative or Accusative Case, even though Nominative and Accusative Cases cannot cooccur with each other. However, it is possible to analyze *-eykey* as a postposition rather than a Dative Case marker as argued in Kuh (1987) and Urushibara (1991). Therefore, so-called Case stacking may not be real Case stacking.

The grammaticality of sentences like (7) and (10), which is the counterpart of (9b) with a medial demonstrative marker *ku*, may appear to raise a problem if we assume that a Korean A-Chain cannot bear two Cases.

(10) ?ku chayk$_i$-i [Mary-ka t$_i$ ilhepeli-ess-tako] sayngkak-toy-n-ta.
      that book-Nom -Nom lose-Past-Comp think-Pass-Pres-Dec
      '*That book is thought that Mary lost t.'

However, there is no problem in accounting for the grammaticality of the sentences. (7) and (10) can be accounted for if we assume that the definite NP *ku chayk* 'that book' with a demonstrative bears not a Nominative Case marker but a focus marker -*i* and the NP has not moved from the embedded object position to the matrix subject position where Nominative Case is assigned, but occurs in an A'-position for a focus/topic element, adjoining to the matrix AGRsP as in (11), where the NP with a topic marker occurs in an A'-position.[18]

(11) a. ku chayk$_j$-un (motun salam-ey uyhay) [Hemingway-ka
      that book-Top all people-by -Nom

---

[18] I assume that Korean topics are base-generated, adjoining to IP (AGRsP), following Cho (1988) (cf. Baltin 1982). Kang (1986) argues that Korean topics are base-generated in an A'-position outside of S' based on the evidence that Korean topic constructions allow for resumptive pronouns and violate CNPC and Subjacency. He argues that the gap in the Korean Topic construction is a base-generated empty pronoun. Moon (1989) argues, too, that in Korean Topic constructions with a gap in the subject or object position the topic is base-generated in SPEC of CP and the coreferential null subject or object is *pro*, which is identified by the sentential topic in SPEC of CP. Similarly to Kang, she takes the fact that there is no Subjacency violation with *wh*-extraction from *wh*-islands in Topic constructions with a gap and that a resumptive pronoun can occur in the position of gaps to be evidence that sentential topics are base-generated in SPEC of CP. Y.-S. Kim (1988) argues, however, that Korean topics do not occur in SPEC of CP, based on the fact that *wh*-phrases have a wider scope than topics in constructions with both a *wh*-phrase and a topic. She suggested a different analysis of Korean Topic constructions, assuming the VP-internal subject hypothesis. She suggested that in Korean Topic constructions with an object gap, movement occurs: the object moves to SPEC of IP; in Topic constructions with a subject gap the subject remains in SPEC of VP. Whether one assumes the base-generation approach like Kang and Moon among others or the movement approach for Korean Topicalization, *ku chayk-i* 'that book-Foc' in (7) and (10) will occur in an A'-position and it will not bear two Cases under my analysis of *ku chayk-i* 'that book-Foc' as a topic-like focused element.

e$_i$ ssu-ess -tako]   sayngkak-toy-n-ta.
write-Past-Comp think-Pass-Pres-Dec
'*That book is thought (by everybody) that Hemingway wrote t.'

b. ku chayk$_i$-un [Mary-ka   e$_i$ ilhepeli-ess-tako] sayngkak-toy-n-ta.
that book-Top   -Nom   lose-Past-Comp   think-Pass-Pres-Dec
'*That book is thought that Mary lost t.'

This analysis is reasonable, since the definite NP *ku chayk-i* 'that book-Foc' in (7) and (10) has a functional role to set the domain within which the comment or predication holds (cf. I.-H. Lee 1987; H.-S. J. Yoon 1987; Cho 1988) as in (11a) and (11b).[19] If the NP functions as a discourse topic in an A'-position, the Chain of the NP will not bear two Cases, and hence will not involve a Chain Condition violation as in (11a) and (11b). However, the indefinite NP *chayk* 'book' in (9a) and (9b) can't be analyzed as a topic-like element because only definite or generic nouns can be topics (Kuno 1972; Gundel 1974; Li and Thompson 1976; Schachter 1976; Bak 1977; Fuller 1985; Moon 1989). This way both the grammaticality of (7) and (10) and ungrammaticality of (9a) and (9b) can be accounted for under the assumption that an NP cannot move from a Case position to another Case position (cf. Watanabe 1993).[20]

However, the ungrammaticality of (9a) and (9b) can hardly be accounted for under the assumption that an NP can move from a Case position to another Case position, as suggested by Yoon & Yoon (1991) and J.-M. Yoon (1991). This indicates that Korean A-Chains cannot bear multiple Cases. Therefore, it is hard to justify their analyses of Korean ECM

---

[19] In (7) and (10) a resumptive pronoun can occur in the position of the empty category coreferential with the topic as shown below:

(i) ? ku   chayk$_i$-i [Hemingway-ka   *kukes$_i$*-ul   ssu-ess-tako]   sayngkak-toy-n-ta
       that book-Foc   -Nom it-Acc   write-Past-Comp   think-Pass-Pres-Dec
'*That book is thought (by everybody) that Hemingway wrote it'

(ii) ? ku   chayk$_i$-i [Mary-ka   *kukes$_i$*-ul ilhepeli- ess-tako]   sayngkak-toy-n-ta.
       that book-Foc   -Nom it-Acc   lose -Past-Comp   think-Pass-Pres-Dec
'*That book is thought that Mary lost it.'

If Kang (1986) and Moon (1989) are right, (i) and (ii) provide a piece of evidence that *ku chayk* 'that book' in (7) and (10) functions as topic.

[20] J.-S. Lee (1992) argues that the null expletive occurs in Korean. Based on this argument I assume that the null expletive occurs in the matrix subject position of (7) and (10).

constructions based on the assumption that Korean A-Chains can bear multiple Cases.

Another problem with the Raising to SPEC of CP analysis is that it cannot account for why ECM is impossible in the non-ECM constructions as exemplified in (12):

(12) a. Mary-nun [$_{CP}$[$_{C'}$ [$_{IP}$ namphyen-i   nappu-ass]-tako]] kopaykha-ess-ta.
      -Top   husband-Nom bad-Past-Comp   confess-Past-Dec
    'Mary confessed that her husband was bad.'

   b. *Mary-nun [$_{CP}$[$_{C'}$ [$_{IP}$ namphyen-ul   nappu-ass]-tako]] kopaykha-ess-ta
      -Top   husband-Acc bad-Past -Comp confess-Past-Dec
    'Mary confessed that her husband was bad.'

According to the Raising to SPEC of CP analyses suggested by Yoon & Yoon (1991), J.-M. Yoon (1991), and J.-S. Lee (1992) the embedded subject of (12b) should be able to raise to SPEC of CP and receive Accusative Case, because there is nothing to prevent it from raising to SPEC of CP and receiving Accusative Case in their framework. However, this is not borne out. The embedded subject of (12b) cannot bear Accusative Case.

A common problem with all the above-mentioned previous analyses is that they assume an exceptional syntactic configuration for ECM, where there is no SPEC-head or head-complement relation under which ordinary Nominative and Accusative Case-marking occurs.

4. An Alternative Account
4.1. Three-Layered Case Theory

To solve the problem discussed in the previous sections, I will suggest another way to deal with Case alternation in the Korean ECM construction, using Watanabe's (1993) Three-Layered Case Theory in the framework of the minimalist approach (Chomsky 1993).

Watanabe (1993) proposed a Three-Layered Case Theory, arguing that a new feature [F] is created on AGR during the process of Case checking and the [F] feature can be checked off only by a higher functional category.[21] In the Three-Layered Case Theory, Case positions are defined as in (13):

(13)   *a* is a Case position iff the maximal projection HP of which *a* is SPEC is a sister to an appropriate [F] feature checker, where the head of HP has a Case- bearing head adjoining to it. (Watanabe 1993: 76)

In the Three-Layered Case Theory not all SPEC positions of AGRP are Case positions. Only the SPEC position of an AGRP which is a sister to a functional head can be a Case position. To avoid a crash at LF, a derivation must have a configuration as shown in (14), where X is a functional head bearing a Case feature and Y an appropriate checker of an [F] feature created on AGR (Watanabe 1993: 56).

(14)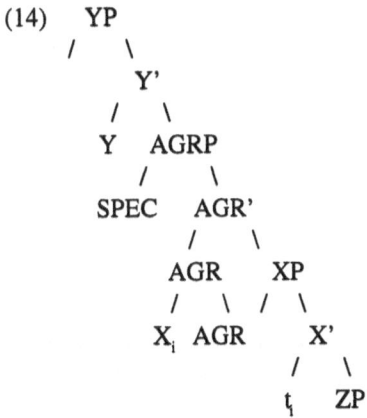

Now, let us think of how the Three-Layered Case Theory deals with English ECM constructions. In this theory the SPEC position of the embedded AGRsP in an English ECM construction is not a Case position, because there is no functional head in a sister relation to AGRsP of the embedded clause of the English ECM construction, unlike a Control construction.[21]

(15) a. Mary believes [$_{AGRsP}$ him to be honest]
      b. *Mary believes [$_{AGRsP}$ PRO to be honest]

(16) a. Mary tried [$_{CP}$ e [$_{AGRsP}$ PRO to be honest]]
      b. *Mary tried [$_{CP}$ e [$_{AGRsP}$ him to be honest]]

In (15a) the embedded subject *him* moves to SPEC of the matrix AGRoP at LF for Case checking, since English AGRo is assumed to have a weak NP-feature, and is licensed by the Accusative Case feature of the matrix verb. In (15b) PRO can't have its null Case licensed,[22] since SPEC of the embedded AGRsP is not a Case position. Hence, the sentence is

---

[22] In the English Control construction SPEC of the embedded AGRsP is a Case position, because there is a functional head C in a sister relation to the embedded AGRsP which can check off the [F] feature arising on the embedded AGRs during the process of Case checking.

ungrammatical. In (16a) SPEC of the embedded AGRsP is a Case position, because there is a functional head C in a sister relation to the embedded AGRsP of the Control construction. Therefore, Case checking occurs in SPEC of the embedded AGRsP. (16a) is grammatical, since the null Case of PRO matches the null Case feature of the infinitival Tense. However, in (16b) the Case feature of the embedded subject *him* does not match the NP-feature of the infinitival Tense, since *him* does not bear null Case, whereas the infinitival Tense bears a null Case feature. This is why (16b) is ungrammatical. This is how the Three-Layered Case theory works.

4.2. Proposal

In this section, I will show how Korean ECM constructions can be accounted for in terms of the Three-Layered Case Theory. Unlike its English counterpart the Korean ECM construction has CP in the embedded clause.

(17) a. Mary-ka [$_{CP}$[$_{C'}$ [$_{AGRsP}$ John-ul cengcikha-ess]-tako]] mit-ess-ta.
 -Nom -Acc honest- Past -Comp believe- Past-Dec
 'Mary believed that John was honest.'
 b. Mary believed [$_{AGRsP}$ him to be honest]

Therefore, according to Watanabe's theory, the SPEC position of the embedded AGRsP of the Korean ECM construction should be a Case position, since in the Korean ECM construction there is a functional head C that can check off an [F] feature arising on AGRs during the process of Case checking in SPEC of AGRsP. If SPEC of the embedded AGRsP of the Korean ECM construction is a Case position, the Three-Layered Case Theory will wrongly predict that the Korean ECM construction is ungrammatical, contrary to the fact, since the Accusative Case feature of the embedded subject NP does not match the NP-feature (Nominative Case feature) of the embedded Tense.

To solve this problem I suggest that the complementizer node selected by bridge verbs like *mit-* 'believe' has no semantic feature and so can be deleted,[23] whereas the complementizer node selected by non-bridge verbs has semantic features like a factive or noun feature and so cannot be deleted.

---

[23] According to Chomsky and Lasnik (1993) PRO receives null Case from the infinitival Tense.

This suggestion is based on the arguments of the different semantic contents of different complementizer systems by Iatridou (1991) and Hegarty (1991a; 1991b; 1992) (cf. Progovac 1988; Laka 1990; Melvold 1991).

Iatridou (1991) argues that complementizer nodes show differences in syntactic licensing of CP recursion, depending on whether they have semantic content or not. Iatridou considers conditionals with *then* in English or *dan(n)* in Dutch (German) to be of category CP as in (18), with the *if*-clause adjoined to CP.

(18)
```
           CP
          /  \
        if... CP
             /  \
           then  C'
                /  \
               C   consequent
```

When the conditional CP occurs as a clausal complement, CP recursion is yielded, as in (19).

(19) We all believe [$_{CP}$ that [$_{CP}$ if it rains then the party will be canceled]]

Iatridou argues, however, that when *then* is absent, then the conditional is of category IP, with the *if*-clause simply adjoined to IP, and then no CP recursion occurs in the complementation of the conditional. Iatridou argues that the complementizer node in an L-marked CP with no semantic content or feature specification beyond that of an ordinary affirmative complementizer can embed a conditional with *then*, allowing CP recursion as in (20a), whereas the complementizer node with semantic content or feature specification beyond that of an ordinary affirmative complementizer cannot embed a conditional with *then*, as in (20a), but it can embed a conditional without *then*, as in (20b).

---

[24] Chomsky (1981) stipulates that verbs such as *believe, consider*, etc., called bridge verbs, have an idiosyncratic lexical property of triggering S' (CP)-deletion for governing and Case-marking the subject of the embedded infinitival clause.

(20)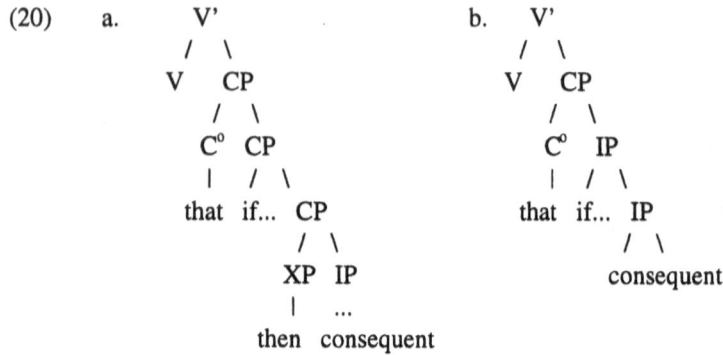

The complementizer node that can embed a conditional with *then* as in (20a) must have no semantic content so that the verb can license the lower CP. Bridge verbs like *believe* select the complementizer node that has no semantic content or feature specification beyond that of an ordinary affirmative complementizer, allowing CP recursion with the complementation of the conditional with *then* as in (20a), whereas verbs whose complements express factive content or negative verbs select the complementizer node that has a semantic content or a feature specification beyond that of an ordinary affirmative complementizer, disallowing the CP recursion structure in (20a) (cf. Hegarty 1992).

Melvold (1991) and Hegarty (1991a; 1991b; 1992) account for the difference in *wh*-adjunct extraction out of propositional complement clauses and factive complement clauses in terms of the presence or absence of semantic or feature content in the complementizer system of the complement clause. Melvold argues that in the SPEC of the CP of the factive complement clauses a factive null operator is present, blocking adjunct extraction, whereas in the SPEC of the CP of the propositional complement clauses there is no null operator, allowing adjunct extraction. Hegarty argues that *wh*-adjunct extraction out of complement clauses is sensitive to the semantic or feature content of the complementizer itself.

These arguments suggest that all complementizers are not of the same kind. The complementizer selected by bridge verbs like *believe* has no semantic content, whereas the complementizer selected by factive verbs like *forget* has semantic content or a feature specification beyond that of the ordinary affirmative complementizer. I assume, based on the arguments of Iatridou (1991) and Hegarty (1991a; 1991b; 1992), that the complementizer -*tako* selected by Korean bridge verbs has no semantic content or feature, whereas the complementizers -*tako*, -*um*, etc. selected by Korean factive verbs have a factive feature.[24] I also assume that the complementizers -*um* and -*ki*, which head nominal constructions,[25] allowing for the attachment of the Nominative or Accusative Case marker, have a noun feature, whereas -*tako*, which does not allow for the attachment of the Case markers, has no noun feature (cf. H.-J. Yoon 1991; Jung 1992).[26]

The following Korean examples show that the subjects of the embedded clauses in Korean cannot bear an Accusative Case marker when the complementizers have a factive or noun feature.

(21) a. Mary-nun namphyen-i/ul cengcikha-ess -tako sayngkakha-ess-ta.
    -Top husband-Nom/Acc honest-Past-Comp think-Past-Dec
    'Mary thought that her husband was honest.'

  b. Mary-nun namphyen-i/*ul aphu-ass-tako kopaykha-ess-ta.
    -Top husband-Nom/*Acc sick-Past-Comp confess-Past-Dec
    'Mary confessed that her husband was sick.'

  c. Mary-nun namphyen-i/*ul aphu-ass-um-ul ic-ess-ta.
    -Top husband-Nom/*Acc sick-Past-Comp-Acc forget-Past-Dec
    'Mary forgot that her husband was sick.'

  d. Mary-nun namphyen-i/*ul kenkangha-ki-lul pala-ss-ta.
    -Top husband-Nom/*Acc healthy-Comp-Acc wish-Past-Dec
    'Mary wished that her husband would be healthy.'

The complementizer -*tako* in (21a), which has no noun feature, heads the non-factive complement. Therefore, it is assumed to have neither a noun nor a factive feature. The complementizer -*tako* in (21b) heads the factive complement clause. Therefore, the complementizer is assumed to have a factive feature. The complementizer -*um* in (21c), which has a noun feature,

---

[25] Bridge verbs are verbs like *mit*- 'believe' and *sayngkakha*- 'think'. Factive verbs are verbs like *kopaykha*- 'confess' and *ic*- 'forget'. The factive verb *ic*- 'forget' can select -*um*, but not -*tako*, whereas the factive verb *kopaykha*- 'confess' can select either -*tako* or -*um*.

[26] The constructions ending with the morphemes -*ki* and -*um* have been considered to be nominal constructions which have sentential structures internally (cf. H.-B. Lee 1970; I.-S. Yang 1972; N.-K. Kim 1974; S.-W. Lee 1983; H.-J. Yoon 1991; Jung 1992 among others). There has been considerable controversy over the status of -*um* and -*ki*. Some (cf. N.-K. Kim 1974 among others) have argued that they are sentential nominalizers and others (cf. I.-S. Yang 1972; S.-W. Lee 1983; H.-J. Yoon 1991; Jung 1992 among others) have argued that they are complementizers. I assume that -*um* and -*ki* are complementizers.

[27] H.-J. Yoon (1991) argues that when the complementizer of an embedded clause bears a factive feature, *wh*-adjunct extraction is not available, whereas *wh*-adjunct extraction is possible when the embedded complementizer lacks a factive feature.

heads the factive complement clause. Therefore, it is assumed to have both a noun and a factive feature. The complementizer -*ki* in (21d), which has a noun feature, heads the non-factive complement clause. Therefore, it is assumed to have only a noun feature. An Accusative Case marker on the embedded subject is possible only when the complementizer has no semantic content or feature. I take this fact to indicate that the complementizer node that has a semantic content or feature is present through the derivation and blocks ECM, whereas the complementizer node that has no semantic content can be deleted with the CP and so does not block ECM for the embedded subject.[27] Under this suggestion a mismatch does not arise between the embedded subject bearing an Accusative Case feature and the Nominative Case feature of the embedded Tense in the Korean ECM construction (17a), since if the CP of the embedded clause is deleted, SPEC of the embedded AGRsP cannot be a Case position according to the definition of the Case position in (13), repeated here as (22).

(22)   *a* is a Case position iff the maximal projection HP of which *a* is SPEC is a sister to an appropriate [F] feature checker, where the head of HP has a Case-bearing head adjoining to it.
(Watanabe 1993: 76)

Then our problem is solved. But one remaining problem is to explain how the CP can be deleted when there is a complementizer in the COMP position.
    J.-M. Yoon (1989; 1991) has claimed that it is impossible for CP to be deleted in Korean ECM constructions, since the complementizer is present (cf. J.-Y. Yoon 1990). One solution to the problem is COMP-lowering. Hong (1985: 46) argued that "the Korean complementizer is always cliticized

---

[28] Due to the Full Interpretation Principle (Chomsky 1986; cf. Chomsky 1993), which requires that every element of a structure at PF and LF must receive an appropriate interpretation, illegitimate PF or LF objects that lack appropriate phonetic or semantic contents should not be present at PF or LF. If they are present, the derivation crashes at PF or LF. Thus, the complementizer node that has no semantic content should not be visible at LF. One way to achieve this is to delete the complementizer node after COMP-lowering before Case checking occurs in SPEC of the embedded AGRsP. Another way is to raise the V-T-AGR complex together with the lowered COMP to the original C position after Nominative Case checking in SPEC of the AGRsP. This raising is motivated by the need to have the [F] feature, created on AGR during the process of Case checking, checked off by the complementizer node. After the raising of the COMP and V-T-AGR complex to the C position, the complementizer node cannot be deleted due to the presence of the V-T-AGR complex in the complementizer node and the selectional relationship between the matrix verb and the form of the overt complementizer.

to the verb", because Korean complementizers are not free morphemes but bound morphemes which can be used only when attached to the end of verbs (cf. Yim 1988). Based on Lasnik's (1981) morphological filter banning an affix which is not lexically supported, I will assume that the complementizer in Korean ECM constructions is lowered to the INFL position and attached to the end of the verb of the lower clause when that verb raises to the INFL position. In this I agree with Hong (1985), even though I disagree with her on how to account for Case-marking in Korean ECM constructions.[28]

J.-S. Lee (1992: 17) made a claim against CP-deletion, saying that it is not clear if the trace of COMP can be deleted after COMP-lowering because of the general selectional restriction between the matrix verb and the embedded COMP. However, there is no problem with the selectional restriction even though the trace of COMP is deleted with CP, because the complementizer -*tako* itself is not deleted.

Therefore, I will maintain the CP-deletion approach in accounting for Case- marking in Korean ECM constructions, based on the Three-Layered Case Theory in the spirit of the minimalist approach. One might wonder why a Korean complementizer–which is realized as a verbal suffix—is base-generated in the COMP position and then lowered, whereas other verbal inflectional features such as AGR and Tense are attached to a verb and *raised* with the verb. The reason is that a complementizer is not a verbal feature, whereas other inflectional features like AGR and Tense are verbal features (Chomsky and Lasnik 1993).

Let us see how the Korean ECM construction can be accounted for under this alternative approach. (23) shows the derivational steps for the Korean ECM construction (17a).

(23) a. (Underlyingly)
 $[_{CP} [_{AGRsP} [_{TP} [_{AGRoP} [_{VP} \text{Mary-ka} [_{CP} [_{AGRsP} [_{TP} [_{AGRoP} [_{VP} \text{John-ul}$ cengcikha-ess]]]] -tako] mit-ess]]]] -ta]

---

[29] Hong (1985) suggested that S' (CP)-deletion optionally applies at S-structure in the Korean ECM construction after complementizer cliticization to account for Case alternation between Nominative Case and Accusative Case of the embedded subject in constructions like (17a). She also suggested that Korean AGR is an optional Nominative Case-assigner. However, a problem with this suggestion is that Accusative Case-marking on the embedded subject occurs in an exceptional syntactic relation different from that for Nominative and ordinary Accusative Case-marking. Another problem is the ad hoc stipulation of S'-deletion by Korean bridge verbs.

b. (Before SPELL-OUT)

[$_{CP}$ [$_{AGRsP}$ [$_{TP}$ [$_{AGRoP}$ [$_{VP}$ Mary-ka [$_{CP}$ [$_{AGRsP}$ [$_{TP}$ [$_{AGRoP}$ [$_{VP}$ John-ul t_i]] cengcikha-ess$_i$+AGRo +T+ AGRs +tako$_k$]] t_k] t_j]] mit-ess$_j$ +AGRo +T+AGRs +ta]] t_i]

'Mary believed that John was honest.'

c. (LF)

```
                    CP
                    │
                    C'
                   / \
              AGRsP   C
              / \     │
            NP  AGRs' mit-ess_j+AGRo+T+AGRs+ta
            │   / \
       Mary-ka_i TP  t_AGRs
                │
                T'
               / \
          AGRoP   t_T
          / \
        NP   AGRo'
        │    / \
   John-ul_k VP  t_AGRo
            / \
          NP   V'
          │   / \
         t_i AGRsP V
             / \    │
           NP  AGRs' t_j
           │   / \
          t_k' TP  AGRs
               │    │
               T'  cengcik-ha-ess_i +AGRo+T+AGRs+tako
              / \
         AGRoP   t_T
          │
         AGRo'
         / \
        VP  t_AGRo
        / \
```

```
NP      V
 |      |
 t_k    t_i
```

If the CP of the embedded clause of an ECM construction is deleted, SPEC of the embedded AGRsP in the ECM construction cannot be a Case position under the Three-Layered Case Theory, since there is no functional head in a sister relation to the embedded AGRsP which can check off an [F] feature arising on the embedded AGRs during the process of Case checking. Therefore, the embedded subject of the ECM construction (17a) will not be checked in SPEC of the embedded AGRsP. It has to move to SPEC of the matrix AGRoP, where it is checked against the NP-feature (Accusative Case feature) of the matrix verb. Since its Accusative Case feature matches the NP-feature (Accusative Case feature) of the matrix verb, it is licensed. Therefore, the derivation converges at LF. In this way Case-marking in Korean ECM constructions can be accounted for, avoiding problems pointed out earlier.

Next, let us consider how Nominative Case can be licensed on the subject of the complement clause of bridge verbs like *mit-* 'believe' in Korean. If the COMP is lowered and the complementizer node selected by the bridge verb is deleted due to the lack of semantic content, SPEC of the embedded AGRsP is not a Case position according to the definition of the Case position (22) under the Three-Layered Case Theory, even though the embedded Tense bears a Nominative Case feature. Therefore, in that case, Nominative Case cannot be licensed on the embedded subject. The COMP position must be present for Nominative Case checking to occur in SPEC of the AGRsP of embedded clauses under the Three-Layered Case Theory.

There is no problem, however, in licensing Nominative Case to the embedded subject, since the complementizer node does not have to be deleted, because the lowered COMP can raise to its original position when the embedded subject bears a Nominative Case feature. If the COMP lowered to the verb raises back to the original COMP position together with the V-T-AGR complex in order to have the [F] feature created on AGRs checked off, the complementizer node filled with the complementizer cannot be deleted due to the selectional relationship between the matrix verb and the form of the overt complementizer of the embedded clause and because of the presence of V-T-AGR in the complementizer node. In this case, SPEC of the embedded AGRsP can be a Case position according to the definition of a Case position (22). No Case conflict arises between the Nominative Case feature of the embedded subject and the NP-feature of the embedded Tense during the process of Case checking. The [F] feature on AGR can be checked off by the functional head C. Therefore, all the relevant features are properly checked off and so the derivation converges at LF.

5. Extension to an Account of Case Alternation in Korean Periphrastic Causative Constructions

The present approach can be extended to an account of Case alternation in Korean Periphrastic Causative constructions. Consider the examples in (24).

(24) a. John-i [Mary-lul/ka hakkyo-ey ka-key]   ha-ess-ta.
 -Nom -Acc/Nom school-to go-Comp do (CAUSE)-Past-Dec
 'John made Mary go to school.'

 b. John-i [Mary-lul/ka chayk-ul ilk-key]   ha-ess-ta.
 -Nom -Acc/Nom book-Acc read-Comp do (CAUSE)-Past-Dec
 'John made Mary read the book.'
 (J.-S. Lee 1992: 88)

In (24) the embedded subject NP *Mary* can have either Accusative or Nominative Case.

I agree with J.-S. Lee (1992) in considering that Korean Periphrastic Causative constructions have bi-clausal structures, even though I disagree with him on how Case alternation occurs in the constructions.[29] I suggest that the complementizer node for the complementizer -*key* selected by the matrix verb *ha-* 'do' in the Periphrastic Causative construction lacks a factive or noun feature and so it can be deleted. With this suggestion, Case alternation in Periphrastic Causative constructions can be accounted for straightforwardly in the same way as in Korean ECM constructions. Consider the version of (24) where the embedded subject bears an Accusative Case feature. In (24) the Accusative Case feature of the embedded subject NPs does not match the NP-feature (Nominative Case feature) of Tense in the embedded clauses. However, the complementizer node of the embedded clause can be deleted after COMP-lowering. After that, SPEC of the embedded

---

[30] J.-S. Lee (1992) suggested that the embedded subject of Periphrastic Causative constructions raises to SPEC of CP to receive Accusative Case from the matrix verb. J.-S. Lee's analysis adequately accounts for the way in which the embedded subject of Korean Periphrastic Causative constructions can be assigned Accusative Case. However, under his approach Accusative Case-marking on the embedded subject is exceptional, since it occurs in a configuration different from that for Nominative and ordinary Accusative Case-marking. See J.-S. Lee (1992) for a detailed discussion of his account of Case-marking in Korean Periphrastic Causative constructions.

AGRsP is not a Case position any longer. Therefore, the embedded subject with an Accusative Case feature moves to SPEC of the matrix AGRoP for Case checking. Since the matrix AGRoP is a sister to Tense, which is a functional head that can check off an [F] feature arising on AGRo during the process of Case checking, SPEC of the matrix AGRoP is a Case position according to the Three-Layered Case Theory. The Accusative Case feature of the embedded subject NP matches the NP-feature of the matrix verb and so it is licensed at SPEC of the matrix AGRoP.

If the complementizer node is not deleted, SPEC of the embedded AGRsP becomes a Case position where the embedded subject bearing a Nominative Case feature can have its Case feature checked by the NP-feature of the embedded Tense. This way Case alternation on the embedded subject position of the Periphrastic Causative construction can be accounted for.

There are cases, however, where the embedded subject NP can have only Accusative Case in Korean Periphrastic Causative constructions, as exemplified in (25).

(25) a. John-i [Mary-lul/*ka yeyppu-key] ha-ess-ta.
  -Nom -Acc/*Nom pretty-Comp do (CAUSE)-Past-Dec
  'John caused Mary to be pretty.'

  b. John-i [pang-ul/*i nelp-key] ha-ess-ta
  -Nom room-Acc/*Nom wide-Comp do (CAUSE)-Past-Dec
  'John caused the room to be wide.'
  (J.-S. Lee 1992: 88)

J.-S. Lee (1992) observed a correlation between the embedded predicate in the Periphrastic Causative constructions and the appearance of the AGR element -*si*, which is an honorific verbal suffix: no AGR element can show up in the embedded clause when the embedded predicate is not a Case-assigner as in (26); whereas an AGR element *can* show up in the embedded clause when the embedded predicate is a Case-assigner or a potential Case-assigner as in (27).

(26) a. John-i [emeni-lul/*ka alumtap (-?*si) -key]
  -Nom mother Acc/*Nom pretty-?*Hon -Comp

  ha-ess-ta.
  do (CAUSE)-Past-Dec
  'John caused mother to be beautiful.'

b. John-i [apeci-lul/*ka   sulphu (-?*si) -key]
   -Nom   father-Acc/*Nom sad-?*Hon   -Comp

   ha-ess-ta.
   do (CAUSE)-Past-Dec
   'John caused father to be sad.'

c. John-i [sensayngnim-ul/*i cap-hi (-?*si) -key]
   -Nom   teacher-Acc/*Nom catch-Pass-?*Hon- Comp

   ha-ess-ta.
   do (CAUSE)-Past-Dec
   'John caused the teacher to be caught.'
              (J.-S. Lee 1992: 113)

(27) a. John-i [apeci-lul/ka   (hakkyo-lul) ka-si-key]
        -Nom   father-Acc/Nom school-Acc go-Hon-Comp

   ha-ess-ta.
   do (CAUSE)-Past-Dec
   'John caused father to go to school.'

b. John-i [sensayngnim-ul/i chayk-ul ilku-si -key]
   -Nom   teacher-Acc/Nom book-Acc read-Hon-Comp

   ha-ess-ta.
   do (CAUSE)-Past-Dec
   'John caused the teacher to read the book.'
              (J.-S. Lee 1992: 112)

I suggest in agreement with J.-S. Lee that the reason that the embedded subjects in (25) cannot bear Nominative Case is that the embedded clauses in (25) lack AGRs, since the embedded predicates in (25) are not Case-assigners as in (26). However, my account differs from J.-S. Lee's (1992). J.-S. Lee assumes that AGR is a Nominative Case-assigner and so the embedded subjects in (25) cannot be assigned Nominative Case, since there is no AGR in the embedded clauses of (25). I assume, however, that Tense bears a Nominative Case feature and that Case checking occurs in SPEC of AGRP only via mediation of AGR in Korean. With this suggestion we can account for why Nominative Case is impossible and only Accusative Case is possible for the embedded subjects in (25a) and (25b). Suppose that the embedded subjects have a Nominative Case feature as shown in (28).

(28) a. *John-i [$_{CP}$ [$_{TP}$ [$_{VP}$ Mary-ka yeyppu-key]]] ha-ess-ta.
   -Nom   -Nom pretty -Comp   do (CAUSE)-Past-Dec
   'John caused Mary to be pretty.'

   b. *John-i [$_{CP}$ [$_{TP}$ [$_{VP}$ pang-i   nelp-key]]] ha-ess-ta.
   -Nom   room-Nom wide-Comp   do (CAUSE)-Past-Dec
   'John caused the room to be wide.'

Since the embedded clauses lack AGRs in (28), there is no Case position in these clauses where the embedded subject NPs can have their Nominative Case feature checked, even though these clauses have Tense that bears a Nominative Case feature. Therefore, the derivations crash at LF. The embedded subjects in (28) cannot raise to SPEC of the matrix AGRsP even if Korean Tense is assumed to bear multiple Nominative Case features, since they cannot skip SPEC of the matrix AGRoP, which is another Case position, due to the Shortest Move Principle (Chomsky 1993; Chomsky and Lasnik 1993; cf. Rizzi 1990), which prohibits an element from skipping over another element of the same kind. If the embedded subjects in (28) stop at SPEC of the matrix AGRoP, a mismatch in Case features between the embedded subjects and the matrix verbs cause the derivations to crash. However, when the embedded subject has an Accusative Case feature as shown in (25), the embedded subject NP moves to SPEC of the matrix AGRoP at LF, where it can have its Accusative Case feature checked against the Accusative Case feature of the matrix verb. After CP-deletion the LF representation of (25a) looks like (29).[30]

(29)

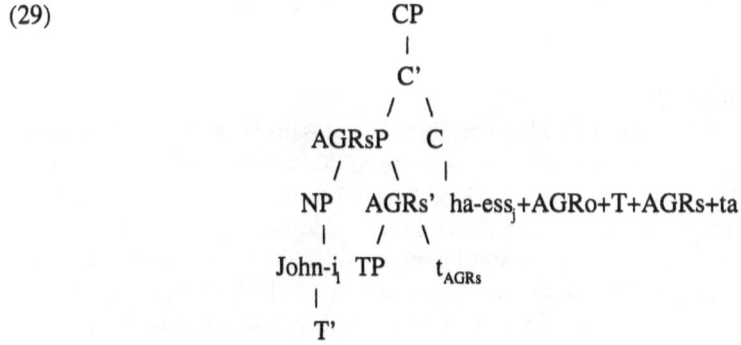

[31] The complementizer node is deleted with CP due to the Full Interpretation Principle, since it lacks a semantic feature like a factive or noun feature. The option of the V-T-C complex raising to the COMP position does not take place in this case, since there is no [F] feature arising on embedded AGRs because of the absence of AGRs in the embedded clause.

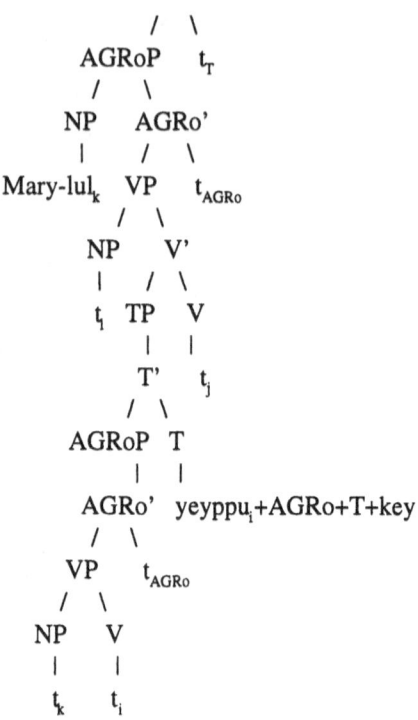

The NP-feature of the embedded Tense transfers to the embedded AGRo that adjoins to it and deletes with this AGRo at LF (cf. Watanabe 1993). Therefore it does not cause the derivation to crash at LF. Hence, the derivation can converge at LF.

6. Conclusion

Chomsky (1993) suggests that the Accusative Case-marked embedded subject of ECM constructions raises to SPEC of the matrix AGRoP so that ECM can fall in the general SPEC-head relation. However, this suggestion is not extended to Korean ECM directly due to a violation of the Chain Condition and the Last Resort Principle, since the raising of the embedded subject from SPEC of the embedded AGRsP to SPEC of the matrix AGRoP is a movement from a Case position to another Case position, which is not allowed in Korean.

Watanabe's (1993) Three-Layered Case Theory cannot deal with Korean ECM straightforwardly either. Watanabe's theory predicts that SPEC of the embedded AGRsP of the Korean ECM construction is a Nominative Case position due to the presence of an overt complementizer in the embedded

CP. Therefore, under his theory the embedded subject with an Accusative Case feature cannot move to SPEC of the matrix AGRoP without violating the Chain Condition and the Last Resort Principle. If the embedded subject bearing an Accusative Case feature stays at SPEC of the embedded AGRsP where Nominative Case is licensed, the derivation crashes due to a mismatch in Case features. Therefore, Watanabe's theory wrongly predicts that the Korean ECM construction is ungrammatical.

To avoid this problem I have suggested that CP-deletion occurs after COMP-lowering in Korean ECM constructions due to the lack of the semantic content of the complementizer node selected by Korean bridge verbs. After CP-deletion SPEC of the embedded AGRsP of the Korean ECM construction is no longer a Case position according to the Three-Layered Case Theory. I have argued that with this suggestion it is possible for the embedded subject of the Korean ECM construction to raise to SPEC of the matrix AGRoP without violating the Chain Condition and the Last Resort Principle and that Korean ECM can be accounted for in terms of the SPEC-head relation in the framework of the Three-Layered Case Theory based on the minimalist program. I have also shown that this approach can be extended to account for Case alternation in Korean Periphrastic Causative constructions.

References

Bak, S.-Y. Topicalization in Korean. The University of Hawaii *Working Papers in Linguistics* 9.2, 63-88, 1977.

Baltin, M. A Landing Site Theory of Movement Rules. *Linguistic Inquiry* 13, 1-38, 1982.

Bayer, J. COMP in Bavarian Syntax. *The Linguistic Review* 3, 209-274, 1984.

Bennis, H. and L. Haegeman. On the Status of Agreement and Relative Clauses in West Flemish. In *Sentential Complementation*, edited by W. de Geest and Y. Putseys, Dordrecht: Foris. 33-53, 1984.

Carlson, G. N. *References to Kinds in English.* Ph.D. dissertation. The University of Massachusetts, Amherst, 1977.

Cho, E. *Some Interactions of Grammar and Pragmatics in Korean.* Ph.D. dissertation. The University of Illinois, Urbana, 1988.

Choe, H.-S. *Restructuring Parameters and Complex Predicates—A Transformational Approach.* Ph.D. dissertation. MIT, 1988.

Chomsky, N. *Lectures on Government and Binding.* Dordrecht: Foris, 1981.

Chomsky, N. *Knowledge of Language: Its Nature, Origin and Use.* New York: Prager, 1986.

Chomsky, N. Some Notes on Economy of Derivation and Representation. In *Principles and Parameters in Comparative Grammar*, edited by R. Freidin, Cambridge, Mass.:MIT Press, 1991.

Chomsky, N. A Minimalist Program for Linguistic Theory. In *The View from Building 20*, edited by K. Hale and S. J. Keyser, Cambridge, Mass.: MIT Press, pp. 1-52, 1993.

Chomsky, N. Bare Phrase Structure. *MIT Occasional Papers in Linguistics 5*, 1994.

Chomsky, N. *The Minimalist Program.* Cambridge, Mass.: MIT Press, 1995.

Chomsky, N. and H. Lasnik. Principles and Parameters Theory. In *Syntax: An International Handbook of Contemporary Research*, edited by J. Jacobs, A. van Stechow, W. Sternefeld, and T. Vennemann, Berlin: de Gruyter, 1993.

Diesing, M. Bare Plural Subjects and the Stage/Individual Distinction, ms., The University of Massachusetts, Amherst, 1988.

Fuller, J. *Topic and Comment in Hmong.* Ph.D. dissertation. The University of Minnesota, Twin Cities, 1985.

Gundel, J. K. 1974. *The Role of Topic and Comment in Linguistic Theory.* Ph.D. dissertation. The University of Texas, Austin. Reproduced by IULC, 1977.

Haegeman, L. Subject Pronouns and Subject Clitics in West Flemish. *The Linguistic Review* 7, pp. 333-363, 1990.

Haegeman, L. *Theory and Description in Generative Grammar: A Case Study in West Flemish.* Cambridge University Press, 1992.

Han, H.-S. *The Configurational Structure of the Korean Language.* Ph.D. dissertation. The University of Texas, Austin, 1987.

Hegarty, M. *Adjunct Extraction and Chain Configurations.* Ph.D. dissertation. MIT, 1991a.

Hegarty, M. Adjunct Extraction without Traces. In *Proceedings of the Tenth West Coast Conference on Formal Linguistics*, edited by D. Bates, pp. 209-222, 1991b.

Hegarty, M. Familiar Complements and Their Complementizers: On Some Determinants of A'-Locality, ms., The University of Pennsylvania, 1992.

Hong, S.-S. *A and A-bar Binding in Korean and English—A Government and Binding Approach.* Ph.D. dissertation. The University of Connecticut, Storrs, 1985.

Iatridou, S. *Topics in Conditionals.* Ph.D. dissertation. MIT, 1991.

Jonas, D. and J. D. Bobaljik. Specs for Subjects: The Role of TP in Icelandic. In *MIT Working Papers in Linguistics* 18, edited by J. D. Bobaljik and C. Phillips, pp. 59-98, 1993.
Jung, Y.-J. *A Restrictive Theory of Functional Categories and Their Parametric Variation*. Ph.D. dissertation. The University of Washington, 1992.
Kang, Y.-S. *Korean Syntax and Universal Grammar*. Ph.D. dissertation. Harvard University, 1986.
Kim, N.-K. *Studies in the Syntax of Korean Complementation*. Ph.D. dissertation. The University of Washington, 1974.
Kim, Y.-S. *Licensing Principles and Phrase Structure*. Ph.D. dissertation. The University of Wisconsin, Madison, 1988.
Kratzer, A. Stage-Level and Individual-Level Predicates, ms., The University of Massachusetts, Amherst, 1989.
Kuh, H. Plural Copying in Korean. In *Harvard Studies in Korean Linguistics* II, edited by S. Kuno et. al., Seoul: Hanshin, pp. 239-250, 1987.
Kuno, S. Functional Sentence Perspective, *Linguistic Inquiry* 3.3, pp. 269-320, 1972.
Kuno, S. Subject Raising. In *Japanese Generative Grammar: Syntax and Semantics* 5, edited by M. Shibatani, New York: Academic Press. pp. 17-49, 1976.
Laka, I. *Negation in Syntax: On the Nature of Functional Categories and Projections*. Ph.D dissertation. MIT, 1990.
Lasnik, H. Restricting the Theory of Transformations: A Case Study. In *Explanation in Linguistics*, edited by N. Hornstein and D. Lightfoot, London: Longman, pp. 152-172, 1981.
Lee, E.-J. Exceptional Case Marking in Korean. In *MIT Working Papers in Linguistics* 12, edited by T. Green and S. Uziel, pp. 113-127, 1990.
Lee, H.-B. *A Study of Korean Syntax: Performatives, Complementation, Negation, Causation.* Ph.D. dissertation. Brown University, 1970.
Lee, I.-H. Double Subject Constructions in GPSG. In *Harvard Studies in Korean Linguistics* II, edited by S. Kuno et. al., Seoul: Hanshin. pp. 287-296, 1987.
Lee, J.-S. *Case Alternation in Korean: Case Minimality*. Ph.D. dissertation. The University of Connecticut, Storrs, 1992.
Lee, K. Korean A-chains and the chain condition. In *Proceedings of the Twelfth Eastern States Conference on Linguistics*, edited by M. Przezdziecki and L. Whaley, pp. 161-172, 1996.
Lee, K.-H. *A Study on the Case Marker 'ul/lul' in Korean*. Seoul: Tower, 1988.

Lee, S.-W. *Syntax of Some Nominal Constructions in Korean*. Ph.D. dissertation. The University of Wisconsin, Madison, 1983.
Li, C. N. and S. A. Thompson. Subject and Topic: A New Typology of Language. In *Subject and Topic*, edited by C. N. Li, New York: Academic Press, pp. 457-490, 1976.
Martin, R. On the Distribution and Case Features of PRO, ms., The University of Connecticut, Storrs, 1992.
Massam, D. *Case Theory and the Projection Principle*. Ph.D. dissertation. MIT, 1985.
Melvold, J. Factivity and Definiteness. In *MIT Working Papers in Linguistics* 15, edited by L. L. S. Cheng and H. Demirdache, pp. 97-117, 1991.
Moon, G-.S. *The Syntax of Null Arguments with Special Reference to Korean*. Ph.D. dissertation. The University of Texas, Austin, 1989.
Progovac, L. *A Binding Approach to Polarity Sensitivity*. Ph.D. dissertation. The University of Southern California, Los Angeles, 1988.
Rizzi, L. *Relativized Minimality*. Cambridge, Mass.: MIT Press, 1990.
Schachter, P. The Subject in Philippine Languages. In *Subject and Topic*, edited by C. N. Li, New York: Academic Press, pp. 491-518, 1976.
Stowell, T. *Origins of Phrase Structure*. Ph.D. dissertation. MIT, 1981.
Ura, H. Varieties of Raising and the Feature-Based Bare Phrase Structure Theory, *MIT Occasional Papers in Linguistics* 7, 1994.
Urushibara, S. *Ey/Eykey*: A Postposition or a Case Marker? In *Harvard Studies in Korean Linguistics* IV, edited by S. Kuno et. al., Seoul: Hanshin, pp. 421-431, 1991.
Watanabe, A. *AGR-Based Case Theory and Its Interaction with the A-bar System*. Ph.D. dissertation. MIT, 1993.
Yang, D.-W. The Minimalist Theory and the Structure of Korean, Lecture presented at the Second Seoul International Conference on Generative Grammar. Seoul, Korea, 1993.
Yang, I.-S. *Korean Syntax: Case Markers, Delimiters, Complementation and Relativization*. Ph.D. dissertation. The University of Hawaii, 1972.
Yim, Y.-J. Properties of INFL in Korean. In *Linguistics in the Morning Calm 2: Selected Papers from the 1986 Seoul International Conference on Linguistics*, edited by The Linguistics Society of Korea, Seoul: Hanshin, pp. 631-638, 1988.
Yoon, H.-J. *Functional Categories and Complementation: In English, Korean and Turkish*. Ph.D. dissertation. The University of Wisconsin, Madison, 1991.

Yoon, H.-S. J. Some Queries Concerning the Syntax of Multiple Subject Constructions in Korean. In *Harvard Studies in Korean Linguistics* III, edited by S. Kuno et. al., Seoul: Hanshin, pp. 138-162, 1987.

Yoon, H.-S. J. and J.-M. Yoon. Chain Condition, Ambiguity of Government and Derivational Grammar. In *Proceedings of the Twenty First Annual Meeting of the North East Linguistics Society*, edited by T. Sherer, pp. 415-429, 1991.

Yoon, J.-M. ECM and Multiple Subject Constructions in Korean. In *Harvard Studies in Korean Linguistics* III, edited by S. Kuno et. al., Seoul: Hanshin, pp. 369-381, 1989.

Yoon, J.-M. *The Syntax of A-Chains: A Typological Study of ECM and Scrambling*. Ph.D. dissertation. Cornell University, 1991.

Yoon, J.-Y. *Korean Syntax and Generalized X-bar Theory*. Ph.D. dissertation. The University of Texas, Austin, 1990.

9
Prominence of An Antecedent and Its Effect on Anaphor Binding in Korean

Chan Chung

1. Introduction[1]

Pollard and Sag (1992, 1994) propose that there are two types of anaphors in English: anaphors whose binding possibilities are subject to certain syntactic constraints and anaphors whose binding possibilities are subject to certain discourse or pragmatic constraints. Similar claims are also independently made in Roberts (1987), Reinhart and Reuland (1991, 1993), Baker (1994), and Xue, Pollard and Sag (1994). The dichotomy between syntactic anaphors and discourse anaphors seems to obtain in Korean too.

In this paper, I will make the following proposals. First, in Korean, binding possibilities of syntactic anaphors depend on the *syntactic prominence* of an antecedent. Syntactic prominence is determined by two factors concerning the anaphor and its antecedent: obliqueness and linear order. Second, binding possibilities of discourse anaphors depend on the discourse prominence of an antecedent. Discourse prominence is partially determined by a set of presuppositions (i.e. the presuppositional set in Rooth (1985) and the familiarity presupposition in Heim (1982)) and linear order.

2. Korean Anaphora

The typical pattern of anaphor constructions in Korean is that the antecedent is a subject and the anaphor a complement as in (1a). In such cases, as shown in (1b), the relative order of the anaphor and its antecedent

---

[1] My special thanks go to Carl Pollard for his comments and discussions on an earlier version of this paper. I also thank Peter Culicover and Hyunoo Lee for their comments on the earlier draft of this paper. Of course all errors are mine.

does not affect the possibility of binding: in (1b), the anaphor is scrambled into sentence-initial position and linearly precedes its antecedent.

(1) a. Ku namca-ka caki$_i$-eykey phyenci-lul ssessta.
the man-Nom self-to letter-Acc wrote
'The man$_i$ wrote a letter to himself$_i$.'

b. Caki$_i$-eykey ku namca$_i$-ka ___ phyenci-lul ssessta.
self-to the man-Nom letter-Acc wrote
'The man$_i$ wrote a letter to himself$_i$.'

The sentences in (2) are the reverse of the typical pattern, i.e., the reflexive is a subject, and its antecedent is a complement. I will call this pattern an atypical binding pattern. Both of the sentences in (2) are unacceptable.

(2) a. *Caki$_i$-ka ku namca$_i$-eykey phyenci-lul ssessta.
self-Nom the man-to letter-Acc wrote
Lit. 'Himself$_i$ wrote a letter to the man$_i$.'

b. ??Ku namca$_i$-eykey caki$_i$-ka ___ phyenci-lul ssessta.
the man-to self-Nom letter-Acc wrote
Lit. 'Himself$_i$ wrote a letter to the man$_i$.'

As shown in (3), however, when the anaphor or its antecedent is contrastively focused by focal delimiters such as *nun* and *man* ('only') or by focal stress, acceptability of the atypical binding pattern is much improved to the point of being at least marginal.

(3) A: Ku namca-eykey ku yeca-ka phyenci-lul ssess-ni?
the man-to the woman-Nom letter-Acc wrote-Q
'Did the woman write a letter to the man?'

B: Ani,
'No,'
a. Ku namca$_i$-eykey-nun caki$_i$-man-i___ phyenci-lul
the man-to-Foc self-only-Nom letter-Acc
ssessta.
wrote
Lit.'Only himself$_i$ wrote a letter to the man$_i$.'

b. (?) Ku namca$_i$-eykey-nun caki$_i$-ka___phyenci-lul
   the man-to-Foc   self-Nom letter-Acc

   ssessta.
   wrote
   Lit.'Himself$_i$ wrote a letter to the man$_i$ (but not to the others).'

c. (?) Ku namca$_i$-eykey caki$_i$-man-i___ phyenci-lul
   the man-to   self-only-Nom letter-Acc

   ssessta.
   wrote
   Lit.'Only himself$_i$ wrote a letter to the man$_i$.'

d. (?) Ku namca$_i$-eykey CAKI$_i$-ka___ phyenci-lul ssessta.
   the man-to   self-Nom   letter-Acc wrote
   Lit.'Himself$_i$ (but not the others) wrote a letter to the man$_i$.'

Note that contrastive focus alone does not improve the acceptability of the atypical binding pattern. As shown in (4), when the anaphor precedes its antecedent, the acceptability improvement does not occur. Hence we can say that the improvement via contrastiveness occurs only when the antecedent precedes the anaphor.

(4) A: Ku yeca-ka   ku namca-eykey phyenci-lul ssess-ni?
       the woman-Nom the man-to   letter-Acc wrote-Q
       'Did the woman write a letter to the man?'

    B: Ani,
       'No,'
       a. *Caki$_i$-man-i   ku namca$_i$-eykey-nun phyenci-lul
          self-only-Nom   the man-to-Foc   letter-Acc

          ssessta.
          wrote
          Lit.'Only himself$_i$ wrote a letter to the man$_i$.'

       b. *Caki$_i$-ka   ku namca$_i$-eykey-nun phyenci-lul ssessta.
          self-Nom   the man-to-Foc   letter-Acc wrote
          Lit.'Himself$_i$ wrote a letter to the man$_i$ (but not to the others).'

c. *Caki̇-man-i   ku namcaᵢ-eykey phyenci-lul ssessta.
    self-only-Nom the man-to   letter-Acc wrote
    Lit. 'Only himselfᵢ wrote a letter to the manᵢ.'

d. *CAKIᵢ-ka   ku namcaᵢ-eykey phyenci-lul ssessta.
    self-Nom   the man-to   letter-Acc wrote
    Lit. 'Himselfᵢ (but not the others) wrote a letter to the manᵢ.'

Contrastive focus and linear precedence also improve acceptability in the binding of the reciprocal *selo* ('each other'), as shown in (5):

(5) a. *Seloᵢ-ka   ku namcatulᵢ-ul   piphanhayessta.
        each other-Nom   the men-Acc   criticized
        Lit. 'Each otherᵢ criticized the menᵢ.'

    b. *Ku namcatulᵢ-ul seloᵢ-ka   ___ piphanhayessta.
        the men-Acc   each other-Nom criticized
        Lit. 'The menᵢ, each otherᵢ criticized.'

    c. (?)Ku namcatulᵢ-ul/-un seloᵢ-man-i   ___ piphanhayessta.
        the men-Acc/-Foc   each other-only-Nom   criticized
        Lit. 'Only each otherᵢ criticized the menᵢ.'

    d. (?)Ku namcatulᵢ-un seloᵢ-ka/SELOᵢ-KA
        the men-Foc   each other-Nom/each other-Nom

        ___ piphanhayessta.
            criticized
        Lit. '(Only) each otherᵢ criticized the menᵢ (but not the others).'

The sentences in (6) show that, in general, it is not necessary that an antecedent be a definite.

(6) Nwukwunaᵢ-ka seloᵢ-lul   piphanhayessta.
    everyone-Nom each other-Acc   criticized
    Lit. 'Everyoneᵢ criticized each otherᵢ.'

When the antecedent is an indefinite, however, contrastiveness and linear precedence do not improve acceptability of the atypcal pattern, as illustrated in (7):[2]

(7) a. #Nwukwuna$_i$-lul/-nun selo$_j$-man-i ___ piphanhayessta.
everyone-Acc/-Foc each other-only-Nom criticized
Lit. 'Only each other$_j$ criticized everyone$_i$.'

b. #Nwukwuna$_i$-lul/-nun caki$_i$-man-i ___ piphanhayessta.
everyone-Acc/-Foc self-only-Nom criticized
Lit. 'Only himself$_i$ criticized everyone$_i$.'

The sentences in (8a,b) contain a direct-object antecedent and an indirect-object anaphor, while those in (8c,d) contain an indirect-object antecedent and a direct-object anaphor. This set of data shows that when the antecedent is not a subject, the antecedent must precede its anaphor.

(8) a. Nay-ka ku namcatul$_i$-ul selo$_j$-eyke sokayhaycwuessta
I-Nom the men-Acc each other-to introduced
'I introduced the men$_i$ to each other$_j$.'

b. ??Selo$_j$-eykey nay-ka ku namcatul$_i$-ul ___
each other-to I-Nom the men-Acc

sokayhaycwuessta.
introduced
'To each other$_j$, I introduced the men$_i$.'

c. Nay-ka ku namcatul$_i$-eykey selo$_j$-lul sokayhaycwuessta.
I-Nom the men-to each other-Acc introduced
Lit. 'I introduced each other$_j$ to the men$_i$.'

d. ??Selo$_j$-lul nay-ka ku namcatul$_i$-eykey
each other-Acc I-Nom the man-to

___ sokayhaycwuessta.
introduced
Lit. 'Each other$_j$, I introduced to the men$_i$.'

The last set of data to be considered is cases of so-called long-distance anaphors whose binding possibilities are believed to be determined by discourse or pragmatic conditions.

---

[2] The sentences in (7) are marked with #, which indicates that the sentences are infelicitous. In section 4, I will show that the awkwardness of these sentences results from a presupposition failure.

(9) a. Nay-ka   Mary$_i$-eykey   [$_S$ aphulonun   caki$_i$-ka
        I-Nom   M-to   from-now-on   self-Nom

        motun   il-ul   haynakayahanta-ko]   malhaycwuessta.
        all thing-Acc   must-do-COMP   told
        Lit. 'I told Mary$_i$ that herself$_i$ must do all things from now on.'

   b. *Nay-ka caki$_i$-eykey [$_S$ aphulonun   Mary$_i$-ka
        I-Nom   self-to   from-now-on   M-Nom

        motun   il-ul   haynakayahanta-ko]   malhaycwuessta.
        all thing-Acc   must-do-COMP   told
        Lit. 'I told herself$_i$ that Mary$_i$ must do all things from now on.'

   c. *Nay-ka Mary$_i$-ka/-NUN   caki$_i$-eykey/caki-eykey-man
        I-Nom   M-Nom/-Top   self-to/self-to-only

        [$_S$ aphulonun ___ motun il-ul   haynakayahanta-ko] malhaycwuessta.
        from-now-on   all thing-Acc must-do-COMP   told
        Lit. 'I told (only) herself$_i$ that Mary$_i$ (but not the others) must do all things from now on.'

In (9a), the antecedent *Mary-eykey* is an indirect object of the main verb *malhaycwuessta* ('told'), and the anaphor *caki-ka* is the subject of the embedded clause. In (9b), which is ungrammatical, the anaphor is the indirect object of the main verb and the antecedent is the subject of the embedded clause. In this paper, I do not want to discuss why (9a) is acceptable, while (9b) is unacceptable, since the binding condition on so-called long-distance anaphor is beyond the scope of this paper. The point of this example is to show that the compensation through linear precedence and focalization discussed above only occurs among co-arguments of a lexical head.[3] In (9c), the embedded subject is extracted out of the embedded clause and linearly precedes its anaphor, which is the indirect object of the main verb. Also, the anaphor or/and its antecedent is/are contrastively focused. In this case, however, the acceptability is not improved.

The Korean anaphor binding facts discussed in this section can be summarized as in (10):

---

[3] See Chung (1995) for detailed discussion about long-distance anaphor binding. There I propose that binding possibilities of some instances of so-called long-distance anaphor binding (i.e., anaphor binding beyond the scope of an S-complement or a VP-complement) are determined by the same principle that determines binding possibilities of the given data above, namely by the relative obliqueness and linear precedence between an anaphor and its antecedent. On this approach, (9b,c) are ruled out by a version of principle C.

(10)

	typical pattern Sub_{ant}-$Comp_{ana}$	nontypical pattern $Comp_{ant}$-$Comp_{ana}$	atypical pattern Sub_{ana}-$Comp_{ant}$
effect of linear order	no	yes	yes
effect of definiteness	no	no	yes
effect of contrastiveness	no	no	yes

In (10), the typical pattern is the case where the subject is an antecedent, and a complement is an anaphor. Sentences of this pattern are all acceptable regardless of the effect of linear order, definiteness and contrastiveness. The nontypical pattern is the case where the both the anaphor and its antecedent are complements. Sentences of this pattern are sensitive only to linear order. The atypical pattern is the case where the subject is an anaphor, and a complement is an antecedent. This pattern is sensitive to the effect of linear order, definiteness and contrastiveness.

3. Previous analyses

In this section, I will review some recent studies on anaphor binding in Japanese, a language generally considered to have numerous properties in common with Korean. I will also show how none of these studies can fully account for the Korean data discussed in this section.

3.1 Saito (1992)

In Saito (1992), binding in Japanese is accounted for by the notion of c-command and the properties of a scrambled position. A summary of Saito's theory is given in (11):

(11) At LF, the scrambled position (which is a non-A and non-operator position at S-structure) must satisfy at least one of the following three options: (a) it disappears, (b) it is reanalyzed as an operator position, or (c) it is reanalyzed as an A position.

If one of these options satisfies Principle A, the scrambled sentence containing an anaphor is considered to be grammatical. Saito does not explicitly specify at which level binding must occur, but we can infer that it must be at LF. The grammaticality of the sentences discussed in the previous section is then accounted for as follows. In (1b), the reflexive is adjoined to IP, and the scrambled position occupied by *caki* can satisfy (11a) at LF. In this case, the anaphor is reconstructed into the original position (the position of the trace) at LF, and then the antecedent *ku namca* ('the man') c-commands the reflexive. The sentences in (3) and (5c,d) are grammatical because the position occupied by the antecedent can satisfy (11c) by being reanalyzed as an A-position and becoming eligible to bind the anaphor.

However, the sentences in (2) and (5b) are problematic for this theory. According to Saito, the position of the antecedent can be reanalyzed as an A-position, and the anaphor *caki* is c-commanded by the antecedent. Thus, these sentences are wrongly predicted to be grammatical. To avoid these problems, we may assume that the binding theory applies at both LF and S-structure. However, then a grammatical sentence like (1b) is problematic, as the anaphor is not c-commanded by its antecedent at S-structure. Another problem arises when we consider sentence (8b) which contains a direct-object antecedent and an indirect-object anaphor, and sentence (8d) which contains an indirect-object antecedent and a direct-object anaphor. For example, in (8d), the position occupied by *selo-lul* ('each other') can disappear and the anaphor can be reconstructed into the trace position at LF, making (8d) the same as (8c). Thus, (8d) is wrongly predicted to be grammatical.

From the above discussion, we may conclude that it is hard to account for all the observations in section 1 solely on the basis of differences among scrambled positions and the notion of c-command. Saito's theory must be augmented with some mechanism which can rule out the unacceptable sentences allowed by his theory.

3.2 Yatabe (1993)

In Yatabe (1993), the ungrammaticality of (8b,d), which is problematic for Saito's account, is correctly predicted by the notion of *grammatical command* (*g-command*) and the anaphor binding condition as defined in (12) and (13), respectively:

(12) X *g-commands* Y iff X is a sister to Y or Z dominating Y and (i) X is a subject, or (ii) neither X nor Y is a subject and X precedes Y.

(13) An anaphor must be *g-commanded* by its antecedent within the anaphor's domain.

In (8b,d), neither the anaphor nor the antecedent is a subject. (12ii) and (13) together predict that in this case, the antecedent must precede its anaphor.

However, Yatabe wrongly predicts (2b) and (5b) to be grammatical. According to his analysis, the description of the structure of (2b) is roughly as follows: [[Object] [Subject Verb]]. This structure is subject to (12ii) since neither the object nor the [Subject Verb] constituent is a subject. Here, the object g-commands the subject-verb constituent and also the subject within that constituent, since the object precedes the subject-verb constituent. Thus, Yatabe's theory has the same problem as Saito's.

3.3 Iida (1992)

Following Pollard and Sag (1992, 1994), Iida uses the notion of *obliqueness-command* (*o-command*) to formulate a syntactic condition on *zibun* ('self') binding in Japanese. A summary of her theory is given in (14):

(14) The reflexive *zibun* must simultaneously satisfy both the minimal syntactic constraint in (15) and a discourse constraint based on the notion of deictic perspective: the reflexive takes as its antecedent an NP whose referent is the individual with whom the speaker identifies himself/herself through his/her deictic perspective.

(15) *Zibun* may not *o-command* its antecedent.

In (15), the notion of o-command defined in (17) is based on the notion of *local o-command* defined in (16) which, in turn, is defined by the relative obliqueness of the two arguments, illustrated in (18).

(16) Local O-Command: X *locally o-commands* Y just in case X is less oblique than Y. Here, X and Y are arguments of the same lexical head.

(17) O-Command: X *o-commands* Y just in case X locally o-commands Z dominating Y.

(18) A subject is less oblique than an object.

In other words, Iida's syntactic constraint simply says that a reflexive may not be less oblique than its antecedent or a constituent dominating the antecedent. This syntactic constraint alone would permit unacceptable binding possibilities, but those possibilities are ruled out by the discourse constraint based on the notion of speaker's perspectives. However, the syntactic constraint in (15), adopted for Korean, is too strong because word order variation can sometimes compensate for the violation of the syntactic constraint. That is, the syntactic constraint wrongly rules out sentences (3) and (5c,d). For example, in (3b), the subject reflexive is less oblique than the focused indirect object antecedent, which causes a violation of constraint (15). But the sentence is still acceptable; thus we need to loosen the constraint further to allow sentences like these. Also it is not clear on this approach how the sentences in (8) are accounted for, in which the linear precedence between the anaphor and its antecedent, not their relative obliqueness, plays a crucial role. In sum, a problem of Iida's analysis is that it cannot account for the fact that word order can affect anaphor binding possibilities.

In the following two sections, I suggest a new theory of Korean anaphor binding, based on the notion of *syntactic* and *discourse prominence*, which I will argue provides a better explanation for the anaphor binding facts in Korean.

4. Syntactic prominence and binding of syntactic anaphors

The syntactic factors which determine the relative prominence among the arguments of a lexical head are their obliqueness and linear order. The independent linguistic motivations for each factor are discussed in sections 3.1 and 3.2. Then, in sections 3.3 and 3.4, we discuss the binding principle for syntactic anaphors and relevant phenomena.

4.1 Obliqueness

Pollard and Sag (1992, 1994) assume the obliqueness hierarchy in (19): (Here Subject is less oblique than Primary Object, Primary Object is less oblique than Secondary Object, and so on.)

(19) Subject < Primary Object < Secondary Object < Obliques...

They show that the notion of obliqueness hierarchy plays a crucial role in the account of various linguistic phenomena such as raising control, complement ordering, and binding. Among them, what is directly relevant to the current discussion is their formulation of binding principles. Pointing out some serious problems in GB binding theory, they propose that the binding principles can be reformulated in terms of *local o-command* defined in (16), repeated in (20).

(20) Local O-Command: X *locally o-commands* Y just in case X is less oblique than Y. Here, X and Y are arguments of the same lexical head.

Not every language makes all the distinctions on the obliqueness hierarchy (19). For example, if in a language, Primary Object (PO) and Secondary Object (SO) positions are not syntactically distinguished (e.g. Kinyarwanda, a Bantu language, in Gary and Keenan (1976)), then we can assume that the distinction between the PO and SO on the obliqueness hierarchy does not exist.

In this paper, I assume that the distinction between PO and SO does not exist on the obliqueness hierarchy in Korean, and they are treated as having the same degree of obliqueness. There seems to be at least one independent motivation for this. In Korean, SO can be distinguished from PO by case markers: SO is marked by *eykey* or *hanthey* ('to') whereas PO is marked by *lul*, an accusative case marker. However, in casual speech, this morphological distinction is often not made and both objects exhibit accusative case marking. In this case, unlike English, the order between the objects is free, as shown in (21), and passivization is allowed only when both accusative NPs become nominative ones, as shown in (22):

(21) a. Nay-ka Mary-lul   sakwa-lul   cwu-essta.
         I-Nom   M-Acc   apple-Acc   give-Past
         'I gave Mary an apple.'

     b. Nay-ka   sakwa-lul   Mary-lul   cwu-essta.
         I-Nom   apple-Acc   M-Acc   give-Past
         'I gave Mary an apple.'

(22) a. */??Mary-ka sakwa-lul   cwue-ci-essta.
             M-Nom   apple-Acc   give-Passive-Past
         'Mary was given an apple.'

     b. Sakwa-ka   Mary-lul cwue-ci-essta.
         apple-Nom   M-Acc   give-Passive-Past
         Lit. 'An apple was given Mary.'

     c. Mary-ka   sakwa-ka   cwue-ci-essta.
         M-Nom   apple-Nom   give-Passive-Past
         'An apple was given to Mary/Mary was given an apple.'

Passivization is generally assumed to be a test to distinguish PO from SO. However, even this test does not distinguish between them in Korean. Thus, we may say that at least in this construction, they are morphologically and syntactically indistinguishable.

On the basis of this assumption, I propose the obliqueness hierarchy in (23) for Korean, which says that a subject is less oblique than a complement, and that complements are all equally oblique.

(23)   Subject < Complements < ...

O'Grady (1987) assumes the same type of grammatical relation hierarchy to account for Korean anaphora (i.e., all complements have the same rank on the hierarchy) and shows its advantages. Our theory can make the same predictions as O'Grady's in this respect.

The hierarchy in (23) can account for the asymmetrical binding possibilities for subject antecedents vs. object antecedents illustrated in (1) and (8). That is, when an antecedent is less oblique than its anaphor (e.g. (1) where the antecedent is a subject and its anaphor is an object), the word order does not matter, but when the antecedent and its anaphor are equally oblique (e.g. (8) where the antecedent and its anaphor are both complements), the antecedent must precede its anaphor.

Although relative obliqueness of an anaphor and its antecedent is crucial for the syntactic anaphor binding condition, we cannot explain all binding facts solely depending on the obliqueness of the arguments. In section 3.2, we discuss the other factor affecting syntactic binding possibilities, linear precedence.

4.2 Linear precedence

Space limitations prevent me from engaging in an extensive discussion of how to treat scrambling in Korean. Without further discussion, I will assume that a sentence in Korean has a flat structure, and that clause-internal scrambling results from the lack of linear precedence constraints among constituents at the sentence level.[4]

Even though Korean allows considerable freedom in constituent order, sentences with different constituent orders have distinct discourse functions. Following Givón (1975), Kim (1985) claims that one of the factors most crucial in the constituent order variation in a sentence is the Principle of Information Flow. The principle states that the constituents in a sentence

---

[4] In Chung (1993a, 1995), I have shown that none of the current arguments for the existence of the VP node provide crucial or theory-external evidence for hierarchical sentence structure in Korean, and that all the constructions that have been argued to require the assumption of a VP node turn out to be explicable without it.

tend to be sequentially ordered in such a way that a constituent expressing given information comes first, a constituent expressing new information next, and a constituent expressing unpredictable information last. This is similar to saying that other things being equal, a more prominent constituent linearly precedes a less prominent constituent.[5]

As for anaphor binding, if we assume that an antecedent needs to be more prominent than its anaphor, we can account for the fact that the relative linear order of an anaphor and its antecedent affects binding possibilities. In (8), the anaphor and its antecedent are equally oblique. In this case, the ordering of an antecedent before its anaphor is enough to make the antecedent more prominent than its anaphor, and only (8a,c) are correctly predicted to be acceptable.

4.3 *Prominence-command* and binding of syntactic anaphors

From the discussion in the previous sections, we may conclude that relative prominence of an antecedent, compared with that of an anaphor, has a crucial effect on syntactic anaphor binding in Korean. Then, we can define a new notion of *prominence-command* (*p-command* hereafter) based on the the concept of local o-command in (20).

(24) P-Command: X *p-commands* Y iff
either (i) X locally o-commands Y,
or (ii) X and Y are equally oblique and X linearly precedes Y.

And the concept of *prominence-bind* (*p-bind*) and the syntactic anaphor binding condition in Korean are defined in (25) and (26), respectively, based on the notion of p-command.

(25) P-Bind: X *p-binds* Y iff X and Y are coindexed and X p-commands Y.
(26) Syntactic Anaphor Binding Condition:
A p-commanded anaphor must be p-bound.

Now let us consider the relevant data given in section 1. The sentences in (1) are acceptable because the antecedent *ku namca-ka* ('the man') p-

---

[5] Note that this general word order principle can be easily overridden by other grammatical means such as stress and special syntactic constructions. For example, in many languages, a constituent with stress signals that it carries new information, regardless of its position in a sentence. In English cleft constructions, the focused constituent is extracted to the beginning of a sentence (*It is X that...*).

commands its anaphor *caki-lul* ('self') due to (24i). (7) is also predicted to be acceptable by the same reason.

Sentences (8a,c) also observe (26) due to (24ii), i.e., the anaphor and its antecedent are equally oblique, and the antecedent precedes its anaphor. In contrast, sentences (8b,d) are predicted to be unacceptable. Here the antecedent neither locally o-commands nor precedes its anaphor.

The sentences in (2), (5a,b) and (6) are all unacceptable since the antecedent does not p-command its anaphor, i.e., the antecedent does not locally o-command its anaphor, and they are not equally oblique.

The sentences in (3) and (5c,d) are also predicted to be unacceptable since the antecedent does not p-command the anaphor. Contrary to the prediction, however, they are all acceptable. In section 4, I suggest that even though the sentences in (3) and (5c,d) appear to violate the syntactic binding condition in (26), the antecedent in them becomes prominent enough to antecede an anaphor at the discourse level, by satisying some presuppositions of contrastive focus. In other words, the anaphors in (3) and (5c,d) are discourse anaphors (as apposed to syntactic anaphors) in terms of Pollard and Sag (1992, 1994) or Reinhart and Reuland (1991, 1993), and thus the syntactic anaphor binding condition in (26) does not apply to them. The sentences in (4) and (6) are unacceptable because the discourse anaphors there do not satisfy the discourse binding condition discussed in section 4. In Chung (1994), I tried to incorporate the effect of focus into the notion of p-command. However, I have to acknowledge that this kind of syntactic approach is simply wrong because we cannot account for the effect of focus without considering discourse or pragmatic factors.

Before discussing the factors in discourse anaphor binding, I will digress for a moment and provide an independent motivation for the definition of p-command in (24) in section 3.4, showing that the distribution of the possessor NP and the body-part NP in the inalienable possession construction can be accounted for by the notion of p-command.

4.4 P-command and inalienable possession constructions

The Inalienable Possession construction (IAP hereafter) owes its name to the fact that there is an inalienable body-part relationship between the two accusative NPs: e.g. *John-ul* is the Possessor NP (PS NP hereafter) and *son-ul* is the Body Part NP (BP NP hereafter) in (27).

(27) Mary-ka   John-ul   son-ul   capassta.
      M-Nom   J-Acc   hand-Acc   held
      'Mary held John's hand.'

In the IAP, a PS NP always precedes a BP NP (Yoon (1989), and O'Grady (1991), among others) as shown in (28):

(28)   *Mary-ka son-ul   John-ul capassta.
        M-Nom   hand-Acc   J-Acc   held
        'Mary held John's hand.'

However, the BP NP can precede the PS NP when the PS NP is passivized, as shown in (29b).

(29) a.   John-i   son-ul   cap-hi-essta.
             J-Nom   hand-Acc   be-caught
             'John's hand is caught.'

      b.   Son-ul   John-i   cap-hi-essta.
             hand-Acc   J-Nom   be-caught
             'John's hand is caught.'

The BP NP alone cannot be passivized (Kang (1987), Yoon (1989), O'Grady (1991)), as shown in (30), while it can be passivized when the PS NP is passivized as shown in (29).

(30) a.   *Son-i   John-ul   caphiessta.
             hand-Nom   J-Acc   be-caught
             'John's hand is caught.'

      b.   *John-ul   son-i   caphiessta.
             J-Acc   hand-Nom   be-caught
             'John's hand is caught.'

Note that when both NPs are passivized, the PS NP must precede its BP NP, as shown in (31):

(31) a.   John-i   son-i   cap-hi-essta.
             J-Nom   hand-Nom   be-caught
             'John's hand is caught.' (=(29a))

      b.   *Son-i   John-i   cap-hi-essta.
             hand-Nom   J-Nom   be-caught
             'John's hand is caught.'

In Chung (1993b), I suggested a flat structure analysis of the IAP, and this provides a more restricted way of explaining the scrambling phenomena. As argued by Guéron (1985), the referent of a BP NP depends on its PS NP within a local domain: roughly speaking, in order to identify a BP NP, we need to identify its PS NP first. And this referential dependency of the BP NP makes it similar to anaphora even though it differs from real anaphors such as English reflexives: in the case of real anaphora, there is a coindexing relation between the dependent NP and its antecedent, whereas in the case of the body-part relationship, there is no such relation between the BP NP and the PS NP. In spite of this difference, the BP NP has a referential dependency on its PS NP, and I propose syntactic restriction (32) to account for this type of dependency, based on the notion of *p-command* relation in (24).

(32) A BP NP must be p-commanded by its PS NP.

On my approach, (27) is acceptable because the PS NP *John-ul* and the BP NP *son-ul* are equally oblique, and the PS NP precedes the BP NP. (28) is unacceptable because the PS NP follows the equally oblique BP NP. In (29), the linear precedence between the PS NP and the BP NP does not matter because the PS NP is less oblique than the BP NP. The sentences in (30) are all unacceptable because the BP NP is more oblique than the PS NP. Sentence (31a) is acceptable because the PS NP precedes the equally oblique BP NP, while sentence (31b) is unacceptable because the PS NP follows the equally oblique BP NP.

These observations on the IAP provide an independent motivation for the notion of p-command and indirectly support my suggestions that the relative prominence between an anaphor and its antecedent plays a crucial role in binding of syntactic anaphors in Korean. In the next section, I will return to binding of discourse anaphors mentioned in section 3.3 and discuss the effect of contrastiveness on it.

5. Contrastiveness and binding of discourse anaphors

Roberts (1994) proposes that the crucial factors for binding of a pronominal variable are discourse salience of an antecedent and its familiarity to interlocutors. In this section, I suggest that these two factors are also crucial in determining the binding possibilities of the sentences in (3)-(6).[6] As mentioned already, one of the important characteristics of the sentences in (3), (4), (5c,d) and (6) is that they are all involved with contrastive focus. Jackendoff (1972) and Rooth (1985), among others, propose that a sentence with focus has a presuppositional set (p-set in terms of Rooth (1985)). The p-set can be derived in two steps as in (33):

(33) a. Substitute variables for the focused phrases, giving the presup of the sentence, and
b. Lambda abstract the focus variables to produce a relation, the p-set of the sentence. (Rooth (1985: 11)

For example, (34b) is an answer to (34a), and *Sue* gets informational focus.

(34) a. Who did John introduced Bill to?
b. John introduced Bill to SUE.

Then by (33a), the presup of (34b) is derived as in (35a). And by (33b), the p-set of (34b) is derived as in (35b):

(35) a. introduced'(John', Bill', x)
b. λx introduced'(John', Bill', x)

That is, the p-set is a set of individuals to whom John introduced Bill. Focus in (34b) is called informational focus (Culicover and Rochemont (1983)), since the focused expression carries new information to the hearer. According to Culicover and Rochemont (1983), and Kim (1990), among others, the contrastive focus that we are concerned with in this paper differs from informational focus in that the contrasted expressions carry old information that is presupposed to be familiar to the interlocutors. For example, in (3b), the contrastively focused expression is *ku namca* ('the man'). Then the p-set is (36), which is a set of self-criticizing individuals:

(36) λx criticized'(x,x)

---

[6] This does not mean that the distribution of the discourse anaphors such as *caki* ('self') or *selo* ('each other') is the same as that of the pronouns such as *ku* ('he') in Korean. The sentence in (i) is unacceptable where the reflexive in (3a) is replaced by a pronoun.

(i) */?? Ku namca$_i$-eykey-nun ku$_i$-man-i ___ phyenci-lul ssessta.
　　　　the man-to-Foc　　　he-only-Nom letter-Acc　wrote
　　Lit.'Only he$_i$ wrote a letter to the man$_i$.'

The familiarity presupposition guarantees that the referent of the focused expression, the man, and the target of the contrast, the woman, be members of the p-set. I.e., the p-set must include the referents of the man and the woman, in order for the sentence to be felicitously uttered.

On this approach, it is naturally explained why a sentence with an atypical binding pattern does not allow an antecedent to be an indefinite (e.g. (6)). According to Heim (1982), the difference between definites and indefinites comes from their distinct presuppositions. Definites have familiarity presuppositions while indefinites have novelty presuppositions. Then the sentences in (6) where the antecedents are indefinites are predicted to be infelicitous due to the presupposition failure. Sentences with contrastive focus presuppose the focused expression to be familiar to interlocutors, and an indefinite NP cannot be felicitously used for that expression.

Also note that contrastive focus by itself cannot improve the acceptability of the atypical binding pattern. Comparison between (3) and (4) shows that the effect of contrastiveness must be reinforced by the effect of linear precedence. In (3), if we do not consider the effect of linear precedence or obliqueness, the anaphor and its antecedent are equally prominent at the discourse level, because the anaphor and its antecedent refer to the same individual in the p-set. If we assume that an antecedent needs to be more prominent than its anaphor in order for the involved sentence to be acceptable, as we assumed in section 3.2, then we can explain why the antecedent must precede the anaphor in (3). I.e. other things being equal, a linearly preceding constituent tends to be more prominent than a linearly following constituent.

In this section, the main concern is given to the effect of contrastiveness on binding of discourse anaphors. This does not mean that contrastiveness is the sufficient condition that determines the binding possibilities. In Pollard and Sag (1992, 1994), two crucial factors are suggested that are relevant to discourse anaphor binding: a processing factor such as *intervention* and a discourse factor such as *point of view*. Here, point of view generally refers to various discourse concepts such as empathy (Kuno (1976)), and logophoricity (Sells (1987) and Zribi-Hertz (1989)), through which a particular individual in a clause or discourse may be picked up who is relatively more prominent than the others and thus may be used as a referent of an antecedent. For this paper to be a more complete one, the relationship between contrastiveness and point of view need to be explored and a more general theory on discourse prominence should be provided.[7] I leave this for further study.

6. Summary and conclusion

In this paper, I have investigated anaphor binding possibilities in Korean. What I have proposed is that an antecedent must be more prominent than its anaphor at the syntactic or discourse level to satisfy the anaphor-antecedent dependency. More specifically, I have proposed (i) that the syntactic anaphor binding condition in Korean needs to be reformulated in terms of the notion of syntactic prominence, which is based on the concepts of obliqueness and linear precedence, and (ii) that interaction between the presuppositions of contrastive focus and the effect of linear precedence can make the antecedent more prominent than an anaphor at the discourse level.

Korean has various syntactic and morphological ways of representing relative prominence among constituents. My proposal suggests that those grammatical features and their discourse (or pragmatic) functions affect anaphor binding possibilities in this language.

References

Baker, C. L. Locally Free Reflexive, Contrast, and Discourse Prominence in British English. Paper presented at the Annual Meeting of the Linguistic Society of America. Boston, Massachusetts, Jan. 6, 1994.

Chung, Chan. Korean Auxiliary Verb Constructions Without VP Nodes. *Harvard Studies in Korean Linguistics* V, edited by S. Kuno et al. Seoul: Hanshin, 1993a.

Chung, Chan. A Lexical approach to inalienable possession constructions in Korean. In *Ohio State University Working Papers in Linguistics*, edited by C. Pollard and A. Kathol, 1993b.

Chung, Chan. Grammatical Prominence and Anaphor Binding in Korean. *Chicago Linguistic Society 30*, pp. 117-130, 1994.

Chung, Chan, *A Syntactic Theory of Word Order Variations in Korean.* Draft. Ph.D. Dissertation. Ohio State University, 1995.

Culicover, Peter and Michael Rochemont. Stress and Focus in English. *Language* 59, pp. 123-165, 1983.

Gary, J. and E. Keenan. On Collapsing Grammatical Relations in Universal Grammar. In *Syntax and Semantics*, edited by P. Cole and J Sadock, 1976.

---

[7] Baker (1994) uses the notion of discourse-prominent characters to give a unified account to binding of locally free reflexives (LFRs) in British English. On his account, LFRs in British English are a kind of intensive, and the intensives are appropriate only in contexts where emphasis or contrast is recognized.

Givón, T. Serial Verbs and Syntactic Change: Niger-Congo. *Word Order and Word Order Change*. Austin: University of Texas Press, pp. 47-112, 1976.

Guéron, J. Inalienable possession, PRO-inclusion and lexical chains. *Grammatical Representation*. Dordrecht, Holland: Foris, pp. 43-86, 1985.

Heim, Irene. *The Semantics of Definite and Indefinite Noun Phrases*. Ph.D. Dissertation. University of Massachusetts at Amherst, 1982.

Iida, Masayo. *Context and Binding in Japanese*. Ph.D. Dissertation. Stanford University, 1992.

Jackendoff, R. S. *Semantic Interpretation in Generative Grammar*. The MIT Press, 1972.

Kang, M. Y. Possessor raising in Korean. *Harvard Studies in Korean Linguistics II*, edited by S. Kuno et. al. Seoul: Hanshin, pp. 80-88,1987.

Kim, Alan H. The Functions of Linear Order in Korean Syntax. *Harvard Studies in Korean Linguistics* I, edited by S. Kuno et. al. Seoul: Hanshin, pp. 154-167, 1985.

Kim, Kwang-Sup. Where do Contrastive and Focus Readings Come From? In *Japanese/Korean Linguistics*, edited by H. Hoji. CSLI, Stanford, 1990.

Kuno, Susumu. Subject, Theme, and Speaker's Empathy: A Re-examination of Relativization Phenomena. *Subject and Topic*, edited by C. Li. New York: Academic Press, pp. 417-444, 1976.

O'Grady, William. The Interpretation of Korean Anaphora. *Language* 63, pp. 251-277, 1987.

O'Grady, William. *Categories and Case: the Sentence Structure of Korean*. Amsterdam: John Benjamins Publishing Company, 1991.

Pollard, Carl and Ivan Sag. Anaphors in English and the Scope of Binding Theory. *Linguistic Inquiry* 23, pp. 261-303, 1992.

Pollard, Carl and Ivan Sag. *Head-Driven Phrase Structure Grammar*. University of Chicago Press and CSLI Publications, 1994.

Reinhart, Tanya and Eric Reuland. Anaphors and Logophors: An Argument Structure Perspective. *Long Distance Anaphora*, edited by J. Koster and E. Reuland, Cambridge: Cambridge University Press, pp. 283-321, 1991.

Reinhart, Tanya and Eric Reuland. Reflexivity. *Linguistic Inquiry* 24, pp. 657-720, 1993.

Roberts, Craige. *Modal Subordination, Anaphora, and Distributivity*. Ph.D. Dissertation. University of Massachusetts at Amherst, 1987.

Roberts, Craige. Salience, Centering and Anaphora Resolution in Discourse Representation Theory. Ms. The Ohio State University, 1994.

Rooth, Mats. *Association with Focus*. Ph.D Dissertation. University of Massachusetts at Amherst.Saito, Mamoru. 1992. Long Distance Scrambling in Japanese. *Journal of East Asian Linguistics* 1, pp. 69-118, 1985.

Sells, Peter. Aspects of Logophoricity. *Linguistic Inquiry* 18, pp. 445-480, 1987.

Yatabe, S. *Scrambling and Japanese Phrase Structure*. Ph.D. Dissertation. Stanford University, 1993.

Yoon, J. H-S. The Grammar of inalienable possession constructions in Korean, Mandarin and French. *Harvard Studies in Korean Lingustics III*, edited by S. Kuno et. al. Seoul: Hanshin, pp. 357-368, 1989.

Xue, Ping, Carl Pollard and Ivan Sag. A New Perspective on Chinese ZIJI. *West Coast Conference on Formal Linguistics* 13, pp. 432-447, 1994.

Zribi-Hertz, Ann. Anaphor Binding and Narrative Point of View: English Reflexive Pronouns in Sentence and Discourse. *Language* 65, pp. 695-727, 1989.

10
Affectedness and the Degree of Transitivity in Korean : A Functional-Typological Approach

Jae-Hoon Yeon

Introduction

   Hopper & Thompson's (1980) observation that the more affected the object NP, the higher the transitivity is attested in a wide range of languages. The marking for the wholly affected patient is the accusative and the marking for the partly affected patient is usually non-accusative.
   The methodology we adopt here is a functional-typological approach. Explanations in this paper will be in functional rather than formal terms. We are concerned with how grammatical structures are used in different situations and what the semantic differences are between the different grammatical structures. Functionalism attempts to explain form in terms of function, in terms of the job it does. Functionalists take semantic and pragmatic factors into account in explaining morpho-syntactic behavior. We are interested also in conceptual domains and the way languages conceptualize them. One possible question that the functional-typological approach to grammar may ask is whether these conceptual differences find formal linguistic reflection in one or more languages. For example, the degree of control that the subject or the causee exerts over the action may be formally reflected in languages. Another example is that a conceptual distance between inalienable possession and alienable possession is reflected in morphosyntactic distance. The point of this paper is that the degree of affectedness of the object may also be differently encoded in grammatical structures.
   We regard the concept of transitivity as a continuum, in terms of degrees of transitivity. Hopper & Thompson (1980) proposed that transitivity

is a notion consisting of a number of components which involve certain parameters concerning argument NPs and other parameters such as the punctuality and telicity of the verb, the volitional activity of the agent, and the referentiality and degree of affectedness of the object, etc. These components co-vary with one another to render varying degrees of transitivity of a clause as a whole. Transitivity features are manifested both morpho-syntactically and semantically. In this paper, we are concerned with the degree of transitivity manifested in Korean, especially in terms of the degree of affectedness of the object.

1. Case-Marking Contrast and Affectedness

In Korean, there are cases when we find alternative case-marking between accusative and locative to mark place nouns. Some verbs of motion taking a place-NP as their complement show alternative case-marking. In this case, taking the accusative marker indicates that the motion designated by the verb takes place covering the entire dimension of the NP, while taking the locative marker indicates that the motion takes place at some part of it. Consider (1):

(1) a. Swuni-ka kongwen-ulo ttwi-ess-ta.
 -Nom park -to run-Past-Dec
 'Swuni ran to the park.'

 b. Swuni-ka kongwen-eyse ttwi-ess-ta.
 -Nom park -at run-Past-Dec
 'Swuni ran in the park.'

 c. Swuni-ka kongwen-ul ttwi-ess-ta.
 -Nom park -Acc run-Past-Dec
 'Swuni ran (throughout/the length of) the park.'

(1a) indicates the goal point and (1b) the spatial limits within which the action takes place. The interrelationship between the space and the action designated by the predicate is perceived as partial in (1a-b) but in (1c) the place-NP marked by the accusative is perceived as more total. Example (2) further corroborates this point.

(2) a. Swuni-ka tali - *lo/*eyse/lul kenne - ess - ta.
 -Nom bridge to at Acc go across-Past-Dec
 'Swuni went across the bridge.'

b. Swuni-ka   sewul - *lo/*ey(se)/ul   cina - ass - ta.
   -Nom Seoul   to at   Acc   pass-Past-Dec
   'Swuni passed (went through) Seoul.'

kenne- 'go across' and *cina-* 'pass, go through' are verbs implying "completeness" or "thoroughness" of the action of a verb. In a context in which the predicate has the meaning of completion, the NP may only be marked by the accusative, as shown in (2a) and (2b).

When the predicate is a motion verb as in (3), the locative NP implies the goal point to which the subject moves, and the accusative NP implies the area where the subject's movement takes place.

(3) a. John-i   san-ey   ka-taka   holangi-lul
        -Nom mountain-Loc go-Transf tiger Acc

   manna - ass - ta.
   meet-Past-Dec
   'On the way to the mountain, John met a tiger.'

   b. John-i   san-ul   ka-taka   holangi-lul
       -Nom mountain-Acc go-Tranf   tiger Acc

   manna - ass - ta.
   meet-Past-Dec
   'While John was walking in (traversing) the mountain, he met a tiger.'

In (3a), the subject has not reached the mountain yet, while in (3b), the subject was already in the mountain when he met a tiger. This semantic contrast can also be explained based on the affectedness of the object. Although the action of "going" does not affect the object properly, the locative-marked space in (3a) is not affected by (has not come into contact with) the subject at all, whereas the accusative-marked space in (3b) can be said to be affected (impinged on) by the subject.

The semantic contrast between locative *-ey* and accusative *-ul* is also manifested in the case of time NPs as in (4) (Jeong 1988). While the locative is used with reference to a point in time, the accusative cannot be used in such a case.

(4) a. 2 si - (ey /*lul)   manna - ca.
        o'clock-Loc/*Acc   meet-Let's
        'Let's meet at 2 o'clock.'

b. 2 sikan - (*ey/ul) John-i kongpuha-n-ta.
    hour *Loc/Acc -Nom study -Pres-Dec
    'John studies for two hours.'

While the locative marker indicates a point in time in (4a), the accusative marker indicates a whole period of time in (4b). This contrast may also be interpreted as related to the affectedness of different case-markings.

In quite a large number of languages a distinction is made in case marking according to whether the patient is wholly or partly affected. The marking for the partly affected patient is either a special partitive case or the genitive. The marking for the wholly affected patient is usually the accusative. This kind of alternation can be found in Russian, Finnish and other eastern European languages[1]. (5) is an example from Russian and (6) is an example from Finnish.

(5) Russian (Mallinson & Blake 1981: 65)
    a.   Peredajte   mne   xleb.
         pass   me   bread-Acc
         'Pass me the bread.'

    b.   Peredajte   mne   xleba.
         pass   me   bread-Gen
         'Pass me some bread.'

(6) Finnish (Shibatani 1982: 110)
    a.   Lauri   otti   rahan.
                  took   money-Acc
         'Lauri took (all) the money.'

    b.   Lauri   otti   rahaa.
                  took   money-Partitive
         'Lauri took some money.'

In the above examples, the accusative-marked Patients denote a whole (complete) affectedness whereas the Patients marked with the genitive or the partitive denote a partial affectedness.

2. Affectedness in the Space-Object Constructions.

Now, consider the examples in (7) - (9), where the space-object is marked either with the accusative or the locative, resulting in a semantic

---

[1] Moravcsik (1978) points out that this is an areal feature found in eastern European languages such as Latvian, Lithuanian, Polish, Russian, Finnish, Estonian and Hungarian.

difference. To anticipate the conclusion, the contrast between total affectedness of the object-space and partial affectedness of the locative-space is also found in the pair of constructions[2] which we call "space-object constructions":

(7) a. John-i chaykphyoci - ey   kemun sayk - ul
       -Nom book-cover-Loc   black colour-Acc
       chilha - ess -ta.
       paint-Past-Dec
       'John painted black color on the bookcover.'

   b. John-i chaykphyoci - lul   kemun sayk - ulo
       -Nom book-cover - Acc   black color - Inst
       chilha - ess -ta.
       paint-Past-Dec.
       'John painted the bookcover (in, with) black.'

While (7a) implies that only some space of the bookcover is painted black, (7b) implies that all the bookcover is painted in black. In other words, there could be other colors on the bookcover in (a), but there is only black in (b). The semantic difference between (a) and (b) correlates with the case marking alternation of space-object constructions.

(8) a. John-i pyek - ey sinmunci - lul   puthi - ess - ta.
       -Nom wall-Loc newspaper-Acc paste-Past-Dec
       'John pasted newspaper on the wall.'

   b. John-i pyek - ul sinmunci - lo   puthi - ess - ta.
       -Nom wall-Loc newspaper-with paste-Past-Dec
       'John pasted the wall with newspaper.'

(8a) may imply that John put a piece of newspaper on the wall for one reason or another (not to forget an important article in the newspaper, for instance) whereas (8b) normally means that John papered the wall with newspaper (not with wallpaper).

Example (9) is one of the well known cases which show semantic contrast between accusative and locative case marking of the spacial object. This phenomenon occurs in many languages.

---

[2] The semantic difference between the alternative constructions in Korean is briefly mentioned in Hong (1987:25-8).

(9) a. John-i   cengwen-ey   sonamu-lul   kakkwu-ess-ta.
       -Nom   garden-Loc   pinetree-Acc plant-Past-Dec
       'John planted pinetrees in the garden.'

   b. John-i   cengwen-ul   sonamu-lo   kakkwu-ess-ta.
       -Nom   garden-Acc   pinetree-Inst plant-Past-dec
       'John planted the garden with pinetrees.'

In the semantic structure for (9a) *sonamu* 'pinetree' is in the patient role and *cengwen* 'garden' is in the locative. In (9b), on the other hand, *cengwen* is in the patient role and *sonamu* is instrumental. The difference in semantic roles accompanies the difference in meaning. The only type of tree that exists in the garden is pine in (9b), while we can suppose many other trees, among which pine is just one kind in the garden of (9a). Here again, we can see that the accusative-marked space-object, *cengwen-ul*, is totally affected (cultivated) by the material, the pinetree, whereas the locative-marked space-object, *cengwen-ey*, is only partially affected (cultivated) by the material. This semantic difference is borne out by the contrast in (10):

(10) a. John-un   cengwen-ey   sonamu-lul   kakkwu-ko,
        -Top   garden-Loc   pinetree-Acc plant-and

        Mary-nun   cangmi-lul   kakkwu-ess-ta.
        -Top   rose - Acc   plant-Past-Dec
        'John planted pinetrees in the garden and Mary planted roses.'

    b. John-un   cengwen-ul   sonamu-lo   kakkwu-ko.
        -Top   garden-Acc   pinetree-Inst plant-and

        Mary-nun   cangmi-lo   kakkwu-ess-ta.
        -Top   rose-Inst   plant-past-Dec
        'John planted the garden with pinetrees and Mary planted (some garden) with roses.'

(10a) implies that John and Mary planted pinetrees and roses in the same garden so that two kinds of plants grow in the same garden. On the contrary, (10b) implies that John planted pinetrees in one whole garden and Mary planted roses in **another** (whole) garden.

Some more examples of verbs of this type in Korean are the following:

(11) palu-   'to paste'   cangsikha- 'to decorate'
      teph-   'to cover'   chaywu-   'to fill'
      meywu-   'to fill up'   cosengha-   'to make'

Cross-linguistically, verb groups such as 'paint', 'plant', 'paste', 'spray', etc., show the semantic contrast depending on case marking alternation between space-object and its complement. This contrast is also true of some predicates in Japanese shown in (12) (see Sugamoto 1982: 438):

(12) a. kabe - ni   nuru
          wall on   paint
          'paint on the wall'

      b. kabe - o   nuru
          wall Acc   paint
          'paint the wall'

There are further examples of a contrast between total affectedness of object-space and partial affectedness of locative-space in Indo-European languages.

First of all, in English, the verbs 'spray' and 'plant' are well-known examples as in (13) and (14):

(13) a. John sprayed paint on the wall.
      b. John sprayed the wall with paint.

(14) a. John planted trees in the garden.
      b. John planted the garden with trees.

In general "the locative complement marked as accusative is asserted to be affected by the event in its full extent, whereas the locative marked as locative adverbial is not asserted to be so affected" (Moravcsik 1978). The interpretation associated with (b) has been called "holistic"; it has been asserted that it always correlates with a direct object noun, whereas nouns preceded by a preposition are assigned a non-holistic interpretation (Brown & Miller 1982: 173).

The sentence in (15) has been discussed by Foley and Van Valin (1984: 61).

(15) a. John loaded hay on the truck.
      b. John loaded the truck with hay.

(16) is an example from German and (17) is an example from Russian.

(16) a. Hans pflanzt Bäume im Garten.
'Hans plants trees in the garden'

b. Hans be-pflanzt den Garten mit Bäumen.
'Hans plants the garden with trees'

(17) a. Ivan sejet/posejal   pshenicu v pole.
'Ivan sows/sowed   wheat in the field'

b. Ivan zaseivajet/zasejal pole pshenicej.
'Ivan sows/sowed the field with wheat'

These examples show the same meaning difference, too. In (17b), for instance, there is the implication that the whole of the field was sown with wheat; whereas in (17a) there is no such implication, and it is quite possible that only a small amount of wheat was sown in a small part of the field.

An example with a similar semantic contrast can be found in Hungarian, as in (18) (Moravcsik 1978: 248):

(18) a. János fák - at   ültett a kert - be.
John trees-Acc   plant the garden-into.
'John planted trees in the garden'

b. János be - ültett a kerte - t   fák - kal
John Appl-planted the garden-Acc trees-with
'John planted the garden with trees'

As we have examined so far, many languages generally show the contrast between total affectedness of object-space and partial affectedness of locative-space. The locative complement marked as accusative is meant to be affected by the event in its full extent, whereas the locative marked as locative adverbial is not meant to be so affected. This phenomenon is one aspect of correlations between morphosyntactic features and semantic interpretations with respect to the case-marking alternations for objects.

3. Affectedness and Case-Marking of the Causee

Now, if we look at the two kinds of causative construction distinguished by the alternation in the case marking of the causee, we have a better understanding of the situation. In many languages, there is a high correlation between morphological case and semantic roles. In Japanese, for instance, there are two ways of encoding the causee as in (19).

(19) a.   Taroo-ga   Ziroo-o   ikaseta.
           -Nom   -Acc   go-Caus
           'Taroo forced Ziro to go.'

      b.   Taroo-ga   Ziroo-ni   ikaseta.
           -Nom   -Dat/Inst   go-Caus
           'Taroo got (persuaded) Ziroo to go.'

While (19a) assigns minimal control to Ziroo, (19b) allows that Ziroo may have retained greater control. A similar distinction with the causative of a transitive verb is found in examples (20) and (21):

(20) Bolivian Quechua:
     a.   nuqa   Fan-ta   rumi-ta   apa-√ci-ni.
          I   Juan-Acc   rock-Acc   carry-Caus-1sg.
          'I made Juan carry the rock.'

     b.   nuqa   Fan-wan   rumi-ta   apa-√ci-ni.
          I   Juan-Inst rock-Acc   carry-Caus-1sg.
          'I had Juan carry the rock.'

(21) Hungarian:
     a.   Köhögtettem   a   gyerek-et.
          I-caused-to cough   the   boy-Acc
          'I made the boy cough.'

     b.   Köhögtettem   a   gyerek-kel.
          I-caused-to cough   the   boy-Inst
          'I had the boy cough.' (by asking him to do so)

In these examples, while (a) implies that the causee retains little or no control, (b) implies that the causer worked indirectly on the causee to get him to do something, for instance by persuading him without the use of force.

In the framework of causation, the "total affectedness" is realized in the sense of coercion and direct causation as well as total control over the causee. In causative expressions, the causee marked with accusative case is supposed to be totally affected by the causer, which means the causee has no control or less control over the action in comparison with the causee marked with dative or instrumental case. The dative marked causee in (b) implies that the causee is persuaded or advised to go by the causer, without use of force by the causer.

The distinction between this type of causation and the other non-coercive causation is observed in a number of languages with different case marking of the causee, paralleling the Korean construction in (22):

(22) a. John-i   ai-lul   ka-key ha-ess-ta.
         -Nom   child-Acc   go-Caus-Past-Dec
         'John made the child go.'

   b. John-i   ai-eykey   ka-key ha-ess-ta.
         -Nom   child-Dat   go-caus-Past-Dec
         'John let the child to go.'

Now consider the example (23) from (H. S. Lee 1985):

(23) a. apeci-ka   ai - **lul** matang - eyse nol - key   ha - ess - ta
         father-Nom child-Acc yard - Loc play- Caus-Past-Dec
         'The father forced/ordered the child to play in the yard.'

   b. apeci-ka ai - **eykey** matang - eyse   nol - key ha-ess -ta
                       -Dat
         'The father told/asked the child to play in the yard.'

   c. apeci-ka ai - **ka** matang -eyse   nol - key ha - ess - ta
                       -Nom
         'The father arranged for/permitted the child to play in the yard.'

The above examples differ from each other only in the case marking of the causee. As seen from the translations, the accusative implies a strong enforcement, the dative a simple order or telling, and the nominative a permission or an arrangement. In other words, the variation in the case marking of the causee in the order accusative, dative, and nominative, correspondingly expresses the degree of affectedness of the causee by the causer.

In the causative constructions, the causee marked with the accusative is supposed to be totally affected by the causer, which means the causee has no control over the action in comparison with the causee marked with the dative or instrumental.

All the examples examined thus far show that the accusative case is related to the notion of total affectedness of the object, and that the dative or the adverbial case is related to partial or non-affectedness.

4. Affectedness and Body-Part Object in Possessor-Ascension Constructions

Body-part nouns show interesting facts with respect to case-marking alternation and transitivity. The syntactic behavior of body-part nouns reflects the real-world fact that body parts are physically related (contiguous) with their possessors. We will exemplify below the morphosyntactically peculiar behavior of body part nouns reflecting their semantic and pragmatic characteristics.

The term "Possessor Ascension" has been used to refer to any construction in which the possessor NP is "promoted" to the status of direct object or dative-marked object, while the possessed NP is "demoted" to the status of some sort of oblique phrase (Fox 1981: 323). Examples from English are given in (24):

(24) a. I kicked him in the leg.
     b. I kissed him on the cheek.

Examples of Possessor Ascension can be found in many languages[3]. (25), (26) show examples from Korean:

(25) a. John-i   Mary-uy   son-ul   ttayli- ess - ta.
              -Nom   -Poss   hand-Acc   hit-Past-Dec
         'John hit Mary's hand.'

     b. John-i   Mary-lul   son-ul   ttayli - ess - ta.
              -Nom   -Acc   hand-Acc   hit-Past-Dec
         'John hit Mary on the hand.'

(26) a. John-i   Mary-uy   tung-ul   mil - ess - ta.
              -Nom   -Poss   back-Acc   push-Past-Dec
         'John pushed Mary's back.'

     b. John-i   Mary-lul   tung-ul   mil - ess - ta.
              -Nom   -Acc   back-Acc   push-Past-dec
         'John pushed Mary on the back.'

The Possessor Ascension can take place only when the clause includes body part nouns. Compare the examples in (27) and (28):

---

[3] For detailed data, see Fox (1981).

(27) a. John-i Mary-uy   sakwa-lul mek - ess - ta.
         -Nom -Poss   apple-Acc eat-Past-Dec
         'John ate Mary's apple.'

     b. *John-i Mary-lul   sakwa-lul mek - ess - ta.
         -Nom -Acc   apple-Acc eat-Past-Dec
         'John ate Mary's apple.'

(28) a. John-i Mary-uy   sensayng-ul ttayli - ess -ta.
         -Nom -Poss   teacher -Acc hit-Past-Dec
         'John hit Mary's teacher.'

     b. *John-i Mary-lul   sensayng-ul ttayli - ess -ta.
         -Nom -Acc   teacher -Acc hit-Past-Dec
         'John hit Mary's teacher.'

In similar possessive constructions, body part nouns show different behavior from non-body part nouns. This difference can be explained as follows: Body parts are physically attached to and contiguous with their possessors, and thus when a body part is affected by an action, its possessor is necessarily affected by that action as well.

Given that the affectedness of the possessor in the case of body parts allows the possessor to be interpreted as a direct object, possessor ascension is often not permitted when the clause in question contains a non-action verb, i.e., one which has little or no effect on the object, as in (29) and (30).

(29) a. John-i Mary-uy   moksoli-lul tul - ess - ta.
         -Nom -Poss   voice-Acc   hear-Past-Dec
         'John heard Mary's voice.'

     b. *John-i Mary-lul   moksoli-lul tul - ess - ta.
         -Nom -Acc   voice-Acc   hear-Past-Dec
         'John heard Mary's voice.'

(30) a. John-i Mary-uy   tali-lul   po -ass - ta.
         -Nom -Poss   leg-Acc   see-Past-Dec
         'John saw Mary's leg.'

     b. ?John-i Mary-lul   tali-lul po -ass - ta.
         -Nom   -Acc   leg-Acc   see-Past-Dec
         'John saw Mary's leg.'

(29b) is unacceptable because the possessor is not physically affected by the action of hearing at all. In comparison with the action of hearing, (30b) is not totally unacceptable but sounds awkard because the action of seeing also hardly affects the object.

The sentences from Dutch and English in (31) and (32) (Fox 1981: 327) also exhibit a similar restriction:

(31) Dutch
    a.   Ik   schudde hem de   hand
         I   shook   him the hand
        'I shook his hand.'

    b.   * Ik   zag   hem   de   hand
         I   saw   him   the hand
        'I saw his hand.'

(32)   a.   I hit her on the leg.
        b.   * I saw her on the leg.

Now consider the Luganda data in (33), which show the semantic restriction on possessor ascension (Katamba 1993: 273):

(33)   a.   a-li-menya   okugulu kw-a Kapere
              s/he-Fut-break   leg   of   Kapere
            'S/he will break Kapere's leg.'

        b.   a-li-menya   Kapere   okugulu
              s/he-Fut-break   Kapere   leg
            'S/he will break Kapere's leg.'

(34)   a.   a-li-menya   omuggo gw-a Kapere
              s/he-Fut-break   stick   of   Kapere
            'S/he will break Kapere's stick.'

        b.   * a-li-menya   Kapere omuti
              s/he-Fut-break   Kapere tree
            'S/he will break Kapere's tree.'

(35)   a.   a-li-mu-menya   okugulu
              s/he-Fut-him-break leg
            'S/he will break his leg.'

b. * a-li-mu-menya omuti
s/he-Fut-him-break tree
'S/he will break his tree.'

In the above, we can see the semantic restrictions on possessor ascension. In Luganda, the possessor NP can be promoted to object only if it represents an inalienable possession, e.g. a body-part. Hence, while *okugulu* 'leg' can be turned into an object, *omuggo* 'stick' cannot, since it is not an integral part of Kapere's body. Compare the Luganda case with the English examples in (36):

(36) a. She slapped his face/ She slapped him in the face.
b. She hit his tree/ * She hit him in the tree.

Possessor Ascension is a device to promote a participant from the status of a possessor to that of affected object. We would therefore expect clauses that allow possessor ascension to be high in their degree of transitivity, since a highly affected object entails high transitivity. As seen earlier, Possessor Ascension clauses often contain highly transitive verbs such as 'hit', 'grasp', 'cut' and 'break', while only rarely do they allow such low transitive verbs like 'look' or 'listen'. They also prefer animate nouns as the ascended objects. These facts are consistent with the Transitivity Hypothesis proposed by Hopper and Thompson (1980).

Hopper and Thompson's Transitivity Hypothesis also implies the assumption (37) with respect to the two participants (i.e. Agent, Patient) in the clause in question:

(37) The items referred to by A and P arguments are distinct from each other.

When a body part of the agent participant is expressed as the object or patient argument, one could argue that condition (37) is not satisfied, since in this case A and P would not be physically distinct from one another. Therefore, we would expect that these clauses will be relatively low in transitivity in comparison with clauses with two separate participants. In this respect, Korean body part clauses manifest interesting case marking behavior. Consider examples (38) - (40):

(38) a. John-i son-ul tachi - ess - ta.
-Nom hand-Acc hurt-Past-Dec
'John hurt his hand.'

	b.	John-i son-i tachi - ess - ta.	
		-Nom hand-Nom hurt-Past-Dec	
		'John hurt his hand.'	

(39) a. Mary-ka   elkwul-ul   tey - ess - ta.
        -Nom   face-Acc   burn-Past-Dec
        'Mary burnt her face.'

   b. Mary-ka   elkwul-i   tey - ess - ta.
      -Nom   face-Nom   burn-Past-Dec
      'Mary burnt her face (Mary's face got burnt).'

(40) a. Tom-i   palmok-ul   ppi - ess - ta.
        -Nom   ankle-Acc   sprain-Past-Dec
        'Tom sprained his ankle.'

   b. Tom-i   palmok-i   ppi - ess - ta.
      -Nom   ankle-Nom   sprain-Past-Dec
      'Tom sprained his ankle (= John's ankle got sprained).'

Verbs such as *tachi-* 'hurt', *tey-* 'burn' and *ppi-* 'sprain' usually take the subject's body part as an object. Verbs in this class exhibit an interesting relationship between transitive and intransitive encoding, which can be expressed as in (41) (Yeon 1989):

(41) NPi-Nom NPj-Acc V <--> (NPi) (Poss) NPj-Nom V
         (NPj = body-part)

When a body part of the subject participant is expressed as the object, the object can be marked as either accusative or nominative. The fact that the object NP is marked by the nominative is in tune with the Transitivity Hypothesis. Since the body part object is not distinct from the subject in (38)-(40), these clauses are relatively low in transitivity. We would expect, therefore, that an object low in transitivity could be marked with nominative.

The morphosyntactic behavior of body-part NPs reflects the fact that when a body-part is affected by the action, its possessor is necessarily affected by the action as well. As a result, the affected possessor can be marked with the accusative. The Possessor Ascension can take place only when the clause includes body part nouns. In possessive constructions, body part nouns show different behavior from non-body part nouns. This difference can be explained as follows: Body parts are physically attached to and contiguous with their possessors, and thus when a body part is affected by an action, its possessor is necessarily affected by that action as well.

5. Summary

Many languages, including Korean, generally show a semantic contrast between total affectedness of object-space and partial affectedness of locative-space. The locative complement marked as accusative is meant to be affected by the event in its full extent, whereas the locative marked as locative adverbial is not meant to be completely affected. This is consistent with the typological universal that the marking for the wholly affected patient is the accusative and the marking for the partly affected patient is usually non-accusative (whether locative, genitive or partitive).

Possessor ascension is a device which promotes a possessor NP to the status of affected object. Possessor ascension can take place in Korean when the clause includes body-part nouns. The morphosyntactic behavior of body-part nouns reflects the fact that body parts are physically attached to and contiguous with their possessors; when a body part is affected by an action, its possessor is necessarily affected by that action as well.

In many languages, a distinction is made in case-marking according to whether the patient is wholly or partially affected.

References

Brown, K & J. Miller. *Syntax: Generative Grammar.* Hutchinson & Co. Ltd, 1982.
Comrie, B. Causative verb formation and other verb-deriving morphology. In *Language typology and syntactic description*, edited by T. Shopen. Cambridge: Cambridge University Press, pp. 309-348, 1986.
Croft, W. *Typology and Universals.* Cambridge: Cambridge University Press, 1990
Foley, W. A. & Van Valin, R. D.. *Functional syntax and universal grammar.* Cambridge: Cambridge University Press, 1984.
Fox, B. Body Part Syntax: Towards a Universal Characterization. In *Studies in Language* 5-3, pp. 323-342, 1981.
Greenberg, J. H., C. A. Ferguson and E. A. Moravcsik. *Universals of Human Language.* Vol. 4: Syntax. Palo Alto, Calif.: Stanford University Press, 1978.
Hong, J. S. *Hyentay hankwuk.e tongsakwumun uy yenkwu* (A Study on Korean Verbal Constructions). Seoul: Tower Press, 1987.
Hopper, P. J. and Thompson, S. A. Transitivity in Grammar and Discourse, *Language* 56, pp. 251-299, 1980.

_____. (eds.). *Studies in transitivity (Syntax and Semantics,* 15.) New York: Academic Press, 1982.
Jeong, H. J. 'ey' lul cwungsim ulo pon thossi uy uymi. *Kwukehak* 17. Seoul: Kwukehakhoy, 1988.
Katamba, F. *Morphology.* London: The Macmillan Press Ltd, 1993.
Lee, H. S. Causatives in Korean and the binding hierarchy. In *CLS* 21- 2, edited by Eilfort et. al. Chicago: Chicago Linguistic Society, 1985.
Mallinson, G. and Blake, B. J. *Language typology: cross-linguistic studies in syntax.* Amsterdam: North-Holland, 1981.
Moravcsik, Edith A. On the case marking of objects. In *Universals of Human Language.* Vol. 4: Syntax, edited by Greenberg et. al., pp. 249-89, 1978.
Saksena, A. The affected agent. *Language* 56, pp. 812-826, 1980.
Shibatani, M. Japanese Grammar and Universal Grammar. *Lingua* 57, pp. 103-123, 1982.
Shopen, T. (ed). *Language typology and syntactic description*: Vol. 1-3. Cambridge: Cambridge University Press, 1986.
Sugamoto, N. Transitivity and Objecthood in Japanese. In *Studies in transitivity (Syntax and Semantics,* 15.), e. by: Hopper & Thompson, 1982.
Van Valin, R. D. & W. A. Foley. Role and Reference Grammar.: *Syntax and Semantics* Vol 13, pp. 329-352, 1980.
Watanabe, Y. Transitivity and Evidentiality in Japanese. *Studies in Language* 8-2, pp. 235-251, 1984.
Yeon, J. H. Kwuke cwunglip tongsa kwumun ey tayhan yenkwu (A Study on the neutral-verb constructions in Korean), *Hankul* 203. Seoul: Hankulhakhoy, 1989.
_____. The Degree of Transitivity in Korean: A Functional-Typological Approach, *Language Research* 29-1, pp. 107-136, 1993a.
_____. Causatives and the Encoding of the Causee, *SOAS Working Papers in Linguistics and Phonetics,* Vol. 3, pp. 407-426, 1993b.

11
Coordinated Clauses and their Tense: The Korean Data and the Labelled Deductive Model

Mark Vincent

Introduction[1]

Tense can be omitted on the first clause of certain clause-coordinating structures in Korean. This paper considers this and introduces a new way of looking at natural language interpretation which handles the Korean data at least as effectively as current theories. The framework is based on Labelled Natural Deduction, and the first part of the paper describes the methodology and the motivation for it. The second and major section of the paper investigates the Korean data, with particular focus on the *-ko* linkage device. Other treatments of the optionally missing tense will be considered and compared with the Labelled Deductive view. We also look at some other linkage devices in Korean and conclude by discussing the coordinate~subordinate distinction and its relation to clause union.

1. LDS and Natural Language

Labelled Natural Deduction models the process of natural deduction through the traditional tools of conditional logic, but with the addition of a labelling algebra and metabox discipline which impose strict constraints on the proof process and which keep a record of what is happening as the proof proceeds. Each formula of the conditional logic carries with it a label which records the assumptions used in the proof, the order in which formulae have been applied, and the structure which is developing in the proof. All this serves to make explicit many of the assumptions and steps that are taken as part of a standard proof worked out by Rules of Inference. The deductive

---
[1] Thanks are due to Ruth Kempson for much help with this paper. Also thanks to Ross King and Yeon Jae-hoon for further help, data and intuitions.

process becomes constrained and algorithmic. We can see this in a simple example of *modus ponens* (Conditional Proof):

(1)   a : P
         b : P Q
         ─────────
         b(a) : Q

Equally importantly, the labelling algebra permits us to impose constraints on each item of input in the proof. For example, an assumption might contain a control specification like 'use me last (as the input to some formula)' or 'use me once and only once (in some formula)'. This is a powerful mechanism which provides a high degree of control over what will take place in the proof.

In addition to the labelling algebra, it is the metabox discipline which sets LDS apart from a standard conditional logic. The metabox discipline allows a proof to be broken down into interrelating sections, each containing their own goal specification as to what is to be achieved in that particular section of the proof. All goals are carried down the proof until they have been satisfied, and it is only then that the metabox which contains them can be exited. LDS therefore requires the goal of each part of the proof process to be specified; the overall goal of the proof carries through into any metaboxes contained in it. In this sense the metabox is analoguous to a subroutine in a computer program.

The metaboxes also serve another important function, since they were originally developed to provide a model of temporal logic (Gabbay 1976, forthcoming). A metabox can be seen as containing not only a goal specification, but also a label (like any other item in the proof) which reflects different tasks of reasoning at different points in time.

Through the labelling algebra we can articulate various relations between metaboxes which correspond helpfully to the natural language notions of coordinate, subordinate, relative clause, and the like, with intermediate stages along the way. Metaboxes can be embedded inside others, they can be linked coordinately or can be linked to some item of data inside another metabox while remaining independent. The parallels with natural language will be developed shortly.

So we have a conditional logic, a labelling algebra allowing us to keep a structured record of what is going on and imposing constraints on the proof process, and a metabox discipline which determines how the various proofs and subsystems interact. LDS is a highly procedural approach. The only other thing we need is recourse to standard processes of natural reasoning so that we can operate the system. To summarize, "The defining property of a labelled deductive system is that it enables metastatements about the inference process itself to be encoded in the logic without distorting the logical language." (Kempson 1993a).

2. A Natural Language Application?

It turns out that the methodology of Labelled Deductive Systems can be easily ported to the field of natural language interpretation. Utterance interpretation can be seen as a proof-theoretic process in which the goal is to build a structure which can be assigned some truth value, that is, to build incrementally or proof-theoretically a structure of logical type t. This is the goal of the proof process. The lexical items are seen as having labels corresponding to the words in the language (like 'stone', 'kill'), and each of them is lexically assigned a logical type ('e' or 't'), a logical formula (e.g. 'e > t'[2]), or a control specification on structure building (for example, the content of 'who' as a relative clause marker might be something like 'build a relative clause as a separate database (in its own metabox) linked to the last lexical item'). As the proof proceeds structure is constantly being built up in the labels until the goal is reached and a structure of type t has been obtained.

The natural language application of Labelled Natural Deduction is currently being worked out by Ruth Kempson of SOAS, in collaboration with Dov Gabbay (see works by Kempson and Gabbay in the References). The initial aim of the exercise was to reconstruct utterance interpretation as an on-line, incremental, left to right reasoning procedure in such a way that it could be embedded in the larger task of drawing inference from the direct content of what was said. Great stress is laid on reflecting the underdetermined and context-dependent nature of language, and it is sought to explain the way in which general processes of reasoning can be brought to bear on what is actually said in order to retrieve the desired meaning (Kempson and Gabbay 1993).

3. How LDS works for Utterance Interpretation

Words are combined together by simple steps of *modus ponens*. Names are seen as entities, therefore of logical type e, and predicates are seen as logical formulae. The whole process is combinatorial, driven by the predicates, and this reflects the semantic process of combining meanings. An intransitive verb would be a one place predicate of the formula e > t ('if you give me an

---

[2] The symbol '>' is being used in this paper to represent the logical symbol of implication ('if ... then ...').

NP, then I will give you something which denotes a truth value' (that is, a clause or sentence), much like phrase structure rules backwards: S>NP+V), and naturally enough we can have two place predicates too, such as e>(e>t) or t>(e>t). A simple sentence, being a vehicle for expressing propositions, is something of logical type t (it denotes a truth value), and it therefore satisfies the goal requirement of its metabox which is to create a structure of type t. The hearer is reasoning towards the goal of establishing what this proposition is. A sentence's metabox is assigned a temporal label according to tense and other temporal elements which arise from the words in the sentence. All this is best illustrated by example. We work on the simple sentences 'John kicked Bill' and 'He died', with a simplified version of the LDS formalism. Underlined labels indicate empty labels–that an item has to be chosen by the hearer on the basis of context. This process is signalled by the operation CHOOSE.

(2)
```
S₁                                          GOAL: t
John:                      e
kick:                              e > ( e > t )
    [also assigns value to immediately preceding e, 'use me last']
-ed:
    [assigns temporal label to whole database, s_i precedes s_now or
    similar]
Bill:                              e
kick(Bill):                        e > t
kick(Bill)(John):                  t
    [goal is now achieved, box terminated]
```

```
S₂                                          GOAL: t
He  :
u(pron) :                  e       male(u(pron))
                                   u(pron) not an element of S₂
            CHOOSE u (He) = Bill
Bill:                      e       use last
die:                       e > t
-ed:
die(Bill):                 t
```

Notice the underdetermined nature of the pronoun. The hearer has to make a choice (given certain restrictions such as maleness and locality) as to how the pronoun is to be interpreted. The lexical content of the pronoun instructs the hearer to enrich the content of the utterance by reasoning so that the most likely referent is selected. This is done by virtue of context. The pronoun *he* could refer to some other person not mentioned in the two sentences, but according to the Principle of Relevance (Sperber and Wilson 1986) the nearest available referent *Bill* is selected. This process is formalized under LDS and is typical of the way many aspects of language interpretation work.

Tense, too, is an on-line choice. For some given sentence, there may be a number of temporal interpretations (as with coordinated Korean clauses, as we shall see later), but one is selected by virtue of Relevance applying to the linguistic and non-linguistic context. The other elements in the database (like temporal adverbials and conjunctions) frequently contribute heavily, for example. There are a number of parallels between the interpretation of tense and the behavior of pronouns (Partee 1984), and such things can be accounted for in LDS because it is a formalism designed to handle underdeterminacy.

All the information for interpreting the sentence and assigning structure to it comes from the words that are used themselves and the context upon which reasoning and inference are based. There is no predetermined pattern into which a sentence should fit—structure is built up incrementally as more words are received. The claim is that for the purposes of parsing there is no need for recourse to an external set of syntactic axioms/stipulations. The left to right string of words in the utterance provide stepwise input which is used to build a structural representation. Using parsing vocabulary, this means that the approach is essentially bottom-up. However, it is not exclusively so. Crucially, the methodology is also weakly top-down because of the goal specifications carried through the metaboxes. The reasoning process is goal directed, and utterance interpretation always proceeds in a dynamic way with the goal in view.

4. LDS and the Nature of Language

If the LDS methodology is indeed applicable to natural language, then there are important implications regarding the nature of language which we will mention cursorily. According to LDS, natural language can be seen as an essentially combinatorial procedure which makes use of general abilities of reasoning inherent in human beings. Utterance interpretation consists in assigning structure to the string of words uttered with the overall goal of obtaining a truth value. The inferential effects or implicatures of what has been said can then be evaluated through principles of Relevance (Sperber and Wilson 1986).

This leads naturally to the break-down of the traditional domains of syntax and semantics. Language interpretation is seen as a dynamic process in which both insights of previous work in syntax and semantics interact. (Kempson 1993). Under an LDS framework we are led to expect a significant blurring of the syntax, semantics and pragmatics of natural language. We will argue that this breakdown of barriers gives us an alternative way at looking at Korean coordination which more naturally handles the data.

5. Korean Clause Coordination and Tense

Korean employs various linkage devices for joining clauses together. These attach either directly on to the verb base or on to the 'infinitive' of the main verb in the first clause.

We investigate the fact that some of these linkage devices optionally allow tense to be omitted on the first clause, while others **require** that the tense is omitted and is marked only on the final clause. This may have important implications for our theory of clause union—the group which require tense omission normally show a temporal relation between juncts, whereas the other group do not. Here are examples with -*ko* (in one of its functions) in which overt tense marking on the first clause is optional, and with -*ese* in which tense can be marked only on the final clause:

(3) a. emeni ka   chayk ul   ilk-ko   apeci nun   ca ss e yo
       mother-SUBJ book-OBJ read-AND father-TOP sleep-PAST-POLITE
       'Mom read a book [-tns] and Dad went to sleep [+tns].'

   b. emeni ka   chayk ul   ilk-ess-ko   apeci nun   ca ss e yo
      mother-SUBJ book-OBJ read-PAST-AND father-TOP sleep-PAST
      'Mom read a book [+tns] and Dad went to sleep [+tns].'

(4) a. chinkwu lul manna-se   swul   masi-le   ka ss e yo
       friend-OBJ meet-ANDTHEN   alcohol drink-to go-PAST
       'I met a friend [-tns] and went for a drink [+tns].'

   b. * chinkwu lul manna-ss-ese   swul   masi-le   ka ss e yo
       * friend-OBJ meet-PAST-ANDTHEN   alcohol drink-to go-PAST
       'I met a friend [+tns] and went for a drink [+tns].'

We note that with the -*ko* pattern as above, tense would not be marked on the first clause in normal speech. Overt tense on the first clause becomes more likely for purposes of clarification if the clauses are becoming unwieldy to the extent of creating interpretational difficulties.

5.1. Coordinate and Subordinate

We could use the temporal specification of the first clause of concatenated structures as a syntactic basis for dividing up the Korean connectives. We could put those that optionally permit tense on the first clause into one group ('coordinate'?) and those that do not permit tense into another group ('subordinate'?). The first group we can assign the feature [-temporal] and the second group [+temporal]. Such a classification is found in Shin (1988b), and it looks like this (note that the usage of -*ko* is divided into two, one of which is taken to be temporal, the other not):

(5)   **[+temporal]**
    'before' relation
        -*ese*   'and then', 'and so'
        -*taka*   'and then', '[SHIFT]',
                        'while doing [INTERRUPT]'
        -*kose*   'and then'
        -*ko*   (temporal type, like -*kose*)
    'after' relation
        -*(u)lyeko*   'in order to'
        -*key*   'so that'
        -*tolok*   'so that', 'in such a way that'
        -*koca*   'intending to'
    overlapping relation
        -*(u)myense*   'while'
        -*nulako*   'while doing'

   [-temporal]
        -*ciman*   'but'
        -*(u)na*   'but'
        -*ko*   'and' (spatial enumerative, additive)
        -*kenman*   'even though'
        -*(u)nikka*   'because'
        -*(u)myense*   'although'
            [Taken from Shin (1988b), some glosses partially modified.]

The temporality feature which divides up the connectives in the way shown above may be extended and made the basis for a subordinate/coordinate distinction, but it need not be so used. We will return to this.

We have, then, two problems. The first is to account for the way in which tense is compulsorily omitted (or deleted) on the first clause of certain patterns, but occurs on the latter clause, and the second problem is to account for the other group in which overt tense on the first clause is optional. Firstly we shall discount the view that there is simply some arbitrary tense deletion rule, and then we shall consider a much more substantial theory, that found in Shin Sung-ock's doctoral dissertation.

5.2 Tense Deletion Rules

We could posit that two initially tensed clauses are brought together, and the first one is permitted to drop its tense because the second clause already has it. Such a rule would be most reasonable for those connectives which optionally permit tense omission [-temporal], rather than those which demand it.

We might then claim that the hearer recovers the original underlying structure according to a rule of recoverability of deletion. This would be an algorithmic step.

However, the deletion-rule explanation is unsatisfying on a number of counts. Deletion rules are subject to a Recoverability of Deletion principle which requires the identity of the information deleted. However, there are many examples in which the hearer has to reason pragmatically to interpret the clause with respect to tense. If the Recoverability of Deletion principle is retained, we would have to have arbitrarily many rules according to each possible reading to satisfy the recoverability of deletion principle. A tense-deletion explanation would make it cumbersome to explain the ambiguity that arises when tense is omitted (a better explanation comes through taking into account underdeterminacy).

Furthermore, there are many connectives which rarely or (worse) never occur with overt tense. It complicates the grammar to postulate the existence and deletion of elements that never occur. An alternative without any process of deletion would be preferable.

There are also semantic problems with positing tense on two independent clauses at some underlying level, and these have been outlined elsewhere (Shin 1988b: 131-137; Yang 1981).

5.3 Tense Indexing and Binding

A more satisfying view is that worked out by Shin Sung-ock (Shin 1987, 1988a, 1988b). On this view, tense is treated as either anaphoric or deictic, and the absence of tense on the first clause is explained by binding mechanisms. We will need to outline the position in some detail.

Concatenating devices are divided up according to the features [+/-temporal], [+/- anaphoric], [+/- perfective] (Shin 1988b: 155). For our purposes, it is the temporality feature (whether or not the device carries with it a sequential or overlapping time relationship) which is crucial (see 5). The use of -*ko* is divided into two, one of which has the temporal feature (and is interchangeable with -*kose*), and the other which does not (simply two independent clauses linked by 'and'). These are seen to have different underlying syntactic forms, the first, [+temporal], being subordinate, the other, [-temporal], coordinate. Through the tense indexing and binding mechanisms Shin introduces, the difference in temporal requirements can be explained (whether or not omission of the tense morpheme on the first clause is possible).

Shin discerns two tense markers, -*ess*, which names the past relation, and the null form -0, which is either deictic (representing a non-past tense, like present or future) or anaphoric (being coindexed to some tense in a matrix clause, whether -*ess* or a deictic -0). The past tense marker -*ess* is taken to be an R-expression, and is hence subject to Principle C of the Binding Theory ('R-expressions must be free'), whereas -0 is pronominal (it can either be deictic, and hence free, or it can be anaphoric, coindexed and bound with some tense in the second clause of a concatenated string).

The tense marker on the final clause of a sentence is always deictic, but the tense of an embedded or preceding coordinate clause may be either deictic or anaphoric. In some sentences two interpretations are possible for the embedded clause, depending on whether the -0 is taken deictically or anaphorically (Shin 1988b:105]:

(6) John-i   ka-0-nikka   Mary-to   ka-ss-ta
    John-SUBJ   go-0-BECAUSE   Mary-TOO   go-PAST
    a. 'Mary went there because John went.'
           (anaphoric, -0 is coindexed and bound)
    b. 'Mary went there because John goes.'
           (deictic, -0 is not coindexed)

Note that some connective suffixes block one of these readings (because they are [+temporal]), so that, for example, only an anaphoric interpretation is possible. -*ese* and -*kose* are good example—both tenses have to be coindexed and the first one bound by the second.

[+temporal] connectives (like -*ese* and -*kose*) do not permit tense to appear on the first clause. This is one of the reasons why such constructions are taken by Shin to be subordinate rather than coordinate. The unacceptability of the -*ess* tense morpheme occurring on both clauses is derived from the assumption that *-ess* is an R-expression subject to the Binding Theory. If *-ess* appeared on the first clause it would under this schema be bound by the *-ess* on the higher clause. This is unacceptable because R-expressions cannot be bound like this. They have to be free. Hence the theory correctly predicts the ungrammaticality of:

(7) a. * changmwun-ul   yel-ess-ko,   anc-ass-ta
       * window-OBJ   open-PAST-AND   sit-PAST
       'I opened the window and sat down.'

   b. * John-i   hakkyo-ey   ka-ss-ese
      * John-SUBJ   school-to   go-PAST-ANDTHEN

      Mary-lul   manna-ss-ta
      Mary-OBJ   meet-PAST
      'John went to school and met Mary.'

   c. * hakkyo-ey   ka-ss-umyense   John-i
      * school-TO   go-PAST-WHILE   John-SUBJ

      Mary-lul   manna-ss-ta
      Mary-OBJ   meet-PAST
      'While going to school, John met Mary.'

In contrast to this, the [-temporal] suffixes (including *-ko* in its looser 'and' meaning where sequentiality or simultaneity are not involved and replacement by *-kose* is unacceptable) are taken to be coordinate, and *-ess* can occur on both clauses. The reason why *-ess* is allowed to occur on the first clause as well as the second is that it is not bound by the second *-ess* precisely because of the coordinate structure which Shin assigns these patterns. Because of the presumed coordinate structure, there is no c-command relation between the two clauses.[3]

There are two forms which have both a temporal and non-temporal form. They are *-(u)myense* and *-ko*. In its meaning 'while' it is temporal, whereas in the meaning 'although', 'despite the fact that', it is [-temporal]. Only in the [-temporal] devices is the occurrence of deictic tense allowed

---

[3] Of the [+temporal] connectives, only *-umyense* is considered to be subordinate. All the forms except *-(u)myense*, 'while', and *-(u)nikka*, 'because', are seen to be deictic, and that is why tense can appear on both clauses. If the null tense occurs on the first clause, it can be read as deictic again, referring to a time relation different to that of the final clause. [-anaphoric] devices like *-kena*, 'or else', do not permit anaphoric temporal interpretation of the first clause, which results in maximal temporal independence being maintained [Shin (1988b): 188].

(i.e. overt -*ess* in the first clause). The [-temporal] -*ko* is the one used when enumerating a series of actions, qualities, conditions, for example, and no temporal significance is being attached. The temporal form is used only when those things are being ordered chronologically.

Although the theory is appealing and it neatly handles the [+temporal] category, there are a number of problems with the analysis. The first is that the binding or otherwise of tense morphemes is being used to predict syntactic structure--whether the clauses are subordinate or coordinate. Certain other evidence for the distinction is given, but this is not especially principled or compelling. The behavior of tense morphemes is being used to predict syntactic structure, and the (assumed?) syntactic structure is then being used to explain why the tense morphemes behave as they do.

The naturalness of the indexing/binding explanation is also questionable. It is most unusual for anaphoric elements to look forwards to items yet to appear in the sentence (the anaphoric tense on the first clause being indexed by a tense which occurs after it). This means that the hearer has to wait and hold the first clause in limbo until the tense on the final clause is heard; only then can the first clause be assigned a temporal interpretation. Anaphoric dependencies in language standardly go the other way, as linear phenomena they look **back** to an antecedent that has already occurred in the sentence. Examples of dependencies of the sort Shin is proposing are very rare and are usually limited to occurrence in adjuncts which are parasitic on the main clause. To elaborate on this, we take an example sentence with -*ese*:

(8) chinkwu lul   manna-se   swul   masi le ka ss e yo
     friend-OBJ   meet-ANDTHEN   alchohol drink-to go-PAST
     'I met a friend [-tns] and went for a drink [+tns].'

Now here clause two takes place at some time relative to clause one, that is **after** clause one has taken place, clause two occurs (by virtue of the meaning of -*ese*). For the real time sequence, clause two is dependent on clause one. But, according to Shin, clause one is dependent on clause two for indexing, which means that syntactic dependency goes one way and semantic dependency goes in completely the opposite direction. Even given the supposed independence of syntax and semantics at LF, we would not expect to find the two in direct conflict.

Even if the indexing/binding explanation be accepted for [+temporal] clauses, there are problems when we look at fragments and afterthoughts. A clause with [+temporal] -*ese* ('and then', 'because') can be added **after** a sentence, and rounded off with the polite style particle *yo*, thus:

(9)   kimchi nun   way an   mek ess ci yo? nemwu maywe se yo.
      Kimchee-TOP   why NOT   eat-Q?   too spicy-BECAUSE
      'Why didn't you eat any kimchee? Because it was too spicy.'

Here we have to explain the missing tense, which should be syntactically bound by the preceding clause according to Shin, when there is no syntactic relation between the sentences.

Then there is the behavior of the [-temporal] connectives, notably -*ko*, which is still not adequately explained. Assuming Shin's explanation for the temporal -*ko* is correct, and we allow the unusual anaphoric dependencies for clauses which are subordinate, we still have a problem with the fact that the [-temporal] connectives, while allowing tense morphemes on both clauses, will also allow the tense to be omitted on the first clause. We are still left with the problem of having no convincing explanation of how this might be without recourse to the 'tense-deletion rule' we already discarded. Shin's own explanation here is weak: she proposes the following principle, making a parallel with the noun morphology in which markers appear on either all the nouns in a list or on the last noun only, all other forms being unacceptable:

(10)   In coordinate structures an overt tense form is allowed in both conjuncts or in the last conjunct ... The discussion so far indicates that **anaphoric tense is coindexed and does not require a c-command relation**, as stated below: Anaphoric tense is coindexed with its antecedent. As just noted above **this notion of 'anaphoric' is a bit unusual since the c-command requirement is not necessary**. (Shin 1988b: 208-209, my emphasis)

If the anaphoric tense does not need to be bound here, why should we assume it needed to be bound in the way described for the other structures? Shin's principle undermines the whole system of tense binding which she had previously set up to explain the other data.

Another matter left unaccounted for is the way in which other verbal information like mood and aspect can carry across between clauses. Although Shin sees only two temporal markers, -*ess* and -0, what she sees as the future aspect marker also requires specification on only the final clause. The same applies for imperatives, and there are occasions when even a negative appears to have scope over both clauses, as we will see later. It appears that a whole complex of verbal features needs specification only on the final clause, for some connective devices at least. Are all these other features in the first clause also to be **bound syntactically** by the final clause? That seems highly unlikely.

6. Underdeterminacy, Inference and LDS

An alternative is to regard the aspecto-temporal features of clauses linked by these connectives as underdetermined and proceed to an explanation that way, using the LDS formalism.

6.1 Overt Tense on both Clauses

If overt tense is present on the first clause, then of course there is no problem; context, temporal adverbials, narrative flow and the tense morpheme all contribute to providing a temporal database label for the first clause. The tense morpheme of the first clause completes the database label, and the connective licenses the exiting of the metabox of the first clause. The meaning of the connective determines the nature of the link between the two clauses. Here is an example worked through with LDS (underlined labels again stand for items which are underdetermined and which have to be selected or chosen by the hearer on the basis of context and what is said)[4]:

(11)   Mom read a book and Dad slept

```
s1
    emeni   :              e
    ka
    chayk   :              e
    ul
    ilk     :              e > (e > t)
    ilk(chayk)    :        e > t
    ilk(chayk)(emeni) :    t
    ess

            [completes database label, i.e. s1=s1 precede s(now)]
    ko
            [terminates box, instructs to build second concatenated
                box, s1+s2]
```

---

[4] For the purposes of this paper we ignore case markers and their function in marking arguments for the predicate. We shall assume the predicate combines with its arguments in the correct order.

```
s2
    apeci   :              e
    nun
    ca      :              e   t
    ca(apeci) :            t
    ess
    [sets s2 to precede s(now), i.e. s2 = s2 precedes s(now)]
```

-*eyo* completes the database

As the first clause is being built, temporal information from the context, encyclopedic knowledge and temporal adverbials is being recorded in the metabox label. Then, when the tense morpheme occurs, the label for the database is completed, and the metabox is almost ready to be exited. We have an almost complete proposition; all we need is some sentence-ending marker. The next item in the sentence is the linkage device, *-ko* in this case. This encodes the information that the database is complete, and induces the building of a second database concatenated with it, in the pattern shown:

(12)
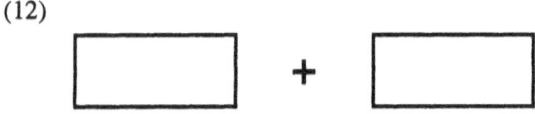

Two basically independent sentences are being coranked and concatenated in some way. We claim that in these structures (those which allow tense to be overtly marked on the first clause), the clauses are regarded as being independent for the purposes of drawing inference. The first clause is complete, and with the appropriate sentence ender could stand alone; it is fully tensed and inflected, and can be used--as metaboxes are--for inference-drawing and the continued process of context selection. The second clause is also able to function in this way. It is this discourse function which tense critically projects.

The independence and co-ranked nature of these linkage patterns is obvious when we look at the connectives that can be used: *-ko* in its additive or spatial enumerative function; *-ciman* for 'but' and a connective for 'or'.

These clauses have maximum independence of all the coordinate structures. Although the tenses of both clauses are usually the same (overtly marked), we can even get different tenses on both clauses, particularly if different temporal adverbials are used on both clauses to strengthen the interpretation:

(13) na nun ilpon ey pelsse ka ss ko   naynyen
      I-TOP Japan-TO already go-PAST-AND next year

   cwungkwuk ey ka keyss e yo
   China-TO   go-FUT
   'I've already been to Japan and next year I will probably go to China.'
   (without the temporal adverbials, this becomes questionable)

That leaves us with two other situations to consider: such sentences when the tense is omitted, and sentences with [+temporal] connectives which **require** the tense to be omitted.

6.2 Compulsory Tense Omission

First, the group which require omission of tense. Let us take an example sentence, and work it through with LDS. Underlining again represents an empty label, a placeholding device, with the content of the label to be chosen by the hearer[5].

(14) I met my friend and went for a drink

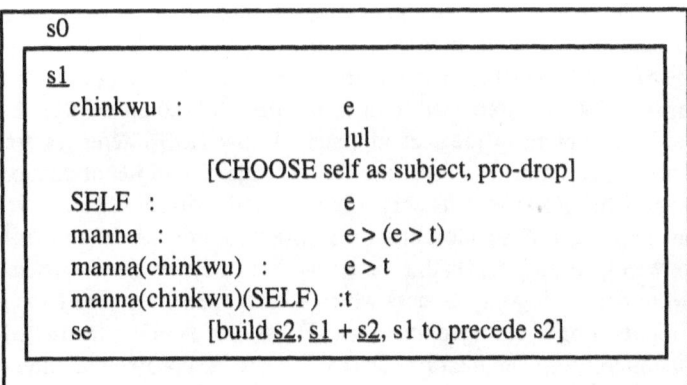

---

[5] Word order, case markers and argument marking by the predicate are again ignored. We also ignore the way arguments are chosen from the context (because of pro-drop), and simply assume that this is done correctly.

```
                              +
┌─────────────────────────────────────────────────────────┐
│   s2                                                    │
│   swul  :              e                                │
│                  [CHOOSE this as object, 'WE' as subject]│
│   masi  :              e > (e > t)                      │
│   masi(swul)  :        e > t                            │
│   masi(swul)(WE)  :    t                                │
│   ess         [CHOOSE s2 precede s(now)]                │
└─────────────────────────────────────────────────────────┘
```

eyo encodes that s0 is complete, all choices are fixed.

As the first clause is being built the hearer is once again recording temporal information which can be drawn from the sentence, pragmatically, from temporal adverbials, context, and narrative flow. This assumes maximum integration of syntactic and pragmatic information in real time processing. The temporal information collected in this manner fill out the database label but they cannot complete it until a tense morpheme appears. The label is therefore left incomplete, and when the connective occurs it instructs the commencement of a new database connected with the first, but with the label of the first database still incomplete. Why should it do this?

The answer seems to be that the absence of the tense morpheme and the incomplete database label is signalling that there is a close relation between the two clauses and that the hearer should not reason with the first clause and draw inferences from it, but that she should wait until she has heard the content of the second clause. Under LDS inferences are drawn over complete databases, and the context (this is a notion of context which comes from Relevance Theory (Sperber and Wilson 1986)) is reshaped constantly, based on the units over which inferences are drawn and the inferences themselves. On this view, context is a dynamic notion, and context selection is an ongoing process which a hearer performs during the process of interpreting a dialogue/utterance. The hearer is being instructed not to draw inferences from the first clause or update the context until after hearing the content of the second clause and therefore being able to work out the relation between them. The hearer is alerted not to choose a context too quickly.

If these suggestions are correct, then it would lead us to expect a closer relationship between the two conjuncts, and also ambiguity concerning the meaning or status of the first clause (its emphasis or place in the utterance) which can only be cleared up when the second clause is heard and inferences are drawn over the larger unit of the whole sentence.

If the two conjuncts are one inferential unit then in LDS terms this means assigning them a joint metabox which has its own label. The incomplete database label on the first clause and the temporal connective signal the building of this additional metabox when the second database is complete. This encompassing metabox has two metaboxes inside it, then, as we can see above, and its label applies to both of them. If this is the case, then we should expect to find sentences in which sentential operators apply over **both** clauses, not just the second, and this is indeed the case, as we have noted above. Here are examples:

(15) a.   achim   mek ko   hakkyo ey ka la
      breakfast   eat-AND   school-TO go-IMPERATIVE
     'Eat you're breakfast and go to school.'

   b.   swul   masi ko (se)   wuncen ha ci ma sey yo
      alcholol drink-AND   drive-DON'T!
     'Don't drink and drive!'

In (15a) the imperative has force over both conjuncts, this is a command to eat breakfast, as well as a command to go to school. With the LDS explanation of an extra metabox this feature is easy to assign over both clauses, and the clauses are treated inferentially as one unit. Note that this construction cannot be regarded as subordinate (which the tense indexing and binding explanation would claim), because if it were the imperative would not carry over into the first clause.

(15b) is an example of the temporal -*ko* which cannot occur with tense, and here it is the whole sentence, or rather the relation between the two clauses which is being negated. It is the combination of drinking and driving which is being forbidden, not merely one conjunct, so the whole unit joined by -*ko* (which, being tenseless, instructs the building of the surrounding metabox) is being negated.

As we have already mentioned, it is not just past tense that is omitted on the first clause, other aspecto-temporal elements also occur only on the final clause, supporting the idea of a metabox with a label which applies over both clauses:

(16) ilpon ey   ka kose   cwungkwuk ey ka keyss e yo
      Japan-TO   go-AND(then)   China-TO   go-FUT
      'I will go to Japan and (then) I will go to China.'

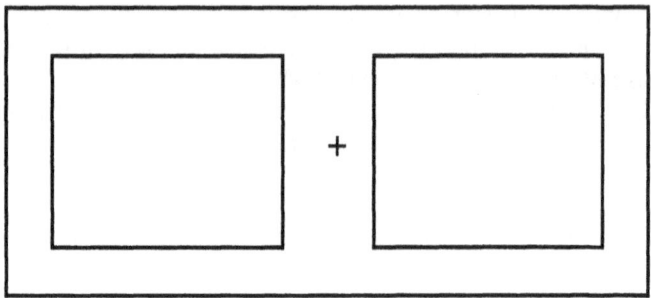

The ambiguity in [+temporal] connective patterns is relatively restricted, but still the hearer clearly makes choices about the two clauses and the relation between them based on context and the content of the sentences. Ambiguity can be cleared up by insertion of lexical items which disambiguate the intended interpretation, and the ambiguity arises from the content of the sentences and the way they are understood to relate to each other, rather than there being an entirely different temporal interpretation. Here are two examples:

(17) a. oythwu-lul   ip-0-kose   cip-ul   naka-ss-ta
         coat-OBJ   wear-AND(then)   house-OBJ   go out-PAST
         1. 'He put on his overcoat and left the house.'
         2. 'He left the house wearing his overcoat.'

   b. cim-ul   tul-0-kose   ku salam-ul   ttalaka-ss-ta
       baggage-OBJ   lift-AND(then)   that man-OBJ follow-PAST
       1. 'I picked up my baggage and followed him.'
       2. 'I followed him, carrying my baggage.'

The status of the first clause in the whole context of the utterance is quite different for each of the readings of the three sentences above. In the first reading, the first clause is more independent from the second, and functions as an event in a narrative about what the subject did. The second reading gives a different interpretation in which the first clause functions more like an adverbial describing the manner or state in which the second clause was carried out. This is worked out by pragmatic means and by inference from the context, but we notice that the first clause can't be evaluated properly until the second has been heard.

The non-occurrence of tense on the first clause is seen as carrying out a discourse function, therefore. The first clause's incomplete label is a flag which procedurally instructs the hearer not to draw pragmatic inferences at that stage but to wait until the second clause has been heard, and then to treat the whole sentence as a composite inferential unit.

By modeling the hearer's process of utterance interpretation through LDS we can capture these intuitions directly. The model does this for us, making the correct predictions as a result of the incomplete database label. The boxes are not merely restricted to being in coordinate/subordinate relation; there are at least three possibilities: a, two independent label and box pairs; b, one box contained within another; c, two independent boxes sharing a composite label.

By this means we are not obliged to make the temporality feature of Korean connectives the basis of a syntactic distinction between subordinate and coordinate. Doing that forces us into making an artificial distinction into two categories which the data do not seem to fit. For example, such an analysis predicts that -*ko* clauses when temporal ('and then. . .' and similar interpretations, also the simultaneous) are subordinate, and the only other evidence that can be cited for this is the fact the conjuncts cannot be reordered and the meaning kept the same. This also applies to English 'and' in one of its uses, however, yet it is not normally claimed that our analysis should change from coordinate to subordinate just because of that, but rather that the 'and' is low in specificity, and is underdetermined.

As Kuno has pointed out in Japanese (Kuno 1973), there appears to be a continuum of distinctions between coordinate and subordinate, and the breakdown into two rigid categories is too simplistic. LDS not only gives us more ways to articulate relations between clauses (something which this paper has not developed), but also a way of handling the low specificity and underdeterminacy of many connective patterns.

6.3 Optional Tense and Underdeterminacy

Now we have those sentences which have no tense marking to consider. We need to establish more clearly the possible ambiguity in such sentences, because this leads us naturally to expect underdeterminacy. Note that this is **not** just 'semantic vagueness' of some unspecified kind, outside the remit of linguistic analysis, it is another of the many examples of the underdetermined content of natural language expressions. Most frequently we have no tense / present tense (the present tense marker is a null form) marked on the first clause, and some other tense on the final clause, usually past, and the ambiguity consists in whether the first clause is interpreted as past or present.

Our claim is that this results purely and simply from underdeterminacy, and that the hearer has to reason on the basis of context towards the correct interpretation (based on Relevance). On many occasions it is temporal adverbials which identify the correct reading, and this is shown in the following two sentences, identical except in the adverbs they contain:

(18) a. Sue nun **ecey**   hakkyo ey ka ko   John un **onul** ka ss ta
       Sue-TOP yesterday school-TO go-AND John-TOP today   go-PAST
       'Sue went to school yesterday, and John today.'

   b. Sue nun **nayil**   hakkyo ey   ka ko   John un
      Sue-TOP tomorrow   school-TO   go-AND   John-TOP

      ecey   ka ss ta
      yesterday   go-PAST
      'Sue goes to school tomorrow and John went yesterday.'

Examples like this could be found with other connectives, but *-ko* is a particularly good example because it is maximally ambiguous due to its two forms [+temporal] and [-temporal].

We claim that the non-occurrence of an overt tense marker on the first clause signals that there is likely to be underdeterminacy, that inferences should not be drawn yet, and the hearer should wait for more information from the final clause. Here the situation is more complex, because we don't necessarily wish to stipulate that we have a metabox around both clauses in the way that we did for the [+temporal] connectives, since here it is possible for the clauses to be temporally independent. This time, the non-occurrence of tense alerts the hearer to the possibility of the clauses being either inferentially dependent (with a surrounding metabox) or independent (without a metabox). Sometimes there is a three way ambiguity, as demonstrated below:

(19) a. Chelswu nun   phiano lul   chi ko   nolay lul   pull ess ta
        Chelswu-TOP   piano-OBJ   play-AND   song-OBJ   sing-PAST
        'Chelswu played the piano and sang.'

   b. John-i nolayha-0-ko chwum-ul chwu-ess-ta
      'John sang a song and he danced.' (independent listing)
      'John sang a song first and then he danced.'
      'John sang a song and danced at the same time.'

Looking at the first sentence in (19), there are three interpretations: 1) additive, the two clauses being linked non-temporally, a listing of separate or independent things; 2) simultaneous, Chelswu is singing to his own playing; 3) sequential, John plays the piano first, and then he sings afterwards. The interpretations can be disambiguated by adding other items in the sentence (for example, adding 'at the same time' would single out the simultaneous reading). In the temporal sequential reading (replaceable by -*kose*), the speaker would be alerted to the possibility of different readings by the non-occurrence of tense on the first clause, and then, while hearing the second, would be working out on the basis of context and narrative flow that the temporal reading was intended. Note that the reading with maximal independence is the additive, and this is the only one in which tense is allowed on the first clause. If the speaker wishes to stress temporal independence and disambiguate the utterance, he could do so by putting overt tense on the first clause. Without tense, all three readings are possible, there is clear underdeterminacy and the hearer has to select a reading by Relevance.

Because of the highly underdetermined nature of these patterns, we would expect there to be ambiguities concerning the scope of questions, negation and imperatives also. This is indeed the case, and the hearer has to choose whether to treat the two clauses inferentially as one (with a surrounding metabox) or as two independent clauses with the scope of the question only over the final clause. Here are examples (the first a modified translation of Kuno's Japanese example (Kuno 1973):

(20) a.   John i   syassu lul   pes ko   oskeli ey   ke syess e yo?
          John-SUBJ shirt-OBJ   take off-AND hanger-ON hang-PAST?
   a. 'After taking his shirt off, did John hang it on a hanger?'
   b. 'Did John take his shirt off and hang it on a hanger?'

   b.   syassu lul   pes ko   oskeli ey   ke sillay yo?
        shirt-OBJ   take off-AND hanger-ON hang-'WANNA'?
   'Do you want to take your shirt off and hang it on a hanger?'

In the second example, the hearer is instructed not to build inferences until after the second clause has been heard, at which point (because of content and context) she builds a metabox around the whole structure and interprets it as one inferential unit.

It has also been claimed that when -*ko* is used in the active sequential sense, negation functions to negate the temporal sequence (thus applying over the whole structure as one inferential unit), and when there is a causal sense present, the negation denies the causal link (as we observed in the previous section) (Kang 1991).

Here is another sentence in which the second clause is being influenced by the content of the first. Again, we want the whole structure to be treated as one inferential unit.

(21) wuli nun kasum ul   coi ko   ku uy   hapkyek
      we-TOP chest-OBJ worry-AND he-POSS pass

   sosik ul   kitali ko iss ess ta
   news-OBJ are waiting-PAST
   'While worrying we were waiting for the news that he
   had passed [the exam].'

Finally in this section, a couple of example sentences of a very different kind, those in which the clauses are not linked as one inferential unit in this way (they are non-temporal). The occurrence of certain lexical items of contrast and emphasis (like *to*, 'too, also', and *nun* (TOPIC)) will signal this reading, but on other occasions the interpretation has to be worked out by the hearer because of the underdeterminacy.

(22) a. wucheykwuk ey to   ka-ko   unhayng ey to ka ss e yo
         post office-TO-TOO go-AND bank-TO-TOO go-PAST
         'I've been both to the post office and to the bank.'

     b. os to   eps-ko   ton to eps e yo
         clothes-TOO   haven't-AND   money-TOO haven't
         'I have neither clothes nor money.'

In all these cases of underdeterminacy and in the instances of ambiguity that we have highlighted, the hearer is reasoning towards and interpretation as she parses what is said. The presence of tense markers or their absence on the first clause provides a mechanism for controlling the way in which this takes place, as we have seen. The hearer is constructing an inference structure on the basis of what is said and the surrounding discourse. This inference structure will be used to draw inferences from, and as the basis for the context for what follows.

7. Conclusion

I have deliberately given these explanations in a pragmatic way with functional motivation since LDS was set up to model the pragmatic process of utterance interpretation. However, making only the uncontroversial assumption that this process is one of drawing inferences, modeling this using labelled deduction has provided a richer concept of structure than syntactic theories standardly provide--in particular richer than familiar concepts of X-bar driven tree structure. Thus, with the addition of labels and the metabox discipline to conditional logic, syntax, semantics and pragmatics can be brought together and used to provide us with helpful insights into linguistic phenomena like that of Korean coordination, giving us an explanation which appears to be more satisfying than those to which previous frameworks have led.

References

Foley, William A and VanValin, Robert D Jr. *Functional Syntax and Universal Grammar.* Cambridge Studies in Linguistics 38. Cambridge: Cambridge University Press, 1984.

Gabbay, Dov. *Investigations in Modal and Tense Logics with Applications to Problems in Philosophy and Linguistics,* 1976.

Gabbay, Dov. forthcoming. *Labelled Deductive Systems.* Oxford: Blackwell.

Gabbay, Dov and Kempson, Ruth. *The Tale of the Missing Operators: a Preliminary Report.* Imperial College and SOAS ms, 1992.

Kang Choonwon. *A Study on -ko Constructions in Korean.* PhD dissertation, Georgetown University, 1991.

Kempson, Ruth. Semantics versus Syntax? Shifting Perspectives on Natural Language Content. In *The Pergamom Encyclopedia of Language and Linguistics* edited by Asher, K., Aberdeen: Aberdeen UP, 1993.

Kempson, Ruth and Gabbay, Dov. *How we Understand Sentences. And Fragments too: Natural Language Interpretation as Labelled Natural Deduction.* SOAS draft ms, 1993.

Kuno, Susumu. *Japanese Syntax.* Cambridge: MIT Press, 1973.

Lee Keedong. *A Korean Grammar on Semantic-Pragmatic Principles.* Seoul: Hankwuk Munhwasa, 1993.

Shin Sung-ock. *Tense and Aspect in Korean.* PhD dissertation, University of Hawaii, 1988.

Sperber, Dan and Wilson, Deirdre. *Relevance: Communication and Cognition.* Oxford: Blackwell, 1986.

SEMANTICS, PRAGMATICS and GRAMMATICALIZATION

12
A Pragmatic Analysis of the Postpositional Marker *Nun*

Seungja Choi

Introduction

For over twenty years, the problem of the postpostional marker *nun* in Korean and its Japanese counterpart *wa* has been amply addressed in a vast literature on the subject. While most of the work in the 1970s was devoted to the semantics or discourse functions of these markers, research in the 1980s proposed syntactic accounts in the framework of government-binding theory utilizing a non-lexical category, the complementizer. A fairly standard syntactic account is that sentence-initial topics in Japanese and Korean are dominated by S' (CP) (Saito 1985, Hoji 1985, Kang 1986). The main focus of that research was to distinguish the position of topics and scrambled elements. None of these analyses, however, has accounted for what licenses the distribution of these markers syntactically. The first such attempt was Whitman (1989), in which he claims that the topic phrase in Japanese and Korean occupies the SPEC position of the projection headed by a modal element, and furthermore he proposes that the category Modal or Mood in Japanese and Korean is the highest category S (IP).[1] However, a close examination of his data reveals that Whitman's hypothesis of the licensing relationship between Modal and Topic phrases cannot be maintained; embedded topics can occur without a modal element in Korean. In this

---

[1] The phrase structure that has been widely adopted in the Government-Binding literature assumes two levels: the first level, X(consists of a head (X-zero, represented as X(or simply X) plus X(s subcategorized COMPLEMENTS. X may be instantiated by a lexical item from a major word class, e.g. N, V, or A, or by a so-called FUNCTIONAL element, e.g. INFLECTION (abbreviated INFL or I) or COMPLEMENTIZER (COMP or C) The second level, X(consists of the X(just defined plus a phrase that is not subcategorized, but is referred to as the SPECIFIER (SPEC) of X(.

paper, I will argue that the felicity of *nun*-marked phrases is a function of the accessibility of the discourse entity to which the *nun*-marked NP is used to refer.

1. Whitman (1989): Co-occurrence Relation between Modals and Topic Phrases

Whitman (1989) claims that topic phrases in Korean are limited just to those embedded clauses where modals are also possible, and he argues that this fact can be explained by the hypothesis that topic phrases occupy the SPEC position of the projection headed by a modal element: that is, it is the modal element which licenses the topic being marked with *nun*.

1.1 Quotative Complementizer -*ko* in Korean and -*to* in Japanese

It is well known that in most embedded clauses, topic marking in Japanese and Korean is generally disallowed on a non-contrastive reading (from Whitman, quoted from Lee & Im 1983):

(1) ab. [Kaul -i / *-un   o-nun   soli-ka]$_{NP}$
    Autumn-NOM/TOP come-PRES sound-NOM

    tul-li-n-ta.
    hear-PASSIVE-PRES-IND
    'The sound of autumn coming can be heard.'

(2) ab. [Ney cwucang-i /*-un olh-ass-um-ul]$_{NP}$ wuli-nun
    your claim-NOM/TOP right-PAST-COMP-ACC we-TOP

    nacwungey-ya kkaytal-ass-ta.
    later- only   realize
    'Only in the end did we realize the rightness of your claim.'

(3) ab. Kore wa [John ga /*wa   yonda] hon desu.
    this   NOM/ TOP   read   book is
    'This is the book that John read.'

However, in Japanese -*to* clauses, non-contrastive topic marking is allowed, as shown by example (4) from Kuno (1989):

(4) Taroo-wa [[ore-wa oobaka da] to]   iw-ta.
     Taroo-TOP I -TOP biggest.fool be COMP   say-PERF
     a. 'Taroo said that I am the biggest fool.'
     b. 'Taroo said, "I am the biggest fool."'

Whitman notes that similar facts hold for the Korean quotative complementizer -*ko* 'that'[2], as shown by (5) (from Whitman 1989):

(5) Chelswu-nun, [sayngsen-un taykwu-ka coh-ta-ko]   hay-ss-ta.
     Chelswu-TOP fish-TOP   cod-NOM   good-INDIC-C say-PAST-IND
     'Chelswu said that as for fish, cod is the best.'

On the basis of these observations, Whitman argues that only the complementizers which co-occur with post-tense modals permit embedded non-contrastive topics.[3] He further claims that this fact can be explained if a licensing relationship between modals and topics is posited in Japanese and Korean. A close examination of the data, however, reveals that the hypothesis of the licensing relationship between modals and topics in Korean is not tenable.

1.2 Factive Complementizer *Kes*

Quotative complements are well known to be root-like contexts. Therefore Whitman's argument hinges on his interpretation of the factive complementizer *kes* '(fact) that' and the complementizer *cwul* 'that'. The complement of *kes* may be headed by an attributive form of Tense as in (6a), or by Indicative-*ta* + (Present) Attributive -*nun* as shown in (6b).[4] When the latter option is chosen, a modal suffix (the Indicative -*ta*) is embedded under the complementizer. Whitman argues that only when the latter option is chosen is an embedded topic possible in a *kes*-complement. The following contrast was presented as evidence:

---

[2] Bhatt & Yoon (1991) point out that the function of complementizer -*ko* in Korean is quite different from lexical complementizers in English in that, while in English lexical complementizers function both as Mood (or clause-type indicator) and Subordinators, the function of -*ko* is simply to indicate verbal subordination.

[3] In this paper, the term "post-tense modal" refers to the non-periphrastic modals, which are not tensed and appear outside the position of Tense and Aspect morphology, such as Indicative -*ta* or the Propositive modal -*ca*.

[4] Whitman (1989) states that it is undesirable to analyze -*nun* in -*ta*-*nun* (*kes*) as the true Attributive Present ending ('processive modifier' in Martin 1992's terminology), because this ending does not alternate with the Past and Future attributive endings. He suggests that it is preferable to analyze this suffix as a fixed attributive form.

(6) a. *Chelswu-nun, [sayngsen-un taykwu-ka coh-un-kes-ul]$_{CP}$
Chelswu-TOP   fish -TOP   cod-NOM good-PRES-C-ACC

palkyenhay-ss-ta.
discover -PAST- IND

b. Chelswu-nun [sayngsen-un taykwu-ka coh-ta-nun-kes-ul]$_{CP}$
Chelswu-TOP fish-TOP   cod-NOM good-IND-ATT-C-ACC

palkyenhay-ss-ta.
discover-PAST-IND
'Chelswu discovered that as for fish, cod is the best.'

Notice, however, that not just the topic marker, but even the nominative marker is disallowed in a *kes*-complement when the modal suffix *-ta* is absent in certain contexts, as indicated in (7a) and (7b):

(7) a. *? Chelswu-nun [kolay-ka   phoyutongmul-i-n-kes-ul]$_{CP}$
Chelswu-TOP [whales-NOM mammals-be-PRES-COMP-ACC

al- ass -ta^5
discover-past-IND

b. Chelswu-nun [kolay-ka   phoyutongmul-i-la-nun-kes-ul]$_{CP}$ al-ass-ta
Chelswu-TOP whale-NOM mammals-be-IND-ATT-COMP-ACC
'Chelswu found out that whales are mammals.'

(8) a.? Chelswu-nun   [Swuni-ka   ttokttokha-n-kes-ul]
Chelswu-TOP Swuni-NOM smart -ATT-COMP-ACC

palkyenhay-ass-ta
discover-past-IND

---

^{5} An anonymous reader points out that *?(7a) sounds quite acceptable when the matrix verb is replaced by *moll-ass-ta* 'didn't know' and becomes fully acceptable when the accusative marker after the COMP is replaced by *to* 'also'. This might be due to the fact that the sentence with *moll-ass-ta* gives a sense of sudden realization. However, even for those speakers who find (7a) with *moll-ass-ta* quite acceptable, the (8b) version is still preferable.

b. Chelswu-nun [Swuni-ka   ttokttokha-ta-nun-kes-ul]
   Chelswu-TOP Swuni-NOM   smart-IND-ATT-COMP-ACC.

palkyenhay- ass-ta
discover-past-IND
'Chelswu discovered that Swuni was smart.'

Whitman's analysis would suggest that the contrast between the (a) versions and (b) versions in (7) and (8) indicates that nominative marking is only possible when the complement *kes* is headed by the modal *-ta*. However, observe the following data:

(9) a. kyengchal-un [Bronco-ey phi-ka   mut-e-iss-nun-kes -ul]
       police -TOP   Bronco-at blood-NOM stained- ATT-COMP-ACC

   palkyenhayssta.
   discovered

   b. *Kyengchal-un [Bronco-ey phi-ka   mut-e-iss-ta-nun-
       police-TOP   Bronco-at blood-NOM stained-Modal-ATT-

   kes-ul]   palkyenhayssta.
   COMP-ACC discovered
   'Police discovered that a blood stain was on the Bronco.'

In contrast to (7) and (8), the nominative maker occurs without the modal *-ta* in (9a). The asymmetry between (7), (8) and (9) indicates that there is no co-occurrence relationship between nominative marking and the modal *-ta*. The data in (1) through (9) indicate that what is relevant here is the nature of the relationship between the matrix verb and the proposition of the complement. A modal suffix *-ta* must be present in a *kes*-complement when the proposition of the complement is an abstract state (i.e., knowledge). In contrast, when the content of the complement is a concrete state (i.e., that which has already happened, or that which has been directly perceived through the action of the matrix verb) the modal suffix *-ta* is absent as in (9a). The following data also support the above generalization:

(10) a. kemchal-chuk-un   [O.J. Simpson-i   Nicole Simpson-ul
        prosecutors-part-TOP O.J.Simpson -NOM Nicole Simpson -ACC

   cwuki-ess-ta- nun -kes-ul]   ettehkey cungmyengha -l- kka?
   kill-PAST-IND-ATT-COMP-ACC how   prove   - will- Q

290 • *Seungja Choi*

   b. *kemchal-chuk-un   [O.J.Simpson-i   Nicole Simpson-ul
      prosecutors-part-TOP   O.J.Simpson- NOM Nicole-   ACC

      cwuki- n-kes-ul]   ettehkey cungmyengha-l-kka
      kill-ATT-COMP-ACC how   prove   will-Q
      'How will the prosecutors prove that O.J. Simpson killed Nicole Simpson?'

The proposition that O.J Simpson killed Nicole Simpson is presupposed knowledge that has not yet been proved. It is not something that could be directly discovered like a stain of blood on a car. It is a proposition that is conjectured, and therefore the modal -*ta* must be present. Hence, the ungrammaticality of (10b).

    In order to make a more systematic case for the above argument (specifically, that the occurrence or absence of the modal -*ta* in a *kes*-complement crucially depends on the relationship between the matrix verb and the proposition of the complement) it will be necessary to consider whether or not the grammaticality judgment for sentences like (7a) improves when the pragmatic context changes. For example, imagine the following scenario: According to our pragmatic knowledge of the world, suppose that whales were regarded as fish up to the point in time when Chelswu, a marine biologist, examined a whale and discovered for the first time that whales are mammals. In this context, the sentence in (7a), repeated again below as (11), becomes fully acceptable.

(11)   Chelswu-nun [kolay-ka   phoyutongmul-i-n-kes-ul]$_{CP}$
       Chelswu-TOP [whales-NOM mammals-be-PRES-COMP-ACC

       al- ass- ta.
       discover-past-IND.

Let us imagine another scenario: Suppose that a woman named Jessica entered a male-only military academy disguised as a man under the name of Jerome. One day a cadet, John, saw Jerome undressed and discovered that Jerome was a woman. In this situation, both the (a) and (b) versions are acceptable:

(12)   a. John-un [Jerome-i   yeca-i-n-kes-ul]$_{CP}$
           John-TOP Jerome-NOM   woman-be-PRES-COMP-ACC

          al-ass-ta.
          discover-PAST-IND

b. John-un [Jerome-i   yeca-i-la-nun-kes-ul]$_{CP}$
   John-TOP Jerome-NOM woman-be-IND-ATT -COMP-ACC

   al-ass-ta
   discover-PAST- IND
   'John discovered that Jerome was a woman.'

This raises doubts about Whitman's argument that the ungrammaticality of (6a) is due to the absence of a modal -*ta* and presence of the topic marker. What is relevant in (6a) and (6b) is the nature of the complement, just as in the cases of (7) - (12). The proposition that "as for fish, cod is the best" is not something that one can directly and instantly perceive like a stain of blood on a car (as in the case of (9a)) or the sex of a person (as in the case of (12a)). Rather it is knowledge that one can only gradually come to grasp through much experience eating fish. Therefore, in this case the modal suffix -*ta* must be present in a *kes*-complement, which accounts for the asymmetry between (6a) and (6b).

At this point, one might wonder if the structure -*ta-nun kes* in (6b), (8b) or (12b) etc. might be the abbreviation of -*ta* + -*ko ha-* + -*nun* + *kes* with the deletion of the Quotative Complement -*ko* plus the verb *ha-* 'say'. There are two reasons against this analysis: First, in cases like ' ... -*ta-nun mal* 'word'/ *sosik* 'message'/ *phyenci* 'letter' etc., it is clearly the result of the optional deletion of -*ko ha-* from -*ta* + -*ko ha-nun mal /sosik/ phyenci*, etc. Unlike these cases, however, in cases like (6b), (8b) or (12b) the "unabbreviated form" cannot be fully acceptable. Observe the following contrast between (13) and (8b), repeated here as (14b):

(13) a. Kkok   tolao- keyss-ta - nun   mal ul
        definitely return-will-IND-PRES word-ACC

   namki-ko   ku nun   salaci-ass-ta.
   leave-and he-TOP   disappeared

   b. Kkok tola-okeyss-ta -ko ha nun mal ul namki-ko   ku nun
      salaci-ass-ta.
      'Leaving a word that he would definitely come back, he disappeared'

(14) a. Chelswu-nun [Swuni-ka ttokttokha-ta-nun-kes-ul]
                              smart-IND-ATT-COMP-ACC
      palkyenhay- ass-ta
      discover-PAST-IND

b.?* Chelswu-nun [Swuni-ka ttokttokha-ta-ko ha-nun-kes-ul] palkyenhay-asta.
'Chelswu discovered that Suni was smart.'

Second, unlike cases like '...-ta-nun mal/sosik /phyenci, etc., -nun in -ta-nun-kes does not alternate with the Past and Future attributive endings. Therefore, as Whitman suggests, it seems preferable to analyze this suffix as a fixed attritutive form. For example, observe the following contrast between (15) and (16):

(15) tolao-keyss-ta-(ko ha)-nun / -n / -ten   ku mal-ul
     return -will-IND-(C-say)-PRES/PAST/RET\the-word-ACC

   chelsekkathi   mit-ko,   Swuni-nun sip nyen-ul   mayil-kathi
   without doubt   believe-and Swuni-TOP ten-year-ACC everyday

   ku-lul   kitali-ass-ta.
   him-ACC   wait-PAST-IND
   'Believing his word that he would come back, Swuni waited for him everyday for ten years.'

(16) Chelswu-nun [Swuni-ka ttokttokha-ta- nun / *-n /*-ten -kes -ul] palkyenhay-ass-ta.

These examples show that there is a clear difference between cases like -ta ko ha-nun mal/sosik, etc. and cases like -ta-nun kes. Thus, the structure -ta-nun kes cannot be analyzed as the result of optional deletion of -ko ha- from -ta ko ha-nun kes.

Whitman's claim (i.e., that an embedded topic is possible in a kes-complement only when the complement is headed by a modal, the Indicative -ta and the Present Attributive -nun) is falsified by the data in (17) - (18), which show that embedded topics can occur in a kes-complement without modals. Thus, there is no licensing relationship between modals and embedded topics.

(17) cikum-kkaci [sayngsen-un kotunge-ka   ceyil yengyangqka-ka
     now until   fish-TOP   mackerel-NOM   most nutrition-NOM

   manh-un-kes ulo]$_{CP}$allyecye-o-ass-una,   choykun yengyangsa
   many-PRES-C as known -come-PAST-but, recent   nutritionist

   tul-uy yenkwu-ey uyhamyen, [yene-ka   ceyil yengyangqka-ka
   PL-of research-by according to salmon-NOM   best nutrition-NOM

manh-un-kes ulo]   palphyotoy-ess-ta.
many-PRES-C as   reported-PAST-INDIC
'Until now, mackerel was known as the most nutritious fish. According to the recent research of nutritionists, however, it was reported that salmon is the most nutritious fish.'

(18) a. [ai-tul   kyoyuk-un   kacengkyosa-lul   twu-nun-kes pota,
        children education-TOP tutor-ACC   have-AT-C than

   hakkyo-ey   ponay- nun- kes -i   te   coh-ul-kes-ulo]
   school-to   send-ATT-COMP-NOM   more   good-FUT-COMP-as

   sayngkaktoy-pni-ta.
   is thought-HON-IND
   'I think that as for children's education, sending them to school is better than to have tutors.'

At this point, one might raise a question as to whether or not the topic NP, *ai-tul kyoyuk-un* 'as for the children's education' in (18a) really occurs inside the complement clause. One piece of positive evidence for the occurrence of the topic NP inside the complement clause is the fact that in (18b) the topic NP can occur after *kacengkyosa-lul twu-nun-kes pota* 'than to have tutors'[6]:

(18) b. [kacengkyosa-lul twu-nun-kes   pota,   ai-tul   kyoyuk-un
        tutors -ACC have-PRES-C than   child-PL education-TOP

   hakkyo-ey   ponay-nun-kes-i   te   coh-ul-kes-ulo]
   school-to   send-PRES-C-NOM   more   good-FUT-C-as

   sayngkak toy-pni-ta.
   be thought-HON-IND

---

[6] Unlike (18), the sentence (17) cannot be tested on whether or not the topic phrase *sayngsen-un* occurs inside the complement clause, because *sayngsen-un* is the type of topic phrase which is not argument of the predicate. This type of topic phrase invariably disallows scrambling of other constituents over it, both in main clauses and in embedded clauses. In sum, non-argument topic phrases always occur in sentence-initial position:

* Taykwu-ka, sayngsen-un   coh-ta.
  cod-NOM   as for fish   best-IND

1.3. Complementizer *Cwul*

Whitman's second argument involves the complementizer *cwul* 'that', which has nominal properties and, like *kes*, is preceded by attributive forms of Tense. However, unlike *kes*, Whitman notes that *cwul* allows its complement to contain a topic. The complementizer *cwul* also disallows embedding of the non-attributive modals, the indicative -*ta*, the suspective -*ci*, etc. Contrast (6a) repeated as (19a) below, and (19b):

(19) a. *Chelswu-nun, [sayngsen-un   taykwu-ka   coh-un-kes-ul]CP
Chelswu-TOP fish -TOP   cod-NOM   good-PRES-C-ACC

palkyenhay-ss-ta.
discover-PAST-IND

b. Chelswu-nun, [sayngsen-un taykwu-ka coh-un-cwul (lo)]
Chelswu-TO fish-TOP   cod -NOM good-PRES-C (as)

al-ass-ta.
know-PAST-IND
'Chelswu thought that as for fish, cod is the best.'

With regard to this fact, which appears to disconfirm Whitman's hypothesis that embedded topics are possible exactly where an embedded modal head is possible, Whitman argues that the complementizer *cwul* allows its complement to contain a non-attributive form of Tense followed by the Future modifier ending -*ul* /-*l*, and furthermore, that this attributive Future suffix -*ul*/-*l* is a modal, an option that is not available for *kes* :

(20) a. Chelswu-nun, [ku phyenci-ka   o-ass-ul-cwul (lo)] cp
Chelswu-TOP that letter-NOM   come-PAST-FUT-C-(as)

al-ass-ta.
know-PAST-IND
'Chelswu thought that the letter would have come.'

b.?*Chelswu-nun, [ku phyenci-ka   o-ass-ul kes-(ul)]cp
Chelswu-TOP the letter-NOM   come-PAST-FUT-C

al-ass-ta.
know-PAST-IND
'Chelswu knew that the letter would have come.'

Thus, he argues that if *-ull-l* is a modal, the contrast between (20a) and (20b) explains the contrast between (19a) and (19b) on the basis of the hypothesis that topics are possible only in embedded clauses with modal heads. This attributive future suffix *-ull-l* does indeed receive a modal rather than a temporal interpretation denoting the speaker's supposition when it follows overtly realized Tense. Therefore it is not unreasonable to assume that this attributive Future suffix *-ull-l* is a modal. However, it is not clear how the contrast between (20a) and (20b) explains the contrast between (19a) and (19b), because *kes* can also select a complement headed by a modal element such as *-ta*. Furthermore, Whitman fails to observe two facts: First, when the complement of *cwul* contains a non-attributive form of Tense followed by *-ull-l*, as in the case of (20a), *al-* is interpreted as 'think', and when *al-* is interpreted as 'think', the missing particle after *cwul* is *ulo* 'by, as'. However, when *al -* is interpreted as 'know', the missing particle after *cwul* is Accusative *-ul*. Therefore, contrary to Whitman's assumption, (20a) and (20b) do not form a minimal pair. Second, the future suffix *-ul /-l*, which we have identified as a modal, can also occur in *kes-*complements when the complement is embedded under certain verbs like *chwucengtoy-* 'is conjectured', as indicated by (21) where the *kes-*complement allows a non-contrastive topic and the non-attributive Tense form *-ass-* followed by a modal (the attributive future suffix *-ul*):

(21). cengpu poko-ey   uyhamyen   Kwangcwu sathay eyse cwuk-un
government report according to Kwangju   event in   die-ATR

salam-i   450 myeng i-lako ha-na, [silcey samangca swu-nun
people-NOM 450 people is-as say-but real   casualty number-TOP

i pota   te   manh-ass-ul-kes ulo]   chwucengtoy- n- ta.
this than more many -PAST-FUT-COMP-as conjectured-PRES-IND
'According to the government report, 450 people died in the Kwangju Incident, but it was conjectured that the real number of casualties was more.'

Furthermore, (20b) becomes grammatical when it is marked by *ulo* and the matrix verb is replaced by a non-factive verb such as *sayngkakha-* 'think':

(22) Chelswu-nun, [ku phyenci-ka o-ass-ul kes-ulo]$_{CP}$ sayngkakhay-ss-ta.
Chelswu-TOP the letter-NOM come-PAST-FUT-C think-PAST-IND
'Chelswu thought that the letter would have come.'

The grammaticality of (21) and (22) lead us to conclude that the deviance of (20b) cannot be attributed to a syntactic constraint that claims the complementizer *kes* does not allow its complement to contain a non-attributive form of Tense followed by the future modifier ending *-ul/-l*. There is no difference between the complementizer *kes* and *cwul* in terms of their ability to contain modals, whether it is the Indicative *-ta* or the future modifier/ modal *-ul/-l*. Consequently, Whitman's second argument involving a non-existent asymmetry between *cwul* and *kes* with respect to modals is not valid and therefore Whitman's hypothesis of the co-occurrence relationship between modal and topic phrases is not tenable.

Instead, we must assume that a syntactically ungrammatical construction is ungrammatical in all contexts and cannot be "amnestied" by semantic, pragmatic or discourse factors. I argue that the deviance of (20b) is the result of a semantic conflict. In (20b) the complement is embedded under *al-* 'know' and the modal interpretation of *-ul/-l* in the complement denotes the speaker's conjecture. Thus, embedding a complement with the modal *-ul/-l* (which denotes the speaker's conjecture) under factive verbs such as *palkyenha-* 'discover' or *al-* 'know' (the meaning of which is incompatible with a speaker's conjecture) naturally results in a semantic anomaly. On the other hand, *sayngkaktoy-* 'is thought' in (18), *al-* 'think' in (20a) and (22) and *chwucengtoy-* 'is conjectured' in (21) are compatible with the modal *-ul/-l*, since these verb forms denote a speaker's conjecture, and hence the grammaticality of (18), (20a), (21) and (22).[7]

A further piece of evidence against Whitman's hypothesis emerges in the data in (23), where a non-contrastive topic occurs in the embedded clause of an *-(u)m* nominalization. Observe the contrast between (2b) and (23) (from a letter by missionary Park):

[7] The complement clauses in (17), (18), (19b), (20a), (21) and (22) are all marked by a lexical case *ulo* whereas in (20b), the complement clause is accusative-marked. Within the framework of GB, there is a difference between inherent lexical case such as the Instrumental *ulo* and structural case such as the Accusative *-lul*. Based on this fact, one might wonder if, instead of a semantic explication, the data in (17) - (22) can be explained more simply in terms of case-marking. There are two reasons against this case-marking explanation:

1) Unlike other theta-assigning postpositions like *eyse* 'at' or *hanthey* 'to', this instrumental *ulo*, I propose, is not present at D-structure, where this inherent Case is assigned to the complements directly by the verbs, but is inserted at S-structure for the purpose of Case realization.

While there is much debate on nominative Case assignment, a fairly standard account for accusative Case assignment in Korean claims that it is agentivity of the verb which is responsible for accusative Case:

(i) An NP is assigned accusative Case by an [+agentive] V under government. However, the verbs *chwucengtoy-* 'is conjectured' in (21), *allyeci-* 'is known' in (17), *al-* 'think' in (19b) and (20a), are all [-agentive]. Therefore, the complement cannot be assigned accusative Case under these verbs. Instrumental marker *ulo* on these complements is a realization of inherent Case assigned to these complements by the verbs. However, following Chomsky (1986), I assume there is a distinction between Case assignment at D-structure and Case realization at S-structure. According to Chomsky, an NP is assigned inherent Case at D-structure by the lexical category that governs and theta-marks it; and such an inherent Case is realized at S-structure under government by the Case marker, which is either the Case-assigning category (P, N, or V) or an inserted preposition. A similar analysis which splits the Case Assigner and Case realizer has been proposed for the dative/locative marker on experiencers in Korean by Y.J. Kim (1990) and a similar difference between Case marker/prepositions has been described in Chichewa by M. Baker (1988). In these analyses, the DAT/LOC marker in Korean and the instrumental prepositions in Chichewa are not present at D-structure, where inherent Case is assigned to these NPs directly by the verbs. Similarly, I propose that instrumental markers *ulo* on the complements in (17)-(22) are not present at D-structure. Rather, these Case markers are inserted at S-structure to realize the inherent Case assigned to them at D-structure. Therefore, unlike other postpositions in Korean, they are neither theta-markers nor Case assigners of the complements. Due to limitations of space, I will not go into the details of motivation and evidence, but one fact can be observed: Unlike other theta-assigning postpositions, this *ulo* cannot be used independently without verbs:

1)   A: nwukwu-hanthey   ku   chayk-ul   cwu-ess-ni?
           who   to   the book-ACC   give-PAST-Q
           'To whom did you give the book?'

        B: Yenghuy-hanthey.
           Yenghuy-to
           'To Yenghuy.'

(23) [Warai salam-tul-eykey philyoha-n-kes-un kihoy-wa
Warai people-PL-to need -PRES-thing-TOP opportunity-and

tongki-lul puyeha-nun-kes- i- m -ul]
motivation-ACC provide-PRES-COMP-COP-COMP-ACC

kkaytal-ass-upni-ta.
realize-PAST- HON-INDIC
'We realized that what is needed for the Warai people is to give them opportunity and motivation.'

The -(u)m nominalizer never allows modals including the future modifier -ull-l, which we have interpreted as a modal. However, as indicated in (23), the non-contrastive topic marker nun occurs in -(u)m nominalization clauses. The above discussion of the nominalizers kes, cwul, and -(u)m clearly demonstrates that Whitman's hypothesis of a licensing relationship between modals and topic phrases cannot be maintained.

Latent in Whitman's hypothesis is the assumption that topic sentences in Japanese and Korean are instances of CP, and that CP topic sentences have the topic phrase in the SPEC of CP and a derived lexical overt head in the position of COMP. These assumptions, in turn, are made on the analogy of Germanic V2 languages. The exhibition of verb second phenomena in these languages suggests that CP topic sentences must be projected from an overt lexical head at s-structure. CP topic sentences thus have the topic phrase in the SPEC/CP position, and a derived lexical (overt) head in the position of COMP. Whitman argues that CP topic sentences in Korean and Japanese in fact share the property that they are headed by an overt X(category at s-structure and that, while the lexical head in Germanic V2 languages is Tense (Travis 1984, Pollock 1989), it is the category Modal

---

2) A: ai-tul kyoyuk-un ettehkey sayngkakhay?
child-PL education-TOP how think
'How do you think about the children's education?'

*? B: hakkyo ey ponay-nun-kes-i te coh-ul-kes-ulo.
school-to send-PRES-COMP more good-FUT-COMP-as
'(I think) that sending them to school is better.'

2) The discussion of kes-complements above has already shown that the nature of the relationship between the matrix verb and the proposition of the complement plays a role in allowing the modal suffix -ta in the complement. For these reasons, the semantic explication in which the semantics of the matrix verb and the complement play a role is more consistent and explanatory.

that heads topic sentences in Japanese and Korean. The resulting analysis of IP structure for Korean and Japanese proposed by Whitman is given in (24):

(24)   MP (IP)
            /   \
        SPEC   M((I()
                /   \
           Mood(I ()   TP
                      / \
                   Tense   VP

Thus, the status of the category Modal or Mood in Korean and Japanese is parallel to the status of the category Tense in Germanic and Romance languages. The basic clause structure of CP posited for these languages by Pollock (1989) is given in (25):

(25)

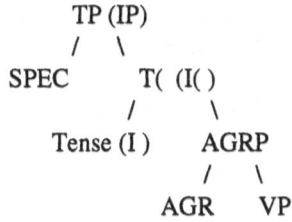

         TP (IP)
          / \
      SPEC   T((I( )
              /   \
          Tense (I) AGRP
                    /   \
                  AGR   VP

If CP topic sentences must be projected from an overt lexical head, with the result that topic sentences in Korean need not be projected by a modal head, then this, in turn, leads us to question a fairly standard account of topic phrases in Japanese and Korean: namely, that sentence-initial topics in these languages are in the SPEC of CP position (Saito 1985, Hoji 1985 for Japanese, Kang 1986 for Korean). We have seen that the syntactic account with the hypothesis of a licensing relationship between modals and embedded topics cannot be maintained. In the following section, I propose a pragmatic account of the topic marker *nun*.

2. Accessibility of the Discourse Entity as a Felicity Condition

An examination of the above data reveals that the modal is irrelevant to the distribution of embedded topic phrases. Instead, what is relevant is that one of the discourse conditions that must be met by a felicitous topic marked by *nun* is that the discourse entity to which the *nun*-marked topic refers has relatively high accessibility or assumed familiarity. Natural languages show various phenomena which require familiarity or accessibility of the discourse entity as a felicity condition (e.g., English inversion). There are many ways in which familiarity or accessibility of the discourse entity can be obtained (see Prince 1981a, 1981b, 1991; Horn 1986). In this paper, however, I will discuss only two phenomena: outbound anaphora in English and contrastive topics in an embedded clause in Korean and Japanese. Both of these phenomena will show that assumed familiarity or relative accessibility can be obtained through CONTRAST. That is, by virtue of being in contrast, an entity can acquire more relative accessibility and hence assumed familiarity.

2.1 Outbound Anaphora

In discussing outbound anaphora, exemplified in (26) ((27), Ward, et. al. (1991) convincingly demonstrate that the felicity of outbound anaphora, as with anaphora in general, is a function of the accessibility of the discourse entity to which the anaphor in question refers, and that pragmatic factors such as contrast and topicality serve to increase the salience or accessibility of discourse entities evoked by word-internal elements. The first attempt to rule out word-internal antecedents for anaphoric elements is found in Postal (1969: 230), where contrasts such as (26a) and (26b) are discussed:

(26) a. Hunters of animals tend to like them. [them = animals]
     b. *Animal hunters tend to like them.

(27) a. *Max is an orphan and he deeply misses them. (orphan = 'a child whose parents have died') (Postal 1969:206, ex. 3a)

   b. *The best pork comes from young ones. (pork = 'meat from pigs)
   c. *Smokers really shouldn't do so. (Postal 1969: 217, ex. 65b)

On the basis of such data, Postal argues that coreferential pronouns (e.g., (27a)), 'identity of sense' pronouns (e.g., (27b)), and the pro-VP *do so* (e.g., (27c)) cannot be anaphorically related to words that constitute 'part of the meaning' of another word in the sentence. Even if a word is morphologically present within another word, Postal claims it still cannot serve as an antecedent for these anaphoric elements, as illustrated in (26b) and (27c). Thus, words such as 'animal hunters' constitute a type of ANAPHORIC ISLAND ('a sentence part ... which cannot contain the antecedent structure for anaphoric elements lying outside' (Postal 1969: 205). Advocates of the LEXICAL INTEGRITY HYPOTHESIS claim that the existence of anaphoric islands follows from the hypothesis that syntactic processes do not have access to the internal structure of words. Because word-internal components are not visible to syntactic operations, there is no way for an anaphor to be coindexed with a word-internal antecedent. Cases of outbound anaphora are thus predicted to be categorically ungrammatical (cf. Pesetsky 1979, Kiparsky 1982, and Mohanan 1986). Watt (1975), however, notes that outbound anaphora is permitted when the antecedent bears contrastive stress, as in (28a-d) (from Ward et. al. 1991):

(28) a. For a SYNTAX slot, I'd rather see someone with more extensive coursework in it. (Judith Levi discussing various subdisciplines of linguistics; January 18, 1987)

b. Patty is a definite KAL KAN cat. Every day she waits for it. (Television advertisement for Kal Kan; January 28, 1987)

c. Cliff Barnes: Well, to what do I owe this pleasure?
Ms. Cryder: Actually, this is a BUSINESS call, and I'd like to get right down to it. ('Dallas': 1987).

d. All the NIXONites I know are for putting all the Agnewites in cold storage till 1976; but HE HIMSELF doesn't care a fig. (Watt 1975: 106)

Watt claims that the contrast between Nixon and Agnew marked prosodically by a pitch accent on Nixon 'exposes' the antecedent in a way a deaccented antecedent would not. Likewise, in (28a) the speaker is contrasting syntax with other subdisciplines of linguistics, and in (28c) the second interlocutor contrasts business with pleasure. Watt also argues that 'exposed' antecedents result in reduced processing effort (1975:105). However, it has been noted that the function of prosodic prominence is not to expose linguistic strings, but rather to highlight, or focus, the discourse entities to which those strings refer. (Wilson & Sperber 1979; Prince 1981b, 1986; Rooth 1985; Pierrehumbert & Hirschbert 1990).

Citing a series of psycholinguistic experiments (McKoon et. al. 1990), Ward et. al. (1993) convincingly demonstrates that the degree to which outbound anaphora is felicitous is determined by the relative accessibility of the discourse entities evoked by word-internal lexical elements, rather than by any principle of syntax or morphology and that the relative accessibility or salience of the discourse entities is increased by pragmatic factors.

More specifically, a discourse entity is more accessible when the entity stands in salient opposition to some other entity, as shown in (28a)-(28d). It has also been claimed by Ward et. al. (1993) that the notion of topicality serves to increase the accessibility of discourse entities to the extent that the outbound anaphora is more felicitous. One assumption that has to be made clear in this analysis is that this view of anaphora sees it as a relation between a linguistic anaphor and its nonlinguistic referent in the discourse world. This contrasts with the earlier prevailing view of anaphora as essentially a relation between linguistic elements.

The phenomenon of outbound anaphora seen above clearly indicates that the accessibility of a discourse entity can be increased enough to render outbound anaphora felicitous, when the entity stands in contrast to some other discourse entity.[8] This result, in turn, indicates that anaphora, like the notion of topic, requires the familiarity of a particular discourse. Familiarity develops syntactically and/or pragmatically.[9] When the anaphor has a linguistic antecedent, it is predictable and hence familiar: this is the case of syntactic development (i.e. surface anaphora). Pragmatic development of familiarity can occur in several ways: when the discourse entity is visible in reality at the time of discourse, i.e. 'deep' anaphora (cf. Sag & Hankamer 1984), when the discourse entity is pragmatically presupposed (cf. Kartunnen 1976; Stalnaker 1977), or when the discourse entity is in a salient partially ordered set-relationship to previously evoked referents or in contrast to other entities, as we have seen above.

2.2 *Nun* -Marked Topics in Embedded Clauses

It is well known that *nun*-marked topics in Korean and *wa*-marked topics in Japanese are disallowed in most embedded contexts, as shown by (1) and (2), repeated here as (29a) and (29b), and by Japanese examples from Kuno (1973):

(29) a. [Kaul-i /-*un   o-nun   soli-ka] $_{NP}$ tulli-n- ta.
        Autumn-NOM/-TOP come-PRES sound-NOM hear-PRES-IND
        'The sound of autumn coming can be heard.'

---

[8] In Baker (1995), Locally free reflexives in British English, which are anaphors in the sense that they are referentially defective NPs--which entails that they cannot be used deictically, are subject to two conditions: a contrastive requirement and a discourse prominence requirement. It is interesting to note that contrast plays a role in this type of anaphora also.

[9] 'Topichood' is also claimed as a relevant factor in Backward Pronominalization in Gundel (1976).

b. [Ney cwucang-i/-*un   olh-ass-um-ul]$_{NP}$ wuli-nun
   your claim-NOM/-*TOP right-PAST-COMP-ACC   we-TOP

   nacwung-ey-ya   kkaytal-ass-ta.
   end-in-only   realize -PAST-IND
   'Only in the end did we realize the rightness of your claim.'

c. [Kyewul-i/-*un   o-myen] CP pom- i   mel-ci   anh-ta
   winter-NOM/-*TOP   come-if   spring-NOM far-COMP not-IND
   'If winter comes, spring is not far off.'

(30) a. John wa   sono hon o   yon-da.
        John TOP this book ACC read-PAST
        'John read this book.'

     b. *Kore wa [John wa   yonda] hon   desu.
        this TOP John TOP read   book is
        'This is the book that John read.'

     c. Kore wa [John ga   yonda] hon   desu.
        this TOP John NOM   read   book is
        'This is the book that John read.'

(31) a. Kuzira wa   hoyuu-doobutu de aru.
        whale TOP   mammal   is
        'A whale is a mammal.'

     b. *Kuzira ga   hoyuu-doobutu de aru.
        whale NOM   mammal   is

     c. *[Kuzira wa hoyuu-doobutu de aru] koto wa yoku shirarete iru.
         whale TOP mammal   is   fact TOP well known   is

     d. [Kuzira ga   hoyuu-doobutu de aru] koto wa yoku shirarete iru.
         whale NOM mammal   is   fact TOP well known   is
        'The fact that a whale is a mammal is well known.'

However we have seen that some embedded clauses do allow *nun*-marked topics in Korean and *wa*-marked topics in Japanese as indicated in (4), (5) and (6b) repeated here as (32), (33) and (34), respectively.

(32) Taroo-wa [[ore-wa   oobaka   da] to]   iw-ta.
     Taroo-TOP I -TOP   biggest.fool be COMP   say-PERF
     a. 'Taroo said that I am the biggest fool.'
     b. 'Taroo said, "I am the biggest fool."'

(33) Chelswu-nun, [sayngsen-un taykwu-ka coh-ta-ko]$_{CP}$ hay-ss-ta.
      Chelswu-TOP fish-TOP   cod-NOM good-IND-C   say-PAST-IND
      'Chelswu said that as for fish, cod is the best.'

(34) Chelswu-nun, [sayngsen-un taykwu-ka coh -ta -nun -kes- ul]cp
      Chelswu-TOP   fish-TOP cod-NOM good-IND-ATT-COMP-ACC

      palkyenhay-ss-ta.
      discover-PAST-IND
      'Chelswu discovered that as for fish, cod is the best.'

We have tried to show that the co-occurrence relationship between topic phrases and modals cannot explain the occurrence of embedded topic phrases.

In what follows, I propose a pragmatic account of embedded topic phrases. The assumption concerning the pragmatic framework that I will be adopting is a revised view of anaphora. One standard view of anaphora and of reference in general involves a direct relation between linguistic elements; both the antecedent and the anaphor must be present in the given sentence(s) as words. In my analysis, however, reference is viewed as a relation that holds between language and one or more entities in a constructed representation, or model, of the ongoing discourse (see Karttunen 1976, Grosz 1977, Webber 1979, and Sidner 1979, *inter alia*).

I propose that *nun*-marked topics in Korean and *wa*-marked topics in Japanese are allowed in any embedded clause, as well as in root clauses, only if the relative accessibility of the discourse entity is high. Pragmatic factors that affect the accessibility of discourse entities are at least three: topicality/discourse prominence, partially ordered set-relationship to a previously evoked entity (cf. Prince 1991), and contrast. In this paper, I will discuss just two of them: topicality and contrast. Recall sentence (31c), repeated here as (35):

(35) *[Kuzira wa hoyuu-doobutu de aru] koto wa yoku shirarete iru
       whales- TOP mammals   is   fact TOP well known is
      'It is well known that whales are mammals.'

However, now imagine the following scenario: A mother is scolding her child, who has returned from school with a poor score on his biology test; one of the questions the child got wrong is about whales. The mother says,

(36) [Kuzira wa   hoyuu dootbutu de aru] koto o   kimi wa
     whales-TOP mammals   is   that ACC you TOP

   shira-nakatta ka
   know-not   Q
   'Didn't you know that whales are mammals?'

In this context, where *kuzira* 'whale' has been the topic, (36) is much better than (35) and many native speakers accept it. Consider the following sentence from advertisements in Christian publications about prayer:

(37) ceca-nun   [kito-la-n   sayngmyeng-uy hohup-i-m -ul]
     author-TOP   prayer-as-TOP   life -of   breathing-be-COMP-ACC

   ciksiha-myesayngmyenglyek   iss-nun   kitolon-ul
   look in the face-and power of life be-PRES theory of prayer-ACC

   cenkayha-n-ta.
   develop-PRES-IND
   'Emphasizing that prayer is the breathing of life, the author develops an invigorating theory of prayer.'

Here, *kito* 'prayer' is the topic of the whole page in which publications about prayer were advertised. Thus, topicality renders the embedded topic in (37) felicitous. The following example in (38) shows that a *nun*-marked topic can occur even in a relative clause in which, Whitman claims, clause-final modals *-ta*, *-ca*, *-kwun*, etc. may not occur, and therefore topics are disallowed:

(38) [[kito-nun   salm-uy   thayto-i-mye   cwunim-kwa-uy
      prayer-TOP   living-of   attitude-be-and Lord-with-of

   kyocey-i-ko   yengcek   wuntong   - i- m- ul]
   fellowship-is-and   spirtitual movement-be-COMP-ACC

   seltuklyek-iss-key kangcoha-ko-iss-nun] i   chayk-un   kito-ey
   convincingly   emphasize-be-PRES   this book-TOP prayer

   kwanhan   tto   hana-uy cwumoktoy-nun kyocay-i-ta.
   - about   another   one-of noteworthy   text-be-IND
   'This book, which convincingly emphasizes that prayer is an attitude of living, fellowship with the Lord, and a spritual movement, is yet another noteworthy textbook.'

Another context in which *wa* is allowed in embedded clauses is when the two subjects or objects are contrasted. In this respect, Japanese and Korean show the same pattern. Observe the following examples from Kuno (1973): ((30a) - (30c) are repeated below as (39a)-(39c)):

(39) a. John wa sono hon o yon-da.
 John-TOP this book ACC read-PAST
 'John read this book.'

 b. * Kore wa [John wa yonda] hon desu.
 this TOP John TOP read book is

 c. Kore wa [John ga yonda] hon desu.
 this-TOP John NOM read book is
 'This is the book that John read.'

(40) Kore wa [John wa yonda ga Mary wa yomanakatta]
 this TOP John TOP read but Mary TOP read-not-PAST

 hon desu.
 book is
 'This is the book that John read but Mary didn't.'

Kuno attributes the grammaticality of (40) to the fact that John is in contrast with Mary. However, Kuno's statement simply *describes* the fact. It is not explanatory. Why does 'being in contrast' suddenly make the sentence felicitous? The context in which (39a) might be uttered is when John has been talked about or implied. In other words, John has been or is the topic. Therefore, John acquires the relative accessibility and hence the grammaticality of (39a). On the other hand, (39b) and (39c) can be uttered when the book has been or is the topic. Consequently, in such a context 'John' does not have high relative accessibility, hence the ungrammaticality of (39b). But in (40), by virtue of being in contrast, the relative accessibility of John and Mary is increased as in the case of outbound anaphora in English. Hence, *wa* is felicitously used. Observe the following Korean examples showing the same pattern:

(41) a. Ku sihem i [John *un / i tteleci-n] sihem ita.
 that exam NOM John-*TOP/NOM fail-PAST exam is
 'That exam is the one that John failed.'

b. Ku sihem i [John un tteleci-ko Mary nun puth-un]
that exam NOM John fail- and Mary pass-PAST
sihem ita.
exam is
'That exam is the one that John failed but Mary passed.'

Notice that even when a contrasted element does not occur explicitly the sentence is felicitous, as long as the *wa*-marked phrase is interpreted contrastively. That is, in this case the *wa*-marked phrase is contrasted implicitly with some other entity in the discourse which became salient (from Hoji 1985):

(42) John-ga [np [s Bill-wa /*-wa Mary-ga   sasotta] baa]-e itta.
      John NOM   Mary NOM invited bar-to went
      'John went to the bar where Mary invited Bill.'
      '*John went to the bar where as for Bill, Mary invited him.'

3. Conclusions

We have found unsupportable the syntactic hypothesis of a licensing relationship between modals and topic phrases which says that topic phrases occur in constructions with overt heads in COMP, and that this overt head is a modal element in Japanese and Korean. Instead, this paper has argued that the relative accessibility of the discourse entity referred to by the *nun*-marked element makes the occurrence of *nun*-marked phrases, whether topic or contrastive, more felicitous. Previous semantico-pragmatic accounts of Japanese *wa* and Korean *nun* have pointed out that the phrase marked by these markers represents 'given' (Kuno 1973), 'identifiable' (Iwasaki 1987), 'assumed familiarity' (Hinds 1987), 'set-anaphoric' (Miyagawa 1987), and 'contrastiveness' (Sohn 1986). However, none of these researches captured the link between contrast and the familiarity of the discourse entity. Some researchers, finding that the two usages are not entirely separable, sidestep this baffling problem simply by asserting that the contrastive use is a subcase of the topic use or vice versa.

The discourse entity to which the topic NP refers must be 'salient' or 'accessible', whether by being directly evoked or by indirect routes. That much is well known. In this paper, I have confirmed that the discourse entity becomes more accessible when the entity is in contrast with some other entity in the discourse. Two phenomena, outbound anaphora in English and the topic phrase in an embedded clause in Korean and Japanese, indicate that this seems to be a universal linguistic phenomenon. Given the correlation between 'contrast' and 'the relative accessibility of the discourse entity', I propose that the shared core of the two seemingly distinctive functions of *wa/nun* is the accessibility of the discourse entity and, accordingly, I have presented 'topic' *wa/nun* and 'contrastive' *wa/nun* as one unified phenomenon.

References

Bhatt, Rakesh and James Yoon. On the composition of COMP and parameters of V2. *Proceedings of WCCFL*, 1991.

Baker, C.L. Contrast, discourse prominence, and intensification, with special reference to locally free reflexives in British English. *Language*, vol. 71, no. 1, 1995.

Baker, M. Theta Theory and the Syntax of Applicatives in Chichewa. *Natural Language and Linguistic Theory* 6, pp. 353-389, 1988.

Chafe, Wallace L. Givenness, contrastiveness, definiteness, subjects and topics.*Subject and Topic*, edited by Charles N. Li. New York: Academic Press, pp. 21-55, 1976.

Chay, Wan. Cosa 'nun' uy uymi [The semantics of the particle 'nun']. In *Kwuke uy thongsa uymilon*, edited by Ko Yengkun. Seoul: Tower Press, 1983.

Chomsky, N. *Knowledge of Language: Its Nature, Origin, and Use*. New York: Praeger, 1986.

Grosz, Barbara. *The representation and use of focus in dialogue understanding*. Berkeley, CA: University of California dissertation, 1977.

Gundel, Jeanette. Stress, Pronominalization and the Given-New Distinction. *Papers from the Seventh Annual Meeting of the North Eastern Linguistic Society*. M.I.T, 1976.

Hinds, John. Thematization, assumed familiarity, staging, and syntactic binding in Japanese. In *Perspectives on Topicalization: The Case of Japanese wa*, edited by Hinds, Maynard, and Iwasaki, pp. 83-106, 1987.

Hoji, Hajime. *Logical form constraints and configurational structure in Japanese*. University of Washington Ph.D. dissertation, 1985.

Horn, Lawrence. Presupposition, theme, and variation. *Papers from the Parasession on Pragmatics and Grammatical Theory*. Chicago: CLS, 1986.

Iwasaki, Shoici. Identifiability, scope-setting, and the particle *wa*: A Study of Japanese spoken expository discourse. In: *Perspectives on Topicalization*, edited by Hinds, Maynard and Iwasaki, pp. 107-141, 1987.

Kang. Y.S. *Aspects of Korean syntax and parameters in Universal Grammar*. Harvard University Ph.D. dissertation, 1986.

Karttunen, Lauri. Discourse referents. In: *Syntax and semantics VII : Notes from the linguistic undergraound*, edited by James McCawley. New York: Academic Press, pp. 363-86, 1976.

Kim, Y.J. The Syntax and semantics of Korean Case: The Interaction between lexical and syntactic levels of representation. Harvard University Ph.D. dissertation, 1990.

Kiparsky, Paul. Lexical phonology and morphology. In: *Linguistics in the morning calm*, edited by In Seok Yang , Seoul: Hanshin, pp. 3-91 1982.

Kuno, Susumu. *The Structure of the Japanese language*. Cambridge: The MIT Press, 1973.

_____. *Danwa no bunpoo*. Tokyo: Taishuukan, 1978.

_____. *Shin nihon bunpoo kenkyuu*. Tokyo: Taishuukan, 1982.

_____. Blended Quasi-Direct Discourse in Japanese. In: *Japanese syntax*, edited by W. Poser , Palo Alto, CA: CSLI, 1989.

Lee, I.-P. & H. -I. Im. . *Kwuke Munpeplon* [Korean Grammar]. Seoul: Hakyen-sa, 1983

Martin, Samuel. *A Reference Grammar of Japanese*. New Haven: Yale University Press, 1975.

_____. *A Reference Grammar of Korean*. Rutland, Vermont: Charles E. Tuttle Co, 1992.

Maynard, Senko. The given/new distinction and the analysis of the Japanese particles, -wa and -ga. *Papers in Linguistics* 14, pp. 109-130, 1981.

Miyagawa, Shigeru. Wa and the WH Phrase. In: *Perspectives on Topicalization : The Case of Japanese 'wa'* (Typological Studies in Language, Vol 14), edited by Hinds, Maynard and Iwasaki, Amsterdam: John Benjamins Publishing Co, pp. 185-220. 1987.

Mohanan, K.P. *The theory of lexical phonology*. Dordrecht: Reidel, 1986.

Pesetsky, David. Russian morphology and lexical theory. Cambridge, MA: MIT ms, 1979.

Pierrhumbert, Janet, and Julia Hirschberg. The meaning of intonational contours in the interpretation of discourse. In *Intentions in communication*, edited by Phil Cohen, Jerry Morgan and Martha Pollack, Cambridge, MA: MIT Press, pp. 271-311, 1990.

Postal, Paul. Anaphoric islands. *Chicago Linguistic Society* 5, pp. 205-239, 1969.

Prince, Ellen. Toward a taxonomy of given/new information. In: *Radical Pragmatics*, edited by Peter Cole, New York: Academic Press, pp. 223-254 1981a.

_____. Topicalization, focus-movement, and Yiddish-movement : A pragmatic differentiation. *Berkeley Linguistic Society* 7, pp. 249-264, 1981b.

_____. On the syntactic marking of presupposed open propositions. *Chicago Linguistic Society* 22 (*Papers from the parasession on pragmatics and grammatical theory*), pp. 208-22, 1986.

_____. On the topicalization of indefinite NPs. *Journal of Pragmatics* 16, pp. 167-177, 1991.

Pollock, J.-Y. Verb Movement, UG. and the Structure of IP. *Linguistic Inquiry* 20: 3, 1989.

Rooth, Mats. *Association with focus*. University of Massachusetts (Amherst) Ph.D.dissertation, 1985.

Sag, Ivan.A., and Jorge Hankamar. Toward a theory of anaphoric processing. *Linguistics and Philosophy* 7, pp. 325-345, 1984.

Saito, Mamoru. *Some Assymmetries in Japanese and their theoretical consequences.*MIT Ph.D. dissertation, 1985.

Sidner, Candace. *Toward a computational theory of definite anaphora comprehension in English discourse.* MIT Ph.D. dissertation, 1979.

Sohn, H.-M. Theme-prominence in Korean. *Linguistic Expeditions*. Seoul: Hanshin Publishing Co, 1986.

Stalnaker, R.C. Pragmatic Presuppositions. In *Proceedings of the Texas Conference on Perfomatives, Presuppositions, and Implicature*, edited by A. Rogers, B. Wall and J. Murphy. Arlington, VA: CAL, pp. 135-148, 1977.

Travis, L. *Parameters and Effects of Word order Variation.* MIT Ph.D. dissertation, 1984.

Ward, Gregory; Richard Sproat; and Gail McKoon. A pragmatic analysis of so-called anaphoric islands. *Language*, vol. 67, no. 3, 1991.

Watt. W. The indiscreteness with which impenetrables are penetrated. *Lingua* 37, pp. 95-128, 1975.

Webber, Bonnie. *A formal approach to discourse anaphora.* New York: Garland Press, 1979.

Whitman, John. Topic, Modality, and IP Structure. *Harvard Studies in Korean Linguistics* III, pp. 341-356, 1989.

Wilson, Deirdre, and Dan Sperber. Ordered entailments: An alternative to presuppositional theories. In *Syntax and semantics XI: Presupposition*, edited by Choon Kyu Oh and David Dinneen, pp. 299-323. New York: Academic Press, 1979.

13
Conditional Forms and Meanings in Korean

Chang-Bong Lee

1. Introduction[1]

The conditional constructions in Korean are formed by the change of verb forms in the protasis; that is, by attaching conditional markers (verbal suffixes) to the verb stem. Among these conditional markers *-(u)myen* and *-tamyen* are the two most frequently used in forming conditional constructions in Korean. The paper aims to study the forms and meanings of these two conditional markers and their functional division of labor within Korean grammar.

Bak (1987) examined the semantic properties of these two conditional markers and discussed their differences in pragmatic function. His main argument was that *-(u)myen* is the unmarked ubiquitous conditional marker used in what he calls 'given' conditionals as well as in 'irrealis'. and 'counterfactual' conditionals, whereas *-tamyen* is restricted to mark only 'irrealis' and 'counterfactual' conditionals. In a similar vein, Bak also claimed that, unlike English conditionals, a 'given' situation can also be a conditional target in Korean; that is, even the realis situation is subject to conditionality in Korean.

In the first half of this paper, I argue against Bak's above claim and advocate the following points; a) I claim that *-(u)myen* is not a ubiquitous conditional marker in Korean, b) I bring evidence to show that the presence of *-(u)myen* does not necessarily constitute a conditional clause: it will be shown that *-(u)myen* can be used to express both a temporal clause for future reference and a 'given that *p*' clause. Finally, having proven that not every occurrence of a *-(u)myen* clause constitutes a conditional construction,

---

[1] I thank Sabine Iatridou for leading me into research on the topic of conditionals in Korean and for her valuable comments on an earlier version of this paper. I also wish to thank Young-Suk Lee for presenting this paper at the ICKL meeting in London on my behalf.

I argue that the fact that *-(u)myen* is compatible with the 'given' (realis) situation in some examples should not lead to the conclusion that even the realis situation can be a conditional target in Korean.

In the second half of the paper, I discuss the functional division of labor between *-(u)myen* and *-tamyen*. First, I start the discussion by noting their difference in (morpho)syntactic form. I observe that *-tamyen* can be characterized as a Korean version of what Inoue (1983) called 'a cleft-conditional', often paraphrased as 'if it is the case that...' or 'if it is true that...' in English. I note that this cleft-conditional feature provides the *-tamyen* clause with a 'quotative' feature. This semantic feature allows speakers to create a hypothesis by quoting what is believed by somebody other than the speaker. I observe that in this context *-tamyen* is typically chosen over the plain *-(u)myen* for rhetorical purposes. Second, I discuss the 'hypothetical feature' of *-tamyen* clauses. I argue that the choice between *-(u)myen* and *-tamyen* is determined by the speaker's subjective attitude toward the content of the protasis or the whole conditional sentence; that is, *-tamyen* is favored over *-(u)myen* when the content of the protasis is viewed as an unexpected and remote possibility (highly hypothetical), whereas *-(u)myen* prevails over *-tamyen* to mark an expected or immediate possibility (less hypothetical). I also note that this hypothetical feature of *-tamyen* explains why it prevails over *-(u)myen* when the content of the protasis describes an unrealistic situation with a counterfactual flavor.

2. The Semantics of *-(u)myen*
2.1. The Domain of Conditionality in Korean

The general consensus on the conceptual domain of conditionals in natural language is that only the irrealis domain is subject to conditionality and that the speaker's positive conviction is excluded in its target since it belongs to the realis domain, as argued by Akatsuka (1985, 1986). Bak (1987) challenged this long-standing generalization by arguing that Korean is exceptional in this generalization in that even the realis situation can be a conditional target in Korean. His argument was based on the observation that *-(u)myen* clauses, traditionally believed to be the prototypical conditional clause in Korean, can be used to represent the speaker's positive conviction in the realis domain in some examples.

The first set of data discussed by Bak are those in (1) below (from Bak (1987:167))[2].

(1) a. pom-i   o-**myen**,   isa-lul   ha-l   yeyceng-i-ta
        spring-NOM   come-**if**   moving-ACC   do-MOD   plan-be-DEC

   'If(when) spring comes, I am going to move.'

b. yel si-ka   toy-**mye**   cong-i   wullin-ta.
      10 o'clock-NOM   become-**if**   bell-NOM   ring-DEC
      'If (when) it gets to be 10 o'clock, the bell rings.'

Bak argued that the antecedents in (1) above represent given events that must occur in the course of time due to the nature of things; therefore the fact that *-(u)myen* is appropriate in this context clearly shows that given situations can be conditional targets in Korean. I argue, however, that the above sentences do not constitute examples of conditionals.[3] Notice that the most appropriate interpretation of each example in (1) above should be temporal, and not conditional. For instance, in (1a), the fact that spring comes is so natural that nobody will assume it as a possibility; that is, this situation is not subject to conditionality. The speaker does not mean, by uttering this *-(u)myen* clause, that under the condition (possibility) that spring comes he will move, but rather he/she means that when (after) spring arrives he/she will move.

The next set of data is the most interesting and puzzling. Bak (1987) observed that in some deictic contexts *-(u)myen* can be used to describe a situation which the speaker already knows. Consider (2) (Bak 1987:168).

---

[2] I use the following abbreviations in the glosses.

NOM-nominative	ACC-accusative	DEC-declarative
HON-honorific	PAST-past	Q-question
NEG-negation	FUT-future	TOP-topic
IMP-imperative	PRS-present	PROP-propositive
MOD-modifier ending	SUPP-supposition	QUO-quotative

[3] Lukoff (1982) also observed that those phrases consisting of a noun denoting a period of time or a point of time plus a verb like *toy-* (to become) or *o-* (to come) realized by *-(u)myen* in the antecedent clause should be translated as temporal; that is, something like 'when it gets to be. . .'. Let us examine two of his examples. It is worth noting that the temporal interpretation of those sentences which are syntactically of conditional form is most often found with reference to future events.

   (1) yelumpanghak-i   toy-**myen**   san-ina   pata-lo   nolle   kanta
       summer vacation-NOM   become-**if**   mountain-or   sea-to   to play   go-DEC
       ' When summer recess starts, they go on vacation to the mountains or seashore.'

   (2) pom-i   o-**myen**   nal-i   kilecy-eyo
       spring-NOM   come-**if**   day-NOM   become longer-DEC
       'When spring comes over, the days grow longer.'

(2) a. ney-ka   enni-**myen**   ceyil-i-ya?
        you-NOM   elder sister-if   best-be-Q
        'Given that you are my elder sister, can you do anything?'

   b. Hyeng-i-**myen**   hyeng-tapkey   hayngtongha-y
       elder brother-be-**if** elder brother-like   behave-IMP
       'Given that you are my elder brother, behave like my brother.'

The speakers uttering the above sentences patently know the content of the antecedent clause. For instance, (2a) can be felicitously uttered by a younger sister to her older sister in the appropriate context; for instance, when she is upset about her sister's arrogant or bossy attitude. This seems to be a genuine example showing that even a positive conviction can be a conditional target in Korean.

However, once again, I argue that these examples do not constitute conditionals, despite the presence of *-(u)myen*. Under the situation that the speaker obviously knows the content of the *-(u)myen* clause in the realis domain, the use of a *-(u)myen* clause in this case does not evoke IF-conditional meaning; rather, it creates a 'given that *p*' reading. For instance, in (2b), the younger brother talking with his real older brother would not entertain the possibility of the hearer being his brother as a condition unless he were insane or joking for sarcastic purposes, since the relationship of brotherhood is innately given. Under this situation the only available reading for the *-(u)myen* clause is the 'given that *p*' reading.

There are a plenty of examples to demonstrate this type of *-(u)myen* clause in Korean. Consider the following examples.

(3) a. (receiving $10 from a friend)
        sip pwul i-**myen**   chwungpwunha-y
        $10   be-**if**   enough-DEC
        'Given $10, it is enough.'

   b. (knowing that his wife just delivered a baby girl)
       ttal-i-**myen**   ettayyo?   ttal-i-myen   te   coha-yo
       daughter-be-**if**   what's wrong?   daughter-be-if   more   good-DEC
       'Given that we got a baby girl, what's wrong with that? It's better to have a daughter'

Both of the examples in (3) above show that the *-(u)myen* clause is used to create a 'given that *p*' type of clause. For instance, the husband can felicitously utter (3b) to his wife to answer her question "Honey, aren't you disappointed that we had a girl instead of a boy?" Since both the husband and the wife already know the sex of their child after delivery, the use of -(u)myen clause in this case cannot evoke the conditional reading. What the -(u)myen clause does in this case is to mark the given situation (we got a baby girl).[4]

However, it is important to notice that what decides the type of reading in the use of -(u)myen is the speaker's subjective attitude toward the content of the -(u)myen clause at the time of utterance. The same sentence with -(u)myen can be read either as an ordinary conditional sentence or as a 'given that p' type of composite sentence depending on the attitude the speaker takes toward its content at the time of utterance. Consider the following example.

(4)   nayngcangko-ey   maykcwu-ka iss-**umyen**, hancan   hayyaci.
      fridge-in   beer-NOM   exist-**if**, a cup   have to drink
      'Given that we have beer in the refrigerator, we have to drink some.'
      'If there is some beer in the refrigerator, we will have to drink some.'

The speaker uttering (4) above can express two different attitudes depending on the context at the time of utterance[5]. Suppose that the speaker is on his way back home with his friend in the evening. He is not sure whether he stored some beer in the refrigerator in the morning. In this situation, what he intends to say by uttering (4) is something like 'I am not sure whether there is some beer in the refrigerator. However, if there is some, surely we should drink some.' Now, let us imagine a different context. Suppose that the speaker and his friend arrive at his home. He has not been home for some days, and thus he is not sure what will be inside the refrigerator. However, he just hopes that there is some beer so that he and his friend can enjoy a drink. He opens the refrigerator door to check and notices that there is indeed some beer. In this situation, what the speaker intends to say by uttering the -(u)myen clause is something like 'I was not sure what would be inside the refrigerator. I am so happy to find some beer. Given that we have some beer in the refrigerator, we surely should enjoy drinking some.'

---

[4] From a discourse point of view this -(u)myen clause is used to mark the given knowledge (shared knowledge) between the speaker and the hearer as a given topic.

[5] The fact that one morphosyntactically uniform sentence (-(u)myen clause) can be read in two different ways convinces us that the conditional sentence in Korean is not definable morphosyntactically. This Korean fact supports Akatsuka's (1985: 628) claim that conditionals should be identified by considering the speaker's attitude toward the situation described in the antecedent clause or in the whole conditional construction.

Reflecting upon the observations so far, we realize that the fact that in some examples -*(u)myen* clauses can represent the realis situation should not lead us to conclude that the realis domain can be a conditional target in Korean; we have verified that such examples do not constitute conditionals. The discussion of -*(u)myen* clause data thus contradicts Bak's claim, while confirming Akatsuka's (1985) position that the conceptual domain of conditionals is universally the irrealis world.

2.2. -*(U)myen* in the Lexicon

In the previous section we observed that -*(u)myen* clauses can create non-conditional readings like temporal clauses and 'given that *p*' clauses in addition to conditional clauses. In light of this fact, the question arises as to how -*(u)myen* should be stored in the Korean lexicon. There are two possible positions. One is to take the view that there are three different kinds of -*(u)myen* stored separately in the lexicon; that is, -*(u)myen$_1$* (conditional), -*(u)myen$_2$* (temporal) and -*(u)myen$_3$* (given). The other is to take the view that there is only one kind of -*(u)myen$_c$* stored in the lexicon and that the non-conditional readings it creates are side-effects found in the appropriate discourse context. Here I opt for the second position based on the following argument.

If we think of -*(u)myen* as a separate marker for the non-conditional readings it evokes, we would expect it to be interchangeable with a more prototypical marker for creating such non-conditional clauses. For instance, -*(u)myen* would be expected to replace the more typical temporal clause marker -*(u)l ttay* (roughly *when* in English). However, we find that a -*(u)myen* clause cannot always be interchangeable with a temporal -*(u)l ttay* clause, as in (5).

(5)   cip-ey   tochakha-yess-**ul ttay (#-umyen)**, cenhwa-ka wass-eyo
            home-at   arrive-PAST-**when (#if)**,   telephone-NOM came-DEC
            'When (I) arrived at home, a telephone rang.'

In (5), the -*(u)myen* clause can never be interpreted as a temporal clause. With the past tense form of the verb in the antecedent clause, the -*(u)myen* clause is only interpreted as conditional. Consider (6).

(6) a. Chelswu-ka   cip-ey tochakha-yess-**umyen**, cenhwaha-l-keya.
       Chelswu-NOM home-at arrive-PAST-**if**,   call-will-DEC
       'If Chelswu arrived at home, (he) will call.'

   b. Chelswu-ka   cip-ey tochakha-yess-**ul ttay (#-umyen)**,
      Chelswu-NOM home-at arrive-PAST- when(#if),

      cenhwaha-yess-ta.
      call-PAST-DEC
      'When Chelswu arrived at home, (he) called (me).

Notice in (6) that the *-(u)myen* clause cannot replace the *-(u)l ttay* clause to describe the simultaneous temporal relation between the two past events. The use of the *-(u)myen* clause with the past tense form of the verb creates only the conditional reading as in (6a). If we take the position that Korean has *-(u)myen$_t$* as a separate form in the lexicon, we have no answer to explain why (6b) with *-(u)myen* should be bad.[6]

The same story holds of *-(u)myen$_g$* with respect to its possibility as a separate marker for a 'given that *p*' clause. We observe in (7) that *-(u)myen* cannot always be used to mark a given situation the speaker patently knows.

(7) (Noticing that the displayed car is black)
    a. #I cha-ka   kkamansayk-i-**myen**,   maum-ey   tul-eyo.
       this car-NOM black-be-**given that**   mind-to   come-DEC
       'Given that this car is black, I like it.'

---

[6] At this point we should note that all those examples where the *-(u)myen* clause is interpreted as temporal are when the verbal expression in the protasis refers to the future tense, as seen in the earlier examples in (1). Strictly speaking, the situation in the future is not in the realis domain, no matter how obvious it is in terms of its possible realization; it is not yet realized. Actually, the possibility of a conditional clause being interpreted as a temporal clause when it predicts a future event is also observed in English. Reilly (1986) points out that in English there are certain instances in which a *when* temporal and a conditional clause (*if* clause) are roughly synonymous. One such case is typically found when the content of the protasis refers to a predictive future event, as in (3) below (Reilly 1986:313):

(3) When/If the strawberries are in, we'll make fresh strawberry pie.

    b. I cha-ka   kkamansayk-i-**nikka (-mulo)**   maum-ey   tul-eyo.
                                    -since (because)

Notice in (7) that the speaker patently knows the content of the antecedent clause as a given situation. In this situation *-(u)myen* is expected to be able to mark the situation as given. However, we find that in this context *-(u)myen* cannot function as such a marker. Instead we find that only those markers creating a *since* or *because* clause are allowed, as in (7b). If *-(u)myen* were a separate 'given that *p*' clause marker, it would be predicted to function as such a marker whenever the content of the clause describes a given situation. However, we realize in (7) that this prediction is not borne out. This suggests that we view the 'given that *p*' reading of *-(u)myen* as one of the side-effect readings of *-(u)myen$_c$* only in particular discourse contexts. It remains as an important topic to explicate in what context *-(u)myen* creates the 'given that *p*' reading; that is, the grammar that explains why the use of *-(u)myen* in the contexts of (3) and (4) is allowed to create such a reading but not in (7). I leave this topic for future research.

Based on the observations so far, I conclude that there is only one form of *-(u)myen* stored in the lexicon and that the non-conditional readings it creates are side-effect readings found only in the appropriate (discourse) context.

3.   The Functional Division of Labor between *-(u)myen* and *-tamyen* Clauses

When we conceive isolated examples of *-(u)myen* and *-tamyen* clauses, they look interchangeable with no semantic difference because they are both equally translatable by an IF-clause in English.

(8)   Nayil   Chelswu-ka   Sewul-ey   o-**myen (n-tamyen)**,
       tomorrow   Chelswu-NOM   Seoul-to   come-**if**,

       manna-keyss-eyo
       meet-will-DEC
       'If Chelswu comes to Seoul, I will meet him.'

However, a closer look at the form of each clause and its associated semantic features will reveal that these two clauses map two different semantic and/or pragmatic functions, such that one is exclusively used in a context where the other cannot be used, or one is preferred over the other for rhetorical purposes.

3.1. 'Cleft-conditional' -*tamyen* Clauses

The starting point for locating a difference between -*(u)myen* and -*tamyen* is found in their morphosyntactic form. Unlike the plain -*(u)myen*, -*tamyen* is, in origin, a contracted form of -*tako hamyen* which consists of the complementizer *ko* followed by the conditional form of the verb *ha-* (='say'). Assuming that the contracted form preserves the underlying meaning associated with the full form, then we predict that -*tamyen* clauses evoke a conditional meaning like 'if somebody says that. . .'

Inoue (1983) introduced the terms *cleft* and *non-cleft* conditional clause to characterize the forms of conditional construction in Japanese. She noted that Japanese is equipped with both *cleft* and *non-cleft* conditionals as exemplified in (9) below (Inoue 1983: 252).

(9) a. Tokyo-ni sum   -e ba   kuruma-ga   ir-ana-i
        Tokyo-in live -if   car-NOM   need-not-Nonpast

   b.   -(no) nara (ba)
   'If (one) lives in Tokyo, (one) does not/will not need a car.'

According to Inoue, the -*e ba* clause in (9a) is an example of a *non-cleft* form consisting of the tenseless verbal ending -*e* followed by the conditional marker -*ba*, while (9b) is an example of *cleft* form consisting of the complementizer *no* followed by *nara*, the conditional form of the nonpast copula -*da*, followed by the optional -*ba*.

Comparing the structural features of -*tamyen* clause in Korean with the Japanese data in (9) above, I observe that the -*tamyen* clause parallels the *(no) nara (ba)* clause.[7] One important piece of evidence to demonstrate the cleft-conditional feature of the -*tamyen* clause is the fact that the -*tamyen* clause must contain a tense or mood marker inside the verbal conjugation, unlike -*(u)myen* clauses. For instance, consider the data in (10).

---

[7] It is worth noting here that the cleft-conditional forms in the two languages differ in two respects. One is that in Japanese, as Inoue reported, the conditional marker -*ba* is optional, but such a possibility is never allowed in Korean; e.g., **Nayil Chelswu-ka Sewul-ey o-n-ta(ko) ha-* , *manna-keyss-eyo*. In this example, the conditional marker -*(u)myen* must be present after the verb stem *ha-*. The other difference is that the conditionalized verb is the copular verb -*da* in Japanese, while it is the verb *ha-* (= 'say') in Korean. It might be worth researching the semantic and/or pragmatic differences of the cleft conditionals associated with this formal difference between the two languages.

(10) a. Chelswu-ka   Seoul-ey ka-**myen**, na-to ka-l-keya
        Chelswu-NOM Seoul-to go-**if**,   I-too go-will-DEC
        'If Chelswu goes to Seoul, I'll go, too.'

   b. Chelswu-ka Seoul-ey ka-**n-tamyen**, na-to kal-ke-ya
                                 -PRES
   c. *Chelswu-ka Seoul-ey ka-**tamyen**, na-to kal-ke-ya
   d. *Chelswu-ka Seoul-ey ka-ta.
   e. Chelswu-ka Seoul-ey ka-n-ta.

We observe that unlike the -(u)myen clause in (10a), -tamyen cannot be attached directly after the infinitival stem form *ka-* ('to go') as in (10c). There should be a tense morpheme like -n- between the stem and -tamyen as in (10b). This restriction is directly explained by the fact that we do not have an independent sentence like (10d) whereas (10e) is fine. What this shows is that the -tamyen clause is attached only after a full and quotable form of an independent sentence.

The following set of examples in (11) shows that the -tamyen clause can be used to quote the independent clause with a full range of tense, aspect, and modal variation because it originally contained the complementizer -ko (roughly English *that*) attached after the declarative ending form -ta.

(11) a. Chelswu-ka Sewul-ey ka-ss-**tamyen**, cikum cip-ey   iss-ul-keya
                                        -PAST   now home-at stay-FUT-SUPP
        'If Chelswu went to Seoul, he may be at home.'

   b. Chelswu-ka Sewul-ey ka-n-**tamyen**, ku-uy canglay-ka
                                   -PRES   his   future-NOM
      kekceng i-ta
      worry-DEC
      'If Chelswu is going to go to Seoul, I worry about his future.'

   c. Chelswu-ka Sewul-ey ka-koiss-**tamyen**, ppalli mak-ayaha-eyo
                                      -PRESPRO quickly prevent-have to-DEC
      'If Chelswu is in the middle of going to Seoul, we should interrupt him.'

d. Chelswu-ka Sewul-ey ka-ss-ess-**tamyen,** way amwuto
                        -PAST PERFEC   why nobody

   ku-lul mos poass-ni
   him-ACC not saw-Q
   'If Chelswu had gone to Seoul, why did nobody see him?'

To summarize this section, I have argued that the underlying structure of -*tamyen* clauses parallels what Inoue (1983) identified as 'a cleft conditional' usually paraphrased in English as "if it is true that. . ." or "if it is the case that. . .".

3.2. The Pragmatic Functions of -*tamyen* Clauses

3.2.1 -*tamyen* as a 'Factual Conditional' Marker. In the following discussion, I note a discourse context where the structural feature of the-*tamyen* clause as a cleft-conditional clause is pragmatically utilized. The context we note is what Iatridou (1990) identified as a 'Factual Conditional' (FC) context. According to Iatridou (1990), this type of conditional is typically found in a conversation like the following (Iatridou 1990: 58):

(12) a. A: Bill is very unhappy.
     b. B: If he is so unhappy, he should leave.

What differentiates this type from other types of conditionals is that only this type carries the presupposition that somebody believes the content of the IF-clause to be true. For instance, in (12b), the content of the IF-clause is believed by speaker A. In other words, the FC IF-clause does not merely specify the circumstances in which the consequent is true, but assumes that the circumstances under which the consequent is true are the actual ones for some person. This some person is usually an addressee but it can be somebody else not participating in the discourse. For this reason, Iatridou calls this type a 'Factual Conditional'.[8]

---

[8] The term 'Factual Conditional' is not a good one because the adjective 'factual' may mislead some readers into thinking that the context where this type of conditional is used describes a fact rather than an imaginable situation. However, as we will notice later, this type is mainly used to quote somebody else's subjective belief or opinion, independent from its factuality. I propose to use the term 'Quotative conditional' instead, since the adjective 'quotative' well expresses the typical context where this type of conditional is used; that is, in quoting somebody else's belief or opinion.

Let us examine one such context in Korean. Consider (13).

(13) A: Yenghuy-ka   Hankwuk-ey   tolao-l kes-kath-a
       Younghee-NOM   Korea-to   return-FUT seem-DEC
       'I think Younghee will return to Korea.'

   B: Yenghuy-ka   Hankwuk-ey   tolao-(?myen)-**n-tamyen**
       Younghee-NOM   Korea-to   return-PRES-**if**

       way   acikto   cenwha-ka   eps-ni?
       why   still   call-NOM   not exist-Q
       'If Younghee is going to return to Korea, why is there still no call from her?'

In (13) the speaker B cites the speaker A's belief or opinion about Younghee in the form of a -*tamyen* clause in his/her conditional statement. The use of -*(u)myen* clause in this case is not impossible, but rather infelicitous; it lacks the appropriate rhetorical effect to express the speaker's challenging attitude against the hearer's belief or opinion. Notice in (13) that the speaker B expresses doubt by asking a question, while taking the hearer's belief as a mere hypothesis by quoting it under a -*tamyen* clause. The use of a -*(u)myen* clause in this context fails to provide this rhetorical effect.

This line of observation shows that the -*tamyen* clause may be said to be a realized form of what Iatridou (1990) called 'Factual Conditionals' (FC). The fact that Korean reserves a distinctive conditional marker for the FC type of conditional strongly supports Iatridou's original motivation in identifying this as one of the important types of conditionals in English. It is an interesting observation that one type of conditional construction in one language is realized as a separate form in the grammar of the other language.

Based on this initial observation, it is predicted that -*tamyen* will occur when the presupposition requirement for the FC type is met; that is, in the context where the content of the antecedent is believed by somebody other than the speaker himself/herself. This prediction is borne out by the tendency for a -*tamyen* clause to be used frequently to represent a third party's feeling or opinion about which the speaker has no controlled judgment over the possible realization or truth of the described situation.[9]

Consider the following example.

(14) A: Chelswsu-ka   ttokttokhan-kes-kath-a
       Chelswu-NOM   smart-seem to be-DEC
       'I think Chelswu is smart.'

B: Chelswu-ka   ttokttokha-**tamyen** (?**myen**),
    Chelswu-NOM   be smart-**if**

    way   tayhak-ey-nun   mos   ka-ss-ni?
    why   college-to-TOP   cannot   go-PAST-Q
    'If Chelswu is smart, why did he fail to get into college?'

In (14) speaker A expresses his/her own subjective opinion about Chelswu's intelligence. Speaker B strongly challenges the addressee's view by providing the counter evidence in question form, granting that what the speaker A said might be true. In this context -*tamyen* is much preferred over -*(u)myen* to quote what the addressee has just said as a mere hypothesis and argue from that point.

3.2.2. The Hypothetical Feature of -*tamyen*. In the previous section we observed that a -*tamyen* clause is used rhetorically to quote the hearer's belief as a mere hypothesis in the middle of the discourse. In this section we will observe that -*tamyen* is not restricted to this kind of discourse-bound context. We will observe that the speaker can felicitously use -*tamyen* without necessarily repeating the belief or statement of others participating in the discourse as long as the speaker views the content of the antecedent clause

[9] The felicitous use of -*tamyen* in this context is also extended to quote the belief or opinion of others not participating in the discourse. Consider (4).

(4) A: (Upon hearing the news about Younghee from a friend)
        Yenghuy-ka   Mikwuk-ey   kongpwuha-le   ka-ntay
        Younghee-Nom   U.S-to   to study   go-QUO
        'They say that Younghee is going to the U.S to study.'

   B: cengmal? Yenghuy-ka   Mikwuk-ey kongpwuhale   ka-**n-tamyen**,
        really   Younghee-Nom   U.S-to   study-to   go-**if**

        kaki-ceney   songpyelhoy-lat   hayyaci.
        going-before   farewell party-even   have to-SUGG
        'Really? If Younghee is going to the U.S to study, why don't we
        have a farewell party before her departure?'

In this example the content of the -*tamyen* clause is believed neither by the speaker nor by the addressee. Notice that the content of the -*tamyen* clause is based upon news heard about Younghee from other people. In this situation, then, it is somebody else not participating in the actual discourse who believes the content of the -*tamyen* clause. We find that even in this situation the use of -*tamyen* is felicitous carrying the same rhetorical effect we observed in (13). Speaker B here accepts the content of the antecedent clause as a mere hypothesis since it just entered his/her knowledge as what Akatsuka (1985) terms *newly learned information*.

as being more *hypothetical* from his/her own subjective point of view; that is, *-tamyen* is chosen over *-(u)myen* by the speaker to mark the protasis as more hypothetical.

Comrie (1986) proposed 'hypotheticality' as one of the important parameters to explain crosslinguistic variation in conditionals. He defined the term 'hypotheticality' as the degree of probability of realization of the situations referred to in the conditional and more especially in the protasis. [10] What decides the degree of hypotheticality in the conditional construction is the speaker's subjective attitude toward the content described in the protasis or in the whole conditional construction.

Consider the following example.

(15) pwukhan-i   haykmwuki-ka   iss-**tamyen**,
                                               -(**?umyen**)
     North Korea-NOM nuclear weapon-NOM   have-**if**,

   namhan-ppwunanila   ilpon-eyto   khun   wihyep-i
   South Korea-not only Japan-to   big   threat-NOM

   toyl-kes-kath-ayo
   become-FUT-seem-DEC
   'If North Korea has nuclear weapons, it will be a big threat to Japan as well as to South Korea.'

Notice in (15) that the nature of the situation described in the protasis is something few speakers can regard as a probabilistic situation with any confidence unless he/she is a political figure exposed to the relevant information. This situation then belongs to the hypothetical realm of the speaker's own world of beliefs with no crucial evidence available. This leads him/her to choose *-tamyen* over the plain *-(u)myen* to express his/her hypothetical attitude toward such situation.

This initial observation predicts then that the speaker will be led to choose *-tamyen* over *-(u)myen* when the content of the protasis is viewed as an unexpected or remote possibility, whereas *-(u)myen* is favored when

---

[10] Comrie (1986: 88) adds that hypotheticality is a continuum with no clear-cut divisions and that different languages simply distinguish different degrees of hypotheticality along this continuum, the choice of form often being determined by subjective evaluation rather than by truth-conditional semantics. I argue that Korean is one such language where the degree of hypotheticality is expressed by the different choice of two available conditional markers; that is, *-tamyen* is chosen over *-(u)myen* when the content described in the protasis is considered more hypothetical.

it is considered as an expected or immediate possibility. In the following example, we observe that the truth-conditionally identical sentence is conditionalized by the two different available markers, -(u)myen and -tamyen, depending on the speaker's subjective view of its hypotheticality. Consider (16).

(16) a. [A and B are both lecturers and expect their work-study student Jin to come soon to work according to his work schedule:]
A: I-il-un   Jin-i-ka   o-myen (#n-tamyen) sikhi-psita
   this work-TOP Jin-SUBJ come-if   let him do-PROP
   'As for this work, if Jin comes, let's have him do it.'

B: kulehkey   ha-psita.   kumpang   o-ltheynikka
   so   do-PROP   soon   come-SUPP
   'Let's do so, since he is about to come soon.'

b. [A and B are both lecturers and have a lot of work to do. They hope their work study student will come to work for them. However, they are not sure since it is snowing heavily:]
A: (Looking out the window and realizing there is heavy snow coming down)
   ilehkey   nwun-i   o-nuntey   Cin-i-ka o-l-kkayo?
   this way   snow-NOM   come-while   Jin-NOM come-will-Q
   'While it is snowing this much, will Jin come (do you think)?'

B: kulsseyyo. Cin-i-ka   o-n-**tamyen** (?**myen**),
   Well.   Jin-NOM   come-**if**

   towum-i   manhi   toy-ltheyntey.
   help-NOM   much   become-SUPP
   'Well. If Jin comes, it will be a lot of help.'

Notice in (16) that a truth-conditionally identical sentence is marked by two different conditional markers. In (16a) speaker A views the content of the protasis as something expected as an immediate possibility and in this context -(u)myen prevails over -tamyen. In fact, the use of -tamyen is almost infelicitous in this context.

On the contrary, in (16b), the possible realization of the same content in this context is not immediately expected and thus viewed as a less probabilistic (highly hypothetical) situation by the speaker. This hypothetical context leads the speaker B to choose -tamyen over -(u)myen in (16b). This observation confirms that the choice between the two conditional markers is governed by the speaker's subjective attitude toward the content of the protasis in the individual discourse context, such that *-tamyen* is chosen over *-(u)myen* when the conditionalized context is more hypothetical.

Now let us note one last context where *-tamyen* prevails over *-(u)myen*. Bak (1987) noted that one of the important contexts where *-tamyen* is favorably used over *-(u)myen* is where the content of the protasis expresses an unrealistic hypothesis with a counterfactual flavor. Consider (17).

(17) nayil   cikwu-ka   mangha-n-**tamyen** (**?-myen**), ne-nun mwues-ul
      tomorrow earth-NOM collapse-**if**,   you-TOP what-ACC

   ceyil ha-ko siph-ni
   most want to do-Q
   'If the earth collapses tomorrow, what do you want to do most?'

The content described in the protasis in (17) is an unrealistic hypothesis with a counterfactual flavor. Here it is not impossible to use *-(u)myen* instead of *-tamyen*. However, it conveys the sense of the immediate possibility of such a situation rather than expressing its unrealistic nature. In this context *-tamyen* is favored over *-(u)myen* and carries the hypothetical attitude by the speaker toward the content of the protasis.

I find that this tendency is much stronger in the preferential use of *-(i)lamyen* (the allomorphic variant of *-tamyen* for the copular verb *i-* (= 'to be')) over the plain *-(u)myen*. *-(i)lamyen* is exclusively used to mark unrealistic or even counterfactual antecedent clauses and in this context *-(u)myen* is not appropriate.

(18) nay-ka superman-**ilamyen** (**#imyen**) Payktwusan-ey
      I-NOM   superman-be-**if**   Payktwu mountain-to

   nalaka-ltheyntey
   fly-would be able to
   'If I were a superman, I would fly to Mt. Payktwu.'

The above two examples show that *-tamyen* is strongly favored over the plain *-(u)myen* to hypothesize an unrealistic or even counterfactual situation.

This tendency of favoring *-tamyen* to mark unrealistic situations with a counterfactual flavor is consistent with the (highly) hypothetical feature of *-tamyen*. Unrealistic situations with a counterfactual flavor are obviously something every speaker puts in the (highly) hypothetical realm of his/her belief world and this is surely compatible with the (highly) hypothetical feature of *-tamyen*.

3. Summary and Closing Remarks

This paper has studied the forms and meanings of two conditional markers, *-(u)myen* and *-tamyen*, presenting two main strands of argument. First, I argued that *-(u)myen* is not a ubiquitous conditional marker in Korean and, contra Bak (1987)'s position, that Korean is not exceptional in its domain of conditionality; that is, the realis domain cannot be a conditional target in Korean. Second, I argued that the *-tamyen* clause is characterized as a cleft-conditional clause and that this structural feature explains its felicitous use over *-(u)myen* in what Iatridou (1990) calls 'Factual Conditional' contexts where the speaker quotes what the addressee has just said in the previous discourse.

The other feature of *-tamyen* is that it is favored over *-(u)myen* when the speaker views the content of the protasis as (highly) hypothetical. We observed that *-tamyen* is favored over *-(u)myen* to mark an unexpected and remote possibility or an unrealistic situation with a counterfactual flavor (more hypothetical), whereas *-(u)myen* prevails over *-tamyen* when the content of the protasis is viewed as an expected or immediate possibility.

The observations made in this paper make two contributions in the crosslinguistic study of conditionals. One is that Korean provides an example of a language where one and the same morpheme functions as a 'given that *p*' clause marker as well as a conditional marker. The other is that Korean is a language that employs two different conditional constructions to express different degrees of hypotheticality. If it turns out that there are other languages with the same pattern as Korean conditionals, it will be important for typological study to attempt to identify what aspects of grammar are shared by these languages.

References

Akatsuka, N. Conditionals and the Epistemic Scale. *Language* 61: 3, 1985.
Akatsuka, N. Conditionals are Discourse-bound. In: *On Conditionals*, edited by E. Traugott, et. al., Cambridge: Cambridge University Press, 1986.
Bak, Sung-Yun. Conditionals in Korean. In *Harvard Studies in Korean Linguistics II.*, edited by Susumu Kuno, et. al., Seoul: Hanshin Pub. Co, 1987.
Comrie, B. Conditionals: a Typology. In *On Conditionals*, edited by E. Traugott, et. al., Cambridge: Cambridge University Press, 1986.
Iatridou, S. *Topics in Conditionals*. MIT Ph.D. dissertation, 1990.

Inoue. An Analysis of a Cleft Conditional in Japanese–Where Grammar meets Rhetoric. *Journal of Pragmatics* 7, pp. 251-62, 1983.

Lee, Chungmin. Conditional Constructions in Korean. *Proceedings of the XIIth International Congress of Linguists*, pp. 451-54, 1991.

Levinson. *Pragmatics*. Cambridge: Cambridge University Press, 1983.

Lukoff, Fred. *An Introductory Course in Korean*. Seoul: Yonsei University Press, 1982.

Reilly, J. The Acquisition of Temporals and Conditionals. In *On Conditionals*, edited by E Traugott, et. al., Cambridge: Cambridge University Press, 1986.

Traugott, E. et. al. *On Conditionals*. Cambridge: Cambridge University Press, 1986.

14
Towards a Unified Analysis of *khenyeng*

Yoon-Suk Chung

Introduction[1]
There have been many studies of so-called delimiters[2] in Korean. Major works have centered on ten such delimiters (Seng 1979, Hong 1983, Kim 1989, to name a few): *(i)nama* 'though, even', *(n)un* 'only concerned', *to* 'also, even', *(i)lato* 'even the last choice or recourse', *man* 'only, exactly', *mace* 'even, indeed, including', *pwuthe* 'from', *(i)ya* 'when it comes to', *cocha* 'even, in addition, indeed, including', and *kkaci* 'up to, even'.

In this paper I discuss *khenyeng*, which has also been traditionally classified as a delimiter with two 'distinct' senses, each of which has different syntax. I provide a unified syntactic and semantic analysis[3] of these two allegedly distinct senses. I argue that *khenyeng* is a "proposition conjunction" and a negative polarity trigger (hence, negative conjunction). I also argue that *khenyeng* is a scalar operator, and that a uniform treatment of the semantics of the *khenyeng* construction can be formulated in terms of the scalar semantics developed in Fillmore et. al. (1988), Kay (1990), and Kay (1992).

The organization of the paper is as follows. Section 1 reviews Choy's (1929/1961) descriptive work—the only serious work on *khenyeng* to date. Section 2 introduces more *khenyeng* examples, showing that Choy's description is not correct. Section 3 and section 4 give a unified analysis of

[1] I am grateful to Charles Fillmore, David Peterson, and especially Paul Kay for valuable comments on a previous version of this paper. Thanks are also due to Ross King for proofreading the final version of this paper. All shortcomings that remain are, of course, my responsibility.

[2] The definition of delimiter will be provided below.

[3] Space does not allow me to investigate the pragmatics of *khenyeng* in this paper.

the form and meaning of *khenyeng*, respectively. The conclusions and the directions for further study are provided in section 5.

1. Previous studies

The *khenyeng* sentence begins with a fragment, followed by *khenyeng*, followed by a full clause, as in (1).

(1)   <u>fragment</u>   <u>khenyeng</u>   <u>full clause</u>
        sippwul   khenyeng   ilpwul-to mos patassta
        ten dollars   let alone   one dollar-even not received
       'I did not receive one dollar, let alone ten dollars.'

In his seminal descriptive grammar of Korean, Choy (1929/1961) characterizes *khenyeng* as an 'auxiliary particle'[4], whose semantic function in a sentence is to add certain auxiliary meanings, such as focus, emphasis, etc. to a word or a phrase to which it is attached. In the subsequent works in the transformational generative tradition, however, the term 'auxiliary particle' has been replaced by 'delimiter' since its semantic function is reinterpreted as delimiting or specifying the meaning of the element it follows.[5]

According to Choy (1929/1961), *khenyeng* is used, loosely speaking, when the result of one event, compared to that of the another event in the sentence, is so obvious that the speaker does not need to mention it. Choy's loosely expressed statement of the two senses of *khenyeng* may be put, I hope, more explicitly as follows.

As illustrated in (2) below, the first sense of *khenyeng* (K_1, henceforth) concerns the case in which the speaker is explicit about the implausibility of the more likely state of affairs expressed in the post-*khenyeng* negative full clause, implicating the impossibility of the less likely state of affairs expressed in the pre-*khenyeng* fragment. As represented in (3), the second 'apparent' sense (K_2, henceforth) concerns the case in which the expected state of affairs in the fragment is denied and the unexpected contrary state of affairs is affirmed in the positive full clause.[6]

---

[4] The somewhat awkward 'auxiliary particle' and its congener 'delimiter' are due to lack of a suitable corresponding term in English.

[5] For example, see Yang (1972). However, the term delimiter does not show any substantial difference from and is no better than the traditional one, auxiliary particle, since the meaning of a noun phrase, for example, is not 'limited' by its immediately following delimiter. Yet in the remainder of the paper I will continue to use the term delimiter since a better term does not at present suggest itself to.

(2) chenwen-khenyeng paykwen-to an toyessta[7]
    thousand won-let alone hundred won-even not come to
    'It did not come to one hundred *won*, let alone one thousand *won*.'

(3) sang-khenyeng pel-ul patasseyo
    prize-instead of punishment-Acc got
    'Instead of being rewarded, I got a punishment.'

Choy (1929/1961) goes on to say that the meaning of the verb in the K_1 sentence usually represents 'impossibility', and that the parts flanked by K_1 are of the same kind. On the other hand, the parts conjoined by K_2 are of a different kind and the verb in the K_2 sentence is only predicative of the post-*khenyeng* part of the sentence.

Choy's (1929/1961) description of *khenyeng* is summarized as follows:

(4) analysis of *khenyeng* by Choy (1929/1961)
    khenyeng is a lexical item with two different meanings and syntactic environments such that
    a) in the K_1 case, the impossibility of the less likely state of affairs is followed by the implausibility of the more likely state of affairs,

---

[6] Choy (1929/1961) actually presents a third sense as well. However, this meaning is unfortunately not available in current Korean. Following is one of the instances he cites:

(i) *onyen-khenyeng sipnyen-i cinassta
    five years-to say nothing of ten years-Nom passed
    'Ten years have passed, to say nothing of five years.'

I am not sure why there is a discrepancy in acceptability between Choy and current Korean. It may be that the third sense of *khenyeng* Choy points out disappeared in the course of time (in half a century) or his observation might be influenced by the Japanese equivalent of *khenyeng*, *dokoroka*, which displays exactly these three senses. Incidentally, (i) becomes acceptable when a comparative verb is attached to the verb, about which more will follow in section 3.2. Now compare (i) and (ii).

(ii) onyen-khenyeng sipnyen-to te cinassta
    five years-to say nothing of ten years-even more passed
    'As many as ten years have passed, to say nothing of five years.'

[7] Abbreviations made in the paper include Contr 'Contrast', Nom 'Nominative', Nml 'Nominalizer', Acc 'Accusative', Pst 'Past', Top 'Topic', Q 'Question ending', and Inf 'Infinitive'.

while in the K_2 case, denial of the expected state of affairs is followed by affirmation of the unexpected contrary state of affairs,
b) words conjoined by K_1 are of the same kind, while words conjoined by K_2 are of two different kinds,
c) the verb of the K_1 sentence is predicative of the word preceding *khenyeng* as well as the one following *khenyeng*, while the verb of the K_2 sentence is only predicative of the word following *khenyeng*.

In the next sections, I will show that the distinction of two forms and meanings associated with *khenyeng* expressions is unnecessary and may be replaced by a unitary account.

2. More examples

To arrive at a fuller understanding of the formal and semantic properties of *khenyeng*, we need to consider more examples that contain *khenyeng* expressions. Although Choy (1929/1961) only provides *khenyeng* examples that conjoin NPs, as shown in (2) and (3), the range of syntactic categories connected by *khenyeng* is not so limited. In addition to NPs, as illustrated by another examples in (5), *khenyeng* can usually conjoin any two like categories including adverbial phrases (6), postpositional phrases (7), and verb phrases (8).

(5)   a. tayhakkyo-nun[8]-khenyeng cwunghakkyo-to colep mos haysseyo
        college-Contr-let alone middle school-even graduation cannot did
        'He could not graduate from middle school, let alone college.'

      b. chingchan-un-khenyeng kkwucwung-ul tulesssupnita
        praise-Contr-instead of scolding-Acc got
        'Instead of being praised, I got a scolding.'

---

[8] As (2) and (3) show, the examples Choy (1929/1961) provides lack the subdued focus delimiter *nun* before *khenyeng*. Korean dictionaries (say, Hankulhakhoy 1991) say that *nun* comes in when the speaker wants to emphasize the word that precedes *khenyeng*. The idea is that *nun* is optional in this construction. However, this remark is incorrect since the delimiter *nun* must be present, for example, after the adverbial or the postpositional phrases. Moreover, the presence of *khenyeng* sounds more natural even after the noun phrases, as in (2) or (3). Therefore, it would be preferable to say that *nun* drops in a very restricted syntactic environment, say, after the noun phrases. I will not go into more detail about *nun* since consideration of the issue involved is not relevant to the points I wish to make.

(6) a. manhi-nun-khenyeng cokum-to epsta
a lot-Contr-let alone a little-even do not have
'I do not have a little, let alone a lot.'

b. cacwu-nun-khenyeng acwu ittakumssik nathanakonhaysseyo
frequently-Contr-instead of very once in a while would show up
'Instead of frequently, he would show up once in a great while.'

(7) a. hayswuyokcang-ey-nun-khenyeng swuyengcang-ey-to an kasseyo
beach-to-Contr-let alone   swimming pool-to-even not went
'I did not go to a swimming pool, let alone a beach.'

b. tayhaksayng-mankhum-un-khenyeng kotunghaksayng-pota-to
college student-as-Contr-let alone   high school student-as-even

yenge-lul   mos hanta
English-Acc cannot speak
'He cannot speak English as well as a high school student, let
alone as well as a college student.'

(8) a. ssu-ki-nun-khenyeng   ilk-ci-to   mos hayssta^9
write-Nml-Contr-let alone read-Nml-even cannot did
'He could not read, let alone write.'

b. ku-ka ka peli-ese   sepsepha-ki-nun-khenyeng siwenhayyo
he-Nom go away-since sorry-Nml-Contr-instead of glad
'Instead of feeling sorry, I am glad that he has gone.'

c. ku-nun pap-ul mek-umyense-nun-khenyeng cha-lul masi-myense-to
he-Top meal-Acc eat-while-Contr-let alone tea-Acc drink-while-even

TV-lul mos ponta
TV-Acc cannot watch
'He cannot watch TV while drinking his tea, let alone while eating
his meal.'

Contrary to Choy's (1929/1961) claim that the K_1 type verb has a predicative scope over the NPs preceding as well as following *khenyeng*, there are also cases of K_1 sentences in which the verb does not serve as a predicate of the pre-*khenyeng* NP. Compare (9) with (10).

---

[9] Verbal nouns are considered as a kind of verb phrase in this paper in order to give a consistent explanation of verb phrases.

(9) a. pwule-nun-khenyeng   yenge-to   mos hanta
       French-Contr-let alone English-even cannot speak
       'He cannot speak English, let alone French.'

   b. pwule-lul   mos hanta
      French-Acc cannot speak
      'He cannot speak French.'

   c. yenge-lul   mos hanta
      English-Acc cannot speak
      'He cannot speak English.'

(10) a. pi-nun-khenyeng   kwulum-to kkici   anhassta
        rain-Contr-let alone cloud-even cloud up did not
        'It was not cloudy, let alone rainy.'

   b. * pi-ka   kkici   anhassta
        rain-Nom cloud up did not
        'It was not rainy.'

   c. kwulum-i   kkici   anhassta
      cloud-Nom cloud up did not
      'It was not cloudy.'

   d. * pi-to   kwulum-to kkici   anhassta
        rain-also cloud-also cloud up did not
        'It was neither rainy nor cloudy.'

Unlike (9a) and (9b), the verb *kki-* 'cloud up' in (10a) cannot serve as a predicate of the pre-*khenyeng* NP *pi* 'rain'. This is shown by the ungrammaticality of (10b) in which the verb *kki-* 'cloud up' cannot have *pi* 'rain' as a possible argument. The grammaticality of (10a) thus shows that even when the NPs require different verbs, they can be connected in a *khenyeng* sentence by the verb that subcategorizes for the post-*khenyeng* NP. The point may be sharpened by the comparison of examples (10d) and (10a). The difference in grammaticality between (10d) and (10a) may be attributed to the predication of the verb whose scope is assigned by the construction involved. That is, the verb in (10d) is predicative of the first NP as well as the second NP, while the verb in (10a) is only predicative of the post-*khenyeng* NP. As we will see in section 3.1, this observation is significant since it is directly relevant to one of our arguments that *khenyeng* is a proposition conjunction, not merely a constituent conjunction.

To summarize, *khenyeng* can conjoin pairs of maximal phrases of a wide range of syntactic categories, not merely NPs. And when conjoining NPs, *khenyeng* does not require that the first NP be an argument of the verb which subcategorizes for the second NP.

Khenyeng can also appear embedded in a sentence. For example, in (11a), the *khenyeng* construction modifies the NP, *mankhum* 'degree'.

(11) a. talli-ki-nun-khenyeng kelul swu-to epsul mankhum phikonhayssta
    run-Nml-Contr-let alone walk ability-even not degree tired
    'I was so tired that I could not walk, let alone run.'

  b. cekum-un-khenyeng   saynghwal-to mos hal cikyengita
    saving-Contr-let alone living-even   cannot do in condition
    'He hardly makes his living, let alone saving money.'

  c. kukes-un ilop-ki-nun-khenyeng   acwu haylowun chayk-ita
    that-Top good-Nml-Contr-instead of very harmful book-be
    'Instead of being good, that is a harmful book.'

Having briefly shown, by considering more examples, that Choy's description of *khenyeng* is not correct, I will take up the syntactic and semantic features of *khenyeng* in turn.

3. Grammar of *khenyeng*
3.1. *Khenyeng* is a conjunction

The first argument that I want to make on the syntactic side is that *khenyeng* is a conjunction, not a delimiter as is widely assumed in the literature. Even though *khenyeng* may not be a canonical conjunction, there is evidence both for the claim that *khenyeng* is a type of conjunction, and that it is not a delimiter.

Arguing against *khenyeng* as a delimiter requires considering a possible family of syntactic characteristics of delimiters. As Chay (1977) observes, however, even the ten widely studied delimiters mentioned in the Introduction do not share the same syntactic properties[10]. Except for *(n)un* 'only concerned', *to* 'also, even', and *(i)ya* 'when it comes to', delimiters tend to have fairly restricted distributions, and to have the particular semantic function of expressing the speaker's attitude. I will therefore take the focus delimiters *(n)un*, *to*, and *(i)ya* as representative delimiters.

It may be true that *khenyeng* shares some syntactic properties with the focus delimiters in that it is neither preceded nor followed by the

---

[10] For some suggested syntactic properties of delimiters, see Hong (1983).

nominative, accusative or genitive case markers, and that it can replace them in appropriate syntactic environments. Nevertheless, *khenyeng* shows remarkable differences from the focus delimiters in several ways.

The first difference can be adduced from a general constraint concerning delimiters, namely, that there is a restricted ordering among them. Yang (1972) classifies delimiters into three sub-categories based on their distributional properties and their mutual co-occurrences: X-lim (*mace* 'even, indeed, including', *mata* 'each', *kkaci* 'up to, even', *pwuthe* 'from')[11], Y-lim (*man* 'only, exactly', *pakk-ey* 'only'), Z-lim ((*(n)un* 'only concerned', *to* 'also, even', *(i)ya* 'when it comes to', *(i)na* 'and, or', *(i)lato* 'even the last choice or recourse'). Yang then argues that when the three kinds of delimiters co-occur, X-lim always precedes Y-lim, which always precedes Z-lim.

According to Yang (1972), the focus delimiters including *(n)un* are Z-lim, coming last in a string of delimiters.[12] No other delimiters are permitted to follow Z-lim, as shown by (12a). If *khenyeng* is a delimiter, it should not follow *nun*, either. The grammaticality of (12b), therefore, demonstrates that *khenyeng* cannot be considered a delimiter.[13]

(12) a.* Mimi-nun-to   yeyppu-ci anhta
       Mimi-Top-also pretty-Nml not
       'As for Mimi, she is not pretty, either.'

   b. Mimi-nun-khenyeng Swumi-to   yeyppu-ci anhta
      Mimi-Contr-let alone Swumi-even pretty-Nml not
      'Swumi is not pretty, let alone Mimi.'

Secondly, *khenyeng* is never immediately preceded by an adverb or an infinitive form of verbs, as is common for the focus delimiters.[14] For example, the adverb *manhi* 'much' and the infinitive form of verbs *-e* can

---

[11] Yang made a mistake in classifying *kkaci* 'up to, even', *pwuthe* 'from' as X-lim. According to this classification, for example, the string *kkaci-pwuthe* 'even from' should be ruled out, since both elements of the string belong to X-lim, but it is okay. I will not go into more detail about this issue, since it is not related to any of my points.

[12] Hong (1983) gives a different classification of delimiters, but the delimiter *nun* is still Z-lim here.

[13] One may argue that *khenyeng* is a delimiter which comes in the last, fourth position in an arrangement of delimiters, thereby proposing another syntactic delimiter slot. I reject this idea since *khenyeng* would then be the only delimiter that occupies the position. Proposing another slot for the delimiters is not economical for the overall organization of the grammar.

be followed by the focus delimiter *to* as in (13a) and (14a) but not by *khenyeng* as in (13b) and (14b), respectively.

(13) a. manhi-to cokum-to epseyo
　　　much-also a little-also not have
　　　'I have neither a little nor much.'

　　b. *manhi-khenyeng cokum-to epseyo
　　　much-let alone a little-even not have
　　　'I do not have a little, let alone much.'

(14) a. ilk-e-to　　　tul-e-to po-ci　　　mos　hayssta
　　　read-Am-also listen to-Inf-also try-Nml cannot did
　　　'I had the experience of neither reading nor listening to (it)'

　　b. *ilk-e-khenyeng　tul-e-to po-ci　　　mos　hayssta
　　　read-Am-let alone listen to-Inf-even try-Nml cannot did
　　　'I did not have the experience of listening to, let alone reading (it).'

Thirdly, as is the case for the focus delimiters, *khenyeng* cannot be immediately preceded by most postpositional phrases such as locative, instrumental, etc. For example, the delimiter *to* can follow the locative case marker, *eyse* 'in, at' in (15a) but *khenyeng* cannot in (15b).

(15) a. i kos-eyse-to　　ce kos-eyse-to　　tampay-lul
　　　this place-in-also that place-in-also tobacco-Acc

　　　phiwul swu　　epssupnita
　　　smoke possibility not exist
　　　'You are not permitted to smoke here or there.'

　　b. *i kos-eyse-khenyeng ce kos-eyse-to　tampay-lul
　　　this place-in-let alone that place-in-even tobacco-Acc

　　　phiwul swu　　epssupnita
　　　smoke possibility not exist
　　　'You are not permitted to smoke there, let alone here.'

The last reason to reject the delimiter account concerns the fact that focus delimiters can follow a wide variety of verbal connectives, while

---

[14] The rest of the negative evidence was already hinted at in the foregoing examples which show *khenyeng* usually following the delimiter *nun*. Thus, I omit a detailed explanation.

khenyeng cannot. Consider (16), in which one of the verbal connectives, *-(u)lyeko* 'in order to', can precede the delimiter *to* but not *khenyeng*.[15]

(16) a. cenyek-ul   mek-ulyeko-to   chyeta po-lyeko-to
       dinner-Acc eat-in order to-also look at try-in order to-also

   ha-ci anhassta
   do-Nml did not
   'He did not intend to eat or look at the dinner.'

b. *cenyek-ul   mek-ulyeko-khenyeng   chyeta po-lyeko-to
    dinner-Acc eat-in order to-let alone look at try-in order to-even

   ha-ci anhassta
   do-Nml did not
   'He did not intend to look at, let alone eat the dinner.'

Observing that there exists evidence to doubt *khenyeng*'s status as a delimiter, we turn our attention to some positive observations available, suggesting treatment of *khenyeng* as a type of conjunction. First, as shown by the wide variety of examples given in (5)-(8), *khenyeng* usually serves to connect two grammatically equal phrases such as NPs, ADVPs, and VPs, etc. Secondly, the *khenyeng* construction shows properties that are typically associated with coordination constructions. For the *khenyeng* construction, for example, topicalization as in (17a), relative clause formation as in (17b), and clefting as in (17c) are possible.[16] The examples in (18) show comparable sentences containing a canonical coordinate conjunction.

---

[15] All the (b) examples of (13)-(16) are acceptable when the delimiter *nun* is inserted before *khenyeng*. This observation might suggest a possibility that *nun-khenyeng* is a compound delimiter in the making. The fact that nothing can intervene between *nun* and *khenyeng* also seems to suggest its compound nature. However, there are independent positive properties of the *khenyeng* construction which are directly indicative of a conjunction, as will be discussed below.

[16] However, the other canonical coordination tests—clause conjunction, gapping, and conjunction reduction—fail to apply because a *khenyeng* sentence cannot have more than one-paired focus.

(17) a. i chayk-khenyeng ku sinmwun-to Mimi-nun han sikan-ey mos
that book-let alone this paper-even Mimi-Top one hour-in cannot

ilkeyo
read
'Mimi cannot read a paper in an hour, let alone a book.'

b. Mimi-ka ttayli-ki-khenyeng yokha-ci-to anhun namca
Mimi-Nom hit-Nml-let alone yell at-Nml-even not man
'The man who Mimi did not yell at, let alone hit.'

c. cikum Mimi-ka mekko issnun kes-un soykoki-khenyeng twaycikoki-
now Mimi-Nom eating thing-Top beef   -let alone pork

to   anita
-even not
'What Mimi is eating now is not pork, let alone beef.'

(18) a. i chayk-kwa ku sinmwun-ul Mimi-nun han sikan-ey mos ilkeyo
book-and-paper-Acc   Mimi-Top one hour-in cannot read
'As for this book and that paper, Mimi cannot read them in an hour.'

b. Mimi-ka ttayli-kena yokha-ci-to   anhun namca
Mimi-Nom hit-or   yell at-Nml-also not man
'the man who Mimi neither hit nor yelled at.'

c. cikum Mimi-ka mekko issnun kes-un soykoki-ttonun twaycikoki-ita
now Mimi-Nom eating thing-Top beef-or   pork-be
'What Mimi is eating now is pork, or beef.'

Yet there are other cases which resist a strict coordinate conjunction account, forcing us to admit that *khenyeng* is a more tolerant type of conjunction. First, recall the case seen in (10), which is repeated as (19):

(19) a. pi-nun-khenyeng   kwulum-to kkici   anhassta
rain-Contr-let alone cloud-even cloud up did not
'It was not cloudy, let alone rainy.'

b. * pi-ka   kkici   anhassta
rain-Nom cloud up did not
'It was not rainy.'

c. kwulum-i   kkici   anhassta
   cloud-Nom cloud up did not
   'It was not cloudy.'

d. * pi-to   kwulum-to kkici   anhassta
     rain-also cloud-also cloud up did not
     'It was neither rainy nor cloudy.'

Since they do not share the same verb, as shown in (19b) and (19c), the two NPs in (19a) cannot be literally said to be connected by *khenyeng*. Moreover, *khenyeng* sentences sometimes comprise two independent verb phrases with their own verbs. An example of such a case can be seen in (20) in which the pre-*khenyeng* part is composed of its separate verb and object:

(20) ton-ul pel-ki-nun-khenyeng   sonhay-lul pwassta
      money-Acc earn-Nml-Contr-instead of damage-Acc suffer
      'Instead of making money, I suffered damage.'

Rather, *khenyeng* is better thought of as combining two propositions with the first syntactically realized as a clause fragment. There is evidence that *khenyeng* sentences are composed of two independent propositions. In order to prove this, we have only to show that the pre-*khenyeng* part of a sentence is not part of the clause headed by the verb which occurs after *khenyeng*.

The first piece of evidence comes from the clause-bound subject-honorification agreement phenomenon. Our assumption predicts that the honorification of the verb, for example, must agree with a post-*khenyeng* NP, not with a pre-*khenyeng* NP. The following sentences bear out our prediction.

(21) a. halapenim-kkeyse-nun-khenyeng   tongsayng-to
         grandfather-Nom[hon]-Contr-let alone younger brother-even

         theynis-lul an   chiko isseyo
         tennis-Acc not playing be
         'My younger brother is not playing tennis, let alone my grandfather.'

      b. *halapenim-kkeyse-nun-khenyeng   tongsayng-to
          grandfather-Nom[hon]-Contr-let alone younger brother-even

          theynis-lul   an chiko kyeyseyyo
          tennis- Acc not playing be[hon]
          'My younger brother is not playing tennis, let alone my grandfather.'

(21a) is grammatical since the non-honorific form *isseyo* 'be' agrees in honorification with the non-honorific NP *tongsayng* 'brother' in the post-*khenyeng* part, but not the honorific NP *halapenim* 'grandfather' in the pre-*khenyeng* part, while (21b) is ungrammatical since the honorific form *kyeysi-* 'be [hon]' cannot agree in honorification with its non-honorific subject *tongsayng*.

Secondly, the appearance of tense or a passive morpheme in the fragment shows that the pre-*khenyeng* part belongs to a separate clausal fragment from the post-*khenyeng* full clause.

(22) chenpwul-i   ket-hi-ki-nun-khenyeng   paykpwul-to
      1000 $-Nom collect-pass-Nlm-Contr-let alone 100 $-even

      mos   kethyesseyo
      cannot   be collect
      '100 dollars were not collected, let alone 1000 dollars.'

(23) i chayk-un   cal ssu-ess-ki-nun khenyeng   mwusun malinci
      this book-Top well write-Pst-Nml-Contr-let alone what speech

      al   swu-ka   epsta
      know   possibility-Nom not exist
      'This book is not clear, let alone well-written.'

To summarize this subsection, with the negative and positive evidence presented above, I have shown that there is some doubt as to the status of *khenyeng* as a delimiter. It is more appropriate to treat *khenyeng* as a conjunction, albeit a non-canonical one.

3.2. Khenyeng is a negative polarity trigger

Now I would like to show that *khenyeng* is a negative polarity trigger. As illustrated by the (a) examples of (5)-(8), sentences containing K_1 usually have explicit negative adverbs *mos* 'cannot', or *an* 'do not' before the verbs. K_1 sentences can also have such intrinsically negative verbs as *eps-* 'not exist', *molu-* 'not know', *silphayha-* 'fail', *tteleci-* 'fail', *pwucok-* 'short of', and *elyew-* 'doubtful', etc. Consider the examples in (24).

(24) a. ku-nun pwule-nun-khenyeng   yenge-to   molunta
         he-Top French-Contr-let alone English-even not know
         'He does not know English, let alone French.'

b. kummeytal-un-khenyeng   unmeytal-to   ttanun tey-ey
   gold medal-Contr-let alone silver medal-even win opportunity-in
   silphayhayssta
   failed
   '(He) failed in winning a silver medal, let alone a gold medal.'

c. ponkosa-nun-khenyeng   yeypikosa-to
   college entrance exam-Contr-let alone preliminary exam-even
   ttelecyesseyo
   failed
   '(He) failed in a preliminary exam, let alone a college exam.'

d. kyelsung-un-khenyeng   cwunkyelsung-to elyepkeyssta
   final-Contr-let alone semifinal-even   doubtful
   '(He) will not make the semifinals, let alone the finals.'

Notice also that an inequality of comparison, as mentioned in footnote 6 and repeated as (25a), and a rhetorical question (25b), which distribute a negative message throughout a sentence, can be expressed in the K_1 sentence.

(25) a. onyen-khenyeng   sipnyen-to   te   cinassta
        five years-to say nothing of ten years-even more passed
        'As many as ten years have passed, to say nothing of five years.'

   b. nwuka ne-eykey chenpwul-un-khenyeng   paykpwul-ilato
      who you-to one 1000 dollars-Contr-let alone hundred dollars-even
      cwukeyss-nunya?
      give-Q?
      'Who would give you one hundred dollars, let alone one thousand dollars?'

Since all the (a) examples of (5-8), and (24)-(25) are negative affect sentences, it is tempting to say that K_1, hastily extending to K_2, is a syntactically negative polarity item, appearing in the negative polarity context.[17] The apparent argument that K_1 is a negative polarity item seems to be supported, for example, by the fact that *amwuto* 'anyone', a representative negative polarity item in Korean, can occur in a sentence, as illustrated in (26).

---

[17] In fact, Lee (1992) assumes, without any arguments, that *khenyeng* is a negative polarity item.

(26) Mimi-nun-khenyeng amwu-to   an wassta
　　　Mimi-Contr-let alone anyone-even not came
　　　'No one came, let alone Mimi.'

This claim, however, turns out to be wrong when we consider K_2 examples. As illustrated in the (b) examples of (5)-(8), K_2 occurs without any accompanying negative form. Or, to be more exact, morphologically explicit negative morphemes must not appear in K_2 examples. Compare (27a) and (27b).

(27) a. chingchan-un-khenyeng kkwucwung-ul tulesssupnita
　　　　 praise-Contr-instead of scolding-Acc got
　　　　 'Instead of being praised, I got a scolding.'

　　　b. *chingchan-un-khenyeng kkwucwung-ul an tulesssupnita
　　　　 praise-Contr-instead of scolding-Acc not got
　　　　 'Instead of being praised, I did not get a scolding.'

If K_2 is also a negative polarity item, it must appear within the scope of an appropriate trigger. But there is no negative polarity trigger, for example, in (27a). Rather, K_2 is a negative polarity trigger with scope over the preceding clausal fragment. The evidence is as follows:

If, as we assume, *khenyeng* is a proposition conjunction, then a K_2 sentence such as (28a) is semantically combined from the two sentences (28b) and (28c).

(28) a. sang-un khenyeng   pel-ul   patasseyo
　　　　 prize-Contr-instead of punishment-Acc received
　　　　 'Instead of being rewarded, I got a punishment.'

　　　b. sang-ul   mos patasseyo
　　　　 prize-Acc not received
　　　　 'I was not rewarded.'

　　　c. pel-ul   patasseyo
　　　　 punishment-Acc received
　　　　 'I got a punishment.'

Comparison between (28a) and (28b-28c) shows that *khenyeng* semantically corresponds to the negative morpheme. It follows that a morphologically explicit negative form cannot normally appear in the pre-*khenyeng* part of a sentence. Consider example (29).

(29) *chingchan-ul mos tutki-nun-khenyeng kkwucwung-ul tulesseyo
praise-Acc cannot hear-Nml-Contr let alone scolding-Acc heard
'I got a scolding, let alone not a praise.'

If a morphologically explicit form occurs, the propositional meaning of the pre-*khenyeng* part is in conflict with that of the post-*khenyeng* part, since under normal circumstances, for example, 'being praised' implies 'not receiving a punishment.'

Returning to K_1 examples, we also find evidence for K_1 as a negative polarity trigger. First, unless we can find any convincing argument that the forms and meanings of K_1 and K_2 are unrelated, diachronically or synchronically, it would not make much sense to claim that K_1 is a negative polarity item, while K_2 is a negative polarity trigger.

Second, if the negative polarity phenomenon in Korean is clause-bound as is generally assumed (cf. Choe (1988)), and the pre-*khenyeng* part is a clause-reduced fragment separated from a full clause of the post-*khenyeng* part, as argued earlier, (26), repeated as (30), should be ruled out, since *khenyeng* occurs outside the scope of its potential negative polarity trigger, *an* 'not'.

(30) [Mimi-nun-khenyeng] [amwu-to an wasseyo]
Mimi-Contr-let alone anyone-even not came
'No one came, let alone Mimi.'

Thirdly, viewing *khenyeng* as a negative polarity trigger with its preceding clausal fragment in its scope predicts the variation whether K_1 and K_2 cases differ superficially in that the full clause is negative only in the former. The recognition of this difference between K_1 and K_2 is significant since it, together with the argument that *khenyeng* is a conjunction, simplifies the schema of the syntax of *khenyeng* as in (31):

(31) [[X K] [Y]]

In the formula (31), X is a variable representing a clausal fragment and Y is another variable representing a full clause, and X is always a negative polarity environment while Y is not (K represents *khenyeng*).

4. Semantics of *khenyeng*

Now that we have looked at the syntactic properties of *khenyeng*, we turn our attention to the semantics of *khenyeng*. We must first note that the semantic interpretation of the *khenyeng* construction ties in with the syntactic arguments that we made above; namely, *khenyeng* is a conjunction and a negative polarity trigger. Since *khenyeng* serves as a negative conjunction, the syntactic schema of (31) must be interpreted as (32).

(32) 'not X' and 'Y'

Formally, this interpretation can be represented by the semantic schema (33), which, together with the syntactic schema (31), reads as 'the sentence meaning of [[X K] [Y]] is the sum of the denotation of 'not X' and the denotation of 'Y'.

(33) ¬||X|| & ||Y||

It should be emphasized here that the notation of ||X|| & ||Y|| is taken to represent propositions and not syntactic forms like clause or clausal fragments. For example, ||X|| is merely syntactically chosen as a fragment in order to highlight the focused element in the preceding context which is present or assumed in the discourse. The argument that ||X|| is a focused element accords with the distributional fact that no other particles except for the subdued focus delimiter *(n)un* can precede *khenyeng*.

The suitable semantic interpretation, therefore, requires the interpreter to reconstruct a semantic clause from a fragment, constructing two sentences. For example, the following sentences (34a) and (35a) must be reconstructed as (34b-c) and (35b-c), respectively, since one of the potential preceding contexts of (34a) and (35a) may be, for example, (36a) and (36b), respectively.

(34) a. chenpwul-un-khenyeng   paykpwul-to   mos patasseyo
         1000 dollars-Contr-let alone 100 dollars-even not   received
         'I did not receive 100 dollars, let alone 1000 dollars.'

       b. chenpwul-ul   mos patasseyo
         1000 dollars-Acc not received
         'I did not receive one thousand dollars.'

       c. paykpwul-ul   mos patasseyo
         100 dollars-Acc not   received.'
         'I did not receive one hundred dollars.'

(35) a. chingchan-un-khenyeng kkwucwung-ul patasssupnita
       praise-Contr-instead of   scolding-Acc   received
       'Instead of being praised, I got a scolding.'

   b. chingchan-ul mos patasssupnita
      praise-Acc   not received
      'I was not praised.'

   c. kkwucwung-ul patasssupnita
      scolding-Acc received
      'I got a scolding.'

(36) a. chenpwul-ul   patasssupni-kka?
       1000 dollars-Acc received-Q
       'Did you receive one thousand dollars?'

   b. chingchan-ul patasssupni-kka?
      praise-Acc   received-Q
      'Did you get a praise?'

It should, however, be noticed at the same time that the meaning of the whole *khenyeng* sentence is not merely the sum of the meanings of its conjoined propositions. For example, (34a) is more than a sum of (34b) and (34c), even though they are not different truth-conditionally. And the meaning difference is obviously attributable to the presence of the meaning of *khenyeng*. Now is the time to elucidate the semantic function of *khenyeng*, which is crucial in the interpretation of the *khenyeng* construction.

I argue that the semantic function of *khenyeng* is to serve as a scalar operator which has the entire sentence under its scope. In other words, *khenyeng* requires the interpreter to construe two propositions as scalar such that the propositions expressed correspond to distinct points on a scale. What I have in mind as a scale here is a simple one-dimensional one, along the lines of Fillmore et. al. (1988), Kay (1990) and Kay (1992), since what are put in contrast are pair-focused propositions, not multiple paired-focused constituents.[18]

Let us now make concrete by way of an example what we conceive as an one-dimensional scale. For example, suppose that there is a directed contextual scale along with there are two distinct points α and β, ---α----β--->, where β outranks α in informativeness. Then, two propositions, ¬ ‖X‖ and ‖Y‖, correspond to α and β on the contextual scale since the second proposition

---

[18] For an informal discussion and formal characterization of a more complex scale, see Fillmore et. al. (1988).

entails the first proposition. The scale is now interpreted if some quantity has reached the point β on the scale, then it has, *a fortiori*, reached the point α. In order to see how this scale can account for the actual data, I will repeat relevant examples below.

(37) a. chenpwul-un-khenyeng   paykpwul-to   mos patassta
      1000 dollars-Contr-let alone 100 dollars-even not received
      'I did not receive 100 dollars, let alone 1000 dollars.'

   b. chingchan-un-khenyeng kkwucwung-lul patasssupnita
      praise-Contr-instead of scolding-Acc   got
      'Instead of being praised, I got a scolding.'

For example, in (37a), if I did not receive $100, it entails that I did not receive $1,000. Likewise, in (37b), if one has reason to believe I got a scolding, he has more reason to believe that I was not praised. Hence, the semantic function of the construction is to suggest that the first proposition expressed as the clausal fragment follows logically from asserting the second proposition expressed as a full clause.

As indicated in Fillmore et. al. (1988), an advantage of the scale is to supply semantic constraints on the acceptability of the sentence types with a scalar operator. For example, the difference between (38a) and (38b) can be accounted for by a scale.

(38) a. chenpwul-un-khenyeng   paykpwul-to   mos patassta
      1000 dollars-Contr-let alone 100 dollars-even not received
      'I did not receive 100 dollars, let alone 1000 dollars.'

   b. *paykpwul-un-khenyeng   chenpwul-to   mos patassta
      100 dollars-Contr-let alone 1000 dollars-even not received
      'I did not receive 1000 dollars, let alone 100 dollars.'

(38b), in contrast with (38a), is ungrammatical since it encounters interpretive problems caused by interchange of the pair of compared propositions. In other words, (38b) violates the semantic constraint that a stronger proposition must follow the weaker proposition in the *khenyeng* construction. Even though *khenyeng* itself does not determine the nature of the scale, it requires, as part of its intrinsic semantic properties, that the interpreter set up some scalar order of the compared propositions.

Having said this, it seems that what we need to explain the semantics of the *khenyeng* sentence is a kind of semantic entailment relation since it explains well, for example, the relationship that "I did not receive $1,000; *a fortiori*, I did not receive $100". However, the *khenyeng* sentence involves more than a simple logical entailment relation. That is why we have put a qualification 'contextual' in the expression 'contextual scale'. We will now defend why the scale must be understood as pragmatic, not semantic in the *khenyeng* construction.

As Fillmore et. al. (1988) argue, the justification for viewing the scale as contextual in nature is found in the cases in which, while the semantic entailment relation holds between the two conjoined propositions, the entire *khenyeng* sentence is still unacceptable. Consider (39), which is bad regardless of the context:

(39)   # ywuksipsa-uy seyceykopkun-un i-nun-khenyeng sosswu-to anita
         sixty four-of cube root-Top two-Contr-let alone prime-even not
         'The cube root of sixty four is not prime, let alone five.'

The interpretation of (39) fails, even though 'not being a prime number' entails 'not being the number two'. The reason that (39) is pragmatically odd is not that the entailment relation does not hold, but that it does not hold within the same scale. In other words, (39) implies that since we have reason to believe that the cube root of sixty-four does not enter the scale, we have all the more reason to believe that the cube root of sixty-four does not reach some non-lowest point on the scale. But since two is the lowest point, the sentence is pragmatically odd. Thus the conclusion that can be drawn from examples such as (39) is that what is involved in a semantic interpretation of the scalar operator *khenyeng* is a sort of special pragmatic entailment relation that presupposes a certain set of contextual conditions shared by the interlocutors.

6. Conclusion

I began by considering the traditional explanation of *khenyeng* as a lexical item with two different meanings, each of which occurs in a different syntactic environment. In this paper, I have demonstrated that the difference is more apparent than real, and I have provided a unified account which treats *khenyeng* as a negative conjunction and a scalar operator. On this account, *khenyeng* is a single lexical item, rather than two semantically unrelated homophonous lexical items.

Interestingly enough, there are several other expressions similar to *khenyeng* in Korean. These include *mal hal nawi epsi* 'needless to say', *mwullon* 'needless to say', *kosahako* 'apart from, let alone, needless to say', *ppwun man anila* 'not only-but also', and *hamwulmye...ilya* 'much more/less, not to mention, let alone', etc. By way of one illustration, consider briefly the scalar operator *kosahako*. At first glance the operator *kosahako* seems to share the same syntactic and semantic properties as *khenyeng*.

(40) a. chenpwul-un kosahako   paykpwul-to   mos patasseyo
    1000 dollars-Contr let alone 100 dollars-even not received
    'I did not receive one hundred dollars, let alone one thousand dollars.'

   b. sang-un kosahako pel-ul patasseyo
    praise-Contr instead of punishment-Acc received
    'Instead of being praised, I got a punishment.'

But a consideration of more data shows that they are not same in every detail. Note the asymmetry, as in (41) and (42).

(41) a. chenpwul-un kosahako   paykpwul-ilato patassni?
    1000 dollars-Contr aside from 100 dollars-even received-Q
    'Did you receive 100 dollars, aside from 1000 dollars?'

   b. * chenpwul-un-khenyeng   paykpwul-ilato patassni?
    1000 dollars-Contr-aside from 100 dollars-even received-Q
    'Did you receive 100 dollars, aside from 1000 dollars?'

(42) a. kwucun nalssi-nun kosahako pappu-ese mos   kakeyssta
    bad weather-Contr aside from busy-since cannot go
    'I cannot go because I am busy, aside from the bad weather.'

   b. * kwucun nalssi-nun-khenyeng pappu-ese mos   kakeyssta
    bad weather-Contr-aside from busy-since cannot go
    'I cannot go because I am busy, aside from the bad weather.'

Time and space precludes a discussion of these issues here. But the study of each of these scalar operators, preferably in comparison with *khenyeng*, will shed light on issues that may have been neglected in this exclusive study of *khenyeng*, and will give a more encompassing and complete explanation of scalar operators in general.

References

Chay, Wan. *Hyentay Kwuke Thukswucosa uy Yenkwu* [A study of special particles in contemporary Korean] = *Kwuke Yenkwu* [Korean Research] 39. Seoul National University: Department of Korean Language and Literature, 1977.

Choe, Hyon Sook. *Restructuring Parameters and Complex Predicates - A Transformational Approach.* Doctoral Dissertation, MIT, 1988.
Choy, Hyenpay. *Wulimalpon* [Korean grammar]. Seoul: Cengumsa, 1929/1961.
Fillmore, Charles. J., Paul Kay and Mary Catherine O'Connor. Regularity and Idiomaticity in Grammatical Constructions: The Case of *Let Alone, Language* 64, pp. 501-38, 1988.
Hankul Hakhoy. *Wulimal Khunsacen* [Great Korean Dictionary]. Seoul: Emwunkak, 1991.
Hong, Saman. *Kwuke Thukswucosa-lon* [A Study of Korean Special Particles]. Taegu: Hakmwun-sa, 1983.
Im, Hongpin, and Iksep Yi [Lee]. *Kwuke Mwunpeplon* [Korean Grammar]. Seoul: Hakyen-sa, 1983.
Kay, Paul. Even, *Linguistics and Philosophy* 13, pp. 59-111, 1990.
_____.At least. In: *Frames, Fields, and Contrasts,* edited by A. Lehrer and E. F. Kittay, Hillsdale: Lawrence Erlbaum Associates, pp. 309-331, 1992.
Kay, Paul and Charles J. Fillmore. Grammatical Constructions and Linguistic Generalizations: the What's X doing Y? Construction. Ms, 1994.
Kim, Sungkon. *Wulimal Thossi Yenkwu* [A Study of Korean Particles]. Seoul: Kenkwuk University Press, 1989.
Ko, Yengkun, and Kisim Nam. *Phyocwun Kwuke Mwunpeplon* [Standard Korean Grammar]. Seoul: Thap Chwulphansa, 1987.
Lee, Chungmin. Frozen Expressions and Semantic Representation. Ms, 1992.
Martin, Samuel E. *A Reference Grammar of Korean.* Rutland: Charles E. Tuttle Company, 1992.
Sohn, Ho-Min. *Korean.* London and New York: Routledge, 1994.
Seng, Kwangswu. *Kwuke Cosa uy Yenkwu* [A Study of Korean Particles]. Seoul: Hyengsel Chwulphansa, 1979.
Yang, In-Seok. *Korean Syntax: Case Markers, Delimiters, Complementation, and Relativization.* Seoul: Paykhap-sa, 1972.

15
From Quotation to Sentence-final Particle: The Analysis of *-ko* in Modern Korean

Sung-Ock S. Sohn

1. Introduction[1]

This paper attempts to examine the interplay between the so-called *ha-* 'say' verb deletion in Korean, illustrated in (1), and the grammaticalization of sentence-final particle *-ko*, illustrated in (2) and (3):

(1)　　A:　Chelswu-ka　　Seoul-ey　　ka-ss-e.
　　　　　Chelswu-NOM Seoul-LOC go-PAST-DEC
　　　　　'Chelswu went to Seoul.'

---> 　B:　mwe-la-**ko**　(hay-ss-e)?
　　　　　what-be-QT
　　　　　'What did you say?'

---> 　A:　Chelswu-ka　　Seoul-ey　　ka-ss-ta-**ko**　(hay-ss-e).
　　　　　Chelswu-NOM Seoul-LOC go-PAST-QT　say-PAST-Q
　　　　　'**I said that** Chelswu went to Seoul.'

---

[1] I would like to thank Ross King and an anonymous reviewer for their valuable comments on an earlier version of this paper. The Yale romanization is used for the transcription of Korean in this paper. The following abbreviations are used:
ACC: Accusative, ATTR: Attributive, AUX: Auxiliary, CIRCUM: Circumstantial, COMP: Complementizer, DAT: Dative, DEC: Declarative, DN: Defective Noun, EMPH: Emphatic, EXC: Exclamatory, HON: Honorific, IND: Indicative, INS: Instrumental, LOC: Locative, MD: Modal, NEG: Negation, PL: Plural, POL: Polite, POS: Possessive, Q: Question, QT: Quotative, RT: Retrospective, SUP: Suppositive, TOP: Topic.

(2)   nay chinkwu-tul cwungey pelsse sey myeng-ina
      my friend-PL among   already three person-even
---> yensang-uy yeca-lang   kyelhonhay-ss-ta-ko.
      older-POS woman-with marry-PAST-DEC-QT
      '**I am telling you that** three of my friends already married women older than they are.'

(3)   Yengi kyelhonsik cwunpi-lul   po-nikka
      Youngi wedding   preparation-ACC see-when
----> cham himtul-te-la-kwu.
       very difficult-RT-DEC-QT
       '**I am telling you** when I observed Youngi's wedding preparation, I found that it is very difficult.'

Example such as (1) above has traditionally been interpreted in terms of the *ha*-verb deletion since the deletion is recoverable from a context. The purpose of this paper, however, is to argue that the omission of the *ha*-verb brings about a new semantic function and reanalysis, leading to the grammaticalization of *-ko* to a sentence-final particle as shown in (2) and (3).

I will argue that in an early stage of grammaticalization, the 'say' verb *ha-* was omitted for an economic reason (i.e. to avoid redundancy), as shown in (1). However, after an extended period of time, the omission created a new semantic function, roughly equivalent to, 'I am telling you that...', which enhances the speaker's point of view. I suggest that once *-ko* was reinterpreted as a point-of-view marker, it spread into sentences like (2) and (3) with no overt verb of saying. This process of change is ongoing in contemporary Korean. The ongoing changes are supported by various pieces of evidence such as coexistence of related forms, ambiguity of meaning, and so on.

To support my view, I will use data mostly from spontaneous conversation in Modern Korean since the analysis of natural discourse provides crucial evidence for synchronic language change.

2. The omission of the 'say' verb *ha-*

It has been often assumed that the deletion of the *ha*-verb in reported speech in Korean is optional (cf. Han 1991: 124). Contrary to this claim, S. Sohn (In press-a; In press-b) has shown that the deletion of *ha-* is not optional, but is constrained by a systematic principle. Analysis of discourse frequency in conversational data reveals that the occurrence of -*ko* without the 'say' verb *ha*- in sentence-final position signals the point view of the speaker, whereas sentences with both -*ko* and the 'say' verb typically indicate the point view of the subject of the *ha*- verb, who is typically not the speaker (cf. S. Sohn In press-b).[2] The contrast between -*ko ha*- and -*ko* in terms of the point-of-view provides counterevidence against the generally accepted claim that the *ha*-verb deletion is unconditional. For instance, compare and contrast the function of -*ko hay* and that of -*ko* in sentence-final position in examples (4) and (5) below.

(4) yelyeses sal i-ntey   kyelhon-ul   hay-ss-   ta-
     16 years old be-CIRCUM   marriage-ACC   do-PAST-DEC

     ko hay-yo.
     -QT say-POL
     '**They say** that she is just 16 years old, but she is married.'

(5) (Campus talk)
---> K: Choy-ssi-ka   com kocip-i   sey-ta-**kwu**,   ku-cyo?
         Choy-surname-NOM   a bit will-NOM strong-DEC-QT that-SUP
         '(**I'm telling you**) People with surname Choi tend to be stubborn, right?'

     J: yey
         'yes'

     K: Kang-ssi-to   sey-ta-**ko**   kule-te-ntey.
         Kang-surname-also be stubborn say-RT-CIRCUM
         '**They say** that people with surname Kang also tend to be stubborn.'

---

[2] The data contains a total of forty-four instances of quotative -*ko* and twelve instances of -*ko ha*- in sentence-final position. (Although the size of the database is not large enough for quantitative analysis, the omission of the *ha*-verb in Modern Korean is widespread in daily conversation and is well attested in previous studies (cf. Hahn 1991, H. Sohn 1994).) The analysis of frequency in my discourse data shows that thirty-eight out of forty-four (86%) occurrences of the sentence-final -*ko* imply first-person's point of view (or second-person's view), and only one out of twelve occurrences of the sentence-final -*ko hay(yo)* indicates the speaker's point of view. The frequent use of the sentence-final -*ko* with first person subject (86%) is a strong indication that a grammaticalization process has been taking place for the quotative constructions in Modern Korean.

M: Kang-ssi-ka   kocip-i   sey-yo.
Kang-surname-NOM   will-NOM   be strong-POL
'Yes, Kangs are strong minded.'

In the above, while the full form -*ko ha(y)*- in (4) indicates that the source of information is from other people, -*kwu* (a variant of -*ko*) in (5) without the *ha*-verb expresses the speaker's own opinion or thought. Unlike a typical quotative marker like (4) which normally expresses repetition of a prior utterance, -*ko* in (5) functions to introduce the speaker's feeling or thought.

The difference between examples such as (4) and (5) can be explained in terms of two types of changes—a) the omission of the 'say' verb *ha*- and b) the grammaticalization of the quotative particle -*ko* into a sentence-final particle. The evidence that sentences (like (1)) without *ha*- are derived from sentences with *ha*- is well attested in Korean both synchronically and diachorinically (cf. Han 1991, King 1994, H. Sohn 1994). The focus of this paper is to examine the process of grammaticalization of -*ko* in terms of reanalysis and analogy. I will show that the deletion of the *ha*-verb leads to the grammaticalization of -*ko* into a sentence-final particle by reanalysis. Furthermore, once -*ko* became reanalyzed as a sentential particle, it was extended analogically into sentences with no overt verb of saying (e.g. -*te-la-ko*). The grammaticalization process is illustrated below.

(6) <u>Stages of grammaticalization of -*ko*</u>

Stage I   [QUOTE]-*ko* (*ha-ta*)
           a. -*ko* was used as a quotation particle
           b. Omission of *ha*-verb was optional.

Stage II   [QUOTE]-*ko*
           (Reanalysis)
           a. -*ko* became a marker of point of view.
           b. -*ko* was reanalyzed into a sentence-final particle.

Stage III [NON-QUOTE]-*ko* (Analogy)
           a. -*ko* was extended to non-quotative sentences.
           b. -*ko* is used as a sentence-final particle (e.g. -*te-la-ko*).

3. The development of sentence-final -ko
3.1. Stage I

In Stage I, -ko functions as a quotation particle (or complementizer), indicating something that was said. The omission of the 'say' verb ha- at this stage is economically motivated (i.e. the principle of least efforts). The issue of when the ha-verb was first omitted (e.g. the date of the first attested example of -ko without ha-) remains unclear since there is no such historical data available. This is presumably due to the fact that the omission began in colloquial form.[3]

Historical data shows that -ko in Modern Korean has been derived from ha-ko 'do/say-and' whose ancestor was Middle Korean ho-ya. According to King (1994), 'the dominant pattern of reported speech from the earliest recorded Middle Korean texts until the 20th century was some variant of {QUOTE + ho-ya + SAY}'. The first attestation of quotative -ko is found in the 19th century (King 1994: 21). The historical development of ho-ya > ha-ko > -ko, which is illustrated below, has been generally accepted among researchers of Korean.[4]

(7) Historical development of -ko
     Form: ho-ya 'do/say-and' --> hoya ---------------------> ha-ko ---> -ko
     Function: verb ------------------> comp(lementizer)--> comp ----> comp

The diachronic development of -ko from the 'say' verb to a complementizer is not unique to Korean. A parallel phenomenon was observed by Lord (1976) in a number of African and Asian languages in which a locutionary verb meaning 'say' has come to function as a complementizer. According to Hopper & Traugott (1993: 15), the process leading to the grammaticalization of a 'say' verb into a complementizer begins when a general verb meaning 'to say' is used to reinforce a variety of verbs of saying in the matrix clause.[5] This paper focuses on the further stage of grammaticalization of -ko (-ko is itself the result of a prior grammaticalization of ha-ko.)

---

[3] Although King (1994) provides a solid explanation for the historical development of the various patterns for reported speech in Korean, there is no discussion of how and when the omission of the matrix 'say' verb ha- took place.

[4] The issue of when hako was reduced to -ko and then reanalyzed as a complementizer is unclear (cf. King 1994: 30). According to King, ho-ya at the second stage is taken to be a non-verbal dummy element.

[5] In Ewe, for example, if the matrix verb is the general verb bé 'say', no further complementizer is needed (Hopper & Traugott 1993: 15).

3.2. Stage II

In Stage II, as the omission of the *ha*-verb became widespread, *-ko* was reanalyzed as a sentence-final particle. This claim is supported by the fact that *-ko* in Stage II is reinterpreted as a point of view marker which typically presents the speaker's own view, whereas *-ko* in the earlier stage (occurring with *ha-*) typically presents third person's point of view (cf. S. Sohn In press-b). In other words, before reanalysis, *-ko* appears in a context of {QUOTE-*ko (hata)*} and functions as a complementizer linking a quoted message and the 'say' verb *ha-* in the matrix clause. (Note that *ha-* was omitted optionally at Stage I.) After an extended period of time, the recurrent pattern of *ha-* omission brings about a new semantic function which enhances the speaker's point of view. The use of *-ko* at this stage is not to report on what others have said, but to express the speaker's point of view, as in (8).

(8) (A discussion about Cheetahs)
A: phoyutongmwul-tul-un ka-se paykophu-ci   anh-umyen an cwuki-e.
    mammal-PL-TOP   go-and be hungry-COMP not-if not kill-DEC
    'Mammals do not go and kill (baby cheetahs) if they are not hungry.'

   palo yeph-ey masissnun key   iss-eto an mek-ko
   just next-LOC tasty   thing   be-though not eat-and

---> an cwuki-n-ta- **ko**.
     not kill-IND-DEC-QT
     '(**I say that**) Even if something tasty is right next to them, they won't kill it.'

   kulentey paykophu-myen cwuki-ketun.
   but   be hungry-if kill-DEC
   'But, they kill (it) if they are hungry.'

In the above, *-ko* is used without *ha*-verb and functions to re-emphasize the speaker's own knowledge about mammals (i.e. 'Mammals do not go and kill baby Cheetahs if they are not hungry.'). Note that there is a clear difference between *-ko* and *-ko ha-* in terms of point of view. For instance, the occurrence of *ha*-verb after *-ko* in utterances like (8) above would indicate a third person's point of view, as illustrated below:

(9) palo yeph-ey   masissnun key iss-eto
     just next-LOC   tasty   thing be-though
---> an mek-ko   an cwuki-n-ta-   **ko hay.**
     not eat-and not kill-IND-DEC-QT say
     '**(They say that)** Even if something tasty is right next to them, they won't kill it.'

Reanalysis creates a new grammatical structure for -*ko* from '[[QUOTE]-*ko*] [*ha-ta*]' to '[QUOTE]-*ko*' (i.e. a shift from a complementizer to sentence-final particle).[6] Furthermore, the mechanism of reanalysis by which the development of the sentence-final -*ko* has been taking place is in line with the phenomenon of main clause deletion in Korean. Historical main clause deletion is commonly observed in Korean (cf. H. Sohn 1986). For example, consider the development of the so-called circumstantial marker -*nuntey(yo)*.[7]

(10) pi-ka   wa-   ss-   **nun tey-yo.**
     rain-NOM   come-PAST-IND tey-POL
     i. 'In the circumstance that it rained.'
     ii. 'My, it rained.'

In the above, the original noun -*tey* (circumstantial marker, cf. Martin & Lee 1969: 361) is restructured as a verbal suffix by way of a historical main clause deletion. According to H. Sohn (1986: 174), discourse meanings such as 'What shall we do?' are easily detectable in (10ii) above depending on the pragmatic or discourse situation. Thus, the restructuring of the noun -*tey* into sentence-final suffix has brought a new discourse function which increases the speaker's involvement. The development of the sentence-final -*ko* is understood to be syntactic restructuring parallel to main clause deletion. Syntactically, the omission of the main verb *ha*- changes a complex sentence into a simple sentence, as in the case of main clause deletion. Semantically, the change brings about the strengthening of the speaker's attitude. H. Sohn (1986: 169) points out that whenever certain syntactic restructuring, including contraction or omission, changes a complex sentence to a simple sentence, speaker's attitude is involved. This claim is supported by the grammaticality of (11a) and the ungrammaticality of (11b) below.

---

[6] Reanalysis has been thought of in terms of shift from one parametric setting to another (cf. Hopper & Traugott 1993: 40).

[7] The example is taken from H. Sohn (1986: 174).

(11) a. na-nun hakkyo-ey ka-llay-yo.
I-TOP school-LOC go-INTENTION -POL
'I intend to go to school.'
(cf. na-nun hakkyo-ey ka-lye-ko hay-yo. 'I intend to go to school.')

b. *John-un hakkyo-ey ka-llay-yo.
'John intends to go to school.'
(cf. John-un hakkyo-ey ka-lye-ko hay-yo. 'John intends to go to school.')

The construction -(u)lye-ko hay-yo, which consists of the suffix -(u)lyeko 'intending to' and the main verb ha-, indicates intention of sentient beings regardless of first or non-first person subjects. However, the contracted form -(u)llay-yo allows only first person subject (or second person in questions). The ungrammaticality of (11b) is explained by the fact that the reanalyzed -(u)llay-yo falls under the domain or the territory of speaker's attitude (H. Sohn 1986: 170). Similarly, the omission of the ha- verb not only changes the grammatical category of -ko from complementizer to sentence-final particle, but also brings to the fore the speaker's subjectivity, thus signaling first person's point of view.

3.3. Stage III

While -ko in Stage II was reanalyzed as a sentence-final particle for quotative sentences, -ko in Stage III was analogically extended to sentences with no overt verb of saying. At this stage, the internal reconstruction of the ha-verb after -ko is not reconstructible, as in (12):

(12) (Exchange students)[8]
Y: kuntey,   hyeng-un   yekise cekung cal   ha-si-nun
by the way you-TOP   here   adapt well do-HON-ATTR

kes   kath-a-yo.
DN   seem-DEC-POL
'By the way, it seems you adapt to this place very well.'

J: molla,
'I don't know.'

na-n   cincca yeki o-l   ttay
I-TOP really here come-ATTR   when

---

[8] I would like to thank Yumiko Kawanishi for the discourse data 'Exchange students'.

maum tantanhi mek-ko wa-ss-e.
mind firmly determine-and come-PAST-DEC
'When I came here, my mind was firmly set.'

yeki wa kaci-ko wancenhi twipakkwe pelli-lyeko
here come-and completely change AUX-in order to

---> cakcengha-ko wa-ss-ta-**ko**.
determine-and come-PAST-DEC-QT
'**I am telling you** my mind was firmly set to change myself completely when I came here.'

The sentence-final -*ko* in J's utterance expresses the internal world of J's belief and attitude. The extension of quotative -*ko* to non-quotative sentences like (12) is explained in terms of analogy. While reanalysis refers to the development of new structures out of old, analogy refers to the attraction of extant forms to already existing constructions (cf. Hopper & Traugott 1993: 56). There is a strong correlation between reanalysis and analogy. The analogy taking place at Stage III would not have been possible without the reanalysis of -*ko* as a sentence-final particle at Stage II. In other words, once -*ko* was reanalyzed as a point-of-view marker (by reanalysis), it was extended to sentences having nothing to do with verb of saying (by analogy).

Note that the semantic function of -*ko* at Stage III is to reinforce the speaker's own opinion or thought rather than to report on other's utterance. For example, the speaker J in (12) above by employing -*ko*, reinforces the message that he really made up his mind to change himself completely. The reinforcement function of -*ko* is supported by the fact that J repeats the message twice without having been asked to do it. Thus, the original quotative -*ko* is used to express the emotive affective attitude which is related to the speaker's subjectivity. The increased subjectivity encoded in sentence-final -*ko* is further evidenced by the frequent use of the sentence ender -*te-la-ko* in spoken Korean (see next section.).

4. The discourse function of -*te-la-ko-(yo)*

The so-called retrospective suffix -*te*- when occurring with -*la* represents the speaker's realization or discovery of a situation which is based on his or her own past observation or experience (Chang 1985: 58-87). The difference in meaning between -*te-la* and -*te-la-ko* in sentence-final position is often very subtle. However, conversational data shows that the message marked with -*te-la-ko* is often associated with an emotionally charged event (cf. Romaine and Lange 1991), an unexpected event, or sudden realization of an event. A few examples are given below.

(13) (Exchange students)
a. Y: ku chinkwu-nun yeki o-n   key
      that friend-TOP   here come-ATTR DN

   kwukminhakkyo   ihaknyen ttay   wa-ss-e-yo.
   elementary school 2nd grade time come-PAST-DEC-POL
   'That friend came here (USA) when he was a second grade at elementary school.'

   toykey   eli-l   ttay wa-ss-canh-a-yo.
   very   young-ATTR   time come-PAST-MD-DEC-POL
   'As you know, he came here when he was very young.'

   kuntey hankwukmal ce pota   hwelssin cal   ha-ko
   but   Korean   me than   much   better speak-and

   yok-to   cal   hay-yo.
   swearing-also   well say-POL
   'But he speaks Korean much better than me and also swears well.'

---> po-nikka   toykey   sinkiha-**te-la-kwu-yo**.
     see-when   very   amazing-RT-DEC-QT-POL
     'I find it amazing when I see this.'

b: J: wenlay   keki   cali   eps-ess-e.
      originally   there opening   be not-PAST-DEC
      'Originally, there was no job opening over there.'

   supervisor-lul   kyeysok   insaha-ko
   supervisor-ACC   continuously   greet-and

---> kyelkwukey kwichanhkey ha-nikka nacwungey toy-**te-la-kwu**.
     finally   bother-   when   later   work out-RT-DEC-QT
     'I kept seeing and bothering the supervisor and finally it worked out (I got a job).'

In the above, -*kwu* (= -*ko*) is attached to the sentence ender -*te-la* and expresses the speaker's surprise at an unexpected discovery. In (13a), for example, -*te-la-kwu-yo* is used in the retelling of an emotionally charged event. As an exchange student from Seoul, J is talking about his experience in the United States. J expresses his surprise at the discovery that the so-called 1.5 generation Korean-American speaks and swears in Korean much better than himself, a native speaker of Korean. The use of -*ko* in such a case has to do with pragmatic strengthening (cf. Traugott 1989) in that by employing

-ko, the speaker seeks articulation of his or her attitude and the interactive communication with interlocutors. The contrast between the effect of -te-la and -te-la-ko is clear in (14) where the speaker uses both.

(14) (Exchange students)
   J: paykhwacem-ey   ka-to   kulehkey
       department store-LOC go-even if that much
---> hwalyeha-ci-n   anh-**te-la-kwu**   yeki-n.
      splendid-COMP-TOP not-RT-DEC-QT here-TOP
      'Even though when I went to a mall, I found that it is not that splendid.'
   Y: kulayyo.
      'That's right.'
   J: cham nollay-ss-e.   mikwuk-i amwu kes-to   anikwu-na.
      very be shocked-PAST-DEC U.S.-NOM any thing-EMPH not-EXC
      'I was really shocked. USA is nothing.'

      kuntey ettehkey sayngkaha-myen kethmosup-ul sinkyeng an ssu-ko
      but   differently think-if   appearance-ACC attention not pay-and

      naysil-man   ttacinun   key mikwukin-uy sakopangsik-i
      substance-only make sure COMP American-POS thinking-NOM

      aninka ha-ko   eccemyen kukey olh-ci   anhna ha-nun
      maybe wonder-and probably that   right-COMP not say-ATTR
---> kulen sayngkak-i   tul-**te-la**.
      that   thought-NOM come to my mind-RT-DEC
      'But, when I think from a different perspective, maybe the American way of thinking is not to care about appearance, but to be concerned about substantiality, and I think probably that kind of thinking is right.'

Example (14) illustrates the motivation behind the speaker's choices between -te-la-ko and -te-la and how these influence the meaning of the discourse. The speaker J uses -te-la-ko for soliciting agreement and interactive communication with his interlocutor, and uses -te-la for a less interactive response. The marker -te-la-ko seems especially useful for expressing the speaker's emphatic attitude. For example, in (14), the speaker used -te-la-ko to express his surprise at the unexpected discovery that malls in the United States are not as splendid as he had expected. This use of -te-la-ko evokes a vivid effect in the speech situation, capturing a positive response from the interlocutor, as illustrated by Y's response *kulayyo* ('That's right'). By using *-te-la-ko*, the speaker thus conveys an emotive (affective) attitude which indicates aspects of the speaker subjectivity. The emotive use of the quotative marker is not unique to Korean alone. Akatsuka (1985) discusses that reported speech in Balkan languages which are normally associated with doubts or inferences can also express the speaker's surprise at actually witnessing some unexpected events. From the speaker's point of view, the proposition marked with *-te-la-ko* is newly learned information and thus may evoke surprise. In other words, the speaker is not fully prepared for the discovery of the event (Akatsuka 1985: 635). By using *-ko*, the speaker expresses such surprise, thus indicating reinforcement.

5. The process of grammaticalization: A case of subjectification

Thus far, I have shown the development of *-ko* into a sentence-final particle in terms of reanalysis and analogy. What is the mechanism which motivates this change? Cross-linguistic typological studies on quotative constructions have revealed that quotative markers have been or are being grammaticalized in a certain direction. For example, in many languages the pragmatic and interactive function of the 'say' verb gives rise to other meanings such as 'know' 'believe' 'hope' 'purpose', etc. (cf. Saxena 1987; 1988, Heine et. al. 1991: 233). According to Saxena (1987), this development is not random, but predictable in that the development of grammaticalized functions is from a general to more restricted one. Specifically, he argues that languages which have the verb 'say' as a comparative marker ('than') also have other functions of the verb 'say' such as 'know' 'believe' 'hope' 'purpose' 'reason', etc., demonstrating that there is an implicational hierarchy. This claim has been justified by the parallelism between the cross-linguistic typological findings and the diachronic single language development (e.g. Sanskrit, cf. Saxena 1987) of the quotative constructions. The Korean quotative construction has been undergoing a similar grammaticalization process. The particle *-ko* can appear in subordinate clauses and carry various semantic functions such as 'believe, hope, purpose, cause, etc.', as illustrated below:[9]

---

[9] Note that the internal reconstruction of *ha*-verb after *-ko* is not possible in sentences (15)-(17).

(15) (BELIEVE)
    kuntey   nay sayngkak-ulo-nun kyelhon-ul   com   nuckey
    by the way my opinion-INS-TOP marriage-ACC a little late
---> hanun-key coh-ta-**ko**.
    do-DN   be good-DEC-QT think
    'In my opinion, I believe that it is better to marry later.'

(16) (HOPE/PURPOSE)
---> Chelswu-nun tayhak-ey   tuleka-keyss-ta-**ko**
    TOP college-GOAL enter-MD-DEC-QT

    yelsimhi   kongpwuhay-yo.
    hard   study-POL
    'Hoping to go to college, Chelswu studies very hard.'

(17) (CAUSE)
    hankwuk-eyse-uy   tayhak saynghwal-i engmang-i-ess-e-yo.
    Korea-LOC-POS   college life-NOM   terrible-be-PAST-DEC-POL
---> waynyahamyen   kosi   kongpwuha-n-ta-**ko**.
    because   exam   study-IND-DEC-QT
    'My college life in Korea was terrible, because I was studying for the (law) exam.'

Note that the original function of the quotative -*ko* is lost in sentences (15)-(17). As discussed earlier, the grammaticalization of -*ko* from quotation to a complementizer (or a sentence-final particle) parallels what Heine et. al (1991: 236) show, namely that in many languages worldwide, verbs meaning 'say' have been, or are being grammaticalized into clause subordinators.[10] More specifically, they suggest the conceptual expansion of the 'say' verb as follows:

(18) The conceptual expansion of the 'say' verb
    SAY> KNOW> BELIEVE> HOPE> PURPOSE> CAUSE

Korean -*ko* shows all the stages of the conceptual domain listed above. For example, sentence (16) above illustrates the occurrence of -*ko* as HOPE/PURPOSE and sentence (17) exemplifies the occurrence of -*ko* as CAUSE.

---

[10] This process is in line with the historical development of -*ko* (i.e. *ho-ya* > *hoya* > *hako* > -*ko*) as illustrated in (7).

Recent studies on grammaticalization have focused on meaning changes and the cognitive motivations behind them (cf. Bybee & Pagliuca 1985, Traugott 1989, Hopper & Traugott 1993). In particular, Traugott (1982: 254) has shown that meaning shift in the process of grammaticalization moves from less personal to more personal whereby 'more personal' means 'more anchored in the context of the speech act, particularly the speaker's orientation to situation, text, and interpersonal relations.' Traugott (1989) has further proposed three general tendencies in semantic-pragmatic changes. Tendency 1 involves a shift from external to internal situation, which also subsumes a shift from concrete to abstract. Tendency 2 includes meaning changes from lexical to textual (i.e., text-construction, a cohesive function). Tendency 3 is stipulated as subjectification, whereby 'meanings tend to become increasingly based in the speaker's subjective belief state/attitude toward the proposition' (Traugott 1989: 35). Traugott's proposal that grammaticalization does not always involve loss of meaning (bleaching, weakening, etc.) stands in contrast with the traditional view on grammaticalization. Previous researchers on this issue have observed that grammaticalization involves 'a process of loss of semantic content' (cf. Hopper & Traugott 1993: 87). Subjectification involves 'increase in coding of speaker attitude, whether of belief, assessment of the truth, or personal commitment to the assertion' (Traugott 1989: 49).

The development of the sentence-final -*ko* illustrates an increase in the coding of speaker informativeness about his or her attitude. It also demonstrates a shift from relatively objective 'utterance' (i.e. 'to say') meaning to a specification of the speaker's subjective attitude (i.e. the use of -*ko* as the speaker's point of view).

Thus far, I have discussed the process of grammaticalization of -*ko* from the perspective on reanalysis and analogy. Stages I, II, III are all observed in Modern Korean. Indication of change in progress (as an ongoing grammaticalization) is supported by the coexistence of ambiguity. That is, in some contexts -*ko* is ambiguous between a quotative and non-quotative interpretation.[11] For instance, consider the following example where the sentence-final -*ko* is ambiguous between REASON as in (19i) and quotation as in (19ii):

---

[11] Thompson and Mulac (1991: 325) postulate that the coexistence of several layers of a set of related grammatical phenomena is strong indication of ongoing grammaticalization.

(19) kulen kyengwu-eynun casik   honsa-lul   aphtwuko
     such case-TOP   children wedding-ACC   before

   swuswulha-nun   swu-to   manh-a-yo.
   plastic surgery-ATTR case-also be many-DEC-POL
   'In such a situation (where parents have deformed faces), there are many cases where parents do plastic surgery before their children's wedding.'

---> saton po-ki-ka   pwukkulep-ta-**ko**-yo.
     in-law see-COMP-NOM   embarrassing-DEC-QT-POL
   i. 'Because it is embarrassing to see their in-laws.'
   ii. 'They say that it is embarrassing to see their in-laws.'

As the grammaticalization of -*ko* to a sentence-final particle continues and the use of -*ko* without the *ha*-verb becomes routinized, -*ko* gains a new meaning. However, the older meaning (i.e. quotation) continues to exist together with the new meaning, thus forming ambiguity as shown in (19).

6. Conclusion

In line with recent studies of grammaticalization which emphasize unidirectionality in semantic changes, the present paper has shown further evidence that the grammatical extension of the Korean quotative marker -*ko* moves toward speaker-based meaning. As discussed in Saxena (1987; 1988), languages may differ regarding the grammaticalized functions of reported speech, but the direction of the development follows a predictable pattern.

Our examination of conversational data has revealed that the omission of the 'say' verb *ha*- in Korean leads to the grammaticalization of -*ko* as a new grammatical category. Reanalysis and analogy are the major mechanism in the grammaticalization process of -*ko*. The particle -*ko*, originally linking a quoted message and the 'say' verb *ha*-, is reanalyzed as a sentence-final particle, which enhances the speaker's point of view. Once -*ko* became a point of view marker, it was extended analogically to sentences with no overt verb of saying, as shown in the sequence of -*te-la-ko*. This process is consistent with cross-linguistic studies revealing that some very general principles underlie the development of reported speech. This result also supports Traugott's (1989) claim that in the process of grammaticalization, meanings tend to move toward greater subjectivity. The grammatical change in sentence-final -*ko* has an important implication for the grammar of Korean in that it gives rise to a new syntactic slot among sentence-final particles. This process also shows significant parallels to historical main clause deletion in Korean. The coexistence of the various stages of grammaticalization of

-ko (such as quotative particle and sentential particle) is a strong indication that the grammaticalization process is an ongoing process in Modern Korean. I hope that further study using quantitative analyses will provide statistical evidence on the ongoing processes involving -ko.

References

Akatsuka, Noriko. Conditionals and the epistemic scale, *Language* 61 (3), pp. 625-639, 1985.

Besnier, Niko. Language and affect, *Annual Review of Anthropology*, Vol 19, 1990.

Bybee, J. & W. Pagliuca. Crosslinguistic comparison and the development of grammatical meaning. In: *Historical semantics*, edited by Fisiak, (Trends in Linguistics, studies and monographs no. 29). Berlin: Mouton de Gruyter, pp. 59-83, 1985.

Cang, Kyenghuy. *Hyentay kwuke uy yangthay pemcwu yenkwu* (A study of modality elements in Korean). Seoul: Tower Press, 1985.

Chui, Kawai. Grammaticalization of the saying verb *wa* in Cantonese, *Santa Barbara Papers in Linguistics*, vol. 5. Dept. of Linguistics, University of California, Santa Barbara, pp. 1-14, 1994.

Han, Kil. *Kwuke congkyel emi yenkwu* (A Study of sentence-final suffixes in Korean). University of Kangwon Press, 1991.

Heine, B., Claudie, U. & F. Hünnemeyer. *Grammaticalization*. The University of Chicago Press, 1991.

Hopper, P. On some principles of grammaticalization. In: *Approaches to grammaticalization*, vol. 1, edited by E. Traugott and B. Heine, pp. 17-36, 1991.

Hopper, P. & S. Thompson. The discourse basis for lexical categories in universal grammar, *Language* 60, pp. 703-752, 1984.

Hopper, P. & E. Traugott. *Grammaticalization*. Cambridge University Press, 1993.

King, J. R. P. History of reported speech in Korean, *Korean Linguistics* 8, pp.1-38, 1994.

Lord, Carol. Evidence for syntactic reanalysis: from verb to complementizer in Kwa. In:, *Papers from the Parassession on Diachronic Syntax*, edited by Steever et. al., Chicago: Chicago Linguistic Society, pp. 197-191,1976.

Martin, S. E. and Y. Lee. *Beginning Korean*. New Haven: Yale University Press, 1969.

Romaine, S. & D. Lange. The use of *like* as a marker of reported speech and thought: A case of grammaticalization in progress, *American Speech* 66:3, pp. 227-278, 1991.

Saxena, Anju. On the grammaticalization of the verb 'say': A typological and diachronic study. Paper presented at the Third Pacific Linguistics Conference, Eugene: University of Oregon, 1987.

_____. On syntactic convergence: The case of the verb 'say' in Tibeto-Burman, *Berkeley Linguistic Society* 14: 375-388, 1988.

Sohn, Ho-min. *Linguistic expeditions*. Seoul: Hashin Press, 1986.

_____. Grammicalization and semantic shift. In *ICKL* (International Circle of Korean Linguistics.) 7, pp. 425-435, 1990.

_____ *Korean*. London: Routledge, 1994.

Sohn, Sung-Ock. The development of the epistemic causality in Korean, *Korean Linguistics* 8, pp. 67-84, 1994a.

_____. Phonological reduction and reanalysis in Korean: A case of incipient grammaticalization, *Chicago Linguistic Society* 30-2, (In press-a)

_____. On the development of sentence-final particles in Korean.Paper presented at the Fifth Japanese/Korean Linguistics Conference, (In press-b)

_____. (with Y. Kawanishi). The grammaticalization of Korean negation: Semantic-Pragmatic analysis of -*canh(a)*. In *Harvard Studies in Korean Linguistics*, 1993.

Thompson, S. & A. Mulac. A quantitative perspective on the grammaticalization of epistemic parentheticals in English. In *Approaches to grammaticalization*, vol. 2, edited by E. Traugott & B. Heine, pp. 313-329, 1991.

Traugott, E. From propositional to textual and expressive meanings: Some semantic-pragmatic aspects of grammaticalization. In *Perspectives in historical linguistics*, edited by Lehmann & Malkiel, Amsterdam: John Benjamins, pp. 245-271,1982.

Traugott, E. On the rise of epistemic meanings in English: An example of subjectification in semantic change, *Language* 65:1, pp. 31-55, 1989.

Traugott, E. & E. König. The semantics-pragmatics of grammaticalization revisited. In *Approaches to grammaticalization*, vol. 1, edited by E. Traugott and B. Heine, pp. 189-218, 1991.

Index

A-position, 173, 226
accusative case-marking, 185
affectedness, 241-42, 244, 248, 251
Akatsuka, 312, 315n, 323n
Anaphor Asymmetry Universal, 172
anaphor binding, 219, 224, 226
anaphor-antecedent (AA) relation, 170, 180, 237
anaphora, 169-70, 179-80, 182
anaphoric island, 300
anaphoric tense, 270
Anti-Superiority Condition, 112, 114, 117, 120, 122, 124-25, 127-28
aspect, 3, 136, 143-44, 146-53, 155-62, 164, 270-71, 275, 320
aspiration, 2, 11, 13, 15-20, 25, 28-29, 31, 35-39, 41-47, 68-69, 73, 75-76, 80-81
assimilation, 37, 39-48, 51-52, 60, 64

atelic aspects, 159
Autosegmental Linking Constraint, 42n, 52

backward pronominalization, 302n
Bak Sung-Yun, 68-69, 72, 77, 197, 311-13, 326-27
Baker, 146, 219
Bantu, 24, 229
binding, 104n, 116, 117n, 171, 220, 231, 234, 266, 268
body-part object, 251
bridge verbs, 200n, 203n, 205n

C-command, 102, 104, 104n, 106n, 112, 121n, 122n, 137n
-ca, 305
case alternation, 134, 136, 139, 185, 208
case assignment, 133, 148, 192n, 297n
case position, 204
case stacking, 195

case-marking, 185, 242, 248
causative suffixation, 67, 78
Cella dialect, 58
chains, 105, 191, 194, 195-98, 213
Chain Condition, 191-92, 194, 212-13
Checking Theory, 186, 192
Chinese, 134
Chomsky, Noam, 2-3, 77, 103, 105, 148, 156, 171, 185-86, 189, 191-92, 198, 205, 211-12
Choy Hyenpay, 331, 332n
-*ciman*, 272
clause coordination, 264
cleft conditionals, 312, 319, 321
cleft constructions, 213n,
Clements, George N., 41-42, 46, 52-54, 72
coalescence, 36-37, 45-47
cocha, 329
coda neutralization, 38
complementation, 146
complementizer, 3, 105-110, 186, 193, 200-05, 190n, 207-09, 211n, 212-13, 285-87, 287n, 294, 296, 319-320, 355-58, 363
complementizer *kes*, 287, 289, 291-92, 294-96, 298
compulsory tense omission, 273
Comrie, Bernard, 151, 324
conditional forms, 311
consonant phonation, 11
consonantal strength, 42
contrastiveness, 234
control, 190n, 192-93, 199-200, 228,
coordination, 140-41, 143-44, 157-59, 259, 264, 281, 338

counterfactual conditionals, 311
cwul, 287, 294

D-structure, 3, 87, 89-91, 93, 101, 104-05, 111-12, 117-18, 120, 122-27
definites, 236
degree of transitivity, 241
delimiters, 220, 329, 335-37
dialects, 12, 160n
discourse anaphors, 234
discourse deletion, 97, 98
discourse prominence, 228
dissimilation, 71-72, 74-76, 78-82
duration adverbials, 135, 136
Dutch, 253

ECM constructions, 185-87, 189, 189n, 190n, 191-94, 197-200, 204-08, 205n, 212-13
Elsewhere Condition, 44, 71
embedded clauses, 88, 91-92, 105, 186, 192-94, 199, 200, 204, 207-09, 224, 267, 296, 300, 304, 307
emphatic lengthening, 46
English, 87, 99, 101-03, 107, 247, 253-54
-*ese*, 264
-*ess*-, 268, 270
event types, 159
experiencer subject, 165
eykey, 229
eyse, 90
Ewe, 355n

factual conditional, 321, 327
features, 37, 39, 41, 44-45, 47,

52-54, 60, 64, 73, 80, 186, 187n, 200, 205, 208, 211, 213, 242, 248, 267, 270-71, 318-19, 335
felicity condition, 299
Finnish, 133, 244
FØ, 14-15
focal delimiters, 220, 337
"free-choice" quantifier, 107-08
fundamental frequency, 11

gapping, 118, 141, 144
geminates, 37, 40
'geminate inalterability', 56
German, 248
Germanic V2 languages, 298
'given' conditionals, 311
glottal approximant, 35
Government Transparency Corollary, 146
grammatical command (g-command), 226

h-deletion, 68, 77, 79, 83
ha-, 351-52, 358
hanthey, 229
head movement, 138, 147
Hopper and Thompson, 241, 254
Hungarian, 248-49

-(i)lamyen, 326
-(i)lato, 329, 336
-(i)na, 336
-(i)nama, 329
(i)ya, 329, 336
Icelandic, 133
inalienable possession, 232
indefinites, 236

inference, 271
Inoue, 312, 319, 321
irrealis, 311-12, 321, 146-47, 150, 153
isomorphism, 176-77, 179-80
Iverson, Gregory, 1-2, 39, 42, 46, 51, 53-54, 63, 76

Jackendoff, R. 173, 234
Japanese, 89, 94, 102, 225, 247, 248, 279, 285-86, 298-99, 302-03, 306, 319

Kay, Paul, 329, 346
Keenan, Edward, 170-71, 174, 176, 229
Kempson, Ruth, 4, 261, 264
-*kena*, 268n
Kenstowicz, Paul, 52, 55-56, 59
kes, 287, 289, 298n
-*key*, 208
khenyeng, 329, 335-36, 338
-*ki*, 203n
Kim, C-W, 11-12, 17, 20, 31, 67-69, 72
Kim-Renaud, Y-K, 1, 2, 6, 21, 32, 36, 38-40, 77
Kinyarwanda, 229
Kiparsky, Paul, 44, 68, 71, 301
kkaci, 329, 336
-*ko*, 157n, 189n, 259, 264-65, 267-70, 272, 275, 286-87, 351, 353
-*ko ha-*, 287n, 353
-*kose*, 267, 268
Kuno, Susumu, 1-2, 98, 116, 119, 197, 236, 277, 279, 286, 302, 306-07

372 • Index

-kwun, 305
Kyengsang dialect, 58

l-gemination, 69, 71, 77, 83
l-spreading, 78, 83
labelled deductive model, 259, 261
labelled natural deduction, 259
Lasnik, Howard, 2, 103, 105, 191, 205, 211
Last Resort Principle, 191-192, 212-213
lax, 16-18
LDS, 259, 262-64, 271, 280
lexical integrity hypothesis, 300
LF-representation, 107
licenser Q, 114
linear order, 228, 230
locally free reflexives, 237n, 302n
Luganda, 253
-lul, 229

-mace, 329, 336
-man, 220, 329, 336
Martin, Samuel, 36, 39, 357
-mata, 336
Maximal Uniformity Condition on Predication (MUCP), 182
Medieval German, 52
metathesis, 36-37, 47
Middle High German, 57
Middle Korean, 82n, 150n
minimalist program, 2-3, 148n, 185-86, 198, 205, 213

modal(s), 4, 285-92, 294-96, 298-99, 307, 320
Moravcsik, Edith, 247-48
mos, 341
movement, 90, 100, 105, 108-09, 114, 117, 128, 138, 146-48, 154-55, 157, 186, 189, 191, 212, 243

neg-incorporation, 118
Neg-NPI Clause Mate Constraint, 87-90, 92, 100-101
negative polarity, 87, 99, 341-42
neutralization, 37-40, 45-47, 63, 68
nominative case-marking, 185
non-ECM constructions, 198
non-telicity, 159
NPI Licensing, 101, 107-108, 117-18, 120, 125, 127
-(n)un, 220, 280, 285, 300, 302, 329, 336
-nuntey(yo), 357

O'Grady, William, 230, 233
O-Command, 227, 229, 231
Obligatory Contour Principle (OCP), 61-62, 64, 64n, 69-70, 70n
oblique case marker, 90
obliqueness, 228-230
obliqueness-command (see o-command)
Old High German, 51-2
optional tense, 277
outbound anaphora, 300
overt licenser, 96
overt tense, 271

P-Bind, 231
P-command, 231-232, 234
p-set, 235-36
pakk ey, 336
partial affectedness, 256
passive, 67, 135
passivization, 229
Pecking Order of Deletion Principle, 98, 100
periphrastic causatives, 208-09
phonation type, 13
phonetic implementation constraint, 38
phonological incorporation, 35
Pollard and Sag, 219, 227-28, 236
possessor ascension, 251-52, 256
preceding segment, 13
predication, 170, 181-82, 197, 334
presupposition, 223n, 235
primary object (PO), 229
primary umlaut, 52, 54
Prince, Ellen, 300-01, 304
principal filter, 180
Principle A, 171, 226
Principle C, 171, 267
Principle of Referential Autonomy, 169, 174, 177, 182
Principle of Relevance, 263
prominence-command, 231
prosodic position, 13
prosodic structure, 11
psych predicates, 143, 164-65
pwuthe, 329, 336

Quechua, 249
quotative complementizer, 286-87
quotative conditionals, 321n

R-expressions, 267-68
raising, 3, 186, 192, 194, 198, 212, 228
realis, 4, 311-12, 314, 316, 327
reanalysis, 5, 352, 354, 356-57, 357n, 359, 362, 364
reciprocality, 172
referentially autonomous, 175, 179
referentially dependent, 169, 172, 175
reflexivity, 172
reinforced, 16-18
Relevance Theory, 274
resumptive pronoun, 197n
Roberts, C., 219, 234
Rooth, Mats, 219, 234-35, 301
Russian, 133, 244, 248

Saito, Mamoru, 103, 225-26, 285, 299
scope ambiguity, 140-41
scrambling, 94, 230, 234
secondary object (SO), 229
secondary umlaut, 52
Sells, Peter, 139, 141, 236
selo, 222, 235n
Shin, Sung-ock, 4, 265-70
siphta, 133
Sohn, Ho-min, 307, 354, 357-58
Sohn, Hyang-sook, 36, 42, 46
Sohn, Sung-ock, 5, 352-53, 356
sonority, 42-3
space-object constructions, 245
Spanish, 99

spell-out, 186
Sperber and Wilson, 263, 274
structure preservation, 41n, 44n
subject antecedents vs. object antecedents, 230
subject-object asymmetry, 101, 112
subject-to-subject raising, 107-09
Syllable Contact Law, 42-43
syllable-final neutralization, 38
syntactic anaphor binding condition, 231, 237
syntactic prominence, 228
syntactic superiority, 112

t-irregular conjugation, 79
-ta, 189n, 287n, 289, 305
-tako hanun kes, 287n, 291-92
-tamyen, 323
-tanun kes, 287n, 291-92
-tamyen, 311-12, 318, 321, 327
target of predication, 181-82
-telako (yo), 359
telicity, 159
+/-temporal, 265
temporal adverbs, 152, 278
tense, 259, 264
tense deletion rules, 266
tense indexing, 266
tense markers, 267
tensing, 44
ternary nuclear sentence, 175
Theta Role Hierarchy Condition, 173
Three-Layered Case Theory, 198-99, 207, 212, 213
to, 280, 329, 336
Toba Batak, 170, 177

topic, 196n, 280, 286, 302n
topicalization, 196n, 338
total affectedness, 256
transitivity hypothesis, 254
translaryngeal harmony, 56n

$ul/l,$, 294, 298
-(u)llay yo, 358
-(u)lyeko, 358
-(u)m, 203n, 298
-(u)myen, 311-14, 316, 318, 326-27
-(u)myense, 268
umlaut blocking, 55
umlaut uniformity, 51
unary nuclear sentence, 175
underdeterminacy, 271, 277-78, 280
uniform identifiability, 176
uniformity condition, 42n, 52, 56, 62, 64
-(u)nikka, 268n

velarization, 69
vowel FØ, 11
VP node, 230n

Watanabe, A., 193, 197-99, 204, 212
wh-expressions, 114, 196n
Whitman, John, 146, 285-87, 289, 292, 294-95, 298-99, 305

Yang, 336
Yatabe, 226
Yoon, James, 146, 156, 158, 193-95, 197-98, 204, 233

CORNELL EAST ASIA SERIES

No. 4 *Provincial Leadership in China: The Cultural Revolution and Its Aftermath*, by Fredrick Teiwes

No. 8 *Vocabulary and Notes to Ba Jin's Jia: An Aid for Reading the Novel*, by Cornelius C. Kubler

No. 16 *Nō as Performance: An Analysis of the Kuse Scene of* Yamamba, by Monica Bethe & Karen Brazell

No. 17 *Pining Wind: A Cycle of Nō Plays*, translated by Royall Tyler

No. 18 *Granny Mountains: A Second Cycle of Nō Plays*, translated by Royall Tyler

No. 23 *Nanking Letters, 1949*, by Knight Biggerstaff

No. 28 *The Griffis Collection of Japanese Books: An Annotated Bibliography*, edited by Diane E. Perushek

No. 29 *Dance in the Nō Theater*, by Monica Bethe & Karen Brazell
Vol. 1: Dance Analysis, Vol. 2: Plays and Scores, Vol. 3: Dance Patterns

No. 32 *Tone, Segment, and Syllable in Chinese: A Polydimensional Approach to Surface Phonetic Structure*, by A. Ronald Walton

No. 36 *The Diary of a Japanese Innkeeper's Daughter*, translated by Miwa Kai, edited & annotated by Robert J. Smith & Kazuko Smith

No. 37 *International Perspectives on Yanagita Kunio and Japanese Folklore Studies*, edited by J. Victor Koschmann, Ōiwa Keibō & Yamashita Shinji

No. 38 *Murō Saisei: Three Works*, translated by James O'Brien

No. 40 *Land of Volcanic Ash: A Play in Two Parts* by Kubo Sakae, revised edition, translated by David G. Goodman

No. 41 *The Dreams of Our Generation and Selections from Beijing's People,* by Zhang Xinxin, edited & translated by Edward Gunn, Donna Jung & Patricia Farr

No. 44 *Family Change and the Life Course in Japan*, by Susan Orpett Long

No. 46 *Planning and Finance in China's Economic Reforms*, by Thomas P. Lyons & WANG Yan

No. 48 *Bungo Manual: Selected Reference Materials for Students of Classical Japanese*, by Helen Craig McCullough

No. 49 *Ankoku Butō: The Premodern and Postmodern Influences on the Dance of Utter Darkness*, by Susan Blakeley Klein

No. 50 *Twelve Plays of the Noh and Kyōgen Theaters*, edited by Karen Brazell

No. 51 *Five Plays by Kishida Kunio*, edited by David G. Goodman
No. 52 *Ode to Stone*, by Shirō Hara, translated by James Morita
No. 53 *Defending the Japanese State: Structures, Norms and the Political Responses to Terrorism and Violent Social Protest in the 1970s and 1980s*, by Peter J. Katzenstein & Yutaka Tsujinaka
No. 54 *Deathsong of the River: A Reader's Guide to the Chinese TV Series* Heshang, by Su Xiaokang & Wang Luxiang, translated by Richard Bodman & Pin P. Wan
No. 55 *Psychoanalysis in China: Literary Transformations, 1919-1949*, by Jingyuan Zhang
No. 56 *To Achieve Security and Wealth: The Qing Imperial State and the Economy, 1644-1911*, edited by Jane Kate Leonard & John R. Watt
No. 57 *Like a Knife: Ideology and Genre in Contemporary Chinese Popular Music*, by Andrew F. Jones
No. 58 *Japan's National Security: Structures, Norms and Policy Responses in a Changing World*, by Peter J. Katzenstein & Nobuo Okawara
No. 59 *The Role of Central Banking in China's Economic Reforms*, by Carsten Holz
No. 60 *Warrior Ghost Plays from the Japanese Noh Theater: Parallel Translations with Running Commentary*, by Chifumi Shimazaki
No. 61 *Women and Millenarian Protest in Meiji Japan: Deguchi Nao and Ōmotokyō*, by Emily Groszos Ooms
No. 62 *Transformation, Miracles, and Mischief: The Mountain Priest Plays of Kyōgen*, by Carolyn Anne Morley
No. 63 *Selected Poems of Kim Namjo*, translated by David R. McCann & Hyunjae Yee Sallee, with an afterword by Kim Yunsik
No. 64 *From Yalta to Panmunjom: Truman's Diplomacy and the Four Powers, 1945-1953*, by HUA Qingzhao
No. 65 *Kitahara Hakushū: His Life and Poetry*, by Margaret Benton Fukasawa
No. 66 *Strange Tales from Strange Lands: Stories by Zheng Wanlong*, edited & with an introduction by Kam Louie
No. 67 *Backed Against the Sea*, by Wang Wen-hsing, translated by Edward Gunn
No. 68 *The Sound of My Waves: Selected Poems by Ko Un*, translated by Brother Anthony of Taizé & Young-Moo Kim
No. 69 *Han Sŏrya and North Korean Literature: The Failure of Socialist Realism in the DPRK*, by Brian Myers
No. 70 *The Economic Transformation of South China: Reform and Development in the Post-Mao Era*, edited by Thomas P. Lyons & Victor Nee
No. 71 *After Apocalypse: Four Japanese Plays of Hiroshima and Nagasaki*, translated & introduced by David G. Goodman

No. 72 *Poverty and Growth in a South China County: Anxi, Fujian, 1949-1992*, by Thomas P. Lyons
No. 73 *The Shadow of Arms*, by Hwang Suk-Young, translated by Chun Kyung-Ja, with a foreword by Paik Nak-chung
No. 74 *Informal Empire in Crisis: British Diplomacy and the Chinese Customs Succession, 1927-1929*, by Martyn Atkins
No. 75 *Barbed Wire and Rice: Poems and Songs from Japanese Prisoner-of-War Camps*, collected by Bishop D. McKendree
No. 76 *Restless Spirits from Japanese Noh Plays of the Fourth Group: Parallel Translations with Running Commentary*, by Chifumi Shimazaki
No. 77 *Back to Heaven: Selected Poems of Ch'ŏn Sang Pyŏng*, translated by Brother Anthony of Taizé & Young-Moo Kim
No. 78 *Singing Like a Cricket, Hooting Like an Owl: Selected Poems by Yi Kyu-bo*, translated by Kevin O'Rourke
No. 79 *The Gods Come Dancing: A Study of the Japanese Ritual Dance of Yamabushi Kagura*, by Irit Averbuch
No. 80 *Korean Adoption and Inheritance: Case Studies in the Creation of a Classic Confucian Society*, by Mark Peterson
No. 81 *The Lioness Roars: Shrew Stories from Late Imperial China*, translated by Yenna Wu
No. 82 *The Economic Geography of Fujian: A Sourcebook*, Volume 1, by Thomas Lyons
No. 83 *The Naked Tree*, by Pak Wan-so, translated by Yu Young-nan
No. 84 *The Classic Chinese Novel: A Critical Introduction*, by C.T. Hsia
No. 85 *Playing With Fire*, by Cho Chong-Rae, translated by Chun Kyung-Ja
No. 86 *I Saw a Pale Horse and Selections from Diary of a Vagabond*, by Hayashi Fumiko, translated by Janice Brown
No. 87 *Kojiki-den, Book 1*, by Motoori Norinaga, translated by Ann Wehmeyer
No. 88 *Sending the Ship Out to the Stars: Poems of Park Je-chun*, translated by Chang Soo Ko
No. 89 *The Economic Geography of Fujian: A Sourcebook*, Volume 2, by Thomas Lyons
No. 90 *Midang: Early Lyrics of So Chong-Ju*, translated by Brother Anthony of Taizé
No. 91 *Battle Noh: Parallel Translations with Running Commentary*, by Chifumi Shimazaki
No. 92 *More Than a Momentary Nightmare: The Yokohama Incident and Wartime Japan*, by Janice Matsumura
No. 93 *The Snow Falling on Chagall's Village: Selected Poems of Kim Ch'un-Su*, translated by Kim Jong-Gil

No. 94 *Day-Shine: Poetry by Hyon-jong Chong*, translated by Wolhee Choe and Peter Fusco
No. 95 *Troubled Souls from Japanese Noh Plays of the Fourth Group*, by Chifumi Shimazaki
No. 96 *Principles of Poetry* (Shi no Genri), by Hagiwara Sakutarō, translated by Chester Wang
No. 97 *Dramatic Representations of Filial Piety: Five Noh in Translation*, by Mae Smethurst
No. 98 *Description and Explanation in Korean Linguistics*, by Ross King
No. 99 *Japan's First Bureaucracy: A Study of Eighth-Century Government*, by Richard J. Miller, revised edition edited by Joan Piggott
No. 100 *Total War and 'Modernization'*, edited by Yasushi Yamanouchi, J. Victor Koschmann and Ryūichi Narita
No. 101 *The Prophet and Other Stories*, by Yi Ch'ŏng-jun, translated by Julie Pickering
No. 102 *Charisma and Community Formation in Medieval Japan: The Case of the* Yugyō-ha *(1300-1700)*, by S.A. Thornton
No. 103 *Inventing Nanjing Road: Commercial Culture in Shanghai, 1900-1945*, edited by Sherman Cochran
No. 104 *Strike Hard! Anti-Crime Campaigns and Chinese Criminal Justice, 1979-1985*, by Harold M. Tanner
No. 105 *Farmers' Dance: Poems by Shin Kyong-nim*, translated by Brother Anthony of Taizé and & Young-Moo Kim

FORTHCOMING
Lives in Motion: Composing Circles of Self and Community in Japan, edited by Susan Long
Ben no Naishi Nikki: A Poetic Record of Female Courtiers' Sacred Duties at the Kamakura-Period Court, by S. Yumiko Hulvey
Early One Spring: A Learning Guide to Accompany the Film Video February, by Pilwun Wang and Sarah Wang

To order, please contact the Cornell East Asia Series, East Asia Program, Cornell University, 140 Uris Hall, Ithaca, NY 14853-7601, USA; phone (607) 255-6222, fax (607) 255-1388, internet: ceas@cornell.edu, http://www.einaudi.cornell.edu/eastasia/EastAsiaSeries.html.

www.ingramcontent.com/pod-product-compliance
Lightning Source LLC
Chambersburg PA
CBHW030215170426
43201CB00006B/93